## ADVANCE PRAISE FOR "THE NEW YORK TI[...] HEALTH AND MEDICINE"

"Dr. Tom Linden has had a long and distinguished career as both a practitioner and teacher of medical journalism. This anthology of samples from The New York Times should serve as an invaluable resource for both the classroom and the reporter. Tom has a perch at the very top from which to select the best teaching moments."

—Tim Johnson, M.D., Chief Medical Editor, ABC News

"Dr. Linden gives readers a behind-the-scenes look at how reporters at a top newspaper cover complex, controversial issues in health and medicine. Better still, he provides solid advice and best practices that journalists can apply to their own coverage of the health beat, whether they're staff writers on a big daily or in Journalism 101."

—Nancy Shute, Contributing Editor,
U.S. News & World Report

"Drawing on the best of the best from the world's leading newspaper, Dr. Linden has created a valuable resource for health journalism students and educators. Aspiring medical reporters would do well to follow along as he pulls apart stories to show how they came together."

—Ivan Oransky, M.D., Executive Editor, Reuters Health

"Medicine is the most important beat in journalism, because people trust and actually act on what is reported to them. Using examples of exceptionally good medical writing, Dr. Linden clearly identifies not only what a journalist must do to justify that trust, but also how to do it."

—Art Ulene, M.D., "TODAY" show's
"Family Doctor" for 23 years

"This powerful and instructive anthology is both an invaluable guide to medical journalism as well as a great read. Dr. Linden offers an insider's tour of health journalism at its finest—from breaking news to blogs, commentary to columns and investigative stories to essays. His behind-the-scenes insights and spot-on analysis make this an essential text for anyone who writes or reads medical news."

—Carol Krucoff, Founding Editor of The Washington Post's
Health Section and Independent Journalist

"This reader offers a privileged learning experience for anyone desiring to be a better health journalist or a more critical consumer of health reportage.

Dr. Linden teaches us how the nation's preeminent health journalists craft stories that illuminate complex concepts."

—Nortin Hadler, M.D., Author of "The Last Well Person," "Worried Sick," and "Stabbed in the Back"

"A rich resource for aspiring medical journalists *and* the growing number of reporters who have had the health beat added to their collection of hats. Dr. Linden's keen eye for the subtle, along with his candid conversations with reporters, provide valuable lessons—ones even the seasoned pro will appreciate."

—Helen Chickering, Health & Science Correspondent, NBC News

# health AND medicine

Tom Linden, M.D.
and the Writers of
The New York Times

A Division of SAGE
Washington, D.C.

CQ Press
2300 N Street, NW, Suite 800
Washington, DC 20037

Phone: 202-729-1900; toll-free, 1-866-4CQ-PRESS (1-866-427-7737)

Web: www.cqpress.com



Cover design: Matthew Simmons, www.myselfincluded.com
Cover photo: ©iStockphoto.com/GeoffBlack; ©iStockphoto.com/jgroup
Composition: C&M Digitals (P) Ltd.

♾ The paper used in this publication exceeds the requirements of the American National Standard for Information Sciences—Permanence of Paper for Printed Library Materials, ANSI Z39.48-1992.

Printed and bound in the United States of America

14 13 12 11 10 1 2 3 4 5

**Library of Congress Cataloging-in-Publication Data**

The New York times reader : health and medicine / Tom Linden, and the writers of the New York Times.
p. cm.
Includes bibliographical references.
ISBN 978-1-60426-482-1 (pbk. : alk. paper)
1. Journalism, Medical. 2. Medical care—Press coverage.
3. Journalism—Authorship. I. Linden, Tom. II. New York times.

PN4784.M4N48 2010
070.4′4961—dc22

2010000031

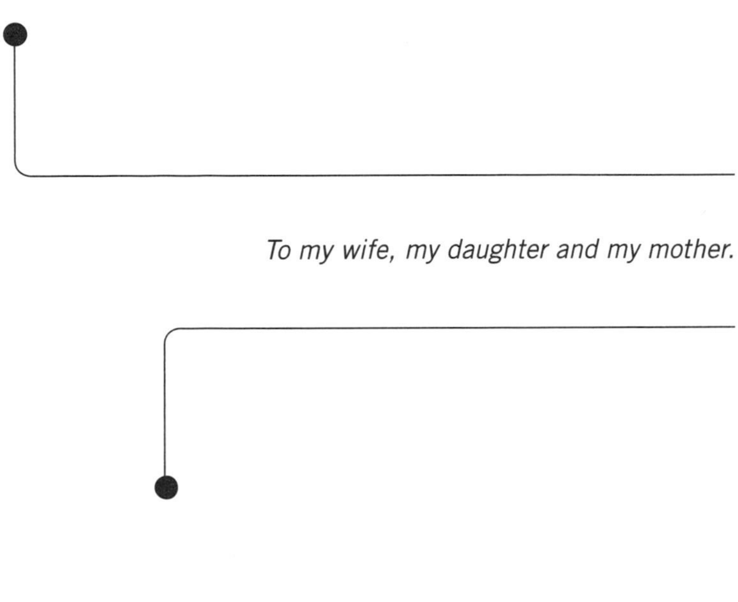

*To my wife, my daughter and my mother.*

# about Tom Linden, M.D.

Courtesy of Rachel Lillis

**Tom Linden, M.D.,** is professor of medical journalism in the School of Journalism and Mass Communication at the University of North Carolina at Chapel Hill. As director of the medical and science journalism program, he administers one of the nation's first master's programs in medical journalism. He was coauthor of "Dr. Tom Linden's Guide to Online Medicine," one of the first medical consumer guides for the Internet. He's worked as a medical journalist for CNBC, KRON-TV (San Francisco) and Fox 11 (Los Angeles), and was coanchor of "Physicians' Journal Update," the flagship news program for the Lifetime Medical Television Network. Before starting medical school, he was a staff writer for The Los Angeles Times. Dr. Linden is currently the medical anchor for "Journal Watch Audio," produced by the Massachusetts Medical Society and the Audio-Digest Foundation.

# contents

# foreword

BARBARA STRAUCH

deputy science editor in charge of health and medical coverage

AS THE MEDICAL EDITOR of The New York Times, I've consistently found that health stories provoke more interest and passion than stories on any other area—from City Hall to cops—that I've been involved with as a journalist.

Medical stories are also among the toughest to report well. Since the days of snake oil salesmen, there's been a long tradition of trying to sell unproven remedies to just about anyone willing to buy them. Such salesmen, of course, have long been replaced with well-trained doctors and researchers and, in many ways, our health and our health care have improved.

Still, in recent years there's been a decline in trust even for modern doctors, who can be rushed and impersonal, leaving patients unsure and afraid. Now, too, we're assaulted with television advertisements from the big pharmaceutical companies, promoting their drugs. On our own, we can easily go onto the Internet and find blogs—full of scary health news, most of it untrue.

So in the midst of this confusion, what makes a good medical story? How can we cut through the hype and tell people not only what really works, but why?

The stories in this book are good examples of how to do that. But I must add, too, that none of these stories, even though they were written by reporters who have covered medicine for years, was easy to do.

Medical reporters have to have multiple talents. First, of course, they have to recognize—and then tell—a good story. They have to persuade people, often at their most frightened and vulnerable moment, to share their stories. At their heart, all good medical stories are human stories. Even those stories centered on the activities in a test tube in a lab should ultimately answer the question: What does this mean for us?

On the most basic level, medical writers must be able to understand complex research, from the intricacies of genetics and stem cells to the molecular biology of cancer—and then explain that research in language normal mortals can understand. This does not mean they need to have taken eight years of biochemistry. It just means they need to have some working knowledge of—and no fear of—basic science. My own major in college? English literature.

Medical writers frequently have to cut through a haze of often-conflicting statistics. Increasingly, as money has become a prime mover of medicine, they also have to understand finance and business. As the nation wrestles with how health care is delivered, medical reporters must know, too, how our health care system works—and how it doesn't. How do politics affect what is funded in medical research? How is it that even those with insurance can go bankrupt if a major illness strikes? How can eight people die from eating peanut butter tainted with salmonella bacteria, even though we have a Food and Drug Administration that is supposed to oversee food safety?

And medical writers must, of course, also know their fields well enough to figure out where the edge of the news is. What's really a breakthrough? What will actually make a difference? And, equally important, they must recognize when a smaller piece of news indicates a widespread trend that has more lasting significance.

For instance, when Denise Grady went to Africa to report on women who die in childbirth, she not only had to work under very difficult circumstances, but also had to push further to find out what was new in this well-known topic. The result was a story rich in detail that not only presented the problem with heart-wrenching and graphic stories of women but also told—and showed—readers how specific countries were trying to address the issue, sometimes by training nondoctors to do such things as C-sections. She found news—and she found news that might, in the end, matter.

Sometimes, too, medical stories matter simply because they explain our world in a way that is clear, illuminating, even fun. In this book, you will find a good example of that as well, also by Denise, who did a 506-word story on a cough. The story was accompanied by photographs and a slide show on the Web mapping the spread of one cough. It was fascinating.

Medical writers are continually bombarded by researchers and public relations people who spin their stories as new. We have to get past those claims and tell our readers why a new discovery does—or does not—move the ball.

We try very hard not to engage in what I call "health gossip." One small study shows a correlation between eating carrots and a reduction in colon cancer. Is that finding real? Or is it just a weak association that, with more rigorous testing, falls apart? What do we *really* know?

There are those who argue that reporting such information—studies about harmless substances such as carrots—doesn't hurt anyone. In fact, if small and insignificant findings are given too much weight—or reported without context—they can do harm. It's tempting for all of us to think that there's one simple thing we can do—eat more carrots, for instance—that will protect us from something horrific such as cancer. But if we settle for the easy answer, we risk never finding the real answer, the real cure. Money, time—and lives—will be wasted.

At times, the meat of medical news is found by telling a story in depth. To do that, you first have to get the subject of your story to agree to let you spend time with him or her, often at a difficult time. For instance, the story that Larry Altman wrote on world-famous surgeon Michael DeBakey gave readers an intimate glimpse of the world of a top surgeon at a crucial time in his life. This kind of story does not happen by accident. Through his years as a reporter, Larry has developed deep relationships with many sources, including Dr. DeBakey. When Larry heard that Dr. DeBakey, at age 97, was saved by the very procedure he had invented, Larry instantly knew it was a good story. And because of the trust that Dr. DeBakey had in him, Larry was able to get the access he needed to tell this powerful story.

It's a medical writer's job to report what doesn't work, but it's equally important to write about what does. In Gina Kolata's story on stroke, part of a series we did on the country's leading causes of illness and death, Gina focused on ways that have been found—though often ignored—to lessen the severity of strokes.

In the end, to my mind, the most important attribute a reporter can have—in any field, but certainly including medicine and health—is curiosity. You have to want to know what is new and why. You have to be curious not only about intellectual developments but also about human hopes, dreams and disappointments. You have to care.

And, like all good reporters, medical writers have to be brave. This is not the kind of bravery that means you are necessarily dodging bullets, although that can happen too. In medical writing, courage often means being willing to go against the grain when necessary, to not automatically swallow the accepted wisdom, even if it comes from the most eminent of researchers. Most people, including reporters and editors, have opinions on health and medicine. Often we're wrong. In this field, as in all areas of journalism, you have to keep an open mind.

No research occurs in a vacuum, and the more we can tell readers about how a certain finding arose, the better. If a study finds a drug works, but the research was largely paid for by the drug company that makes the drug, a reader deserves to know that. If a researcher, however famous, decides to make speeches for and take money from the company that produces a specific drug, we should tell our readers that, too.

In this age, where we can get three different opinions from three different specialists—and then turn on the TV and get yet three more—we need to give our readers solid information, untainted by the influence of money, politics or fad, so they can make informed choices themselves.

And that means we sometimes have to write what we find, not what we think we know.

When Gina Kolata wrote her first story in the series The Forty Years' War, on the nation's long efforts to combat cancer, even some editors at the paper did not initially believe what she found. After all, we are all constantly being told how we are curing cancer. The accepted narrative is that research and drug companies are working miracles.

But, in fact, the numbers told a different story.

And so did Gina.

# preface

AS ALL JOURNALISM TEACHERS KNOW, aspiring writers don't learn the craft simply by reading the work of polished professionals. The best writers can engage readers' minds and inspire students with new ways of thinking about and approaching the subject matter. But to learn to write really well, students need dedicated coaches and guideposts along the way. In producing this book, I've tried to create both a compendium of great writing about health and medicine and a how-to manual that will enable journalism students to tackle this complex beat.

I've drawn on the resources of The New York Times, including its top health and medical reporters and editors. In these pages, you'll find a series of interviews in which five reporters from The Times share their years of experience and offer tips on writing about health and medicine. You'll read insights and commentary from Lawrence K. Altman, Benedict Carey, Gardiner Harris, Gina Kolata and Tara Parker-Pope. In addition, two of their editors, Laura Chang and Barbara Strauch, provide background on how The Times covers the health and medical beat.

With the help of my able research assistant, Audrey Hill, I've selected more than 50 stories about health and medicine that are reprinted in full. They cover topics that span many areas, including genetics, mental health, neuroscience, pharmacology, surgery, fitness and exercise, nutrition, teen sex and the business of health care. A headnote before each story gives readers insight into how the reporter created the piece. Instead of offering readers only the 10-course meal, I try to get students into the kitchen to see how the meal was prepared—what ingredients were used, how they were mixed and what may have been in the cook's mind.

## STRUCTURE OF THIS BOOK

In keeping with the goal of making this book a teaching aid instead of simply an anthology, I've grouped the stories into three parts that reflect the types of writing that medical journalists do: news, features and commentary.

In each part you'll find chapters with some of the best Times writing and reporting. The first section includes stories grouped under the categories of breaking news, news analysis, news briefs, investigative stories and obituaries. The second section focuses on features, with separate chapters on profiles, explanatory stories, perspective pieces, historical stories, series features and narratives. The last section, on commentary, offers examples and analysis of columns, essays, blogs and alternative story forms, or what I call "beyond plain text."

## SPECIAL BOOK FEATURES

This book reflects the insights of many people, not the least of whom are the reporters who wrote many of the stories. In a feature called "A conversation with . . . ," you'll hear directly from Times reporters as they describe the behind-the-scenes work that went into their stories. The reporters also talk about how they got into the field and offer counsel to students who want to follow in their paths.

Interspersed throughout the book you'll find annotated stories that analyze, in some cases line by line, what made the pieces work. Think of this feature, called "StoryScan," as a journalistic anatomy lesson.

Teachers also may appreciate one other special feature of the book. At the end of each chapter, you'll find "Making Connections," questions about the reading material and suggested assignments to put the book's lessons into practice.

Additional Times resources of value for health and medicine writing are on a Web site established specifically for this series, including links to interactive graphics and multi-media presentations that accompanied the stories in this reader. Go to college.cqpress.com/nytimes.

## AUDIENCES FOR THIS BOOK

If you're teaching a course in medical, health or science writing, you can use this book in a variety of ways. Chapter introductions, headnotes and interviews will help students understand how to come up with story ideas, approach topics and write stories. If you're teaching creative nonfiction, many chapters in the features section will be of interest. If your students are in public health or health communication, they'll gain insight into how reporters think and work. Health professionals can use tools in this book to transition into a reporting, writing or communications career. If you're already reporting, either on general assignment or on another beat, this book will jump-start your move to covering health and medicine.

No matter what your background or career goal, this book will give you an inside look into how one of the world's great news organizations covers one of the most popular and challenging beats. And, you'll learn lessons that may help you or your students understand how Times reporters practice their craft.

## ACKNOWLEDGMENTS

My first debt of gratitude goes to my editor, Jane Harrigan, who helped me polish the words and refine the ideas in this book. Through her editing, I've learned that she's a master wordsmith, an inspirational coach and a friend. I also thank Mary Marik, who copyedited the manuscript and further polished my words. Thanks also to Aron Keesbury, former acquisitions editor at CQ Press, who came to me in the winter of 2007–2008 with the idea for this book. I am grateful to my research assistant, Audrey Hill, who is studying for her master's degree in journalism at the University of North Carolina at Chapel Hill; she trolled the voluminous health and medical archives of The New York Times to help me find the stories reprinted in this book. I also thank my colleagues and staff at the School of Journalism and Mass Communication at the University of North Carolina at Chapel Hill; they have provided a sounding board and inspiration for my work as a medical journalism professor. Thanks also to my students who, over the years, have taught me how to better communicate what I know.

Thanks to Holly Stocking, author of The New York Times Reader on science, for her wise counsel, and to CQ Press editorial director, Charisse Kiino, and editorial assistant, Christina Mueller, for their patience and invaluable help in getting this volume to press.

I owe much appreciation to The New York Times editors Laura Chang and Barbara Strauch for helping me understand some of the inner workings of their news organization. Also, thanks to Alex Ward of The New York Times for coordinating interviews with the five Times health and medical reporters featured in this book. Thanks to all The New York Times reporters and writers whose work appears in this book, and very special thanks to Lawrence K. Altman, Benedict Carey, Gardiner Harris, Gina Kolata and Tara Parker-Pope for sharing their thoughts about their work and for allowing me to print their responses to my sometimes intrusive questions.

My most heartfelt appreciation goes to my daughter, Sarah, and my wife, Cindy Rogers, for their never-wavering support and love, without which I would not have been able to complete this book.

# Health and Medicine

# introduction

MEDICINE IS BRIMMING WITH STORIES. Not everyone has an interest in the body politic, but almost everyone has an interest in his or her own body. Readers scour health journalism for information that may have life-or-death implications for themselves or their loved ones. "The stakes as a health reporter are very high," says Tara Parker-Pope, The New York Times health columnist and blogger, in an interview for this book. "People are directly affected by what we do."

Readers of health stories hang on every word; a reporter can make a real difference in people's lives by giving them information they want and tools they can use to make better choices. That's what makes medical and health reporting such a powerful beat.

Of all the general-interest publications in the United States, The New York Times offers the most comprehensive daily coverage of health and medicine (two words this book uses interchangeably). As you'll see from the selections in this book, Times reporters cover a wide range of beats including public health, behavior and neuroscience, infectious diseases, the business of health care, pharmaceuticals, diet and nutrition, and fitness and exercise. These journalists' work is read on paper by more than 1 million people every weekday[1] and online by nearly 20 million people a month, twice as many as visit the next-busiest newspaper Web site.[2]

Because the elements of good medical journalism remain the same no matter what the subject matter, the stories in this book are divided, not by beats, but by types of writing: news, features and commentary. Within each of these three sections, you'll find examples of some of the best health reporting that The Times has to offer. You'll read analyses of what makes pieces tick, and you'll hear reporters talk about how they got their story ideas, what difficulties they faced, and what they like (and don't like) about their work.

In these pages are stories from The New York Times that inspire and educate. You'll also find answers to the question: How did they do that? How, in less than a day, did behavior reporter Benedict Carey write the front-page obituary of an amnesiac who died at age 82 after becoming the most important patient in the history of brain science? How did medical reporter Gina Kolata find the patient who brought home lessons about surviving a stroke? How did Tara Parker-Pope document that vitamins don't do much good, and then how did she deal with the negative reactions her piece generated? And how did public health reporter Gardiner Harris manage to convey a company's response to the nationwide peanut contamination scare in just one word?

## THE HEALTH REPORTER'S ROLES

If you're new to health reporting, the pieces in this book will provide an introduction to medical journalists' many roles. Health reporters translate scientific jargon. They mine a wealth of knowledge among researchers and health professionals and communicate key bottom-line messages to the public. Health reporters—with help from their sources—evaluate the quality of medical research and put it into context for readers. By choosing what to cover and how, health reporters and editors have enormous power to influence the national conversation.

Reporters are, by nature, curious. They ask questions and find answers. If a subject is new to them, they take the time to get educated. When they find a problem in a scientific study or a method of practice, they poke holes in it. Like all reporters, they question authority and refuse to take "no" or "I'm unavailable" for an answer. They pull together disparate findings and come up with new ways of looking. They gain access to places most people never see. They expand their minds as they do their jobs.

All this learning and exploring can be fun, but the health beat has never been easy. And today, with the rise of online journalism, the nature of reporting has changed. Breaking news can become old news in a matter of hours or even minutes. Like reporters everywhere, Times reporters now meet waves of rolling deadlines as they write successive drafts to be posted online. They blog, they post tweets on Twitter (on which The Times has more than 1.6 million "followers" as we go to press). That double-barreled pressure to produce quickly and accurately can take a toll. But new forms of journalism bring new rewards.

In the world of multimedia and social networking, medical reporters get immediate feedback and story ideas from readers. They can share source documents and other background material on the Web so that their audience sees and hears what the reporter saw and heard. Working with a multimedia team, reporters can supplement text stories with interactive graphics, photos, timelines, audio and video. The variety of media empowers journalists and news consumers alike.

## ONLINE OPTIONS

For a glimpse of this huge range of options, go to nytimes.com and click HEALTH. From that landing page, you can head for pieces sorted by both interest (diet, exercise, common diseases) and story type (news, features, blogs). You can get tips on training for a marathon or preventing Alzheimer's disease, take quizzes, watch videos, submit questions to medical experts, or interact with Times bloggers and the people who read them. The site includes Recipes for Health, reviews of health books, summaries of the latest research and the latest political debates, and Decoding Your Health, a special section on how to deal with the onslaught of medical information that bombards us all. Search tools and other interactive tools let visitors to the site customize their own health reports. The online audience shapes the package—but the information still comes from journalists using reporting and writing skills.

The broad range of subjects and approaches requires every health reporter to be a quick study. In one day a medical journalist may move from stories about malaria in Malawi to Botox in Beverly Hills. Principles and practices of good journalism always apply: Reporters need to find and cultivate reliable sources, and not just the obvious ones. They must keep abreast of developments in the field and monitor journals, trade publications and conferences. No matter how complex and technical the subject, reporters have to tell good tales. As Times medical reporter Gina Kolata says in an interview for this book, a story "has to have something about it that captures my imagination," or it won't capture anyone else's.

Medical stories may overlap a number of beats including business, politics and sports. Although The Times closely covers the politics of health care, this book does not focus on policy stories because the skills needed to produce them are the province more of the political reporter than the medical reporter. Instead, the book emphasizes skills that will help the aspiring medical journalist turn stories heavy with numbers and complex concepts into pieces that illuminate not just facts, but people.

For examples in this book, read Lawrence K. Altman's tale in Chapter 6 of the country's most famous heart surgeon, Dr. Michael E. DeBakey, whose life was saved by doctors performing a vascular procedure that DeBakey himself had devised. For pathos, read Pam Belluck's story in Chapter 11 about one family's struggle coping with their 10-year-old daughter's severe mental disorder. Or for internal conflict, take a look at Amy Harmon's story, also in Chapter 11, about a 33-year-old woman with a breast-cancer-causing gene who faces an agonizing choice: have both breasts removed—even though she's symptom free—or do nothing and hope that she dodges the cancer that has struck her mother and generations of family members before her. All these stories explore people's experiences, pulling in readers as they reveal the real-life impact of disease. But medical writing has no one formula to fit all stories; Kolata warns that "the tyranny of the anecdote" can sometimes overwhelm the message of the underlying science. (For more, read the interview with Kolata at the end of Chapter 10.)

## WHAT TO COVER

In breaking news stories a reporter relies less frequently on anecdotes. Readers need information clearly and they need it fast, so the reporter zeroes in on key developments. Every day, health reporters wade through a flood of journal articles, e-mails and press releases, any of which could lead to a story. How to choose what to cover is a huge issue for medical reporters and editors, as is finding the sources and setting the context to put each new development in perspective.

Barbara Strauch, The New York Times health and medical science editor, writes in a Q&A on the paper's Web site that some people mistake small advances in medicine for breaking news: "What's labeled breaking health 'news' is often just a small or incremental finding or—worse yet—insignificant research that's being pushed by drug companies or researchers with a profit motive.

"It's our job to cut through that hype and sort out what is real news that will make a difference to people and their health—and we call on as many resources as we can to help us do that."

The Times devotes lots of coverage to the major illnesses that affect its readers. These include heart disease, cancer and stroke, the major killers of men and women in the United States.[3] Reporters, however, don't have to write about deadly ailments like cardiovascular disease or cancer or chronic diseases like diabetes or arthritis to attract a large audience. Stories about diet, fitness and sex pull in readers and often top the list of the most popular stories on The New York Times Web site.

Strauch writes: "Clearly, figuring out what is news is far from a cut-and-dried process. We often (as in, all day long) have disagreements among ourselves about what the news is and what it means. But news selection is not random, either. There are methods of evaluation that reporters and editors learn through the years to help us figure all this out."

You'll learn about some of those methods in this book.

Most health stories in The Times don't qualify as breaking news. The majority are features, but common to all stories—news and feature—is a nugget of information, a payoff that matters to readers and makes their investment of time worthwhile. As a medical reporter you'll need to figure out that payoff before you write your story. Some journalists call it the message, others the theme or the point; your editor will probably call it the focus (and ask you about it constantly). No matter what you call it, if you don't understand the point, Kolata says, then you don't have a story.

Beyond telling a story that captures readers' interest, medical reporters also educate, teaching people about unfamiliar concepts. That's not always easy for reporters, who deal daily with doctors speaking jargon and scientists whose studies challenge the acumen of the most sophisticated readers—not to mention that today's study might seemingly contradict one reported just last week.

## LEARNING ON THE JOB

Besides understanding complex language and ideas, the health reporter also has to understand the science behind the story. That doesn't mean journalists have to graduate from medical school to be good health reporters. Most health reporters at The Times have learned on the job, just as reporters do on any beat. Times columnist and former reporter, Lawrence K. Altman, is a medical doctor. Another, Benedict Carey, studied math in college and got a graduate degree in journalism, while Gina Kolata studied molecular biology in graduate school and earned a master's in applied mathematics. But some Times health reporters don't have graduate science degrees. Tara Parker-Pope majored in sociology, while Gardiner Harris studied history. The common denominator is that health reporters at The Times have learned how science works and how researchers and doctors think so that they can look science in the eye without fear.

Like all reporters, they have to cover the five Ws (who, what, when, where and why) and H (how), but for the health reporter, the how is different and often more complicated. Health reporters ask doctors and scientists these questions: How does it work? How do you know? How did you do that? How might this information affect people's lives?

Once reporters understand the science, their challenge is to explain it in ways that grab the reader. That's the science lesson, the explanation of how the disease process or basic biology works, and you'll find many examples in this book. Think you'd be bored by reading about how viruses evolve? Check out Carl Zimmer's explanation in Chapter 7. Or follow along in words and pictures as Benedict Carey shows how and why an unusual blind person can navigate an obstacle course. In Chapter 4, read how a team of New York Times reporters mined databases to show how financial relationships between drug makers and doctors may have led to more prescriptions of powerful antipsychotic drugs for children. In all these examples, Times reporters are making medical stories accessible and interesting for general readers. Learning how reporters craft these pieces will help demystify the process and propel you along the path to writing your own compelling stories on the health beat.

# Part I

# news stories

MEDICAL OR HEALTH NEWS STORIES inform readers about recent events or findings in the field. To qualify as news, health information has to be new or updated and come from reliable sources. If contaminated peanut products are sickening consumers, that's news. If the World Health Organization raises the alert level for a disease outbreak, that's news. And if cancer rates change, that too is news. Stories emanate from academia, industry, industry watchdogs, government, health organizations, journals, professional and consumer interest groups and from original reporting by enterprising journalists. The stories may take reporters to professional conferences, government hearings, industry and university laboratories, hospitals, clinics and a host of other locales anywhere in the world.

Medical news stories can be long—more than 1,600 words in the investigative report on the anti-inflammatory drug Vioxx in Chapter 4—or short, as in a news brief. You'll find medical news on the front page, on inside pages, in health or science sections in the newspaper and online. Most hard news stories appear in inverted-pyramid format, with the most important information at the top, but some news stories (like investigative reports) may use elements of a narrative style. The selections in these chapters also include obituaries, which of course begin with the stark news of someone's death, and news analyses, which step back to put recent developments in perspective.

News has a short shelf life. Medical reporters work under intense time pressure, meeting rolling online deadlines and a nightly print deadline. Whether writing about a congressional subcommittee or a speech by the president, reporters have to be quick and accurate. At its best, medical news prose can sing even as it informs.

CHAPTER 1

# breaking news

COVERING BREAKING NEWS IS TOUGH WORK. Reporters often have little more than a few hours to bring themselves up to speed on a topic, interview sources and write the story. Deadlines limit the number of sources a reporter can contact. Often the reporter has to decipher complex studies without the benefit of multiple opinions from impartial experts. In short, writing breaking medical news stories is pressure packed.

As a television medical reporter for CNBC and network affiliates, I covered breaking news all the time. I often got a story assignment at 10 or 11 a.m. and faced a 4 p.m. deadline. Forget about lunch. Forget about deliberation. Take a deep breath, read the seed for the story (be it wire report or journal article) and get cracking. That's the life of the deadline reporter. Not recommended for the faint of heart.

Today, journalists face the additional pressure to post a version of the story on the Web as soon as they can, whether or not they feel ready to write the full story. A daily medical reporter for any medium is dealing with a 24-hour news cycle in which he has to move quickly to find the best angle for his audience, regardless of what others are doing, and to cover the story in a way that only his organization would. Often the real significance of a medical story lies beneath the surface. The ability to see the real point of a story—what's unique, what matters, what will have an impact on people—and to see it fast and know how to pursue it is what distinguishes the great reporter from the average reporter.

To help editors lay out the next edition, reporters for The New York Times submit what they call a "sked" or scheduling line, a description in a couple sentences of the reporter's upcoming story. Editors use the sked line to figure out the story budget. "The sked line might be written by a reporter, or by an editor in consultation with a reporter; it is often adapted from an e-mail the reporter sent the editor early on asking if there is interest," says Laura Chang, Times science editor. To write a good sked line, the reporter has to understand the story's focus.

"If you can't tell me in one or two sentences what your story is about, then you haven't thought it through enough," says medical reporter Gina Kolata, who is interviewed in Chapter 10. "In a newspaper story, you should tell a reader right away why am I reading this and why am I reading this now."

Kolata says reporters need to have a knack for "seeing the story . . . seeing what the point is. Seeing what you want to tell. Seeing why is this interesting right away and glomming onto that."

## Selection 1.1

*In early 2009 Times public health reporter Gardiner Harris covered a congressional committee hearing on a salmonella outbreak traced to contaminated peanuts from a Georgia processing plant. The outbreak had begun five months earlier. Although Harris was one of a number of New York Times reporters who had covered the outbreak, on the day of the hearing he still had to brief himself on the background, review committee documents, listen to testimony and write two to three updated versions for the newspaper's Web site before completing his final story. That's what Harris, in an interview in Chapter 4, calls "simultaneous translation," a tough juggling act to perform in a high-stakes story about a public health blunder in which eight people died and 550 suffered food poisoning.*

*But it's not enough to capture facts. A reporter also needs to convey the drama of the story. Take a look at the second paragraph in Harris' story and the way it uses two simple syllables uttered by the plant manager, "Uh-oh," to convey a whole lot more meaning.*

*"That line kind of summarized the essence of that hearing, which was to show how irresponsible this company had been in handling the responsibility that it had to safeguard the safety of its customers," Harris says.*

*Attention to detail is apparent again a few paragraphs later when Harris describes how a member of Congress brandished a jar of contaminated food and challenged company executives to eat it. When the story says the men were "clearly shaken," we know Harris is giving a firsthand report. By noting that a crowd of photographers and reporters pursued the witnesses out of the hearing room, Harris communicates the charged atmosphere that surrounded the hearing. That's good reporting, the kind you can do on any kind of meeting or hearing, not just in Congress.*

### Peanut Products Sent Out Before Tests

By GARDINER HARRIS

WASHINGTON—The peanut processing company at the center of a salmonella outbreak did not await the results of contamination tests before shipping products to customers, Congressional investigators disclosed Wednesday.

When the plant's manager was told that one such test had shown that the products were tainted with salmonella bacteria, he responded by saying, "Uh-oh," according to documents released by the House Energy and Commerce investigations subcommittee.

Michelle Pronto, an official at the laboratory that did the tests, told the investigators, "When I asked if he could get it back, he said it was on a truck heading to Utah."

---

*Published: February 11, 2009.*

The plant, in Blakely, Ga., owned by the Peanut Corporation of America, shipped contaminated peanut products to distributors who sold them to schools and nursing homes, and the products were included in crackers and cookies made by some of the largest food makers in the world.

The disclosure came at a theatrical hearing of the investigations subcommittee that forced the company's executives into the public eye. Subpoenaed to testify, Stewart Parnell, the president, and Sammy Lightsey, manager of the company's Georgia plant, instead cited their Fifth Amendment rights against self-incrimination.

Shortly after the two settled into their seats, Representative Greg Walden, Republican of Oregon, brandished a large jar wrapped in yellow crime-scene tape and filled with contaminated cookies and crackers and asked the executives, "Would either of you be willing to take the lid off and eat any of these products?"

Clearly shaken, the men demurred and were dismissed a moment later. They swept out of the hearing room and were pursued by a group of photographers and reporters who shouted questions.

Eight deaths and more than 550 illnesses have been associated with the outbreak. It has also led to one of the largest food recalls in the nation's history—including some items that remained in the House Republican cloakroom until Tuesday night, said Representative Bart Stupak, the Michigan Democrat who is the subcommittee's chairman.

On Monday, the Peanut Corporation closed its plant in Plainview, Tex., after tests found salmonella contamination there, too.

Federal investigators raided the Blakely plant on Monday as part of an investigation into whether the company had deliberately shipped contaminated products.

Documents made public on Wednesday by the investigations subcommittee show that the company stopped using a private laboratory because too many tests done there had showed contamination.

Mr. Parnell complained in an e-mail message to Mr. Lightsey that the positive salmonella tests were "costing us huge $$$$$ and causing obviously a huge lapse in time from the time we pick up peanuts until the time we can invoice."

Ms. Pronto, the official at the laboratory that did the tests, J. Leek Associates, said the Peanut Corporation eventually stopped using the lab because it found too much contamination in its samples, according to documents provided by the committee.

"I called Mr. Lightsey to follow up on the recent discussion regarding the confirmed positive," she told committee investigators, "and he confirmed that because of the high coliform results they were going to send samples to a different lab."

Even after the company was identified as the source of the outbreak, Mr. Parnell sent an e-mail message to officials at the Food and

Drug Administration pleading with them to allow the company to continue doing business. He wrote that they "desperately at least need to turn the raw peanuts on our floor into money."

He said the peanuts would be processed by its plant in Texas, which former employees described in interviews with The New York Times as "disgusting."

Despite more than 12 tests in 2007 and 2008 that showed salmonella contamination in his company's products, Mr. Parnell wrote an e-mail message to company employees on Jan. 12 saying, "We have never found any salmonella at all."

As a result of the peanut contamination—one of dozens of similar outbreaks over the past decade—influential members of Congress have pledged major changes in the nation's food protection system. In opening statements on Wednesday, members of the investigations subcommittee said changes would come quickly.

Peter Hurley, a police officer from Portland, Ore., came to the hearing with his wife and three young children, who squirmed throughout the long opening statements of committee members.

Mr. Hurley described how his 3-year-old, Jacob, came down with diarrhea and vomiting in early January. To get him to eat something, Jacob's mother continued to feed him his favorite food, Austin Toasty Crackers With Peanut Butter, "the very food that we later found was the cause of his poisoning," Mr. Hurley said.

Another witness, Jeff Almer, described how his mother, who had overcome cancer and other health problems, checked into a rehabilitation facility in Brainerd, Minn., to overcome a urinary tract infection. There she ate contaminated peanut butter and died.

"Cancer couldn't claim her, but peanut butter did," Mr. Almer said. "She was let down in the worst possible way by the very government whose responsibility it is to protect its citizens."

Both Republican and Democratic members of the panel promised victims' families that they would strengthen the nation's food-safety net.

"I'll just make this commitment to you: We're going to do this, and we're going to do this in your loved ones' memories," said Representative Diana DeGette, Democrat of Colorado.

## Selection 1.2

*Some stories develop on many fronts, and the trick is to pull all the threads together in a "round-up story." If Gardiner Harris in the previous story is doing "simultaneous translation," then Denise Grady in the next story is doing simultaneous translation while juggling at least seven sources across two continents with information provided by seven other Times reporters. Grady is also careful to provide the context that readers need in order to put a potentially alarming story in perspective.*

## World Health Organization Raises Swine Flu Alert Level

By DENISE GRADY

The global spread of swine flu, a pandemic, is highly likely, the World Health Organization said on Wednesday and raised its alert level to Phase 5, the next-to-highest level in the worldwide warning system.

*Notice how Grady defines Phase 5 in the lede. Define terms at their first mention. It would have been less confusing to delete the words "a pandemic" from the lede because at first glance it's not clear whether "pandemic" is modifying "global spread of swine flu" or just "swine flu." This is an important issue because, as the reporter notes later, even the head of the World Health Organization is sending mixed signals as to whether a pandemic has actually begun.*

Phase 5 had never been declared since the warning system was introduced in 2005 in response to the avian influenza crisis. Phase 6 means a pandemic is under way.

The health organization said its decision was based on the continuing spread of swine flu in the United States and Mexico, particularly the increasing numbers of unexplained cases among people not exposed to travelers or to institutions like schools or hospitals where many people have close contact with one another and high rates of transmission might be expected.

Phase 5 had never been declared since the warning system was introduced in 2005 in response to the avian influenza crisis. Phase 6 means a pandemic is under way.

The health organization said its decision was based on the continuing spread of swine flu in the United States and Mexico, particularly the increasing numbers of unexplained cases among people not exposed to travelers or to institutions like schools or hospitals where many people have close contact with one another and high rates of transmission might be expected.

---

*Published: April 29, 2009.*

*Get the first quote as high as possible in the story.*

"All countries should immediately activate their pandemic preparedness plans," Dr. Margaret Chan, director general of the organization, said at a news conference in Geneva. "Countries should remain on high alert for unusual outbreaks of influenza-like illness and severe pneumonia."

*Note how Grady seamlessly moves the story from Geneva to Houston.*

The first death from swine flu in this country—of a 23-month-old child from Mexico who was being treated in Houston—was reported on Wednesday, along with more infections and hospitalizations.

*Get the number of confirmed cases in the U.S. as high up in the story as possible.*

The Centers for Disease Control and Prevention reported 91 confirmed cases from 10 states, up from 64 cases in 5 states on Tuesday.

*The reporter notes the W.H.O. director general's confusion as to whether a pandemic has already begun.*

Dr. Chan emphasized the need for calm, but at times spoke as if a pandemic had already begun, saying, for instance, "W.H.O. will be tracking the pandemic." She also emphasized that developing countries tended to have more severe flu epidemics than rich ones, and said her organization and others would need to make special efforts to help poorer nations.

She called for global solidarity, saying, "After all, it really is all of humanity that is under threat during a pandemic."

*Grady contrasts President Obama's measured response to the more alarmist tone from the W.H.O. director general.*

President Obama, terming the outbreak "cause for deep concern but not panic," took the unusual step of using a prime-time televised news conference, convened to mark his 100th day in office, to deliver a public health message to the American people.

*Don't miss an opportunity to quote the president if he's speaking on point.*

"Wash your hands when you shake hands, cover your mouth when you cough," he said from the East Room of the White House. "It sounds trivial, but it makes a huge difference. If you are sick, stay home. If your child is sick, take them out of school. If you are feeling certain flu symptoms, don't get on an airplane."

With public health officials recommending that schools close if there are more confirmed or suspected cases, Mr. Obama urged parents and businesses to "think about contingency plans" in case of such closings.

He said he was calling on Congress to authorize an immediate $1.5 billion to "support our ability to monitor and track this virus" and to build the supply of antiviral drugs.

*Grady covers this story from both medical and political angles.*

"The more recent illnesses and the reported death suggest that a pattern of more severe illness associated with this virus may be emerging in the U.S.," the C.D.C. said on its Web site. More hospitalizations and deaths are expected, the site said, because the virus is new and most people have no immunity to it.

Dr. Chan said that government preparedness plans could include steps like ensuring that laboratories can test for the disease and that health systems can identify and treat cases, track an outbreak and prevent the virus from spreading in hospitals and clinics. She said governments should also decide on measures like closing schools and discouraging or banning public gatherings.

Mexico, for instance, has prohibited people from eating in restaurants and ordered most stores and other businesses to close for several days starting Friday, a move apparently intended to keep people at home during what is traditionally a long holiday weekend.

*Because the outbreak started in Mexico, it's important to bring that country into the story.*

At a news conference in Mexico City on Wednesday night, Mexico's secretary of health, José Ángel Córdova, also announced that the national government would close all but essential offices during the same time period. The government did not suspend mass transportation or close airports and asked that supermarkets and pharmacies remain open.

*As Grady switches from Mexico City to the U.S., note how she orients the reader to location at the top of each paragraph.*

In the United States, Dr. Anthony S. Fauci, director of the National Institute of Allergy and Infectious Diseases, said the outbreak had caused such concern because officials had never seen this particular strain of the flu passing among humans.

"There is no background immunity in the population, and it is spreading from human to human—all of which has the potential for a pandemic," Dr. Fauci said.

Dr. Richard Besser, acting director of the Centers for Disease Control and Prevention, said that officials had no way of predicting whether the outbreak would become more serious.

"You don't know if this is a virus that will fizzle in a couple of weeks or one that will become more or less virulent or severe in the diseases it causes," Dr. Besser said.

He said officials must follow government plans for a pandemic because of that unpredictability.

"If we could see into the future, it would be wonderful so that we could tailor all our responses specifically to what is occurring," Dr. Besser said.

*The reporter probably filed this story under a rolling deadline. That may explain why she notes here that the number of 91 confirmed cases (first mentioned in paragraph 8) is outdated.*

The disease centers' count of 91 confirmed cases in the United States did not include some later reports by states that confirmed cases after the C.D.C. tally was posted. In addition, there were suspected cases in Louisiana and Delaware. Kits being provided to the states and other countries will allow them to test for the virus on their own and obtain results within a few hours.

New York City added 5 new confirmed cases, bringing its total to 49. All have links to Mexico or St. Francis Preparatory School in Queens, where the virus first surfaced in New York, health officials said. The city identified five more probable cases.

The total in Canada rose to 19, from 16. In Mexico, the number of confirmed cases of the flu rose to 99 from 49, and the number of deaths from confirmed cases of the flu was increased to 8. The number of suspected cases is much higher.

*Note how Grady attends to detail, pointing out that Kathleen Sebelius is holding her first news conference as President Obama's secretary of health and human services. The reporter is seeing both the forest (the big picture) and the trees (the details).*

Kathleen Sebelius focused on the outbreak on Wednesday during her first news conference as the Obama administration's secretary of health and human services. "We're determined to fight this outbreak and do everything we can to protect the health of every American," Ms. Sebelius said.

She noted that the Centers for Disease Control and Prevention had recommended that schools close only if a student is found to be infected. More aggressive steps are under discussion, Ms. Sebelius said, but officials realize that closings can cause problems for families.

"What happens to parents? Where do children go?" she asked.

Dr. Besser, who joined the news conference via a video feed, said the most recent cases included patients of a broad range of ages, with two-thirds of all cases occurring in people under 18.

"There have been five hospitalizations so far, including the child who died. But we have a number of suspect cases that have been hospitalized and we expect that number to go up," he said. Dr. Besser said that a quarter of the nation's stockpile of 50 million treatments of antiviral medicines would be distributed to states by Sunday.

The United States has no plans to close international borders because, Dr. Besser said, such closings are not effective in slowing pandemics. When Hong Kong was hit with severe acute respiratory syndrome, or SARS, "increased border screening on entry and exit was not an effective way of identifying cases or preventing transmission," he said.

Nonetheless, Customs and Border Protection agents have stepped up efforts to spot sick travelers.

Some elected officials have begun to question the decision to leave the borders open. Homeland Security Secretary Janet Napolitano was grilled by senators on Wednesday who asked whether her agency was doing enough to stop the virus from spreading from Mexico. The senators, including John McCain of Arizona and Joseph I. Lieberman of Connecticut, asked several times why the administration had decided against closing the border and banning travel to Mexico.

*The reporter is doing a balancing act as she navigates between the medical and political sides of this story.*

*Reporting was contributed by Sharon Otterman, Liz Robbins and Sewell Chan from New York; James C. McKinley Jr. from Houston; Nicholas Confessore from Albany; Monica Davey from Chicago; Sheryl Gay Stolberg from Washington; Larry Rohter from Mexico City; Marc Lacey from La Gloria, Mexico; and Ian Austen from Ottawa.*

## Selection 1.3

*Breaking medical news can appear anywhere in The New York Times—from the front page, like Denise Grady's swine flu roundup, to the business page, like the next story. In October 2007 Barnaby J. Feder reported on a decision by the medical device company Medtronic to stop selling a cable, which doctors call a lead, for its implanted heart devices. The cable was prone to cracking. At the time of the Medtronic announcement, the defective cable was suspected of contributing to five deaths. The story below is a great example of "news you can use," especially of interest to the quarter of a million people with Sprint Fidelis leads implanted in their bodies. The story also illustrates the close relationship between the business and health beats. Feder explains high in the story how the faulty cable is supposed to work, and what happens when it doesn't. He also provides doctors' advice on options available to patients who have the recalled cable. In medical reporting—even more so than in other reporting—it's crucial to anticipate readers' questions and provide answers whenever possible. Later in the story, Feder details the history of problems with other, similar cardiac devices and the business implications of safety recalls.*

### Patients Warned as Maker Halts Sale of Heart Implant Part

By BARNABY J. FEDER

The nation's largest maker of implanted heart devices, Medtronic, said yesterday that it was urging doctors to stop using a crucial component in its most recent defibrillator models because it was prone to a defect that has caused malfunctions in hundreds of patients and may have contributed to five deaths.

The faulty component is an electrical "lead," or a wire that connects the heart to a defibrillator, a device that shocks faltering hearts back into normal rhythm. The company is urging all of the roughly 235,000 patients with the lead, known as the Sprint Fidelis, to see their doctors to make sure it has not developed a fracture that can make the device misread heart-rhythm data.

Such a malfunction can cause the device to either deliver an unnecessary electrical jolt or fail to provide a life-saving one to a patient in need. In most cases, the defibrillators can be reprogrammed without surgery to minimize the problem.

Medtronic estimated that about 2.3 percent of patients with the Fidelis lead, or 4,000 to 5,000 people, would experience a lead fracture within 30 months of implantation. Those patients will require a delicate surgical procedure to replace the lead, experts said.

---

*Published: October 15, 2007.*

Medtronic said it would stop selling the lead and recall all leads not yet implanted.

Replacing leads on a heart device like a defibrillator is considered by experts to be far more dangerous than replacing the device itself. As a result, doctors said that patients were better off leaving the lead in place except in those instances where it has stopped functioning properly.

The Fidelis lead has been used with Medtronic defibrillators since 2004, and most patients who received Medtronic defibrillators since then have them. Patients who have recently had defibrillators replaced because their batteries were running down may not have the leads because doctors commonly attach replacement defibrillators to the existing leads when possible.

Vice President Dick Cheney uses a Medtronic defibrillator, but it was implanted in 2001, before the Fidelis lead was introduced. The White House declined to comment last night.

Questions about the performance of the Fidelis lead have surfaced before. For example, earlier this year, Dr. Robert G. Hauser of the Minneapolis Heart Institute published an analysis that found, among other things, that a significant number of patients were experiencing "inappropriate" shocks because their defibrillator was firing when not needed. Such jolts can be extremely painful.

Dr. Hauser, who played a central role several years ago in bringing to light malfunctions in defibrillators made by Guidant, said that he discussed his findings earlier this year with Medtronic officials, who said there was not enough data to come to any conclusions. In March, however, the company issued a letter to doctors sharing those concerns.

Last month, when 30 months of data showed a continuing fracture problem, Medtronic began talking with its independent medical advisers about what to do next. "The numbers that we saw were not that bad, but they were worrisome, troubling," said Dr. Douglas P. Zipes, a professor at the Indiana University School of Medicine and a member of the advisory board.

Statistically speaking, there is not enough data to be sure that Fidelis is unusually prone to fracture. But with mounting evidence that there was cause for concern, Medtronic decided to act now. Five deaths have been linked to the fractures as a possible, though not confirmed, contributor.

The numbers suggesting that the problem was significant enough to halt sales of the lead come from two other sources: a clinical trial currently following the progress of 650 patients at 17 hospitals and the mountain of data collected from 25,000 patients in CareLink, Medtronic's system for remotely monitoring implants. Medtronic said that data from fractured leads that have been returned had helped it understand where the malfunctions occur.

Federal safety regulators, who participated in the announcement yesterday, endorsed Medtronic's decision to stop selling the lead.

"Pulling this device from the market is the right thing to do," said Daniel G. Schultz, director of the Center for Devices and Radiological Health at the Food and Drug Administration.

The recall is the latest in a series of setbacks for Medtronic and its two main rivals in the $6 billion global defibrillator market, St. Jude Medical and Boston Scientific, which now owns Guidant. Sales have slumped in the United States in the last two years because of a string of safety recalls and concern among doctors that it is too difficult to identify which patients would benefit from the devices. They can cost $30,000 or more.

Medtronic declined to discuss the potential financial impact of its actions regarding Fidelis prior to a conference call scheduled for this morning with Wall Street analysts. The company, which had $12.3 billion in sales last year, has more than 55 percent of the defibrillator market, and the devices are its biggest product.

Medtronic will cover the cost of a replacement lead for those that have fractured, plus up to $800 in medical expenses that are not covered by insurance. But the company will not pay for procedures to replace functioning leads that patients want taken out to head off possible problems in the future, a company spokesman, Robert Clark, said.

Mr. Clark declined to comment on how many unused leads the company expected to take back and destroy. He said Medtronic would attempt to design a similarly narrow lead to replace the current products.

Medtronic is recommending that doctors switch back to its older Quattro lead, but doctors will have other options from other companies. The biggest long-term financial impact on Medtronic could come not from doctors using other leads but from the possibility that they could switch to complete defibrillator packages from other companies.

Medtronic said that none of its pacemakers used the leads. Pacemakers are devices that, instead of shocking a heart back into a stable rhythm, are meant to ensure a continuous steady beat.

Medtronic developed Fidelis as part of the race among cardiac device companies to develop ever more compact and flexible products that can be implanted more easily and safely.

Whatever happens, Medtronic is hoping to contrast its response with that of Guidant three years ago, when deadly defects were discovered in some of its defibrillators. Guidant, which Boston Scientific acquired in 2006, angered doctors and regulators by failing to quickly disclose the problems.

Since then, the Heart Rhythm Society, the professional group for doctors who implant defibrillators, has developed guidelines for handling product safety problems.

Dr. Schultz at the F.D.A. said the company's actions were an indicator of how much the industry had learned from the mistakes made in handling the Guidant malfunction. Dr. Hauser, the Guidant whistle-blower, agreed. "I think that in the old days, this lead could have continued on the market for a long time, maybe forever," he said.

*Barry Meier contributed reporting.*

## Selection 1.4

*Media organizations place a high priority on breaking news, but breaking the story should mark just the beginning of coverage. Most big stories evolve in a dynamic process that a good reporter (and news organization) follows until its conclusion. Simply keeping track of new developments can be hard enough in the daily deadline rush. But how do you keep a continuing story fresh? How much do you assume your readers already know from previous stories, and how much background do you include? In the report that follows, Barry Meier briefly summarizes the initial defective heart cable story from 2007 and then plows new ground in an update that shows the human impact of what Barnaby Feder wrote about nearly a year and a half earlier.*

## Removing Medtronic Heart Cables Is Hard Choice

By BARRY MEIER

BOSTON—Pulling a medical device off the market is one thing. Removing it from the bodies of thousands of patients is a lot more complicated and dangerous.

Consider the Sprint Fidelis, a heart defibrillator cable. In 2007 its maker, Medtronic, stopped selling it after five patients who had the cables died.

But only now is the full scope of the public health problem becoming clear for the Sprint Fidelis, which is still used by 150,000 people in this country.

In the next few years, thousands of those patients may face risky surgical procedures to remove and replace the electrical cable, which connects a defibrillator to a chamber of the heart.

Medtronic estimates that the cable has failed in a little more than 5 percent of patients after 45 months of being implanted. But as a preventive measure, some patients with working cables are having them removed.

Already, four patients have died during extractions. Experts fear that the toll could quickly rise if such procedures are not performed

*Published: April 6, 2009.*

by skilled doctors at medical centers that have performed many of the operations.

"I think we are just seeing the tip of the iceberg," said Dr. Charles J. Love, a cardiologist at Ohio State University Medical Center in Columbus, who specializes in cable extractions.

For many of the patients around the country who may need the procedure, finding the right medical center will not be easy.

There is little publicly available data on the volumes and success rates of the procedures at the nation's hospitals. Some hospitals disclose their own numbers, but many more do not.

"There are people who are doing this that don't meet the criteria," said Dr. Bruce Wilkoff, a cardiologist at the Cleveland Clinic.

Even experienced cardiologists at well-regarded hospitals, like Dr. Laurence M. Epstein at Brigham and Women's Hospital here, consider the procedure challenging.

Dr. Epstein recently operated on a patient, a 63-year-old man, whose Sprint Fidelis cable had become so overgrown with tissue that it was stuck inside a major vein.

To free it, Dr. Epstein cautiously threaded a catheter-guided laser through the blood vessel to dissolve the entrapping tissue. It was a risky move. The deaths of the four Sprint Fidelis patients at other hospitals apparently occurred when less practiced doctors damaged a vein or the heart, causing extensive bleeding.

Finally, Dr. Epstein pulled the cable out. "This was one of the more difficult ones," said Dr. Epstein, who added that he had removed scores of the Sprint Fidelis cables in the last year without a major complication.

It is not unusual for heart cables, or leads as doctors call them, to eventually wear out or fail, which is why there are doctors who specialize in removing them. What makes the Sprint Fidelis situation stand out is the vast number of patients who got the cable before its recall. A quarter-million people around the world received a Sprint Fidelis in the three years from its introduction in 2004 to its recall in October 2007.

The cable's chief flaw is the tendency for it to crack, creating electrical problems. The defibrillator may fail to give a heart a lifesaving jolt to disrupt a potentially fatal rhythm. Or it may repeatedly discharge, shocking patients for no reason.

Also, when a Sprint Fidelis is used with a device that combines a defibrillator with a pacemaker, the cable's flaw may interfere with the pacemaker's ability to keep a patient's heart beating at a steady rhythm.

Medtronic has given patients some guidance about extractions, like telling them to seek a hospital experienced in the procedure if they decide to have a Sprint Fidelis removed. Though the company has declined to indicate which medical centers have such experience, it recently compiled such a list. Last year, to win approval for a new heart cable from the Food and Drug Administration, the company agreed to provide the F.D.A. with future data from "10 experienced extraction centers," according to agency records. But Medtronic says it does not plan to make such a list public.

"Medtronic believes that a patient's physician is in the best position to make decisions related to patient care, including the most appropriate lead extraction center," the company wrote, in response to a reporter's question.

Experts say patients should ask a hospital how many of the procedures it has performed, and go to medical centers that do at least 50 a year.

Medtronic has been shielded so far from legal claims over the recalled device. More than 1,000 patient lawsuits involving the Sprint Fidelis have been thrown out because of a ruling last year by the Supreme Court. The court held in a ruling involving a different medical device that federal law protects device makers from liability suits involving some products, as long as the F.D.A. has approved their products.

Some Democrats in Congress have vowed to pass legislation that would override the Supreme Court decision. They cite the Sprint Fidelis problem as one reason, also noting the F.D.A. let it onto the market without extensive testing.

Medtronic is supplying replacement cables, but the cost of the operation to implant a cable, which can run $15,000 to $20,000 is being borne by Medicare or private insurers.

A defibrillator cable can last 15 years or more—much longer than a defibrillator, whose built-in batteries may wear out in five years or so. When the cable does eventually wear out, or break, extracting it is not the only option. Often doctors will leave the old one in place, threading a new cable in place alongside.

Those options pose competing risks, experts say. While extracting a cable can be dangerous, leaving it in place can make it more difficult to remove later, because of in-grown tissue.

In the case of the Sprint Fidelis, doctors will be making decisions for a huge number of patients. Medtronic's recent estimates indicate the cables are likely to stop working in thousands of people in the next few years.

Meanwhile, even tens of thousands of additional patients for whom the Sprint Fidelis is still working will need to undergo a procedure in the next few years to have the defibrillators themselves replaced, as the batteries wear out. During replacement procedures, doctors will need to weigh the risk of hoping the cables continue to work or replacing them.

Medtronic has said that whether the Sprint Fidelis is broken or is still working, it should be extracted only as a last resort. The company said it did not know how many Sprint Fidelis cables have been extracted.

Specialists take different approaches on the matter. Dr. Wilkoff of the Cleveland Clinic said he planned to reattach a working Sprint Fidelis when he replaces a defibrillator. Because of the clinic's experience in implanting cable, he said, the failure rate at his hospital has been much lower than at other medical centers.

But other experts like Dr. Epstein, who are concerned about the failure rate, have started pre-emptively removing the cables in some patients. That was the approach he took with his 63-year-old patient, whose life depends on the reliable operation of his heart pacemaker.

Dr. Love of Ohio State, meanwhile, said he had begun routinely removing the Sprint Fidelis when changing defibrillators or pacemakers in younger, more active patients—typically those age 60 or less—because greater physical activity places more stress on a cable, raising the likelihood of its fracturing.

The Heart Rhythm Society, a group representing doctors who implant heart devices, plans to issue guidelines about cable extraction this year. They would urge doctors to perform at least 30 removals under the supervision of an experienced extraction surgeon before operating solo.

But some experts say that it is difficult for doctors to obtain that level of training. And they caution that even well trained physicians need to regularly perform significant numbers of extractions to remain proficient.

The group of device experts, which plans to urge doctors to collect more data about defibrillator cables, has not released a list of hospitals experienced in extractions.

Dr. Epstein said that two of his patients had died of complications during the first 200 extractions of various makes of cables he performed. Since then, he said he had performed 800 procedures without any deaths.

"Of all the procedures I do," he said, "extraction probably has by far the largest learning curve."

## Selection 1.5

*Reporters get breaking stories from lots of venues, including medical conferences. In a December 2006 front-page story, Gina Kolata reported on what she called a "startling" 15 percent drop from August 2002 to December 2003 in the most common form of breast cancer. Scientists at a medical conference attributed the drop to large numbers of women who had stopped taking hormone therapy for menopause. Conferences can be gold mines for reporters who can vet the story with multiple sources close at hand. The downside of conference-based stories is that the reporter runs the risk that a study announced at a conference will not make it through medical journal peer review and, consequently, will never be published. So, what looks like breaking news today may be a nonstory tomorrow. In the story that follows, the study from researchers quoted in Kolata's story did make it through peer review, and their findings were later published in The New England Journal of Medicine. Kolata's reporting is notable for use of multiple sources, including experts other than the investigators whose study was the focus of the story. It's important to seek various perspectives, not only to ensure your story's accuracy but also to distinguish your story from what all the other reporters who interviewed the same experts at the same conference will write. Kolata includes a brief history of both breast cancer and the use of estrogen in postmenopausal women. As she notes, "It's amazing how much knowing a little bit about medical history helps inform what you see today." Also, note that the chart that ran with the story provides a quick, concrete way for readers to grasp the news.*

## Reversing Trend, Big Drop Is Seen in Breast Cancer

By GINA KOLATA

Rates of the most common form of breast cancer dropped a startling 15 percent from August 2002 to December 2003, researchers reported yesterday.

The reason, they believe, may be because during that time, millions of women abandoned hormone treatment for the symptoms of menopause after a large national study concluded that the hormones slightly increased breast cancer risk.

The new analysis of breast cancer rates, by researchers from the M. D. Anderson Cancer Center in Houston and presented at a breast cancer conference in San Antonio, was based on a recent report by the National Cancer Institute on the cancer's incidence.

Investigators cautioned that they would like to see the findings confirmed in other studies, including, perhaps, in data from Canada and Europe, and they would like to see what happens in the next few years.

"Epidemiology can never prove causality," said Dr. Peter Ravdin, a medical oncologist at the M.D. Anderson center and one of the authors of the analysis.

But, he said, the hormone hypothesis seemed to perfectly explain the data and he and his colleagues could find no other explanation.

Donald Berry, head of the division of quantitative science at the cancer center and the senior investigator for the analysis, called the connection between the drop in rates and hormone use "astounding."

---

*Published: December 15, 2006.*

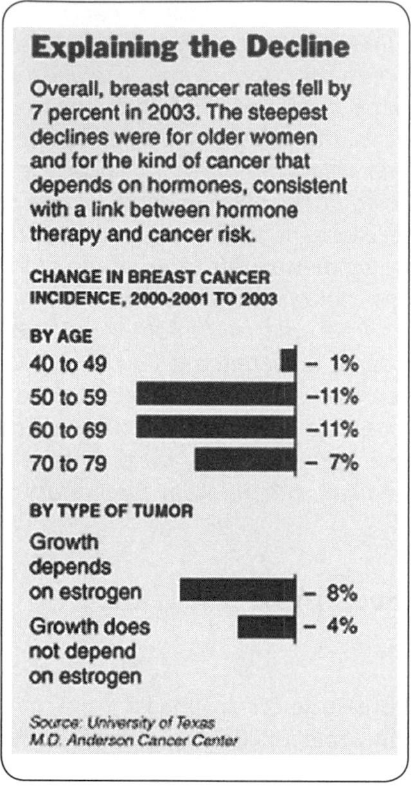

Explaining the Decline
Overall, breast cancer rates fell by 7 percent in 2003. The steepest declines were for older women and for the kind of cancer that depends on hormones, consistent with a link between hormone therapy and cancer risk.
CHANGE IN BREAST CANCER INCIDENCE, 2000-2001 TO 2003
BY AGE
40 to 49
- 1%
50 to 59
-11%
60 to 69
-11%
70 to 79
- 7%
BY TYPE OF TUMOR
Growth depends on estrogen
- 8%
Growth does not depend on estrogen
- 4%
Source: University of Texas M.D. Anderson Cancer Center

The New York Times

Over all, for women of all ages and all breast cancer types, the incidence of the cancer, the second leading killer of women, dropped by 7 percent in 2003, or about 14,000 cases, the researchers said. It was the first time that breast cancer rates had fallen significantly, something experts said was especially remarkable because the rates had slowly inched up, year by year, since 1945.

But the decrease was most striking for women with so-called estrogen-positive tumors, which account for 70 percent of all breast cancers.

In July 2002, the Women's Health Initiative, a large clinical trial looking at the use of one menopause drug, Prempro, made by Wyeth, found that women taking the drug had slightly higher breast cancer rates. The study's findings were a shock to many women and their doctors. Until then, many had assumed that Prempro simply replaced the lost hormones of youth. Within six months, the drug's sales had fallen by 50 percent.

Scientists knew that hormones could fuel the growth of estrogen-positive tumors, which carry receptors for estrogen on their cell surfaces. The hypothesis is that when women stopped taking menopausal hormones, tiny cancers already in their breasts were deprived of estrogen and stopped growing, never reaching a stage where they could have been seen on mammograms.

Other cancers may have regressed, making them undetectable. And, possibly, without hormones, cancers that would have gotten started may never have grown at all.

"This could well be the study of the year in cancer," said Dr. Otis Brawley, director of the Georgia Cancer Center at Emory University. He added that it also might help explain why breast cancer rates were lower for black women than for white women—blacks, he said, were less likely to use hormones for menopause.

Dr. Brawley also said the findings might explain why cancer in black women was more lethal. Hormone-initiated cancers, he said, might be less deadly than those that arise on their own.

Candace Steele, a Wyeth spokeswoman, said in an e-mail message that "breast cancer is a complex disease and the causes are not known."

At this point, she said, "it is simply inappropriate to make any speculative statements" based on the analysis.

And, she added, "clearly, more studies are warranted."

Dr. Berry said that the biggest effect overall was seen in women ages 50 to 69. That, he added, is the group most likely to have been taking menopausal hormones. In them, the incidence of breast cancer, including the type that grows in response to estrogen and the one that does not, fell by 12 percent in 2003, the latest year for which data is available.

The findings of the new analysis were supported by a separate study in California. That study, published in the Nov. 20 issue of the Journal of Clinical Oncology, found an even bigger drop in rates in that state and a correspondingly bigger drop in hormone use starting in July 2002.

Other researchers, who saw Dr. Berry's analysis in advance of its presentation yesterday, said they found the hypothesis convincing.

Susan Ellenberg, a professor of biostatistics at the University of Pennsylvania, said the work was provocative. And, she added, "I certainly don't see any obvious thing that says, 'Oh, this can't be right,' or any obvious flaws."

Until 2002, as many as a third of American women over age 50 were taking menopausal hormones. The drugs could relieve symptoms like hot flashes, and were thought to protect against heart disease. Because the pills were known to slow bone loss, some women used them to prevent osteoporosis. Some women and doctors also believed, without any good evidence, that the pills could keep skin youthful, preserve memory and make women energetic.

The use of estrogen to treat menopause took off in 1966, when a doctor, Robert Wilson, wrote the best-selling book "Feminine Forever" and flew across the country promoting it. He insisted that estrogen could keep women young, healthy and attractive. Women would be replacing a hormone they had lost at menopause just as diabetics replace the insulin their pancreas fails to make.

Before long, the menopause drugs, and in particular Prempro, from Wyeth, a combination of estrogen and progestins, became one of the most popular drugs in history.

The reversal of fortune came in July 2002 when the Women's Health Initiative was halted. Its accumulating data indicated that Prempro was associated with a slight increase in breast cancer and in heart attacks, strokes and blood clots. The drug slightly decreased the risk of hip fractures and colon cancer, but those benefits were not enough to overcome its risks, the researchers said. Health authorities cautioned that similar pills must be regarded as having the same risks as Prempro until proven otherwise.

The very next year, 2003, the National Cancer Institute reported recently, there was a huge decline in breast cancer incidence. It was, Dr. Ravdin said, the largest decline for a single cancer in a single year that he was aware of. He and his colleagues wondered what was going on. The cancer kills an estimated 40,000 women a year and any decline in incidence can be important.

"We looked at all the possible explanations," Dr. Berry said. He ticked them off: less mammography screening. But there was no sign of that. Increased use of drugs like tamoxifen that can prevent breast cancer; no evidence of that.

"There was some notion that it might be statins, but that was essentially debunked," Dr. Berry said.

After July 2002, Dr. Berry said, the rate "dropped each month and it is exactly where you would expect it to be" if the declining use of menopausal hormones were the reason.

Dr. Barnett Kramer, the associate director for disease prevention at the National Institutes of Health, said that hormones were certainly the most plausible explanation for such an immediate effect on incidence. Most breast cancer is fueled by estrogen and studies have found that removing estrogen, with drugs like tamoxifen that block the hormone, sharply reduces breast cancer rates within a year.

That was also the conclusion of Christina Clarke, an epidemiologist at the Northern California Cancer Center, and her colleagues, when they analyzed the cancer's rates in California. The investigators used data they had collected for a National Cancer Institute's program and data from Kaiser Permanente, the health insurer.

Dr. Clarke said that they had data through 2004 and so could ask whether the decrease in cancer incidence in 2003 continued the next year. It did, she said, although it slowed somewhat, as might be expected.

The investigators found that the breast cancer incidence fell even more in California than in the rest of the country—the overall drop was 11 percent in 2003, compared with 7 percent nationally. And, Dr. Clarke said, more women in California also had been using hormone therapy than women in other states.

Kaiser Permanente's prescriptions for hormone combinations like Prempro fell by two-thirds in 2003 and prescriptions for estrogen alone dropped by one-third, Dr. Clarke and her colleagues reported. (Estrogen without progestin can cause cancer of the uterine lining so should only be used by women whose uteruses have been removed. While there is some question about whether estrogen alone increases breast cancer risk, the Women's Health Initiative did not find such an effect.)

The heaviest users of hormone therapy were women in affluent places like Marin County, where high breast cancer rates had long troubled women and researchers. Women in those areas also largely abandoned the treatments after the 2002 report and their cancer rates declined accordingly, Dr. Clarke said.

Dr. Marcia Stefanick, a professor of medicine at Stanford University and chairwoman of the steering committee for the Women's Health Initiative, said she found the hormone argument persuasive and felt it helped clear up the mystery in Marin County.

"Everyone kept saying, 'What is it? What's in the environment?' she said. Now, she said, it is becoming clear. "The best explanation is hormone therapy."

## MAKING CONNECTIONS

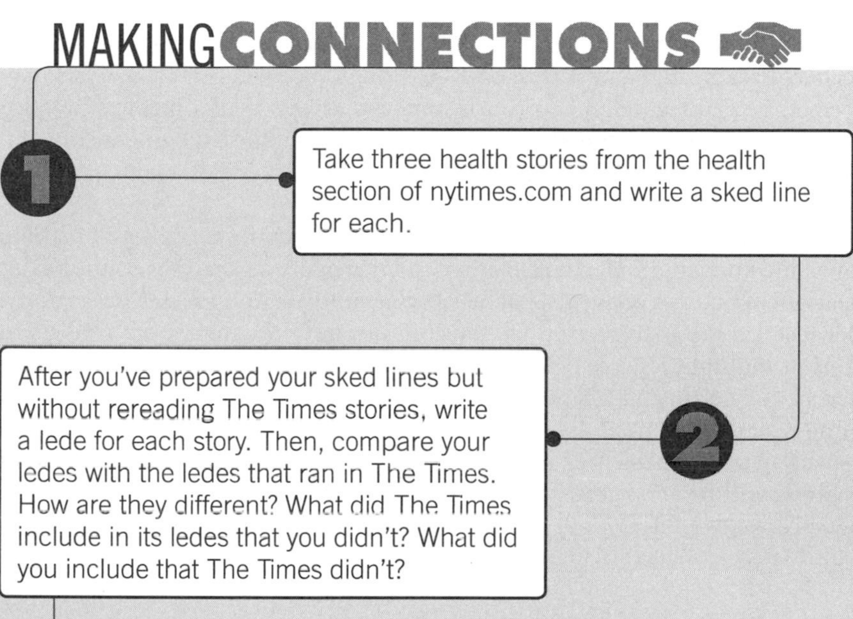

1. Take three health stories from the health section of nytimes.com and write a sked line for each.

2. After you've prepared your sked lines but without rereading The Times stories, write a lede for each story. Then, compare your ledes with the ledes that ran in The Times. How are they different? What did The Times include in its ledes that you didn't? What did you include that The Times didn't?

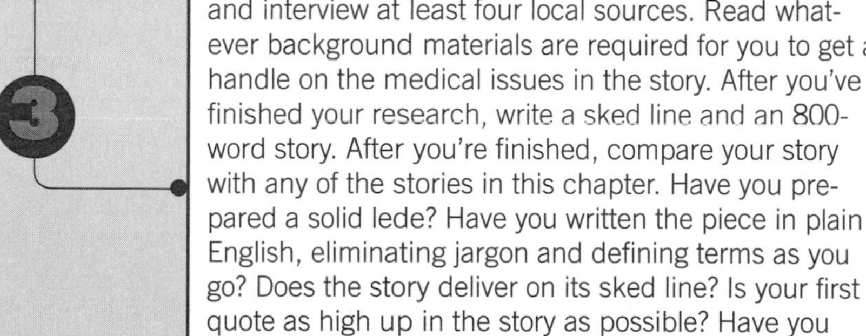

3. Take a breaking health news story in your community and interview at least four local sources. Read whatever background materials are required for you to get a handle on the medical issues in the story. After you've finished your research, write a sked line and an 800-word story. After you're finished, compare your story with any of the stories in this chapter. Have you prepared a solid lede? Have you written the piece in plain English, eliminating jargon and defining terms as you go? Does the story deliver on its sked line? Is your first quote as high up in the story as possible? Have you conveyed the drama of your story as effectively as Gardiner Harris did in his peanut contamination story?

CHAPTER 2

# news analyses

IN THE NEW YORK TIMES, NEWS ANALYSIS IS a staple of political and economic coverage, but it is used sparingly in health coverage. In an analysis the reporter steps away from the chaos of breaking news to give readers background and perspective. Although the writer of an analysis may seem to be making judgments (for instance, that a particular medical practice lacks proof of effectiveness), the writer should base those judgments on fact, not on opinions. To inform readers that the story is a news analysis, editors place a slug with that label above the headline.

To write a good news analysis, a reporter must closely follow breaking news and know the underlying history and issues. News analyses on the health beat often focus on conventional beliefs that collapse upon scientific scrutiny. Because a news analysis is, by definition, not opinion, the reporter needs to consult multiple sources before coming to any conclusions. For example, in her story later in this chapter on foods' effects on health, medical reporter Gina Kolata referenced nine people whom she interviewed (two of them by e-mail) in addition to citing four historical sources. Of course, not every news analysis will be so source heavy, but extensive research does add depth and perspective to a piece.

## Selection 2.1

*This first example of a news analysis resembles a political analysis because health care reform is, after all, a political story. Robert Pear's analysis cuts through the White House hoopla by telling us that the reform proposals are vague and not enforceable and that "none of the savings are guaranteed." To keep readers' expectations realistic, he reviews aborted attempts at health care reform pursued by President Jimmy Carter in 1977 and President Bill Clinton in 1993 and 1994. For sources Pear relies on a health care economist and a political scientist. We don't know where Pear stands on health care reform (and we shouldn't), but we do know that history is on the side of the skeptics. Note how the language in this story differs from language in a straight news story, which would simply report on the president's pronouncements instead of saying he'd "engineered a political coup."*

## News Analysis
# Obama Push to Cut Health Costs Faces Tough Odds

By ROBERT PEAR

WASHINGTON—President Obama engineered a political coup on Monday by bringing leaders of the health care industry to the White House to build momentum for his ambitious health care agenda.

Mr. Obama pronounced it "a historic day, a watershed event," because doctors, hospitals, drug makers and insurance companies voluntarily offered $2 trillion in cost reductions over 10 years. The savings, he said, "will help us take the next and most important step—comprehensive health care reform."

Robert Gibbs, the White House press secretary, said Mr. Obama had told the health care executives, "You've made a commitment; we expect you to keep it."

If history is a guide, their commitments may not produce the promised savings. Their proposals are vague—promising, for example, to reduce both "overuse and underuse of health care." None of the proposals are enforceable, and none of the savings are guaranteed. Without such a guarantee, budget rules would normally prevent Congress from using the savings to pay for new initiatives to cover the uninsured. At this point, cost control is little more than a shared aspiration.

Still, the event was significant. There was something in it for Mr. Obama, and something for the industry—though not necessarily the same thing. Their interests overlap but do not coincide.

For Mr. Obama, the White House meeting was an opportunity to showcase his consensus-building approach, in contrast with the confrontational style of Hillary Rodham Clinton, who at this point in her husband's first term attacked "price gouging, cost shifting and unconscionable profiteering" by the industry in a speech to union members.

Mr. Obama is not cracking the whip on the health care industry so much as wooing it, just as he said he would in the campaign.

For the health care and insurance executives, the savings initiative helps them secure a seat at the table where many decisions about their future will be made in the next year. They also ingratiated themselves with Democrats in the White House and Congress who are moving swiftly to reshape the nation's health care system.

"We came together in a serious way a couple of weeks ago," said David H. Nexon, senior executive vice president of the Advanced

---

*Published: May 11, 2009.*

Medical Technology Association, one of the six health care industry groups that promised to lower costs. "Health care reform is moving very fast. We want to make sure it comes out in a way that's workable and sustainable."

Dennis Rivera, coordinator of the health care campaign of the Service Employees International Union, led efforts to bring the industry groups together, with help from Nancy-Ann DeParle, director of the White House Office of Health Reform.

The consensus-building approach has already yielded some results. Insurance executives have offered to end certain underwriting practices, like refusing to cover individuals with pre-existing conditions or charging women higher rates than men, and they have invited Congress to impose stringent, uniform federal regulation on their industry. But even as insurers and health care providers stand shoulder to shoulder with Mr. Obama in vowing to slow the growth of health spending, they oppose him on other fronts. For example, insurance companies are opposed to a new government-sponsored health plan, which Mr. Obama supports but insurers fear could drive them out of business.

Senator Charles E. Schumer of New York, the third-ranking Democrat in the Senate, welcomed the industry's cost-cutting commitment as "a good-faith gesture." But he said, "It does not mitigate the need for a public plan option in our health care reform bill."

In addition, insurers and health care providers are lobbying strenuously against cuts in their Medicare payments that would produce savings of the type they profess to want. Insurers are fighting Mr. Obama's proposal to cut payments to their private Medicare Advantage plans by a total of $176 billion over 10 years. Doctors are pleading with Congress not to cut costs at their expense, in particular by allowing a 21 percent cut in their Medicare fees scheduled to occur in January. Pharmaceutical companies and makers of medical devices worry that new products may have to pass a cost-benefit test before being approved for coverage under Medicare.

To fulfill Mr. Obama's campaign promise of offering affordable coverage to all, cost control is a political, as well as an economic, necessity. By their own account, Democrats will have difficulty financing coverage for more than 45 million people who are uninsured. The task would be virtually impossible—and new social insurance programs would be unsustainable—if health spending continued to increase at the currently projected rate of 6.2 percent a year for a decade.

The industry says it can shave 1.5 percent off the annual rate of growth through voluntary efforts. But similar efforts to control health costs have been rolled out in the past, without much of a long-term effect.

Henry J. Aaron, a health economist at the Brookings Institution, said that when he heard the industry's promises on Monday, "I had a Rip van Winkle moment, as if I had fallen asleep in 1977 and woke up again this morning."

Mr. Aaron served in the administration of President Jimmy Carter, whose proposal for hospital cost controls prompted the industry to undertake a short-lived "voluntary effort."

After President Bill Clinton proposed an overhaul of the health care system in 1993 and 1994, the growth of health spending slowed, only to surge a few years later.

Drew E. Altman, the president of the Kaiser Family Foundation, offered a historical perspective spanning nearly four decades.

"Neither managed care, nor wage and price controls, nor regulation, nor voluntary action nor market competition has had a lasting impact on our nation's health care costs," Mr. Altman said. "Reformers should not overpromise."

Industry groups sounded constructive and positive on Monday, but the real test will come in a few weeks when lawmakers unveil detailed legislative proposals. "Will they still be supportive?" Mr. Altman asked. "Or will they revert to form and protect their turf?"

Rather than gambling on the answer, some lawmakers want to establish an enforcement mechanism, which would take effect if the industry's voluntary steps did not slow health spending by a specified amount.

Such cost-control devices have proved spectacularly ineffective in limiting the growth of Medicare spending on doctors' services.

## Selection 2.2

*Next is a news analysis on embryonic stem cells that puts political developments in a scientific context. Science reporter Nicholas Wade tells us what President Obama's loosening of funding for embryonic stem cell research will mean to scientists in laboratories across the country. With perspective drawn from the reporter's own experience and from conversations with informed sources, Wade analyzes the president's announcement through the prism of history. In the second paragraph Wade states the focus of his analysis plainly, distinguishing the practical effects of the president's actions from Obama's "soaring oratory" in the lede. Wade spends the rest of the story explaining the implications of the president's announcement while reminding readers that progress in science, including stem cell research, is slow. A good news analysis offers a historical perspective that gives readers a realistic assessment of the significance of current news events.*

## News Analysis
# Rethink Stem Cells? Science Already Has

By NICHOLAS WADE

With soaring oratory, President Obama on Monday removed a substantial practical nuisance that has long made life difficult for stem cell researchers. He freed biomedical researchers using federal money (a vast majority) to work on more than the small number of human embryonic stem cell lines that were established before Aug. 9, 2001.

In practical terms, federally financed researchers will now find it easier to do a particular category of stem cell experiments that, though still important, has been somewhat eclipsed by new advances.

Until now, to study unapproved stem cell lines, researchers had to set up separate, privately financed labs and follow laborious accounting procedures to make sure not a cent of federal grant money was used on that research. No longer. The lifting of such requirements "is just a major boon for the research here and elsewhere," said Dr. Arnold Kriegstein, a stem cell researcher at the University of California, San Francisco.

Dr. George Q. Daley, who studies blood diseases at Children's Hospital in Boston, said that he had derived 15 human embryonic stem cell lines using private money, and that for the first time he could now apply for grants from the National Institutes of Health to study these cells. In the last eight years, his lab has moved from 90 percent N.I.H. support to half N.I.H., half private financing. But private money is now drying up, he said, and new N.I.H. support will be particularly welcome.

However, the president's support of embryonic stem cell research comes at a time when many advances have been made with other sorts of stem cells. The Japanese biologist Shinya Yamanaka found in 2007 that adult cells could be reprogrammed to an embryonic state with surprising ease. This technology "may eventually eclipse the embryonic stem cell lines for therapeutic as well as diagnostics applications," Dr. Kriegstein said. For researchers, reprogramming an adult cell can be much more convenient, and there have never been any restrictions on working with adult stem cells.

For therapy, far off as that is, treating patients with their own cells would avoid the problem of immune rejection.

Members of Congress and advocates for fighting diseases have long spoken of human embryonic stem cell research as if it were a sure avenue to quick cures for intractable afflictions. Scientists have not publicly objected to such high-flown hopes, which have helped fuel new sources of grant money like the $3 billion initiative in California for stem cell research.

---

*Published: March 9, 2009.*

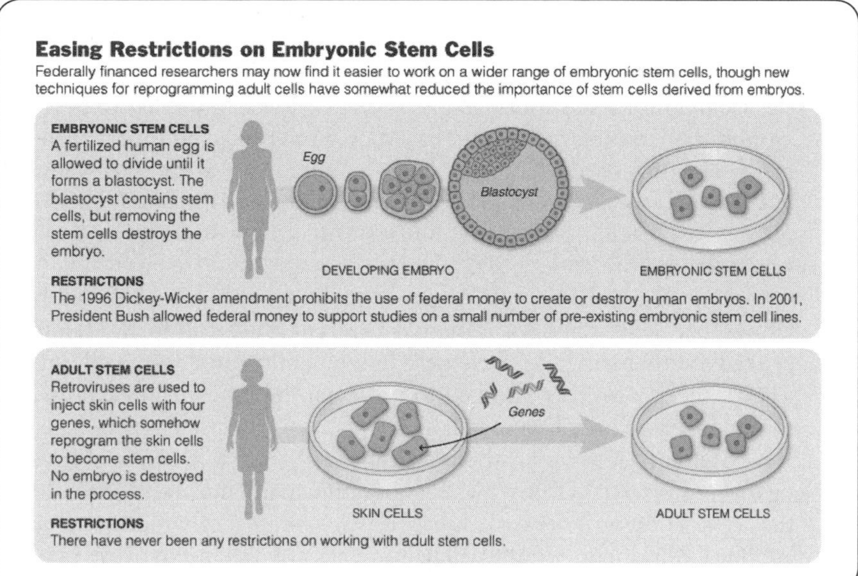

Easing Restrictions on Embryonic Stem Cells
Federally financed researchers may now find it easier to work on a wider range of embryonic stem cells, though new techniques for reprogramming adult cells have somewhat reduced the importance of stem cells derived from embryos.
EMBRYONIC STEM CELLS
A fertilized human egg is allowed to divide until it forms a blastocyst. The blastocyst contains stem cells, but removing the stem cells destroys the embryo.
Egg
Blastocyst
DEVELOPING EMBRYO
EMBRYONIC STEM CELLS
RESTRICTIONS
The 1996 Dickey-Wicker amendment prohibits the use of federal money to create or destroy human embryos. In 2001, President Bush allowed federal money to support studies on a small number of pre-existing embryonic stem cell lines.
ADULT STEM CELLS
Retroviruses are used to inject skin cells with four genes, which somehow reprogram the skin cells to become stem cells. No embryo is destroyed in the process.
Genes
SKIN CELLS
ADULT STEM CELLS
RESTRICTIONS
There have never been any restrictions on working with adult stem cells.

The New York Times

In private, however, many researchers have projected much more modest goals for embryonic stem cells. Their chief interest is to derive embryonic stem cell lines from patients with specific diseases, and by tracking the cells in the test tube to develop basic knowledge about how the disease develops.

Despite an F.D.A.-approved safety test of embryonic stem cells in spinal cord injury that the Geron Corporation began in January, many scientists believe that putting stem-cell-derived tissues into patients lies a long way off. Embryonic stem cells have their drawbacks. They cause tumors, and the adult cells derived from them may be rejected by the patient's immune system. Furthermore, whatever disease process caused the patients' tissue cells to die is likely to kill introduced cells as well. All these problems may be solvable, but so far none have been solved.

Restrictions on embryonic stem cell research originated with Congress, which, each year since 1996, has forbidden the use of federal financing for any experiment in which a human embryo is destroyed. This includes the derivation of human stem cell lines from surplus fertility clinic embryos, first achieved by Dr. James Thomson of the University of Wisconsin in 1998.

President Clinton contemplated but never implemented a policy that would have allowed N.I.H.-financed researchers to study human embryonic stem cells derived by others. Research was able to begin only in August 2001, when President Bush, seeking a different way around the Congressional restriction, said researchers could use any lines established before that date.

Critics said the distinction between the Clinton and Bush policies lacked moral significance, given that each was intended to get around the Congressional ban, based on a religious and moral argument. The proposed Clinton policy amounted to: "Stealing is wrong, but it's O.K. to use stolen property if someone else stole it." The Bush policy was: "Stealing is wrong, but it's O.K. to use stolen property if it was stolen before Aug. 9, 2001."

Mr. Obama has put the proposed Clinton policy into effect, but Congressional restrictions remain. Researchers are still forbidden to use federal financing to derive new human embryonic stem cell lines. They will, however, be allowed to do research on new stem cell lines grown in a privately financed lab.

Stem cell research is the best known of several avenues of investigation into what is known as regenerative medicine. To regenerate the aging body with its own subtle repair systems, of which stem cells are one component, would be far more effective than the brute methods of drugs and surgery used today.

But scientists are still merely at the threshold of understanding how the body's 200 different types of cell interact with one another. It seems likely to be years before biologists know all the settings that must be adjusted in a human cell's chromosomes to make it become a well-behaved cone cell in the retina or a dopamine-making neuron of the type destroyed in Parkinson's.

Despite the new interest in reprogrammed stem cells, human embryonic stem cells are still worth studying, both to track the earliest moments in disease and to help assess the behavior of the reprogrammed cells.

## Selection 2.3

*In the next news analysis, medical reporter Denise Grady uses a new study questioning standard medical procedures to explore the issue of doctors basing practices on untested assumptions. Medical practice isn't always based on scientific proof. As examples, Grady cites two discredited beliefs: that stress leads to ulcers and that hormone treatments prevent heart disease in postmenopausal women. Any journalist can report each new development as it arises. Thoughtful, experienced reporters take the initiative to connect events over time and space and look for deeper meanings. Here, Grady grabs readers with a timely connection—a study reported only two days earlier—and then, in the fourth paragraph, moves from that opening into the story's larger purpose. That's what journalists call a nut graf, one that tells readers the point of the story and why they should care. As you'll see, this analysis succeeds because the reporter uses relevant medical history to make her case. It's also an amazingly short piece for the ground it covers.*

## News Analysis
# When Blind Faith in a Medical Fix Is Broken

By DENISE GRADY

A blocked artery is not a good thing. Public health campaigns have drilled that message into the national psyche. Surely, then, whenever doctors find a closed artery, especially in the heart, they should open it.

Maybe not. A major study, presented Tuesday at a medical conference in Chicago, challenged the widespread use of tiny balloons and metal stents in people who had suffered heart attacks days or weeks before.

Although such treatment can be lifesaving in the early stages of a heart attack, the study found that opening the artery later did no good at all. It merely exposed patients to the discomfort, risk and $10,000 expense of an invasive procedure.

The new report is the latest example of a rigorous experiment turning medical practice on its head by proving that a widely accepted treatment is not the great boon it was thought to be (except maybe to the bank accounts of doctors, drug companies and makers of medical devices).

Ideally, treatments, operations and diagnostic procedures should be thoroughly tested before they come into routine use. But that is not always the case. Drugs and medical devices have to be approved by the Food and Drug Administration, but once they are on the market, doctors can prescribe them in almost any way they see fit, a practice called off-label use.

Migraine drugs are prescribed for weight loss, and heart pills for stage fright; nobody is breaking the law. At least one in five drug prescriptions are for unapproved uses, studies show, with some popular medicines getting more than 90 percent of their use as treatments for which they were never approved. Ideas for such uses may be suggested to doctors by drug companies.

The approval rules for devices are looser than those for drugs, and while there is little data measuring unapproved uses of medical devices, there are hints that off-label use there is even greater. The F.D.A. does not regulate surgery at all.

Some treatments—like opening a closed artery—appeal so strongly to common sense that it becomes irresistible to go ahead and use them without waiting for scientific proof that they are effective. That is especially true if patients are desperate and have few or no other options.

---

*Published: November 16, 2006.*

As the treatments start to catch on, people assume they must work, and it becomes difficult or impossible to study them in the most definitive way—by comparing treated patients with an untreated control group. If most people think a therapy works, who wants to be the control? Doctors may balk at controlled studies, too, calling it unethical to withhold the treatment from patients in the control group.

Dr. Judith S. Hochman, a cardiologist at New York University who directed the recent study on stents, said she encountered exactly that attitude when she was trying to recruit other researchers for her study: some refused to participate, saying it was unethical to leave some patients without stents.

But the counterargument is that it is also unethical to subject people to medicines, operations and invasive tests and treatment without proof that they are safe and effective.

Medical history is strewn with well-intended treatments that rose and then fell when someone finally had the backbone to test them, and the scientific method trumped what doctors thought they knew.

Hormone treatment after menopause, which works for symptoms like hot flashes, was widely believed to prevent heart disease and urinary incontinence. But carefully done studies in recent years have shown that hormones can actually make those conditions worse.

Stomach ulcers were once attributed to emotional stress and too much stomach acid, and were treated with surgery, acid-blocking drugs and patronizing advice to calm down. Then, in the 1980s, two doctors who were initially ridiculed for proposing an outlandish theory proved that most ulcers are caused by bacteria and can be cured with antibiotics.

For decades, women with early-stage breast cancer were told that mastectomies offered them the best chance of survival. But in 1985, a large nationwide study showed that for many, a lumpectomy combined with radiation worked just as well.

"As a nation, we're not doing ourselves any favors by going after the next new thing without doing the studies," said Dr. James N. Weinstein, chairman of orthopedic surgery at Dartmouth and a researcher at its Center for the Evaluative Clinical Sciences, which studies how well various medical and surgical procedures work.

When established treatments turn out to be useless, or worse, harmful, Dr. Weinstein said, "everybody's going to lose trust in the system."

*Gardiner Harris contributed reporting.*

## Selection 2.4

*Medical reporter Gina Kolata says she views a news analysis as an "interesting take on what's going on with a news story." For this piece, her starting point was a large study that found that women who followed a low-fat diet didn't have a significant drop in breast cancer, colon cancer or heart disease. Kolata uses those results for an expansive analysis about how beliefs about food's effects on health have changed during the past 175 years. Like Grady and Pear in previous analyses, Kolata relies on historical research to provide context for her analysis. She says she likes "backing up a little bit, talking about where does this come from, what does this mean, how are people reacting to it." For perspective, she interviews nine experts and weaves in considerable history, including even the "Great Masticator." Although she had the luxury of a 2,000-word story, Kolata's extensive research is still impressive and lends credence to her points.*

### News Analysis
## Maybe You're Not What You Eat

BY GINA KOLATA

In an early 19th-century best seller, a famous food writer offered a cure for obesity and chronic disease: a low-carbohydrate diet.

The notion that what you eat shapes your medical fate has exerted a strong pull throughout history. And its appeal continues to this day, medical historians and researchers say.

"It's one of the great principles—no, more than principles, canons—of American culture to suggest that what you eat affects your health," says James Morone, a professor of political science at Brown University.

"It's this idea that you control your own destiny and that it's never too late to reinvent yourself," he said. "Vice gets punished and virtue gets rewarded. If you eat or drink or inhale the wrong things you get sick. If not, you get healthy."

That very American canon, he and others say, may in part explain the criticism and disbelief that last week greeted a report that a low-fat diet might not prevent breast cancer, colon cancer or heart disease, after all.

The report, from a huge federal study called the Women's Health Initiative, raises important questions about how much even the most highly motivated people can change their eating habits and whether the relatively small changes that they can make really have a substantial effect on health.

---

*Published: February 14, 2006.*

The study, of nearly 49,000 women who were randomly assigned to follow a low-fat diet or not, found that the diet did not make a significant difference in development of the two cancers or heart disease. But there were limitations to the findings: the women assigned to the low-fat diet, despite extensive and expensive counseling, never reached their goal of eating 20 percent fat in the first year—only 31 percent of them got their dietary fat that low. And the study did not examine the effects of different types of fat—a fact that critics say is a weakness at a time when doctors are advising heart patients to reduce saturated fat in the diet, not overall fats.

The researchers also found a slight suggestion that low fat might make a difference in breast cancer but the results were not statistically significant, meaning they may have occurred by chance.

Still the study's results frustrate our primal urge to control our destinies by controlling what we put in our mouths. And when it comes to this urge, it is remarkable how history repeats itself. Over and over again, medical experts and self-styled medical experts have insisted that one diet or another can prevent disease, cure chronic illness and ensure health and longevity. And woe unto those who ignore such dietary precepts.

For example, Jean Anthelme Brillat-Savarin, the French 19th-century food writer, insisted that the secret to good health was to avoid carbohydrates. Brillat-Savarin, a lawyer, also knew the response his advice would provoke.

"'Oh Heavens!' all you readers of both sexes will cry out, 'oh Heavens above!'" he wrote in his 1825 book, "The Physiology of Taste." "But what a wretch the Professor is! Here in a single word he forbids us everything we must love, those little white rolls from Limet, and Achard's cakes and those cookies, and a hundred things made with flour and butter, with flour and sugar, with flour and sugar and eggs!"

Brillat-Savarin continued, "He doesn't even leave us potatoes or macaroni! Who would have thought this of a lover of good food who seemed so pleasant?

"'What's this I hear?' I exclaim, putting on my severest face, which I do perhaps once a year. Very well then; eat! Get fat! Become ugly and thick, and asthmatic, finally die in your own melted grease."

The Frenchman's recipe for good health was only one of many to come. A decade later, the Rev. Sylvester Graham exhorted Americans to eat simple foods like grains and vegetables and to drink water.

Beef and pork, salt and pepper, spices, tea and coffee, alcohol, he advised, all lead to gluttony. Bread should be unleavened, and made with bran to avoid the problem of yeast, which turns sugar into alcohol, he continued. It is also important, he said, to seek out fresh organic fruits and vegetables, grown in soil without fertilizers.

The reward for living right, Graham promised, would be perfect health.

A few decades later came Horace Fletcher, a wealthy American businessman who invented his diet in 1889. He was 40 and in despair: he was fat, his health was failing, he was always tired and he had indigestion. He felt, he said, like "a thing fit but to be thrown on the scrap-heap."

But Fletcher found a method that, he wrote, saved his life: eat only when you are hungry; eat only those foods that your appetite is craving; stop when you are no longer hungry and, the dictum for which he was most famous, chew every morsel of food until there is no more taste to be extracted from it.

Fletcher became known as the Great Masticator, and his followers recited and followed his instructions to chew their food 100 times a minute. Liquids, too, had to be chewed, he insisted. He promised that "Fletcherizing," as it became known, would turn "a pitiable glutton into an intelligent epicurean."

Along with the endless chewing, Fletcher and his supporters also advocated a low-protein diet as a means to health and well-being.

But by 1919, when Fletcher, 68, died of a heart attack, his diet plan was on its way out, supplanted by the next new thing: counting calories. Its champions were two Yale professors, Irving Fisher and Eugene Lyman Fisk, who wrote the best-selling book "How to Live."

"Constant vigilance is necessary, yet it is worthwhile when one considers the inconvenience as well as the menace of obesity," Fisher and Fisk advised their readers.

More recently, of course, the preferred diet, at least for cancer prevention, has been to eat foods low in fat. And that was what led to the Women's Health Initiative, a study financed by the National Institutes of Health comparing low fat to regular diets.

Eight years later, the women who reduced dietary fat had the same rates of colon cancer, breast cancer and heart disease as those whose diets were unchanged.

They also weighed about the same and had no difference in diabetes rates, or in levels of insulin or blood sugar.

It made sense to try the low-fat diet for cancer prevention, said Dr. Elizabeth Nabel, the director of the Women's Health Initiative.

"In the mid- to late 1980's, there was a body of literature that was suggestive that diet might impact the incidence of breast cancer and colorectal cancer," Dr. Nabel said.

For example, studies found that women acquired a higher risk of those cancers if they moved to the United States from countries where incidence of the cancers was low and where diets were low in fat.

And there were animal studies indicating that a high-fat diet could lead to more mammary cancer.

But intriguing as those observations were, there was no direct, rigorous evidence that a low-fat diet was protective.

The Women's Health Initiative study would be the first rigorous test to see if it was. The study investigators decided to follow heart disease rates, as well.

"Think of it," said Dr. Joan McGowan, an osteoporosis expert who is also a project officer for the Women's Health Initiative. "Here was a hypothesis that just a better diet could prevent breast cancer. How attractive was that?"

In the meantime, the notion that fat was bad and that low-fat diets could protect against disease took hold, with scientists promoting it and much of the public believing it. And a low-fat food industry grew apace.

In 2005, according to the NPD Group, which tracks food trends, 75 percent of Americans said they substituted a low-fat or no-fat food for a higher-fat one once a week or more.

So last week, when the study's results, published in The Journal of the American Medical Association, showed that the low-fat diets had no effect, the study investigators braced themselves for attacks.

Dr. Jacques Rossouw, the project officer for the Women's Health Initiative, said the researchers knew that some critics would say the women did not reduce the fat in their diets nearly enough. Perhaps a lower-fat diet would have offered some protection against cancer, Dr. Rossouw said. But, he said, "what we achieved is probably what was achievable."

Other critics said that the study made a mistake in even aiming for 20 percent of calories as fat. Dietary fat should be even lower, they said, as low as 10 percent.

But Dr. Rossouw said this was unrealistic, because try as they might, people are not able to change their eating habits that much.

"You can't do that," he said. "Forget it. It's impossible."

Critics now are telling the investigators that the study was useless because it focused on total fat in the diet, rather than on saturated fat, which raises cholesterol levels. If the women had focused instead on getting rid of fats like butter, had substituted fats like olive oil and had eaten more fruits and grains, then the study might have shown that the proper diet reduces heart disease risk, they claim.

"Lifestyle goes beyond a modest difference in saturated fat," said Dr. Robert H. Eckel, president of the American Heart Association.

Dr. Rossouw responded, "They're telling us that we chose the wrong kind of fat and that we just didn't know."

But, he said: "We're not stupid. We knew all that stuff."

The investigators, he said, had long debates about whether to ask the women to reduce total fat or just saturated fat.

In the end, they decided to go with total fat because the study was primarily a cancer study and the cancer data were for total fat.

If the women had reduced just their saturated fat, their dietary fat content would probably have been even higher, fueling the critics. And, he said, some animal data indicate that polyunsaturated fat may even increase cancer risk.

"We looked at all possible scenarios," Dr. Rossouw said. But, he said, given the study's disappointing findings, he was not surprised by the critics' responses.

Not everyone is attacking the study. Many scientists applaud its findings and say it is about time that some cherished dietary notions are put to a rigorous test. And some nonscientists are shocked by the reactions of the study's critics.

"Whatever is happening to evidence-based treatment?" Dr. Arthur Yeager, a retired dentist in Edison, N.J., wrote in an e-mail message. "When the facts contravene conventional wisdom, go with the anecdotes?"

The problem, some medical scientists said, is that many people—researchers included—get so wedded to their beliefs about diet and disease that they will not accept rigorous evidence that contradicts it.

"Now it's almost a political sort of thing," said Dr. Jules Hirsch, physician in chief emeritus at Rockefeller University. "We're all supposed to be lean and eat certain things."

And so the notion of a healthful diet, he said, has become more than just a question for scientific inquiry.

"It is woven into cultural notions of ourselves and our behavior," he said. "This is the burden you get going into a discussion, and this is why we get so shocked by this evidence."

The truth, said Dr. David Altshuler, an endocrinologist and geneticist at Massachusetts General Hospital, is that while the Western diet and lifestyle are clearly important risk factors for chronic disease, tweaking diet in one way or another—a bit less fat or a few more vegetables—may not, based on studies like the Women's Health Initiative, have major effects on health. "We should limit strong advice to where randomized trials have proven a benefit of lifestyle modification," Dr. Altshuler wrote in an e-mail message.

Still, he said, he understands the appeal of dietary prescriptions.

The promise of achieving better health through diet can be so alluring that even scientists and statisticians who know all about clinical trial data say they sometimes find themselves suspending disbelief when it comes to diet and disease.

"I fall for it, too," says Brad Efron, a Stanford statistician. "I really don't believe in the low-fat thing, but I find myself doing it anyway."

## MAKING CONNECTIONS

1

Find a local medical or health story that pits one point of view against another. Interview as many parties to the dispute as you can find so that you can understand the history and issues involved. Then write a news analysis that makes sense of the controversy.

2

The New England Journal of Medicine and other journals regularly publish what they call review articles. These are articles that summarize the state of thinking about diagnosis and treatment for various diseases or conditions. Using a review article as a jumping-off point, look for a nugget of news in the review. Find and interview local experts. Then write a news analysis translating the academic information in the review article into a story that readers can appreciate and understand.

3

Take another look at Gina Kolata's news analysis, "Maybe You're Not What You Eat." Find another topic where popular belief may clash with medical reality. After you've settled on a topic, do historical research and get informed on how thinking about this topic has changed over the years. Then write a 900-word analysis that makes sense of this issue.

CHAPTER 3

# news briefs

EVERY WEEK MEDICAL RESEARCHERS PUBLISH dozens of studies in the scientific literature, most of them reporting small advances in knowledge on specialized topics. Although these studies are important in the context of science, where research moves incrementally, only a small fraction of them will interest a mass audience. News organizations tend to cover many studies only as news briefs, short stories focused on the nugget of news most likely to have wide interest or impact. Of course it's the reporter's job to find these nuggets in long, complex studies—and then craft short stories that help readers understand.

Editors of the leading medical and science journals say they try to help journalists report intelligently on research findings by making their studies available to reporters several days in advance of journal publication. Reporters who get advance access to journal articles must agree to not publish their stories until a specified release or embargo date. That means reporters can read a study and contact its authors but can't publish stories about the journal article until the embargo expires. Typical embargoes expire the evening before the publication date of the journal. Many of these embargoed journal articles appear in an online aggregation site called EurekAlert! The site contains articles from JAMA, the British Medical Journal, The Lancet, Cell and Science, among others.

Embargoes both help and hurt the quality of health reporting. On one hand, an embargo gives journalists time to read a complicated study and do the necessary reporting to thoroughly understand it, such as interviewing the study's authors and consulting with other experts—all of which would be much harder with the pressure of an imminent deadline. On the other hand, embargoes promote herd journalism in which medical reporters around the world cover the same article in the same time frame—the "if it's Wednesday night, it must be The New England Journal of Medicine story" effect. That's because the NEJM embargo expires Wednesday evening before its official publication date the next day.

The ability of major journals to manipulate the news cycle makes many reporters uneasy. Of course, a reporter can choose not to report on the upcoming NEJM or JAMA article, but then the reporter has to justify that decision to her editor when the competition trumpets the story.

Laura Chang, The Times science editor, says her newspaper tries not to be manipulated by the journals' embargo system: "There are embargoed stories that are being promoted heavily by the journal, by the author, or by the university. For some of those studies we've read them and our reporters have read them and talked to people that they trust and don't think much of the studies. But we know that they're going to get a lot of publicity. So sometimes we will cover such a study in a small way almost to decontaminate the study, to let people know that it's not as significant as it might be portrayed in certain places."

If the journal article is particularly newsworthy, a reporter may be tempted to break the embargo and publish early, but the consequence can be severe. Journals can and do deny access to reporters who don't respect embargo dates. So reporters usually play along with the system. Eventually, newer, peer-reviewed, open-access, online journals like PLoS Medicine may break, the stranglehold. For now, though, Chang says news organizations have little choice but to comply. "I'm not sure the embargo system is going to hold up forever, and I keep waiting for it to crumble," she says. "But it hasn't yet. And until then, we will abide by it."

Each week medical reporters usually cover one or more embargoed stories from the major journals. Most of those stories fall into the Breaking News category that was the subject of Chapter 1. Journal articles from dozens of other reputable but less widely read peer-reviewed journals often miss the radar of the daily medical reporter. However, an enterprising reporter can mine these lesser-known journals—sometimes weeks later—to find nuggets of news. Some of these news items can lead to shorter stories like those featured in a news brief or what some call a news digest.

The key to writing a news brief is to capture the essence of the journal article in a lead sentence. The reporter can then use the next paragraphs to explain the science behind the study before underlining its significance with a short quote from the journal author. If space permits, the reporter can insert another short quote from an expert unaffiliated with the study. This second quote can validate the importance of the study and add credibility to the article.

The New York Times runs these stories in its Science Times section in a weekly feature called Vital Signs. There readers will find stories that many other news organizations either missed or rejected because the journal articles were of limited significance to the general public (although the studies might have generated a lot of interest in specialized scientific circles and for particular groups of patients).

## Selection 3.1

*This 2008 story about an association between diet soda and a disorder called metabolic syndrome is typical of Vital Signs. Because the story by definition is brief, writer Nicholas Bakalar quotes only one source. Bakalar knows that most readers care more about the information in the study than the name of the journal in which the article ran. Still, for those who want more information, Bakalar names the journal in the fifth paragraph—and for those who want a lot more, the online version of his story offers a link to the original study. Because the study's authors found only a correlation between drinking diet soda and metabolic syndrome—but not a causative link—the reporter ends the short story with the researcher asking questions, indicating that scientific scrutiny of this correlation will continue.*

### VITAL SIGNS

### Symptoms: Metabolic Syndrome Is Tied to Diet Soda

By NICHOLAS BAKALAR

Researchers have found a correlation between drinking diet soda and metabolic syndrome—the collection of risk factors for cardiovascular disease and diabetes that include abdominal obesity, high cholesterol and blood glucose levels, and elevated blood pressure.

The scientists gathered dietary information on more than 9,500 men and women ages 45 to 64 and tracked their health for nine years.

Over all, a Western dietary pattern—high intakes of refined grains, fried foods and red meat—was associated with an 18 percent increased risk for metabolic syndrome, while a "prudent" diet dominated by fruits, vegetables, fish and poultry correlated with neither an increased nor a decreased risk.

But the one-third who ate the most fried food increased their risk by 25 percent compared with the one-third who ate the least, and surprisingly, the risk of developing metabolic syndrome was 34 percent higher among those who drank one can of diet soda a day compared with those who drank none.

"This is interesting," said Lyn M. Steffen, an associate professor of epidemiology at the University of Minnesota and a co-author of the paper, which was posted online in the journal Circulation on Jan. 22. "Why is it happening? Is it some kind of chemical in the diet soda, or something about the behavior of diet soda drinkers?"

---

*Published: February 5, 2008.*

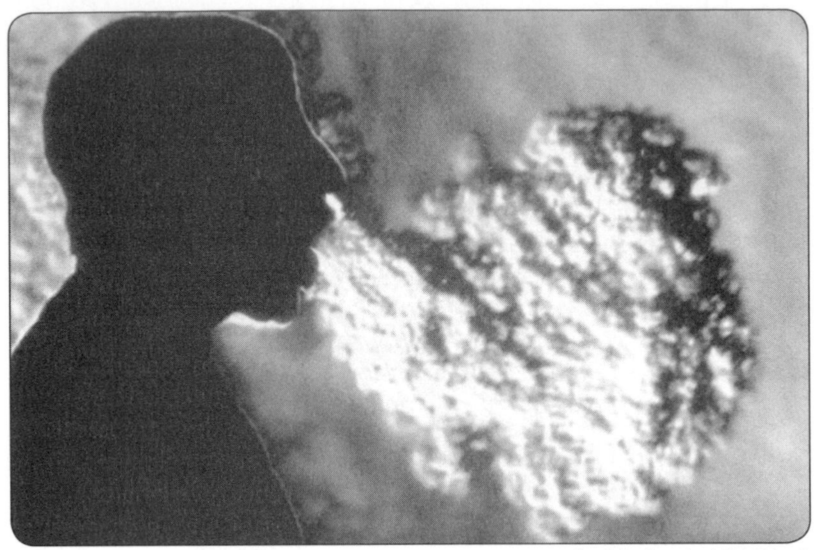

Gary Settles/Pennsylvania State University

## Selection 3.2

*Not every article in major journals is a full-fledged research study. Journals often carry smaller items that can provide a gem of a story for adventurous reporters who don't want to follow the crowd. In the next piece Denise Grady shows us a photo of a cough, an image that she found in a one-page article in The New England Journal of Medicine. The photo and story are newsworthy because few people—even physicians—have ever seen a cough. Notice that even in a short story, good writers take pride in their craft. In her lede Grady takes an image of "dreams in glass jars" from a children's book as a metaphor for a cough caught on camera. She plays with the concepts of visible-invisible, whimsical-ephemeral to describe what defies description in words.*

*In many ways the article reads like an extended caption because the photograph is the main story. A brief—like a caption—necessitates simple explanations. Note Grady's fifth paragraph, which describes in one sentence a scientific process that could have occupied several paragraphs. Rather than going into detail on how the photographic process works, Grady instead lists the elements in the process. For most readers of a news brief, that's ample information.*

### The Mysterious Cough, Caught on Film

By DENISE GRADY

In Roald Dahl's novel "The B.F.G.," the title character, a big friendly giant, captures dreams in glass jars. At Pennsylvania State

*Published: October 27, 2008.*

University, a professor of engineering has captured something less whimsical but no less ephemeral—a cough—on film.

The image, published online Oct. 9 by The New England Journal of Medicine, was created by schlieren photography, which "takes an invisible phenomenon and turns it into a visible picture," said the engineering professor, Gary Settles, who is the director of the university's gas dynamics laboratory.

Schlieren is German for "streaks"; in this case it refers to regions of different densities in a gas or a liquid, which can be photographed as shadows using a special technique.

"In my lab we use this technique a lot," Dr. Settles said. "Often it's used for other things, like in supersonic wind tunnels, to show shock waves around high-speed aircraft."

The process involves a small, bright light source, precisely placed lenses, a curved mirror, a razor blade that blocks part of the light beam and other tools that make it possible to see and photograph disturbances in the air. In the world of gas dynamics, a cough is merely "a turbulent jet of air with density changes." Though coughs spread tuberculosis, SARS, influenza and other diseases, surprisingly little is known about them. "We don't have a good understanding of the air flow," Dr. Settles said.

To map a cough, he teamed up with Dr. Julian Tang, a virus expert from Singapore. A healthy student provided the cough. The expelled air, traveling at 18 miles per hour, mixed with cooler surrounding air and produced "temperature differences that bend light rays by different amounts," Dr. Settles said.

He went on: "The next thing is, you get a couple of people in front of the mirror talking, or one coughs on another, and you see how the air flow moves, how people infect one another. Or you look at how coughing can spread airborne infection in a hospital. This is really a suggestion for how we might study all that. The techniques used in wind tunnels can be used to study human diseases."

Other schlieren images show the churning air and shock waves that emanate from a pistol's firing; an Airedale sniffing a small flower; and the unseen, shimmering world around a candle burning in a breeze.

The final photograph, in a full-scale mock-up of an aircraft cabin, captures in microseconds the flash of an explosion under a mannequin in an airplane seat and the propagation of shock waves into the cabin. The blast was a re-creation of a terrorist's attempt in 1994 to bring down a Philippine Airlines flight with a nitroglycerin bomb. The plane did not crash, but the explosion did kill the passenger seated over the bomb. The simulation used a less intense explosion than the actual bombing.

"The simulation helps to understand how the energy of an onboard blast reverberates around the cabin," Dr. Settles said, "and it is also useful to check the results of computer blast simulations."

# MAKING CONNECTIONS

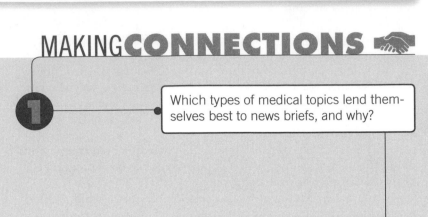

1. Which types of medical topics lend themselves best to news briefs, and why?

2. Compare a short article you've written with the article by Nicholas Bakalar in this chapter. How is your article different? Have you tried to put too much detail into your news brief? Have you given your readers enough information so that they know where to turn if they want to learn more?

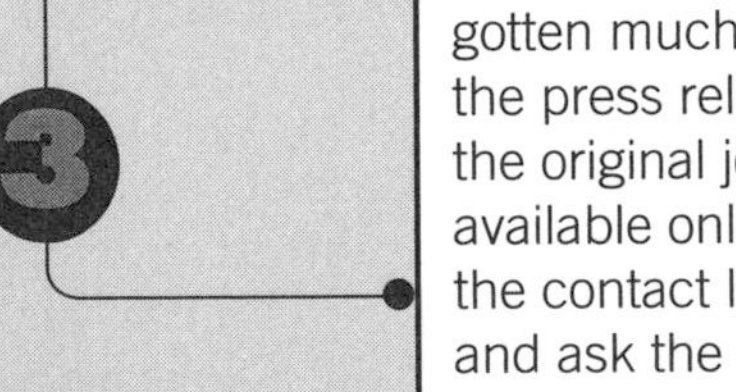

3. Go to the Web site eurekalert.org and search in the medical and science section for a journal article that hasn't gotten much coverage. After you find the press release about the story, read the original journal article. If it's not available online or in your library, call the contact listed on the press release and ask the media liaison to send you a copy of the journal article. After you've read the article, contact the study author and any other people you think will shed light on the subject. Then write a 250-word article.

CHAPTER 4

# investigative stories

INVESTIGATIVE JOURNALISM REQUIRES time and tenacity. Times public health reporter Gardiner Harris, for example, says that he and two fellow reporters and their editors worked for four months trolling public records in Minnesota in order to nail down an association between payments from drug makers and doctors' decisions to prescribe certain psychiatric drugs. Gardiner says their May 2007 story, which you'll read later in this chapter, prompted investigations that, in turn, have led to reforms. As Harris noted in his Times story, "the intersection of money and medicine, and its effect on the well-being of patients, has become one of the most contentious issues in health care."

Most investigations begin when a journalist notices something puzzling—Why are so many antipsychotic drugs being prescribed to children?—and then starts looking for answers. The more difficult the answers are to find, the more detective skills an investigative reporter needs.

Sometimes the information is actually accessible to the public (as was the case with the Minnesota story that Harris and his colleagues reported), but it may be buried in databases, government files or court records where no one has thought to look. Other times, government and private organizations hide documents from public view, and only a whistle-blower can shed light on the truth. Unless subpoenaed by attorneys, closely held private companies and public corporations have no reason to disclose information that they think can hurt them. Even when parties settle in court, they often stipulate that potentially damaging documents can't be released to the public.

Investigative journalists can use the Freedom of Information Act (FOIA) to get public records, but the U.S. Department of Justice notes that FOIA "applies only to federal agencies and does not create a right of access to records held by Congress, the courts, or by state or local government agencies."[1] To obtain state and local documents, a reporter needs to consult state public access laws, which differ in both name and provisions in each state.

Documents, however, are just the beginning of an investigative project. Reporters still need to work the phones, interview experts with a wide range of opinions and expertise, and in many cases analyze documents through computer-assisted techniques. Only then is the reporter ready to move far enough away from that mountain of information to start seeing one main thesis and a story, something that pulls in the reader. That often means putting a face on the story through anecdotes and short narratives. In the months-long process of accumulating information, it can be easy to forget that investigative stories matter only because they have an impact on people's lives.

## Selection 4.1

*In the story that follows, note how the reporters start with a face, that of a 12-year-old girl with an eating disorder who suffered real harm when a doctor prescribed a powerful antipsychotic drug. Both in print and online, that girl is pictured at the top of the story. The lede in the story reels in the reader, but of course an interesting "hook" is not enough. Reporters Gardiner Harris, Benedict Carey and Janet Roberts have to—in Harris' words—"deliver the goods," and they can't wait long to do that.*

*In the sixth paragraph, they provide the context for their case by noting increasing payments to psychiatrists by pharmaceutical companies for consulting and lecturing "have coincided with the growing use in children of a relatively new class of drugs known as atypical antipsychotics." Just two paragraphs later they deliver their thesis: "A New York Times analysis of records in Minnesota, the only state that requires public reports of all drug company marketing payments to doctors, provides rare documentation of how financial relationships between doctors and drug makers correspond to the growing use of atypicals in children."*

*The structure followed in this story is familiar to reporters: Lead with a real person, broaden from that person's experience to the larger issue, deliver facts and context in an organized way, and then return at some point (often at the end) to the person in the lede. It's not a formula in the sense that it can work with every story, but it's a structure that you can modify and use to build your story.*

### Psychiatrists, Children and Drug Industry's Role

By GARDINER HARRIS, BENEDICT CAREY AND JANET ROBERTS

When Anya Bailey developed an eating disorder after her 12th birthday, her mother took her to a psychiatrist at the University of Minnesota who prescribed a powerful antipsychotic drug called Risperdal.

Created for schizophrenia, Risperdal is not approved to treat eating disorders, but increased appetite is a common side effect and doctors may prescribe drugs as they see fit. Anya gained weight but within two years developed a crippling knot in her back. She now receives regular injections of Botox to unclench her back muscles. She often awakens crying in pain.

*Published: May 10, 2007.*

Isabella Bailey, Anya's mother, said she had no idea that children might be especially susceptible to Risperdal's side effects. Nor did she know that Risperdal and similar medicines were not approved at the time to treat children, or that medical trials often cited to justify the use of such drugs had as few as eight children taking the drug by the end.

Just as surprising, Ms. Bailey said, was learning that the university psychiatrist who supervised Anya's care received more than $7,000 from 2003 to 2004 from Johnson & Johnson, Risperdal's maker, in return for lectures about one of the company's drugs.

Doctors, including Anya Bailey's, maintain that payments from drug companies do not influence what they prescribe for patients.

But the intersection of money and medicine, and its effect on the well-being of patients, has become one of the most contentious issues in health care. Nowhere is that more true than in psychiatry, where increasing payments to doctors have coincided with the growing use in children of a relatively new class of drugs known as atypical antipsychotics.

These best-selling drugs, including Risperdal, Seroquel, Zyprexa, Abilify and Geodon, are now being prescribed to more than half a million children in the United States to help parents deal with behavior problems despite profound risks and almost no approved uses for minors.

A New York Times analysis of records in Minnesota, the only state that requires public reports of all drug company marketing payments to doctors, provides rare documentation of how financial relationships between doctors and drug makers correspond to the growing use of atypicals in children.

From 2000 to 2005, drug maker payments to Minnesota psychiatrists rose more than sixfold, to $1.6 million. During those same years, prescriptions of antipsychotics for children in Minnesota's Medicaid program rose more than ninefold.

Those who took the most money from makers of atypicals tended to prescribe the drugs to children the most often, the data suggest. On average, Minnesota psychiatrists who received at least $5,000 from atypical makers from 2000 to 2005 appear to have written three times as many atypical prescriptions for children as psychiatrists who received less or no money.

The Times analysis focused on prescriptions written for about one-third of Minnesota's Medicaid population, almost all of whom are disabled. Some doctors were misidentified by pharmacists, but the information provides a rough guide to prescribing patterns in the state.

Drug makers underwrite decision makers at every level of care. They pay doctors who prescribe and recommend drugs, teach about the underlying diseases, perform studies and write guidelines that other doctors often feel bound to follow.

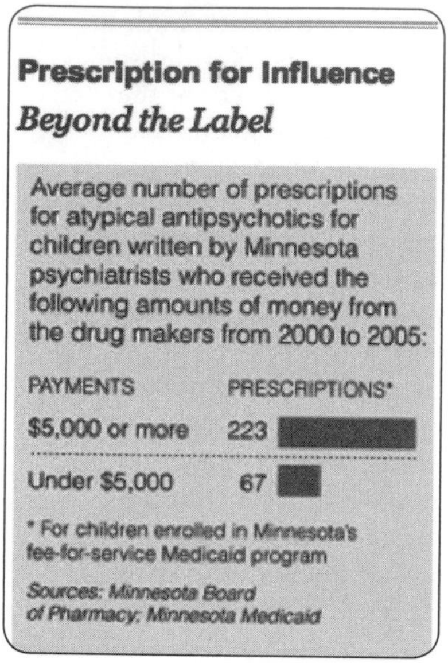

**Prescription for Influence**

***Beyond the Label***

Average number of prescriptions for atypical antipsychotics for children written by Minnesota psychiatrists who received the following amounts of money from the drug makers from 2000 to 2005:

| PAYMENTS | PRESCRIPTIONS* |
|---|---|
| $5,000 or more | 223 |
| Under $5,000 | 67 |

* For children enrolled in Minnesota's fee-for-service Medicaid program

*Sources: Minnesota Board of Pharmacy; Minnesota Medicaid*

The New York Times

But studies present strong evidence that financial interests can affect decisions, often without people knowing it.

In Minnesota, psychiatrists collected more money from drug makers from 2000 to 2005 than doctors in any other specialty. Total payments to individual psychiatrists ranged from $51 to more than $689,000, with a median of $1,750. Since the records are incomplete, these figures probably underestimate doctors' actual incomes.

Such payments could encourage psychiatrists to use drugs in ways that endanger patients' physical health, said Dr. Steven E. Hyman, the provost of Harvard University and former director of the National Institute of Mental Health. The growing use of atypicals in children is the most troubling example of this, Dr. Hyman said.

"There's an irony that psychiatrists ask patients to have insights into themselves, but we don't connect the wires in our own lives about how money is affecting our profession and putting our patients at risk," he said.

## The Prescription

Anya Bailey is a 15-year-old high school freshman from East Grand Forks, Minn., with pictures of the actor Chad Michael Murray on her bedroom wall. She has constant discomfort in her neck that leads her to twist it in a birdlike fashion. Last year, a boy mimicked her in the lunch room.

"The first time, I laughed it off," Anya said. "I said: 'That's so funny. I think I'll laugh with you.' Then it got annoying, and I decided to hide it. I don't want to be made fun of."

Now she slumps when seated at school to pressure her clenched muscles, she said.

It all began in 2003 when Anya became dangerously thin. "Nothing tasted good to her," Ms. Bailey said.

Psychiatrists at the University of Minnesota, overseen by Dr. George M. Realmuto, settled on Risperdal, not for its calming effects but for its normally unwelcome side effect of increasing appetite and weight gain, Ms. Bailey said. Anya had other issues that may have recommended Risperdal to doctors, including occasional angry outbursts and having twice heard voices over the previous five years, Ms. Bailey said.

Dr. Realmuto said he did not remember Anya's case, but speaking generally he defended his unapproved use of Risperdal to counter an eating disorder despite the drug's risks. "When things are dangerous, you use extraordinary measures," he said.

Ten years ago, Dr. Realmuto helped conduct a study of Concerta, an attention deficit hyperactivity disorder drug marketed by Johnson & Johnson, which also makes Risperdal. When Concerta was approved, the company hired him to lecture about it.

He said he gives marketing lectures for several reasons.

"To the extent that a drug is useful, I want to be seen as a leader in my specialty and that I was involved in a scientific study," he said.

The money is nice, too, he said. Dr. Realmuto's university salary is $196,310.

"Academics don't get paid very much," he said. "If I was an entertainer, I think I would certainly do a lot better."

In 2003, the year Anya came to his clinic, Dr. Realmuto earned $5,000 from Johnson & Johnson for giving three talks about Concerta. Dr. Realmuto said he could understand someone's worrying that his Concerta lecture fees would influence him to prescribe Concerta but not a different drug from the same company, like Risperdal.

In general, he conceded, his relationship with a drug company might prompt him to try a drug. Whether he continued to use it, though, would depend entirely on the results.

As the interview continued, Dr. Realmuto said that upon reflection his payments from drug companies had probably opened his door to useless visits from a drug salesman, and he said he would stop giving sponsored lectures in the future.

Kara Russell, a Johnson & Johnson spokeswoman, said that the company selects speakers who have used the drug in patients and have either undertaken research or are aware of the studies. "Dr. Realmuto met these criteria," Ms. Russell said.

When asked whether these payments may influence doctors' prescribing habits, Ms. Russell said that the talks "provide an educational opportunity for physicians."

No one has proved that psychiatrists prescribe atypicals to children because of drug company payments. Indeed, some who frequently prescribe the drugs to children earn no drug industry money. And nearly all psychiatrists who accept payments say they remain independent. Some say they prescribed and extolled the benefits of such drugs before ever receiving payments to speak to other doctors about them.

"If someone takes the point of view that your doctor can be bought, why would you go to an E. R. with your injured child and say, 'Can you help me?' " said Dr. Suzanne A. Albrecht, a psychiatrist from Edina, Minn., who earned more than $188,000 from 2002 to 2005 giving drug marketing talks.

## The Industry Campaign

It is illegal for drug makers to pay doctors directly to prescribe specific products. Federal rules also bar manufacturers from promoting unapproved, or off-label, uses for drugs.

But doctors are free to prescribe as they see fit, and drug companies can sidestep marketing prohibitions by paying doctors to give lectures in which, if asked, they may discuss unapproved uses.

The drug industry and many doctors say that these promotional lectures provide the field with invaluable education. Critics say the payments and lectures, often at expensive restaurants, are disguised kickbacks that encourage potentially dangerous drug uses. The issue is particularly important in psychiatry, because mental problems are not well understood, treatment often involves trial and error, and off-label prescribing is common.

The analysis of Minnesota records shows that from 1997 through 2005, more than a third of Minnesota's licensed psychiatrists took money from drug makers, including the last eight presidents of the Minnesota Psychiatric Society.

The psychiatrist receiving the most from drug companies was Dr. Annette M. Smick, who lives outside Rochester, Minn., and was paid more than $689,000 by drug makers from 1998 to 2004. At one point Dr. Smick was doing so many sponsored talks that "it was hard for me to find time to see patients in my clinical practice," she said.

"I was providing an educational benefit, and I like teaching," Dr. Smick said.

Dr. Steven S. Sharfstein, immediate past president of the American Psychiatric Association, said psychiatrists have become too cozy with drug makers. One example of this, he said, involves Lexapro, made by Forest Laboratories, which is now the most widely used antidepressant in the country even though there are cheaper alternatives, including generic versions of Prozac.

"Prozac is just as good if not better, and yet we are migrating to the expensive drug instead of the generics," Dr. Sharfstein said. "I think it's the marketing."

Atypicals have become popular because they can settle almost any extreme behavior, often in minutes, and doctors have few other answers for desperate families.

Their growing use in children is closely tied to the increasingly common and controversial diagnosis of pediatric bipolar disorder, a mood problem marked by aggravation, euphoria, depression and, in some cases, violent outbursts. The drugs, sometimes called major tranquilizers, act by numbing brain cells to surges of dopamine, a chemical that has been linked to euphoria and psychotic delusions.

Suzette Scheele of Burnsville, Minn., said her 17-year-old son, Matt, was given a diagnosis of bipolar disorder four years ago because of intense mood swings, and now takes Seroquel and Abilify, which have caused substantial weight gain.

"But I don't have to worry about his rages; he's appropriate; he's pleasant to be around," Ms. Scheele said.

The sudden popularity of pediatric bipolar diagnosis has coincided with a shift from antidepressants like Prozac to far more expensive atypicals. In 2000, Minnesota spent more than $521,000 buying antipsychotic drugs, most of it on atypicals, for children on Medicaid. In 2005, the cost was more than $7.1 million, a 14-fold increase.

The drugs, which can cost $1,000 to $8,000 for a year's supply, are huge sellers worldwide. In 2006, Zyprexa, made by Eli Lilly, had $4.36 billion in sales, Risperdal $4.18 billion and Seroquel, made by AstraZeneca, $3.42 billion.

Many Minnesota doctors, including the president of the Minnesota Psychiatric Society, said drug makers and their intermediaries are now paying them almost exclusively to talk about bipolar disorder.

## The Diagnoses

Yet childhood bipolar disorder is an increasingly controversial diagnosis. Even doctors who believe it is common disagree about its telltale symptoms. Others suspect it is a fad. And the scientific evidence that atypicals improve these children's lives is scarce.

One of the first and perhaps most influential studies was financed by AstraZeneca and performed by Dr. Melissa DelBello, a child and adult psychiatrist at the University of Cincinnati.

Dr. DelBello led a research team that tracked for six weeks the moods of 30 adolescents who had received diagnoses of bipolar disorder. Half of the teenagers took Depakote, an antiseizure drug used to treat epilepsy and bipolar disorder in adults. The other half took Seroquel and Depakote.

The two groups did about equally well until the last few days of the study, when those in the Seroquel group scored lower on a standard measure of mania. By then, almost half of the teenagers getting Seroquel had dropped out because they missed appointments or the drugs did not work. Just eight of them completed the trial.

In an interview, Dr. DelBello acknowledged that the study was not conclusive. In the 2002 published paper, however, she and her co-authors reported that Seroquel in combination with Depakote "is more effective for the treatment of adolescent bipolar mania" than Depakote alone.

In 2005, a committee of prominent experts from across the country examined all of the studies of treatment for pediatric bipolar disorder and decided that Dr. DelBello's was the only study involving atypicals in bipolar children that deserved its highest rating for scientific rigor. The panel concluded that doctors should consider atypicals as a first-line treatment for some children. The guidelines were published in The Journal of the American Academy of Child and Adolescent Psychiatry.

Three of the four doctors on the panel served as speakers or consultants to makers of atypicals, according to disclosures in the guidelines. In an interview, Dr. Robert A. Kowatch, a psychiatrist at Cincinnati Children's Hospital and the lead author of the guidelines, said the drug makers' support had no influence on the conclusions.

AstraZeneca hired Dr. DelBello and Dr. Kowatch to give sponsored talks. They later undertook another study comparing Seroquel and Depakote in bipolar children and found no difference. Dr. DelBello, who earns $183,500 annually from the University of Cincinnati, would not discuss how much she is paid by AstraZeneca.

"Trust me, I don't make much," she said. Drug company payments did not affect her study or her talks, she said. In a recent disclosure, Dr. DelBello said that she received marketing or consulting income from eight drug companies, including all five makers of atypicals.

Dr. Realmuto has heard Dr. DelBello speak several times, and her talks persuaded him to use combinations of Depakote and atypicals in bipolar children, he said. "She's the leader in terms of doing studies on bipolar," Dr. Realmuto said.

Some psychiatrists who advocate use of atypicals in children acknowledge that the evidence supporting this use is thin. But they say children should not go untreated simply because scientists have failed to confirm what clinicians already know.

"We don't have time to wait for them to prove us right," said Dr. Kent G. Brockmann, a psychiatrist from the Twin Cities who made more than $16,000 from 2003 to 2005 doing drug talks and one-on-one sales meetings, and last year was a leading prescriber of atypicals to Medicaid children.

## The Reaction

For Anya Bailey, treatment with an atypical helped her regain her appetite and put on weight, but also heavily sedated her, her mother said. She developed the disabling knot in her back, the result of a nerve condition called dystonia, in 2005.

The reaction was rare but not unknown. Atypicals have side effects that are not easy to predict in any one patient. These include rapid weight gain and blood sugar problems, both risk factors for diabetes; disfiguring tics, dystonia and in rare cases heart attacks and sudden death in the elderly.

In 2006, the Food and Drug Administration received reports of at least 29 children dying and at least 165 more suffering serious side effects in which an antipsychotic was listed as the "primary suspect." That was a substantial jump from 2000, when there were at least 10 deaths and 85 serious side effects among children linked to the drugs. Since reporting of bad drug effects is mostly voluntary, these numbers likely represent a fraction of the toll.

Jim Minnick, a spokesman for AstraZeneca, said that the company carefully monitors reported problems with Seroquel. "AstraZeneca believes that Seroquel is safe," Mr. Minnick said.

Other psychiatrists renewed Anya's prescriptions for Risperdal until Ms. Bailey took Anya last year to the Mayo Clinic, where a doctor insisted that Ms. Bailey stop the drug. Unlike most universities and hospitals, the Mayo Clinic restricts doctors from giving drug marketing lectures.

Ms. Bailey said she wished she had waited to see whether counseling would help Anya before trying drugs. Anya's weight is now normal without the help of drugs, and her counseling ended in March. An experimental drug, her mother said, has recently helped the pain in her back.

## Selection 4.2

*Reporters get ideas for investigative pieces from a number of sources, including plaintiffs' attorneys and government reports. In the story that follows, reporter Roni Caryn Rabin relies on both these sources to trace the history of a medical device—a vaginal sling—that some women say made their lives miserable. In this case there's no smoking gun, no irrefutable proof that the device was to blame. The case is still in litigation, but Rabin uses the case to report on a bigger issue with far wider impact—the fact that a company does not have to prove a medical device is safe and effective before getting government approval to sell that device on the market. A manufacturer just needs the Food and Drug Administration to determine that their product is "substantially equivalent" to one already in use. That policy was criticized in a recent Government Accountability Office report. In stories like this one, the reporter has to try to present a balanced account, taking care not to favor one side or the other. The danger is that anecdotes from the plaintiffs are so powerful that readers may not perceive even a response by the manufacturer's attorney as doing much to balance the story.*

# Women Sue Over Device to Stop Urine Leaks

By RONI CARYN RABIN

It was the promise of a quick fix that appealed to Amber Suriani.

She had just turned 40 and was very fit, but whenever she went running or practiced karate—she was working on a black belt—she leaked a bit of urine.

The diagnosis was stress urinary incontinence, and her surgeon recommended a simple procedure to plug the leak by inserting a hammock made of a strip of synthetic meshlike material, called a vaginal sling, under her urethra.

"It was supposed to be a simple 'in one day and out the next' kind of thing," said Ms. Suriani, now 43, who lives in a suburb of Syracuse.

And so it seemed, at least at first. The surgery went smoothly, and the leakage stopped. But several months later, Ms. Suriani developed a persistent, painful and often bloody vaginal discharge.

She was convinced that she had cancer. It did not occur to her that the sling was the source of the problem until a piece of the meshlike tape started working its way through her vaginal wall.

Since then, she has had five operations, each one removing bits of the sling but not the entire thing; another operation is scheduled. She still has chronic discharge and says her sex life with her husband has been affected. She relies on Motrin to get through the day and a sleeping pad to get through the night.

"I feel like I'm never going to be the same again," Ms. Suriani said, adding: "I'm beginning to feel like this has ruined my life. Not just ruining my life, as in 'It will get better,' but ruined, as in 'I'm stuck with this for the rest of my life.' I try to stay positive, but it's getting harder and harder."

Ms. Suriani's lawyer, Matthew Metz of Seattle, said she was one of dozens of women suing the maker of the vaginal sling, called ObTape.

The company, Mentor Corporation, based in Santa Barbara, Calif., and recently acquired by Johnson & Johnson, stopped selling ObTape in 2006 but says there is nothing wrong with the product, which was cleared for sale by the Food and Drug Administration.

John Q. Lewis of Cleveland, a lawyer with the firm Jones Day, which represents Mentor, said that there were risks to any surgical

---

*Published: May 4, 2009.*

procedure and that doctors should have warned patients. He noted that early European studies reported low rates of complications with ObTape.

"It's very unfortunate when anyone reports a complication," Mr. Lewis said. "That being said, these are complications that are well known, that patients are warned about, and are inherent to a surgical procedure that has helped thousands and thousands of people live a better life."

He continued, "The overall benefits of the procedure and this product outweighed the potential risks."

The lawsuits raise new questions about the process by which the F.D.A. reviews new medical devices. While it "approves" drugs, it merely "clears" medical devices with minimal testing if they are deemed "substantially equivalent" to devices already in use.

The process has been criticized by the agency's scientists and in a recent Government Accountability Office report concluding that most devices on the market have never been proved safe and effective.

In ObTape's case, the chain of similarity claims can be traced back to an older product that caused so much harm it was taken off the market. That recall did not stop the F.D.A. from clearing a new generation of vaginal slings whose only claim to safety was their similarity to the flawed device.

A reverse chronology, put together with help from plaintiffs' lawyers and researchers at Public Citizen's Health Research Group, a nonprofit consumer advocacy group, illustrates the pitfalls of the process.

In 2003, Mentor asked the food and drug agency to clear ObTape for the United States market, saying there was essentially no difference between its product and two other vaginal slings already widely in use—Johnson & Johnson's Tension Free Vaginal Tape System and American Medical Systems' Sparc Sling System.

Those slings had been cleared earlier, based on claims that they, too, were much like earlier products—in Johnson & Johnson's case, the Protegen sling, made by Boston Scientific. But that sling had been recalled in 1999, four years before ObTape made its appearance. At the time, the F.D.A. called the Protegen sling an "adulterated and misbranded" product.

Officials at the F.D.A. declined requests for an interview, providing only answers to e-mailed questions. Asked why the agency would clear a product based on a recalled predecessor, they replied, "Any legally marketed device can serve as a predicate for a premarket submission."

In fact, there were significant differences between ObTape and the earlier slings, and once Mentor had cleared ObTape for marketing based on its similarity to other devices, the company promoted its unique features. It obtained a patent and emphasized to surgeons that its new design, based on a European product called Uratape, allowed for a surgical approach that reduced the risk of puncturing the bladder.

Dr. Andrew L. Siegel, a urologist in Hackensack, N.J., who now serves as an expert witness for the plaintiffs suing ObTape, was one of the first surgeons to start using the device. "I was delighted about it," Dr. Siegel said. "It was a great innovation."

But ObTape was different from earlier slings in another way, which became clear only later and had to do with the type of material it was made of.

Many experts say the sling was too dense—not porous enough to allow tissue and capillaries to grow through it so it is fully incorporated in the body, rather than becoming encapsulated and expelled.

Reports of adverse events linked to ObTape soon started pouring in to the F.D.A.—266 in all, starting in 2004, many of them describing problems similar to Ms. Suriani's complaints.

Surgeons like Dr. Siegel started publishing case reports in medical journals and reporting negative experiences with the device. Several described the "malodorous discharge" patients developed after surgery, and said the tape started extruding.

In 2006, doctors at the Virginia Mason Medical Center in Seattle reported in The Journal of Urology that they had stopped using ObTape after observing a 13.4 percent rate of vaginal extrusion.

But Mr. Lewis, the lawyer for Mentor, said the material was tested by company engineers as part of an extensive premarketing process. The 266 reported adverse events represent a small fraction of the 16,000 ObTape slings implanted in the United States, he added, and he pointed to studies finding high complication rates for other slings.

Indeed, the F.D.A. alerted health care providers last year that it had received more than 1,000 reports of complications from nine surgical mesh manufacturers about devices for incontinence and organ prolapse. "Physicians should inform patients about the potential for serious complications and their effect on quality of life, including pain during sexual intercourse, scarring" and other complications, the notice said.

Mr. Lewis said clinical data from Europe supported the ObTape sling's safety and efficacy, and suggested that American surgeons' lack of familiarity with the new surgical technique was responsible for any problems. He noted that in California, a jury recently rejected a claim of negligence against Mentor by Lisa Ann Seeno, now 51, who was hospitalized with an abscess shortly after the device was implanted. (She has requested a new trial.)

Another plaintiff, Suzanne Crews, 69, of Washington State, said she was suing Mentor to spread the word about the risks of trying to repair what was, in hindsight, a problem she could have lived with—minor leaking when she coughed too hard or laughed too loud.

Ms. Crews said she has undergone four operations to remove portions of the tape.

"I'm not like I'm supposed to be," she said. "I just really would be happier if more and more people knew about the problem, and didn't just sit back and say, 'Oh my gosh, I don't know what's happening.' "

## Selection 4.3

*Sometimes the best investigative medical stories piggyback on epidemiologic inquiries. That's the case with the next story. Medical reporter Denise Grady tells us that three people who worked in a Minnesota pork processing plant all presented an unusual set of symptoms. The reporter opens the medical mystery by introducing the setting before telling us about the unusual job that all three workers had. This is the classic medical detective story popularized by the late New Yorker reporter Berton Roueché, who once claimed that the detective story itself "owes its nature to medicine,"[2] explaining that Sir Arthur Conan Doyle derived Sherlock Holmes' method from an Edinburgh diagnostician, Dr. Joseph Ball. In her best Sherlock Holmes style, Grady writes, "And the disease that confronted doctors at the Austin Medical Center here last fall was strange indeed." As in all detective stories, there's a sleuth—in this case epidemiologist Dr. Aaron DeVries—who combs through medical records looking for the link to connect the victims. In probably one of the more disgusting passages that you'll find in The Times, Grady describes the process in which workers got exposed to what doctors believe made the workers sick. Elementary, my dear Watson: It was simply inhalation of aerosolized pig brains. This is the science lesson for this medical detective story.*

## A Medical Mystery Unfolds at Minnesota Meatpacking Plant

By DENISE GRADY

AUSTIN, Minn.—If you have to come down with a strange disease, this town of 23,000 on the wide-open prairie in southeastern Minnesota is a pretty good place to be. The Mayo Clinic, famous for diagnosing exotic ailments, owns the local medical center and shares some staff with it. Mayo itself is just 40 miles east in Rochester. And when it comes to investigating mysterious outbreaks, Minnesota has one of the strongest health departments and best-equipped laboratories in the country.

*Published: February 5, 2008.*

And the disease that confronted doctors at the Austin Medical Center here last fall was strange indeed. Three patients had the same highly unusual set of symptoms: fatigue, pain, weakness, numbness and tingling in the legs and feet.

The patients had something else in common, too: all worked at Quality Pork Processors, a local meatpacking plant.

The disorder seemed to involve nerve damage, but doctors had no idea what was causing it.

At the plant, nurses in the medical department had also begun to notice the same ominous pattern. The three workers had complained to them of "heavy legs," and the nurses had urged them to see doctors. The nurses knew of a fourth case, too, and they feared that more workers would get sick, that a serious disease might be spreading through the plant.

"We put our heads together and said, 'Something is out of sorts,'" said Carole Bower, the department head.

Austin's biggest employer is Hormel Foods, maker of Spam, bacon and other processed meats (Austin even has a Spam museum). Quality Pork Processors, which backs onto the Hormel property, kills and butchers 19,000 hogs a day and sends most of them to Hormel. The complex, emitting clouds of steam and a distinctive scent, is easy to find from just about anywhere in town.

Quality Pork is the second biggest employer, with 1,300 employees. Most work eight-hour shifts along a conveyor belt—a disassembly line, basically—carving up a specific part of each carcass. Pay for these line jobs starts at about $11 to $12 an hour. The work is grueling, but the plant is exceptionally clean and the benefits are good, said Richard Morgan, president of the union local. Many of the workers are Hispanic immigrants. Quality Pork's owner does not allow reporters to enter the plant.

A man whom doctors call the "index case"—the first patient they knew about—got sick in December 2006 and was hospitalized at the Mayo Clinic for about two weeks. His job at Quality Pork was to extract the brains from swine heads.

"He was quite ill and severely affected neurologically, with significant weakness in his legs and loss of function in the lower part of his body," said Dr. Daniel H. Lachance, a neurologist at Mayo.

Tests showed that the man's spinal cord was markedly inflamed. The cause seemed to be an autoimmune reaction: his immune system was mistakenly attacking his own nerves as if they were a foreign body or a germ. Doctors could not figure out why it had happened, but the standard treatment for inflammation—a steroid drug—seemed to help. (The patient was not available for interviews.)

Neurological illnesses sometimes defy understanding, Dr. Lachance said, and this seemed to be one of them. At the time, it did not occur to anyone that the problem might be related to the patient's occupation.

By spring, he went back to his job. But within weeks, he became ill again. Once more, he recovered after a few months and returned to work—only to get sick all over again.

By then, November 2007, other cases had begun to turn up. Ultimately, there were 12—6 men and 6 women, ranging in age from 21 to 51. Doctors and the plant owner, realizing they had an outbreak on their hands, had already called in the Minnesota Department of Health, which, in turn, sought help from the federal Centers for Disease Control and Prevention.

Though the outbreak seemed small, the investigation took on urgency because the disease was serious, and health officials worried that it might indicate a new risk to other workers in meatpacking.

"It is important to characterize this because it appears to be a new syndrome, and we don't truly know how many people may be affected throughout the U.S. or even the world," said Dr. Jennifer McQuiston, a veterinarian from the disease centers.

In early November, Dr. Aaron DeVries, a health department epidemiologist, visited the plant and combed through medical records. The disease bore no resemblance to mad cow disease or to trichinosis, the notorious parasite infection that comes from eating raw or undercooked pork. Nor did it spread person to person—the workers' relatives were unaffected—or pose any threat to people who ate pork.

A survey of the workers confirmed what the plant's nurses had suspected: those who got sick were employed at or near the "head table," where workers cut the meat off severed hog heads.

On Nov. 28, Dr. DeVries's boss, Dr. Ruth Lynfield, the state epidemiologist, toured the plant. She and the owner, Kelly Wadding, paid special attention to the head table. Dr. Lynfield became transfixed by one procedure in particular, called "blowing brains."

As each head reached the end of the table, a worker would insert a metal hose into the foramen magnum, the opening that the spinal cord passes through. High-pressure blasts of compressed air then turned the brain into a slurry that squirted out through the same hole in the skull, often spraying brain tissue around and splattering the hose operator in the process.

The brains were pooled, poured into 10-pound containers and shipped to be sold as food—mostly in China and Korea, where cooks stir-fry them, but also in some parts of the American South, where people like them scrambled up with eggs.

The person blowing brains was separated from the other workers by a plexiglass shield that had enough space under it to allow the heads to ride through on a conveyor belt. There was also enough space for brain tissue to splatter nearby employees.

"You could see aerosolization of brain tissue," Dr. Lynfield said.

The workers wore hard hats, gloves, lab coats and safety glasses, but many had bare arms, and none had masks or face shields to prevent swallowing or inhaling the mist of brain tissue.

Dr. Lynfield asked Mr. Wadding, "Kelly, what do you think is going on?"

The plant owner watched for a while and said, "Let's stop harvesting brains."

Quality Pork halted the procedure that day and ordered face shields for workers at the head table.

Epidemiologists contacted 25 swine slaughterhouses in the United States, and found that only two others used compressed air to extract brains. One, a plant in Nebraska owned by Hormel, has reported no cases. But the other, Indiana Packers in Delphi, Ind., has several possible cases that are being investigated. Both of the other plants, like Quality Pork, have stopped using compressed air.

But why should exposure to hog brains cause illness? And why now, when the compressed air system had been in use in Minnesota since 1998?

At first, health officials thought perhaps the pigs had some new infection that was being transmitted to people by the brain tissue. Sometimes, infections can ignite an immune response in humans that flares out of control, like the condition in the workers. But so far, scores of tests for viruses, bacteria and parasites have found no signs of infection.

As a result, Dr. Lynfield said the investigators had begun leaning toward a seemingly bizarre theory: that exposure to the hog brain itself might have touched off an intense reaction by the immune system, something akin to a giant, out-of-control allergic reaction. Some people might be more susceptible than others, perhaps because of their genetic makeup or their past exposures to animal tissue. The aerosolized brain matter might have been inhaled or swallowed, or might have entered through the eyes, the mucous membranes of the nose or mouth, or breaks in the skin.

"It's something no one would have anticipated or thought about," said Dr. Michael Osterholm, an epidemiologist who is working as a consultant for Hormel and Quality Pork. Dr. Osterholm, a professor of public health at the University of Minnesota and the former state epidemiologist, said that no standard for this kind of workplace exposure had ever been set by the government.

But that would still not explain why the condition should suddenly develop now. Investigators are trying to find out whether something changed recently—the air pressure level, for instance—and also whether there actually were cases in the past that just went undetected.

"Clearly, all the answers aren't in yet," Dr. Osterholm said. "But it makes biologic sense that what you have here is an inhalation of brain material from these pigs that is eliciting an immunologic reaction." What may be happening, he said, is "immune mimicry," meaning that the immune system makes antibodies to fight a foreign substance—something in the hog brains—but the antibodies also attack the person's nerve tissue because it is so similar to some molecule in hog brains.

"That's the beauty and the beast of the immune system," Dr. Osterholm said. "It's so efficient at keeping foreign objects away, but anytime there's a close match it turns against us, too."

Anatomically, pigs are a lot like people. But it is not clear how close a biochemical match there is between pig brain and human nerve tissue.

To find out, the Minnesota health department has asked for help from Dr. Ian Lipkin, an expert at Columbia University on the role of the immune system in neurological diseases. Dr. Lipkin has begun testing blood serum from the Minnesota patients to look for signs of an immune reaction to components of pig brain. And he expects also to study the pig gene for myelin, to see how similar it is to the human one.

"It's an interesting problem," Dr. Lipkin said. "I think we can solve it."

Susan Kruse, who lives in Austin, was stunned by news reports about the outbreak in early December. Ms. Kruse, 37, worked at Quality Pork for 15 years. But for the past year, she has been too sick to work. She had no idea that anyone else from the plant was ill. Nor did she know that her illness might be related to her job.

Her most recent job was "backing heads," scraping meat from between the vertebrae. Three people per shift did that task, and together would process 9,500 heads in eight or nine hours. Ms. Kruse (pronounced KROO-zee) stood next to the person who used compressed air to blow out the brains. She was often splattered, especially when trainees were learning to operate the air hose.

"I always had brains on my arms," she said.

She never had trouble with her health until November 2006, when she began having pains in her legs. By February 2007, she could not stand up long enough to do her job. She needed a walker to get around and was being treated at the Mayo Clinic.

"I had no strength to do anything I used to do," she said. "I just felt like I was being drained out."

Her immune system had gone haywire and attacked her nerves, primarily in two places: at the points where the nerves emerge from the spinal cord, and in the extremities. The same thing, to varying degrees, was happening to the other patients. Ms. Kruse and the index case—the man who extracted brains—probably had the most severe symptoms, Dr. Lachance said.

Steroids did nothing for Ms. Kruse, so doctors began to treat her every two weeks with IVIG, intravenous immunoglobulin, a blood product that contains antibodies. "It's kind of like hitting the condition over the head with a sledgehammer," Dr. Lachance said. "It overwhelms the immune system and neutralizes whatever it is that's causing the injury."

The treatments seem to help, Ms. Kruse said. She feels stronger after each one, but the effects wear off. Her doctors expect she will need the therapy at least until September.

Most of the other workers are recovering and some have returned to their jobs, but others, including the index case, are still unable to work. So far, there have been no new cases.

"I cannot say that anyone is completely back to normal," Dr. Lachance said. "I expect it will take several more months to get a true sense of the course of this illness."

Dr. Lynfield hopes to find the cause. But she said: "I don't know that we will have the definitive answer. I suspect we will be able to rule some things out, and will have a sense of whether it seems like it may be due to an autoimmune response. I think we'll learn a lot, but it may take us a while. It's a great detective story."

## Selection 4.4

*A plaintiff's lawyer motivated to get a public airing for his case will sometimes give documents to a reporter in the hope of instigating an investigative story. Sometimes the seed takes root. In the next story, pharmaceutical industry reporter Alex Berenson received internal drug marketing documents from a lawyer who represented mentally ill patients. The documents led Berenson to write a story detailing Eli Lilly's multiyear promotional campaign suggesting that doctors treat older dementia patients with a drug that was not approved for that use. Note that Berenson does not start this story with an individual's anecdote or narrative. Instead, he leads with a simple statement of the facts and how he came to know them. In the next two paragraphs he gives the company opportunity to rebut the charges. Then, in the fifth paragraph, Berenson provides the scientific context, an important element in any story and especially crucial for a medical investigative piece. If Zyprexa had been approved by the Food and Drug Administration to treat dementia, there would be no story. So letting readers know that the FDA had never approved Zyprexa for treatment of dementia sets up the context for the story. Nearly three years after this story appeared, Lilly paid $1.42 billion to settle criminal and civil probes related to its off-label marketing practices.*[3]

# Drug Files Show Maker Promoted Unapproved Use

By ALEX BERENSON

Eli Lilly encouraged primary care physicians to use Zyprexa, a powerful drug for schizophrenia and bipolar disorder, in patients who did not have either condition, according to internal Lilly marketing materials.

The marketing documents, given to The New York Times by a lawyer representing mentally ill patients, detail a multiyear promotional campaign that Lilly began in Orlando, Fla., in late 2000. In the campaign, called Viva Zyprexa, Lilly told its sales representatives to suggest that doctors prescribe Zyprexa to older patients with symptoms of dementia.

A Lilly executive said that she could not comment on specific documents but that the company had never promoted Zyprexa for off-label uses and that it always showed the marketing materials used by its sales representatives to the Food and Drug Administration, as required by law.

"We have extensive training for sales reps to assure that they provide information to the doctors that's within the scope of the prescribing information approved by the F.D.A.," Anne Nobles, Lilly's vice president for corporate affairs, said in an interview yesterday.

Zyprexa is not approved to treat dementia or dementia-related psychosis, and in fact carries a prominent warning from the F.D.A. that it increases the risk of death in older patients with dementia-related psychosis. Federal laws bar drug makers from promoting prescription drugs for conditions for which they have not been approved—a practice known as off-label prescription—although doctors can prescribe drugs to any patient they wish.

Yet in 1999 and 2000 Lilly considered ways to convince primary care doctors that they should use Zyprexa on their patients. In one document, an unnamed Lilly marketing executive wrote that these doctors "do treat dementia" but "do not treat bipolar; schizophrenia is handled by psychiatrists."

As a result, "dementia should be first message," of a campaign to primary doctors, according to the document, which appears to be part of a larger marketing presentation but is not marked more specifically.

Later, the same document says that some primary care doctors "might prescribe outside of label."

Ms. Nobles said that the company had never promoted its drug for any conditions except schizophrenia and bipolar disorder. Older patients who seem to have dementia may actually have schizophrenia that has gone untreated, Ms. Nobles said.

---

*Published: December 18, 2006.*

Several psychiatrists outside the company said yesterday that they strongly disagreed with Lilly's claim. Schizophrenia is a severe disease that is almost always diagnosed when patients are in their teens or 20s. Its symptoms could not be confused with mild dementia, these doctors said.

Zyprexa is by far Lilly's best-selling product, with $4.2 billion in sales in 2005, 30 percent of its overall revenues. About two million people worldwide received it last year. Based in Indianapolis, Lilly is the sixth-largest American drug company.

The issue of off-label marketing is controversial in the drug industry. Nearly every company is under either civil or criminal investigation for alleged efforts to expand the use of its drugs beyond the specific illness or condition for which they are approved.

Lilly faces federal and state investigations over its marketing of Zyprexa. In its annual report for 2005, Lilly said that it faced an investigation by federal prosecutors in Pennsylvania and that the Florida attorney general's office had subpoenaed the company "seeking production of documents relating to sales of Zyprexa and our marketing and promotional practices with respect to Zyprexa."

Since Lilly introduced Zyprexa in 1996, about 20 million patients worldwide have received the drug, which helps control the hallucinations and delusions associated with schizophrenia and severe mania. But Zyprexa also causes weight gain in many patients, and the American Diabetes Association found in 2004 that Zyprexa was more likely to cause diabetes than other widely used drugs for schizophrenia.

Lilly says that no link between Zyprexa and diabetes has been proven.

As part of the "Viva Zyprexa" campaign, in packets for its sales representatives, Eli Lilly created the profiles of patients whom it said would be suitable candidates for Zyprexa. Representatives were told to discuss the patient profiles with doctors. One of the patients was a woman in her 20s who showed mild symptoms of schizophrenia, while another was a man in his 40s who appeared to have bipolar disorder.

The third patient was "Martha," a widow with adult children "who lives independently and has been your patient for some time." Martha was described as being agitated and having disturbed sleep, but without the symptoms of paranoia or mania that typically marked a person with schizophrenia or bipolar disorder.

Ms. Nobles said that Lilly had actually intended Martha's profile to represent a patient with schizophrenia. But psychiatrists outside the company said this claim defied credibility, especially given Martha's age. Instead, she appeared to have mild dementia, they said.

"It'd be very unusual for this to be a schizophrenic patient," said Dr. John March, chief of child and adolescent psychiatry at Duke University medical center. "Schizophrenia is a disease of teenagers and young adults." Dr. March serves on Lilly's scientific advisory board.

Diagnostic criteria for schizophrenia include delusions, hallucinations, disorganized and incoherent speech, and grossly disorganized behavior. They also include so-called negative symptoms like social isolation and a flattening of the voice and facial expressions.

The documents also show that Lilly encouraged primary care doctors to treat the symptoms and behaviors of schizophrenia and bipolar disorder even if the doctors had not actually diagnosed those diseases in their patients. Lilly's market research had found that many primary care doctors did not consider themselves qualified to treat people with schizophrenia or severe bipolar disorder.

The campaign was successful, the documents show. By March 2001, about three months after the start of Viva Zyprexa, the campaign had led to 49,000 new prescriptions, according to a presentation that Michael Bandick, the brand manager for Zyprexa, gave at a national meeting of Lilly sales representatives in Dallas. Mr. Bandick did not say how many of those new prescriptions were for older patients with dementia.

Over all, sales of Zyprexa doubled between 1999 and 2002, rising from $1.5 billion to $3 billion in the United States. In 2002, the company changed the name of the primary care campaign to "Zyprexa Limitless" and began to focus on people with mild bipolar disorder who had previously been diagnosed as depressed—even though Zyprexa has been approved only for the treatment of mania in bipolar disorder, not depression.

In a 2002 guide for representatives, Lilly presented the profile of "Donna," a single mother in her mid-30s whose "chief complaint is, 'I feel so anxious and irritable lately.'" Several doctors' appointments earlier, she was "talkative, elated, and reported little need for sleep."

Lilly's efforts to promote Zyprexa to primary care doctors disturbed some physicians, the documents show. In August 2001, a doctor in Virginia sent an e-mail message to Lilly and the F.D.A., complaining about a presentation from a Lilly sales representative who had discussed the hypothetical Martha with him.

The representative "presented an elderly female patient who was presented to her physician by her family complaining of insomnia, agitation, slight confusion, and had no physical finding to explain her state," the doctor wrote. The representative then suggested that the doctor prescribe Zyprexa.

"I inquired what Zyprexa was indicated for. She then indicated that many physicians might prescribe an antipsychotic for this patient. I then asked for her package insert and read to her that her product was indicated for schizophrenia and bipolar mania—neither of which the presented patient had been diagnosed with," the doctor wrote.

He added that he had never contacted the F.D.A. before but was "genuinely concerned about the promotion of this powerful drug to my peer community of primary care physicians outside of its approved and intended purpose."

Tara Ryker, a spokeswoman for Lilly, said the company no longer uses "Martha" or "Donna" in its marketing. "We are constantly developing new promotional materials and new profiles," she said.

The Zyprexa documents were provided to The Times by James B. Gottstein, a lawyer who represents mentally ill patients and has sued the state of Alaska over its efforts to force patients to take psychiatric medicines against their will.

Mr. Gottstein said yesterday that the information in the documents should be available to patients and doctors, as well as judges who oversee the hearings that are required before people can be forced to take psychiatric drugs.

"The courts should have this information before they order this stuff injected into people's unwilling bodies," Mr. Gottstein said.

Lilly originally provided the documents, under seal, to plaintiffs' lawyers who sued the company claiming their clients developed diabetes from taking Zyprexa. Last year, Lilly agreed to pay $700 million to settle about 8,000 of the claims, but thousands more are pending. Mr. Gottstein, who is not subject to the confidentiality agreement that covers the product liability suits, subpoenaed the documents in early December from a person involved in the suits.

The "Viva Zyprexa" documents also provide color about Lilly's efforts to motivate its sales force as they marketed Zyprexa—whose generic name is olanzapine—to primary care doctors.

At the 2001 meeting in Dallas with Zyprexa sales representatives, Mr. Bandick praised 16 representatives by name for the number of prescriptions they had convinced doctors to write, according to a script prepared in advance of the meeting. More than 100 other representatives had convinced doctors to write at least 16 extra prescriptions and thus "maxed out on a pretty sweet incentive," he said.

"Olanzapine is the molecule that keeps on giving," Mr. Bandick said.

## Selection 4.5

*Sometimes reporters miss key clues that could blow open big stories. The next story was the first article in The New York Times to point out major problems with the anti-inflammatory drug Vioxx. This 2001 story reported that doctors were concerned that two popular anti-arthritis drugs, Vioxx and Celebrex, were not as safe as originally thought. In the seventh paragraph, reporter Melody Petersen writes that patients taking Vioxx had "four times the risk of heart attacks" compared with "patients taking another pain reliever, naproxen."*

*Yet in the next paragraph she qualifies the findings: "Merck says the research does not show a problem with Vioxx. Instead, the company says, naproxen acted to reduce heart attacks by working much like aspirin."*

*In other words, Merck was saying that the problem wasn't with Vioxx. According to Merck, the problem was that Vioxx was being compared with naproxen, a medication that the company would repeatedly call "cardioprotective." As it turned out, naproxen was not cardioprotective. The problem was that Vioxx was leading to a greater incidence of heart problems. In her story Petersen quoted a Merck vice president who said, "Naproxen had a similar antiplatelet effect to aspirin . . . and those people had fewer heart attacks."*

*That was company spin, but, despite warnings from a few concerned doctors, neither The Times nor other news organizations focused on the dangerous side effects of Vioxx until long after this story was published. In fact, the Merck vice president had the last words in the story: "There is still a tremendous benefit with these drugs." Four years later, Merck would pull the drug off the market as it faced billions of dollars in potential liability. As you'll see in the interview at the end of this chapter, many reporters kick themselves now for taking too long to question the manufacturer's claims despite warning signs that Vioxx was causing major heart problems.*

## Doubts Are Raised on the Safety of 2 Popular Arthritis Drugs

By MELODY PETERSEN

Doctors are beginning to worry that Vioxx and Celebrex, two wildly popular arthritis drugs, may not be as safe as they were initially believed to be.

Research presented to the Food and Drug Administration earlier this year showed that patients taking Vioxx, a Merck & Company drug, had a higher, but still relatively low, risk of heart attacks than patients taking an older pain reliever. The study received little public attention at the time, but the F.D.A. is considering whether to add information on possible cardiovascular side effects to both drugs' labels.

Now Wall Street is becoming aware of the possible problems, with at least one analyst warning that the problem could particularly affect Merck.

The two drugs, which cause fewer ulcers than many other pain relievers, are among the best-selling medicines in the world. And both Pharmacia, which makes Celebrex, and Merck are heavily dependent on the drugs for the sales growth that Wall Street expects.

Celebrex is Pharmacia's biggest-selling drug, generating sales of $2.3 billion in the 12 months ending in March, according to IMS Health. Pfizer co-markets Celebrex with Pharmacia. Merck sold $1.7 billion of Vioxx in the same period, making it the company's second-biggest drug behind the cholesterol medicine Zocor.

---

*Published: May 22, 2001.*

Millions of Americans have tried Vioxx or Celebrex, many of them prompted to request them from doctors after seeing television advertisements paid for by the two companies, which are locked in a fierce marketing battle.

While the data is still limited, a large study sponsored by Merck last year showed that patients taking Vioxx had four times the risk of heart attacks of patients taking another pain reliever, naproxen, which is sold both generically and under the brand names Naprosyn or Aleve. The risk, which appears to increase over time, was still low, however, at about 4 heart attacks per 1,000 patients.

Merck says the research does not show a problem with Vioxx. Instead, the company says, naproxen acted to reduce heart attacks by working much like aspirin.

The information from Merck's study was presented to the Food and Drug Administration in February when the companies asked for changes on their drug labels to reflect data showing that Vioxx and Celebrex caused fewer ulcers than other pain relievers.

In an April 27 report, Richard R. Stover, a pharmaceutical industry analyst at Arnhold & S. Bleichroeder Inc., did his own analysis of what he called "disturbing data" from Merck's study. In an interview, Mr. Stover said he was warning his clients, many of them institutional investors who hold Merck shares, that they should watch the issue carefully since it could hurt the company's stock price.

Some doctors, however, say they are worried about both drugs.

"There must be a warning," said Dr. M. Michael Wolfe, chief of the gastroenterology section at the Boston University School of Medicine and a member of the F.D.A. advisory committee that reviewed the issue earlier this year.

"The marketing of these drugs is unbelievable," Dr. Wolfe added. "I'm sure there are many people out there who are taking these drugs that should not be."

Several doctors say they are worried about the possibility of heart attacks because many of the arthritis patients taking the drugs are elderly and have a higher risk of cardiovascular problems to begin with.

The current debate centers on whether the higher heart attack rate found in patients taking Vioxx is a result of the drug's actually causing damage in some patients or to an absence of the heart-protecting benefits that naproxen may have.

Merck's scientists say that naproxen appears to help reduce heart attacks by stopping or slowing the production of a substance called thromboxane. Thromboxane is thought to cause platelets in the blood to stick together, leading to blood clots.

"Naproxen had a similar antiplatelet effect to aspirin," said Dr. Eve E. Slater, senior vice president of external policy for Merck's research labs, "and those people had fewer heart attacks."

Neither Vioxx nor Celebrex have been shown to have the same heart-protecting benefit.

Dr. Slater also said that Mr. Stover's report was flawed and biased in favor of Pharmacia.

But regulators and some doctors say they still worry that there may be more of a problem with Vioxx.

And even if Vioxx and Celebrex do not damage the heart, the fact that they do not have the heart-protecting benefits of aspirin reduces the ability of the companies to market them as being significantly safer than other pain relievers.

In letters sent to physicians involved in Vioxx clinical trials, Merck recommended last year that doctors consider prescribing low doses of aspirin to patients taking Vioxx if they are at high risk of heart attacks. But those low doses of aspirin could increase the risk of ulcers—the main side effect that both Vioxx and Celebrex were developed to avoid.

The two drugs, known as Cox-2 inhibitors, have been shown to significantly reduce stomach ulcers compared with pain relievers like aspirin and ibuprofen. In rare cases, serious ulcers can lead to death.

So far, no studies have been done to measure whether patients have fewer ulcers if they take low doses of aspirin with either Vioxx or Celebrex.

At an F.D.A. advisory meeting in February, Dr. Maria Lourdes Villalba, a medical officer at the agency, summed up her analysis of Merck's study, saying that the company had proved that Vioxx, which is known generically as rofecoxib, caused fewer serious ulcers than naproxen. But she said that in her opinion, the potential safety advantage was offset by a higher risk of heart problems.

"Over all, there was no safety superiority of rofecoxib over naproxen," Dr. Villalba concluded, "mainly due to an excess of serious cardiovascular events."

Dr. Villalba said that because there were no studies that proved Merck's theory that naproxen worked like aspirin to decrease heart attacks, the F.D.A. was concerned that the higher rate of heart attacks found with Vioxx might have been caused by the drug's producing blood clots.

Both Merck and Pharmacia say that patients taking either Vioxx or Celebrex and low doses of aspirin will still have fewer ulcers than if they were taking a drug combination like ibuprofen and aspirin.

Dr. G. Steven Geis, Pharmacia's vice president for arthritis and cardiovascular clinical research, said, "We believe that if a patient is on low-dose aspirin and needs a drug for arthritis, celecoxib is a good option."

Celecoxib is the generic name for Celebrex.

Dr. Slater of Merck said, "There is still a tremendous benefit with these drugs."

## Selection 4.6

*More than three years after the previous story appeared, The New York Times published an in-depth investigation of how Merck had delayed the recall of Vioxx, despite early warnings that the drug posed a health risk. The article was a team effort by reporters Alex Berenson, Gardiner Harris, Barry Meier and Andrew Pollack. The reporters based much of their story on internal Merck documents provided by company officials and people associated with lawsuits against the company. The Wall Street Journal had previously disclosed some of the records. As in any major investigative piece, the reporters did exhaustive research, which in this case included interviews with Merck researchers, independent researchers, FDA officials, lawyers for both sides, plaintiffs and financial analysts. The team also reviewed at least six studies that pertained to the heart risk posed by Vioxx. In any investigation reporters need to speak to all sides (notice that we don't say "both sides," as most stories have far more than two) and weigh the evidence that they uncover. Reporters should present a balanced account, but if the facts take them in one direction, then the story should reflect that. In this story The Times reporters lay out their takeaway message in the seventh and eighth paragraphs, and the reporters spend the rest of the story providing the evidence to back up their assertions. The story is well researched and well written. (Notice the simple writing, despite the complexity of the subject.) The only disappointment is that The Times and other news organizations had not taken a microscope to this issue years earlier.*

### Dangerous Data
### Despite Warnings, Drug Giant Took Long Path to Vioxx Recall

By THE NEW YORK TIMES

In May 2000, executives at Merck, the pharmaceutical giant under siege for its handling of the multibillion-dollar drug Vioxx, made a fateful decision.

The company's top research and marketing executives met that month to consider whether to develop a study to directly test a disturbing possibility: that Vioxx, a painkiller, might pose a heart risk. Two months earlier, results from a clinical trial conducted for other reasons had suggested such concerns.

But the executives rejected pursuing a study focused on Vioxx's cardiovascular risks. According to company documents, the scientists wondered if such a study, which might require as many as 50,000 patients, was even possible. Merck's marketers, meanwhile, apparently feared it could send the wrong signal about the company's confidence in Vioxx, which already faced fierce competition from a rival drug, Celebrex.

---

*Published: November 14, 2004.*

"At present, there is no compelling marketing need for such a study," said a slide prepared for the meeting. "Data would not be available during the critical period. The implied message is not favorable."

Merck decided not to conduct a study solely to determine whether Vioxx might cause heart attacks and strokes—the type of study that outside scientists would repeatedly call for as clinical evidence continued to show cardiovascular risks from the drug. Instead, Merck officials decided to monitor clinical trials, already under way or planned, that were to test Vioxx for other uses, to see if any additional signs of cardiovascular problems emerged.

It was a recurring theme for the company over the next few years—that Vioxx was safe unless proved otherwise. As recently as Friday, in newspaper advertisements, Merck has argued that it took "prompt and decisive action" as soon as it knew that Vioxx was dangerous.

But a detailed reconstruction of Merck's handling of Vioxx, based on interviews and internal company documents, suggests that actions the company took—and did not take—soon after the drug's safety was questioned may have affected the health of potentially thousands of patients, as well as the company's financial health and reputation.

The review also raises broader questions about an entire class of relatively new painkillers, called COX-2 inhibitors; about how drugs are tested; and about how aggressively the federal Food and Drug Administration monitors the safety of medications once they are in the marketplace.

The decisions about how to test Vioxx were made in a hothouse environment in which researchers fiercely debated how the question should be pursued, and some even now question whether the drug needed to be withdrawn. It also took place amid a fierce battle between Vioxx and Celebrex in which federal regulators said marketing claims ran ahead of the science.

Today Merck faces not only Congressional and Justice Department investigations, but also potentially thousands of personal-injury lawsuits that could tie the company up in litigation for years and possibly cost it billions to resolve.

In late September, more than four years after that May 2000 meeting, Merck announced that it was pulling the drug off the market because a long-term clinical trial showed that some patients, after taking the drug for 18 months, developed serious cardiovascular problems. The data that ultimately persuaded the company to withdraw the drug indicated 15 cases of heart attack, stroke or blood clots per thousand people each year over three years, compared with 7.5 such events per thousand patients taking a placebo.

But the company never directly tested the theory that it used to explain the worrisome results of the clinical trial in 2000. Merck was criticized for what some charged was playing down the drug's possible heart risks; in one case, it received a warning letter from the Food and Drug Administration for minimizing "potentially serious cardiovascular findings." And when outside researchers found evidence indicating Vioxx might pose dangers, Merck dismissed their data.

In 2001, Dr. Deepak L. Bhatt, a cardiologist at the Cleveland Clinic, proposed to Merck a study of Vioxx in patients with severe chest pain. Merck declined, saying the patients proposed for the study did not reflect typical Vioxx users. In Dr. Bhatt's view, the company feared what it might find if it directly examined the dangers of Vioxx, one of Merck's biggest products, with sales last year of $2.5 billion.

"They should have done a trial like this," Dr. Bhatt said. "If they internally thought this drug was safe in patients with heart disease, there was no reason not to do it."

Merck executives said last week that the company acted responsibly, voluntarily withdrawing Vioxx as soon as it had clear evidence the drug was harmful. And they said that even if they had conducted the type of study they discussed internally and rejected in 2000, the company might not have detected Vioxx's risks any sooner.

"Merck wasn't dragging its feet," said Kenneth C. Frazier, the company's general counsel. "It's pretty hard for me to imagine that you could have done this more quickly than we did." The F.D.A., which Merck consulted, also agreed that designing a trial to specifically assess Vioxx's cardiovascular risks would have been difficult and, unless constructed to provide benefits to patients, would have been unethical as well.

But the F.D.A. itself is now under scrutiny for its handling of Vioxx. Congressional investigators are looking at whether the agency, which is charged with protecting Americans from dangerous medicines, was too lax in its monitoring of the mounting evidence against Merck's drug. Internal memos show disagreement within the F.D.A. over a study by one of its own scientists, Dr. David Graham, that estimated Vioxx had been associated with more than 27,000 heart attacks or deaths linked to cardiac problems.

So far, no clinical evidence has linked the next best-selling version, Celebrex, to cardiovascular risks. But its maker, Pfizer, has acknowledged that its other COX-2 drug, Bextra, has been shown to pose risks to patients after heart surgery. Scientists outside the company say there is evidence that Bextra's problems may affect wider groups of patients.

But Merck is the company drawing fire. Senator Charles E. Grassley, the Republican chairman of the Senate Finance Committee, has summoned Merck's chief executive, Raymond V. Gilmartin, to testify this week as part of the committee's investigation of the matter. The Justice Department recently started a criminal investigation of the company, and the Securities and Exchange Commission has begun an informal inquiry.

Some people associated with lawsuits against Merck, and company officials, provided internal Merck documents to The New York Times. The Wall Street Journal previously disclosed some of those records.

Controversy had shrouded Vioxx almost since its introduction in 1999. The drug was among the first of the COX-2 inhibitors, which were developed to reduce pain and inflammation without the risk of ulcers and other gastrointestinal side effects posed by aspirin and other over-the-counter medications. Thousands of Americans die every year from internal bleeding caused by the older drugs.

But when studies on Vioxx and Celebrex became available in 1998 and 1999, many doctors were disappointed. Neither drug alleviated pain any better than the older medicines. And the drugs cost close to $3 a pill; over-the-counter pain relievers, in contrast, cost pennies a dose.

Analysts say, however, that the success of Vioxx was critical to Merck. The patents on several popular Merck drugs expired in 2000 and 2001, opening them to generic competition. Merck badly needed Vioxx to replace those lost sales, said Michael Krensavage, a drug industry analyst at the investment bank Raymond James & Associates. "Vioxx was Merck's savior, it's as simple as that."

## The Critics: Outside Scientists Sounded an Alarm

The data that first alerted Merck to the heart risks with Vioxx arrived in March 2000, derived from a study of 8,100 rheumatoid arthritis patients begun in January 1999. In the study, called Vigor, patients were treated with either Vioxx or naproxen, an older pain reliever. While Vioxx reduced the risk of internal bleeding, it also appeared to raise the incidence of heart problems. Five times as many patients taking Vioxx had heart attacks as those taking naproxen.

Merck disclosed the Vigor data almost immediately and said it believed the difference resulted not from problems with Vioxx but from naproxen's strong protective effect on the heart. Many scientists outside the company found that theory implausible, and a rush to examine Vioxx, as well as Celebrex, began.

In 2001, the first major study critical of the drugs appeared in The Journal of the American Medical Association. The report, written by Dr. Eric J. Topol and cardiologists at Cleveland Clinic, reanalyzed data from several clinical trials of Vioxx and Celebrex. It reported that both drugs appeared to increase the risk of heart attack and stroke, but that the danger from Vioxx appeared higher.

Dr. Topol, the chairman of the clinic's department of cardiovascular medicine, immediately called for trials to specifically determine whether the drugs increased cardiovascular risk. Both Merck and Pfizer rebuffed that request, and said the Cleveland Clinic report was flawed because it failed, among other things, to include data from other studies.

Dr. Topol became a harsh critic of both drugs, but his ire focused on Vioxx and Merck. Even before his 2001 report appeared, he said in a recent interview, company scientists came to Cleveland to try to persuade him not to publish it; Merck officials deny doing so.

A year later, in October 2002, a study by Dr. Wayne Ray, an epidemiologist at Vanderbilt University, found that Medicaid patients in Tennessee who were taking high doses of Vioxx—greater than the recommended long-term dosage of 25 milligrams daily—had significantly more heart attacks and strokes than similar patients who were not taking high doses.

In an interview, Dr. Ray said that he had become concerned about Vioxx's safety as soon as the Vigor data became public. The Tennessee study confirmed his doubts, he said.

"A heart attack in exchange for an ulcer is a poor treatment," said Dr. Ray, who is now consulting with lawyers suing Merck.

But Merck said at the time, and still maintains, that the study from Dr. Ray and others like it did not shake its confidence in Vioxx's safety. Dr. Ray had examined patient records to look for a correlation between patients taking Vioxx and having heart problems, in what scientists call an epidemiological study. But such studies are considered less reliable than clinical trials, which medical researchers consider the gold standard of tests. In clinical trials, scientists enroll patients, carefully control their drug intake and monitor their reactions so that a drug's risks and benefits can be determined.

The quandary facing Merck and others in the Vioxx controversy was how to design a trial that could quickly identify any risks posed by the drug while also conferring some kind of benefit to the patients involved.

Dr. Rory Collins, an epidemiologist at Oxford University, said that examining patient records alone was useful only to find very large differences in risk, like those caused by cigarette smoking. While Dr. Ray's study showed a link between Vioxx and heart attacks, other studies did not, said Dr. Collins, who has conducted studies financed by Merck.

But other researchers were also finding worrisome signs. In 2002, Elucida Research, a small laboratory in Massachusetts, examined the way that Vioxx and other anti-inflammatory drugs interacted with lipids, or fatty compounds found in blood. That laboratory study found that Vioxx damaged the lipids in a way that made them more susceptible to clotting, said R. Preston Mason, the lead investigator on the study.

Meanwhile, more epidemiological studies backed Dr. Ray's findings. In an April 2004 study in the journal Circulation, researchers from Harvard Medical School found that Vioxx raised the risk of heart attacks relative to Celebrex; two months later, several of the same researchers reported in another journal that Vioxx increased the risk of hypertension.

Then, in August 2004, an epidemiological study by an F.D.A. researcher, based on data from 1.4 million patients in the Kaiser Permanente health care system, also showed a heightened cardiovascular risk for Vioxx.

## The Company: An Indirect Road to Assessing Risk

For Merck, the Vioxx episode has been bitter.

Company executives and researchers say that from the moment they were told in March 2000 about the preliminary results from the Vigor trials, they sought every possible explanation for the signs of increased cardiovascular risk. And, they say, they were open to the possibility that Vioxx was at fault.

"We were stunned," by the finding, said Dr. Alise S. Reicin, the Merck researcher who ran the Vigor study. "It's fair to say that we were all concerned."

She and other Merck officials said in interviews last week that nothing in any previous tests of Vioxx, including those submitted by the company in November 1998 to win its regulatory approval, suggested the drug posed a danger of increased heart attacks or stroke. Within days of learning the Vigor results, Dr. Reicin said that she, along with colleagues and academic consultants retained by Merck, were chasing the question of why the rate of heart problems was so high.

One possibility was that it was the result of chance. Another was that the problems were caused by Vioxx. And the third was that naproxen provided heart protection and had skewed the results. Merck researchers looked for data from other studies, aware that studies of two other little-used painkillers in the same class as naproxen had shown cardioprotective effects.

In the spring of 2000, Merck researchers also reviewed safety data from a continuing study in which Vioxx was being used in patients with Alzheimer's disease to test a theory that the painkiller might slow the disease's progress. Dr. Reicin said that there was no evidence in that study, which had started in 1998, that Vioxx posed a risk.

Merck researchers soon concluded that naproxen was cardioprotective. Some academic researchers, including some who consulted for Merck, also supported this theory.

One of them, Dr. Marvin A. Konstam, the chief of cardiology at the New England Medical Center in Boston, said his review of the data suggested Vioxx was safe.

"Based on these data, there was nothing that suggested to me that there was an increase in cardiovascular events with Vioxx," said Dr. Konstam in a recent interview.

But Merck never ran a clinical trial seeking to scientifically establish the heart-protecting properties of naproxen or to quantify how powerful an effect might be. In recent interviews, company officials said they did not believe there was a reason to conduct such tests because the critical issue was not proving naproxen's benefits but determining if Vioxx posed a risk.

Meanwhile, company scientists began to discuss the possibility of designing a trial to directly examine the drug's cardiovascular risks, Merck documents show.

At a meeting in May 2000, a top policy-making group met to discuss ways to defend Vioxx against competing drug makers' accusations that it posed risks. Among the issues they considered was whether to finance the development of a cardiovascular risk study, meeting documents show.

The documents show that Merck's researchers were not in agreement about how, or even whether, a trial could be performed. The documents also make clear that marketing executives were opposed to it.

Mr. Frazier, Merck's top lawyer, acknowledged that the decision to forgo the cardiovascular study was made at the meeting, but said that the decision was not driven by marketing concerns. He added that even if such a study had been undertaken, it would have taken years to produce results and would not necessarily have provided faster answers.

Merck executives opted to take a different road. In early 2000, the company had started a clinical trial to determine whether Vioxx could prevent the recurrence of colon polyps. Merck decided to intensely monitor the cardiovascular condition of patients in that test, known as the Approve trial, as well as subsequent studies. Dr. Reicin said last week that she and others at Merck felt devastated when they learned this past September about the findings from the colon polyp trial. But she said she believed that running the trials as the company did was the best way to learn whether the drug had a problem or not.

"We did our best to think of the most comprehensive study we could have done," she said. "I'm sorry that I didn't know four years ago what I know now, but the data didn't lead us there four years ago."

## The Regulator: Balancing Ethics Against Suspicions

The F.D.A., already under fire for its recent handling of pediatric antidepressants, faces a new round of questions from Congress this week over why it allowed Vioxx to be sold for so long while evidence mounted against it.

For years, drug reviewers at the F.D.A. had raised the possibility that Vioxx might be a danger to the heart, but without being able to answer the question, or even agreeing on the best way to get an answer.

Even before Vioxx's approval, an F.D.A. drug reviewer had written that Vioxx could conceivably hurt the heart. Studies of the drug at that point, however, showed nothing more than a suggestion of a risk.

That suggestion became more powerful when Merck presented the preliminary results of the Vigor study to the F.D.A. in March 2000. In that study, those taking Vioxx were clearly at greater risk than those taking naproxen; Merck officials argued that the difference was a result of naproxen's cardioprotective properties.

"We just didn't buy that," said Dr. Sandra Kweder, deputy director of the F.D.A.'s office of new drugs. Still, data in mid-2000 from other clinical trials did not show a heart risk. Flummoxed, the agency hired a cardiologist to take a careful look at the studies, and it summoned a panel of independent experts to discuss the data publicly.

The panel met in February 2001, and while several members expressed concerns about the heart risks, none suggested that the drug be withdrawn. Doctors on the panel who treated ulcers argued that Vioxx's protective effects far outweighed its possible harm to the heart; cardiologists argued that the drug's possible harm to the heart was a real problem. All agreed that more studies should be done.

The agency consulted with Merck and discussed the idea of a study designed solely to answer questions about the heart risks. As Merck officials had done in May 2000, the agency concluded that such a trial was difficult to envision. Giving placebos and Vioxx to groups of at-risk patients solely for the purpose of comparing side effects would be unethical, Dr. Kweder said.

Besides, Merck already had begun placebo-controlled trials assessing Vioxx's benefits against colon polyps, she said.

But the F.D.A. did require Merck to add to Vioxx's label a warning that patients with a history of heart disease should use the drug with caution.

And the agency underwrote a study at Kaiser Permanente, the giant health maintenance organization, to see if patients given Vioxx had a higher incidence of heart-related problems.

Meanwhile, the marketing battle between Vioxx and Celebrex grew heated. The F.D.A. scolded both drugs' makers for exaggerated claims about their drugs. In September 2001, the agency sent Merck a warning letter stating that Merck's promotional campaign for Vioxx "minimizes the potentially serious cardiovascular findings" in Vigor. The agency required Merck to send letters to physicians across the country "to correct false or misleading impressions and information."

This past August, the results of the Kaiser Permanente study came in and, according to Dr. Graham, who works in the F.D.A.'s office of drug safety, they were damning. Dr. Graham eventually concluded that high doses of Vioxx increased the risk of heart disease 3.7 times.

Dr. Graham contends that his bosses delayed his efforts to have the study published and, in a series of testy e-mail messages, demeaned his conclusions. A message from one superior called his findings "nothing more than a scientific rumor."

Dr. Kweder pointed out that Dr. Graham was unable to tell which patients had taken aspirin and whether patients given Vioxx were already at a higher risk of heart disease before the study started. In the end, she said, Dr. Graham's study did little more than to suggest that Vioxx might harm the heart.

"That's nothing new," Dr. Kweder said. "We knew that from Vigor."

A month later, when Merck informed the agency that the company would withdraw Vioxx, based on the polyp study, Dr. Kweder said agency officials were stunned.

Some experts still contend that Vioxx could be helpful for those at great risk of ulcer who do not have weak hearts. Asked if the agency would have required the drug's withdrawal if Merck had come to a different decision, Dr. Kweder said the agency would have had to examine the polyp study closely "and determine where the benefit might outweigh the risk."

"We haven't done that," she said. "We wish we had had the opportunity to do that."

Some critics say the episode highlights a more systemic problem—that the F.D.A., having approved a drug for the market, does not adequately monitor it afterward for safety problems.

But Dr. Kweder said she had no regrets about the handling of Vioxx. "The case of Vioxx," she said, "is one where the agency left no stone unturned."

## The Plaintiffs: Coming Soon, a Flood of Litigation

Jamie Gregg, a 32-year-old construction worker from Katy, Tex., and father of three boys, had just reported for a job at Houston's Hobby Airport last May 28 when he collapsed, apparently from a heart attack.

He was rushed to the hospital, where a medical team saved his life. But his brain had been deprived of oxygen for so long that Mr. Gregg is now in a nursing home in Lufkin, Tex., fed through a tube, unable to move more than his head or to utter more than a few syllables.

"We really don't know what he's thinking in his head," said his wife, Lisa Gregg, who said she was not sure if her husband even recognized his family.

Mr. Gregg, who had undergone a series of back surgeries, had been taking a high dosage of Vioxx, 50 milligrams a day, for four years to treat back pain. So the day after Mrs. Gregg heard that Vioxx was being withdrawn from the market, she walked into the offices of Goforth Lewis Sanford, a law firm in Houston. That firm, along with W. Mark Lanier, a prominent Houston plaintiffs' lawyer, are now preparing a lawsuit against Merck.

"This has got to be the reason" for her husband's problem, she said. "And if it is the reason, they've got to pay. There's people's lives that have been ruined by this, and I'm one of them."

Stories like the Greggs' underscore the very human nature of Merck's business problems. So far, 375 personal-injury lawsuits, representing 1,000 plaintiff groups, have been filed against Merck, according to the company's third-quarter filing with securities regulators. Some of the suits predate Vioxx's withdrawal. But with people like the Greggs just awakening to the issue, attorneys expect the number to grow markedly.

"From the scope of how many people are affected, it's as big as anything that ever occurred with a pharmaceutical," said Justin G. Witkin, a personal injury lawyer in Gulf Breeze, Fla.

Another plaintiffs' lawyer amassing Vioxx clients is Andy D. Birchfield Jr., of Montgomery, Ala., who noted that fen-phen, the diet drug combination linked to heart valve problems, was used by six million people. "You've got 20 million Americans who took Vioxx," he said. Wyeth, which manufactured two drugs, either of which was combined with a third to make the fen-phen combination, has set aside $16.6 billion to cover its liability.

Some of the first Vioxx cases are expected to go to trial next year. Lawyers and courts are still trying to sort out whether to consolidate the lawsuits and in which courts to try them.

Last Tuesday, about 300 personal-injury lawyers gathered in a ballroom at the Ritz-Carlton Huntington Hotel & Spa in Pasadena, Calif., for a combination strategy session and pep rally on Vioxx claims.

But the plaintiffs' lawyers face a big obstacle in convincing juries that a person's heart attack or stroke was caused by Vioxx, because many people suffer such attacks for many reasons.

Merck has not discussed its defense strategy in detail. But besides arguing that it took the drug off the market as soon as it had solid evidence of Vioxx's dangers, it is also likely to argue in many cases that a person's problems could have other causes. Mr. Gregg, for instance, smoked half a pack of cigarettes a day, his wife said. And since April 2002, the Vioxx label recommended that the 50-milligram dose Mr. Gregg used not be taken for extended periods.

Thomas B. Moore, a Los Angeles lawyer who represents pharmaceutical companies in such matters, although not Merck in this case, predicted that even the estimate by Dr. Graham of the F.D.A. that the drug caused more than 27,000 deaths and heart attacks would not help plaintiffs win cases. "The problem is that David Graham can't name one of them," Mr. Moore said. "He can't name one of those 27,000."

He said Merck did not appear to have hidden any data, but instead disagreed about the interpretation, and had withdrawn the drug voluntarily. "Voluntary withdrawals do much better with jurors than a withdrawal by the F.D.A," he said.

## The Future: Merck's Costs Still Lie Ahead

As if trial lawyers, federal prosecutors and congressional committees were not challenges enough, Merck has had little success introducing new drugs since Vioxx. The company's laboratories, once among the most productive in the pharmaceutical industry, have suffered a long string of failures and the company's new drug pipeline is nearly bare.

Merck's stock has fallen 40 percent since it announced the Vioxx recall in September, lowering its market value by about $50 billion. Merck shares closed Friday at $26.45, up 30 cents.

Merck will not disclose its strategy for resolving the Vioxx-related suits. But analysts who have studied the issue say that Merck may follow the route taken by Bayer, which faced thousands of suits claiming injury from its cholesterol drug Baycol, which was linked to a serious muscle disorder.

Bayer tried to settle most of the stronger suits, while pushing for trials in cases where it felt plaintiffs had overreached and the company had a tactical advantage. Bayer won a crucial case in Texas last year, and its stock has nearly tripled since March 2003, when concerns about its legal liability peaked.

Still, Merck's legal liability could top $10 billion, according to two studies by Wall Street analysts. Merrill Lynch estimated that the company's legal liability would be $4 billion to $18 billion, depending on the number of people who suffered heart attacks while taking Vioxx and how much the company pays to resolve each claim. But that estimate did not include potential punitive damages, Merrill noted.

In an estimate last month, since withdrawn, Sanford C. Bernstein & Company estimated that the company could spend $12 billion. But Richard Evans, the Bernstein analyst, said he withdrew the estimate because the company faced so many uncertainties that an accurate calculation was impossible. He said, though, that he did not think the company faced a serious risk of bankruptcy.

Merck is expected to have $20 billion in sales and $6 billion in profits next year, not counting its Vioxx costs, giving it the financial flexibility to settle thousands of suits. And its legal liabilities and relatively weak prospects for new drugs could actually provide a protective effect, by making Merck an unpromising takeover candidate for other big drug companies.

For now, Merck appears likely to limp along independently, analysts say.

*This article was reported and written by Alex Berenson, Gardiner Harris, Barry Meier and Andrew Pollack.*

## A Conversation with . . . Gardiner Harris

PUBLIC HEALTH REPORTER

© The New York Times

*Gardiner Harris joined The New York Times in 2003, originally as a business reporter covering the pharmaceutical industry. Previously he was a pharmaceutical industry reporter at The Wall Street Journal and covered Appalachia for the Louisville, Ky., Courier-Journal. He graduated from Yale in 1986 with a bachelor's degree in history. The following interview was conducted on the telephone and edited for publication.*

**What do you like best about your job?**

I get to spend a fair amount of time on longer projects and do investigative pieces. Also I think there is an almost boundless interest in health care subjects. Almost whatever I produce or want to produce will find space in the newspaper, and that's not always true in other subjects. My beat really is the intersection of politics and life and death issues.

**What exactly is your beat?**

Public health. It's a specialist beat. You need to know a fair amount about some fairly technical things to be able to tackle it. A fairly high percentage of the stories that I write—70, 80 percent—are self-generated, and a fairly low percentage are assigned.

**How did you get into the beat?**

Accidentally. I was hired by The Wall Street Journal after I had won several national reporting awards. I was fielding a variety of different offers from different newspapers, and the way that The Wall Street Journal managed to lure me there was to give me the pharmaceutical beat. At the time [1999] the pharmaceutical industry was on top of the world, and it was, I thought, the most interesting beat at The Wall Street Journal.

I'd done a fair amount of math in college and some biology, but I remember going to my first scientific meeting put on by Novartis, and it was filled with all these analysts. Some guy with a thick German accent from the company got up there and started talking about their pipeline and their science programs, and I started chuckling because I couldn't understand a word this guy said. I looked around at the other analysts, and they were all busily scribbling notes and apparently were very much on top of what was going on, but I just didn't get it at all. I remember going back to the office, and my boss asked me, "So anything new, anything interesting?" and I was like, "No, we've heard it all before." Of course, I had no idea, but the thought that I was actually going to write a story on that just terrified me. So they gave me a little leeway, and after some months I managed to get to a point where I actually understood a few things that I was being told.

**Do you have a background in public health or medicine or science?**
None of those things.

**You learned on the beat.**
I did.

**What is your favorite story that you've done for The New York Times, and why?**
It was an analysis of payment records to physicians from drug makers in Minnesota. (See story, page 52.) It was my favorite story because it took more effort than any other story that I've ever done here. It took us about eight months of data analysis cranking. It did something entirely original. We managed to compare the money given to doctors with their prescribing history in Medicaid. There was a paragraph in that story that took us about four months to get the goods on. That paragraph said that doctors who take $5,000 from drug makers are more than three times as likely to prescribe antipsychotic medicines to children as doctors who take less than $5,000. It was the first time, and I believe again the only time, that anyone had made a link between what could potentially be at least a controversial prescribing behavior on the one hand and drug maker marketing efforts on the other. That story is what led the [Senator] Charles Grassley staff to start investigating conflicts of interest in medicine, which then led to a series of other stories that really have transformed medicine and continue to transform medicine.

**Going to another story, you were one of the reporters listed for the big front-page 2004 Vioxx story.**
Right. I had been at The Wall Street Journal for many years, and I was their lead pharma reporter. Merck was one of my companies that I covered, so I had known Merck well. So I was able to provide a lot of the context of the history of Merck. We also had an insider who got us a fair amount of the internal correspondence.

The Wall Street Journal had done the first big story on the internal correspondence that came out of litigation about Vioxx. I think their story was before ours and was a great, great story. I think ours did break some new ground.

**What struck me about the story was how you really made it clear that [Merck attempted] to say that naproxen was cardioprotective rather than that Vioxx was risky for the heart.**
That certainly was a strong part of the story. I wrote a lot of stories about Vioxx and Celebrex when they were being launched and was a target of a concerted campaign by both Merck and Pfizer to persuade me of the benefits of these drugs and heard firsthand from Merck during all those years about the cardioprotectiveness of naproxen. What's amazing in retrospect was my

failure to say to them, "Wait just a second, if you're telling me that naproxen is cardioprotective, even if that's the case, why would anybody take Vioxx over naproxen?" Who in their right mind would substitute a heart attack for an ulcer? Why even launch a medicine when there is a competitor that can not only solve your pain, but protect you from heart attacks? In retrospect, it's hard to believe that we even got to where we were. Of course, even at the time Merck executives would answer that naproxen caused far more stomach upset, that many people as a result could not take naproxen. But that seems to me to be a relatively small problem compared to the heart attack risk and, in retrospect, it's what killed the drug.

**You're saying you find it hard to look back and see that you, as a reporter, didn't jump on that until the 2004 story?**
Absolutely. That was a colossal failure on my part and those of my colleagues. Even if we had accepted Merck's interpretation of these data, why didn't we write far more critical stories about that whole class of medicines? We didn't. If you talked to my colleagues at The Wall Street Journal at the time and if you talked to executives within the pharmaceutical industry, I think most of them would say that I was the most skeptical reporter at a big media organization working on the pharmaceutical beat. I wrote a lot of negative stories, but I didn't write that one and I should have.

**What's the hardest part of your job?**
I think the hardest part of any beat reporter's job is getting beat by other reporters. It happens routinely, and you have to admit with your tail between your legs to your bosses that you got beat, and you need to follow in the wake of someone else. The time when I am most depressed is when I get something wrong. It doesn't happen often, but it happens on occasion, and we have to file a correction. Often these corrections result because someone sends an e-mail, often a very caustic e-mail telling me what an idiot I am, and in those cases they're not wrong, and it is very dispiriting. That is probably when I feel my lowest.

**Do you share any of your stories with your sources to make sure you get them right?**
I will sometimes, but it depends. On daily stories, particularly with a hard deadline, it's very hard to do that. You are trying to put together a story in incredibly rapid time. I, like many reporters, tend to overreport. I spend probably too much time trying to get as much information about a subject as I possibly can. I never give myself in those instances adequate time to write the story. So I just have to fly through the writing process. I was trained early on to write very quickly. Nonetheless, it still is a challenge. In those deadline times I often cannot spend the time to go back to sources to read the appropriate paragraphs to make sure that I've gotten it right.

On stories that do not have an immediate deadline, I like to go back to sources. In technical parts of the story, [I] read back those portions to the experts to make sure that I didn't screw it up, that I got it right. But it is an almost endless task to make sure that you have gotten everything right.

**When you say that you share a quote with your source and make sure it's correct, how do you determine that the source isn't trying to change what he said or pull it back?**
The use of quotes in stories is one of the really interesting things about how different reporters do their job. If someone is talking in a public setting in a House hearing or something like that, you don't go back to the source to make sure that you got it right because often I have a recording of those. What was said is what goes in the paper, period. But in many of my stories, the quote comes from an interview I had with them either in person or on the phone. They are often responding to questions that I am asking them about a particular subject. In most cases I will allow people to change their quotes if they feel it doesn't accurately reflect what their belief is on the subject. In most of those cases I am trying to get their best judgment or their opinion about an issue. I want them to feel that I have placed them and their idea in the best light possible. There are other reporters who do this differently. Even if someone stumbles, they will put in the stumble. You can make someone feel stupid. I don't think that that helps the reader. It certainly doesn't help with your sourcing with people. When you do that to people, they tend to not want to talk to you again.

I'm a beat reporter. I have to go back to these people again and again and again, many of them for different stories. I want them to feel that I am giving them their best shot to make their best case. So I allow them to make sure that their quote accurately reflects their thinking and does so in a way that they feel good about.

**Just one more question for you. What's the most fun about your job?**
I have to say this job is not quite as fun as when I was a police reporter in Louisville, when I went out to crime scenes and every day was completely different from the day before. You never really knew what kind of crazy circumstance you were going to find yourself in. So I don't really have that. I do like the struggle for ideas, and I do like working at the frontier of change, of people trying to figure out what's right. My beat right now really is an idea beat. It is about new drugs that are being tried. It's about new public health measures. You don't really know if they work. So it's sort of an exploration.

There are two fundamental processes in my job. One is the reporting part, and the other is the writing part. I've always been one of those guys who was curious and who walked up to the cops standing in front of a police line and asked, "Hey, what's going on?" I also love the kind of crossword puzzle aspect of writing. Writing is putting the pieces together in a coherent way and in a way that provides readers with nice moments and surprises. Having been a student of American history, I still get a great kick out of going up to the Senate, going up to the House and, on occasion, wandering into the White House. I'm still a starry-eyed kid when I go there. I do like my job, and thankfully I say that to my wife and I say that often to my boss. I'm aware of it. It's a fun job. Not every day, but most days.

# MAKING CONNECTIONS

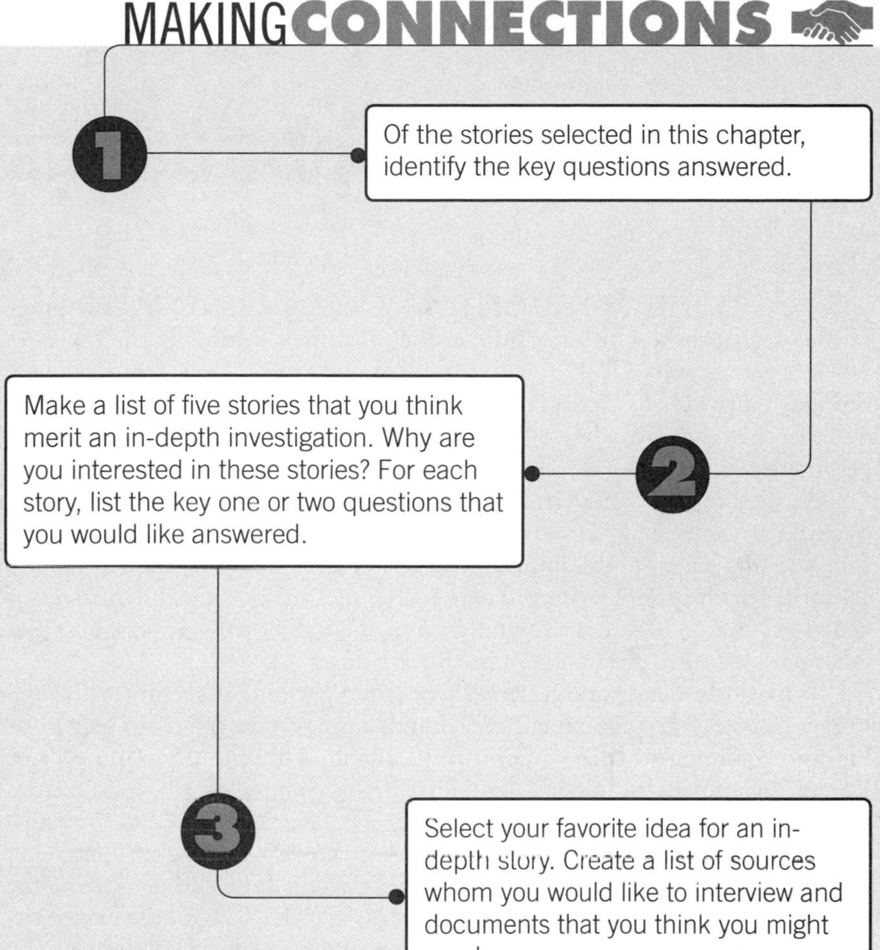

1. Of the stories selected in this chapter, identify the key questions answered.

2. Make a list of five stories that you think merit an in-depth investigation. Why are you interested in these stories? For each story, list the key one or two questions that you would like answered.

3. Select your favorite idea for an in-depth story. Create a list of sources whom you would like to interview and documents that you think you might need.

# CHAPTER 5

# obituaries

THINK OF THE OBITUARY AS AN ABBREVIATED biography—a snapshot of history. Besides documenting a death, obituary writers work to give readers a feel for who the person was. New York Times medical reporter Lawrence K. Altman says his job in an obituary is to "delve into what it is that they did, why they did it and how they did it, and what led them to get interested to do it."

At its simplest, an obituary tells readers who died, when the death occurred and under what circumstances. A profile of the deceased usually follows. In a memorable obituary the writer uses many of the techniques associated with profile writing. These techniques include short narratives or anecdotes that give readers a window into the individual's personality. (See Chapter 6 for a full discussion of profile writing.)

Typical obituaries appear as a short story in the obit section, although longer obits of very prominent individuals may run on the front page. For highly prominent people, the obituary can run a couple thousand words. For less prominent individuals, like those in this chapter, obituaries run from 800 to 1,500 words.

One or more photographs usually accompany the obituary. Action pictures give life to the story since the last thing you want to do is to make the obituary a solemn recapitulation of the deceased's life. Toward the end of the obituary the reporter lists the deceased's survivors and their relationships to the person who died.

Most major news organizations research and write obituaries of highly prominent people well in advance of their deaths. By doing that, the reporter can avoid deadline pressure and take time to interview family, friends and colleagues of the individual and, in some cases, even have the opportunity to speak to the individual.

In an obituary about a prominent researcher or physician, the reporter explains the individual's scientific achievements in language simple enough for a layperson to understand. This explanation often leads to one or more science lessons in which the writer gives readers a concise explanation of the process or procedure underlying the science behind the individual's major accomplishments.

## Selection 5.1

*The next story, an obituary of Dr. Donald F. Gleason, follows the typical formula. In the lede the reporter tells us who died and why that individual was well known. By the second or third paragraph we learn the cause of death. The real heart of the story is Gleason's scientific contribution, a method for tracking the aggressiveness of prostate cancer. The level of detail in this science lesson is often dependent on the significance of the individual's contributions. In this case the explanation of the Gleason score takes five paragraphs. If the story had been about Dr. Jonas Salk, who developed the first successful vaccine against polio, the science lesson would have been much longer.*[1]

## Donald F. Gleason, 88, Dies; Devised Prostate Test

By LAWRENCE K. ALTMAN

Dr. Donald F. Gleason, who devised the Gleason score, which has been used to help determine the aggressiveness of prostate cancer in millions of men, died on Dec. 28 in Edina, Minn. He was 88.

The cause was a heart attack, according to the University of Minnesota, where he taught. He was also former chief of pathology at the Minneapolis VA Medical Center, which was affiliated with the university and where he did most of the research that led to the score.

Dr. Gleason devised his scoring system in the 1960s through his observations of the cellular architecture of the prostate, the gland that produces seminal fluid. The score is considered the most reliable indicator of the potential for prostate cancer to grow and spread. It helps provide a prognosis and guide treatment, and it is a reference standard in clinical trials testing new therapies.

"Every prostate cancer patient knows his Gleason score," said Dr. Bruce Roth, a professor of medicine and urological surgery at Vanderbilt University and an official of the American Society of Clinical Oncology. "It is remarkable that the Gleason score remains the standard test despite the millions of dollars spent on trying to develop molecular tests to displace it."

The score is based on a pathologist's microscopic examination of prostate tissue that has been chemically stained after a biopsy. Under a standard microscope, the cells can show in various patterns.

To determine a Gleason score, a pathologist assigns a separate numerical grade to the two most predominant architectural patterns of the cancer cells. The grade depends on how far the cells deviate from normal appearance. The numbers range from 1 (the cells look nearly normal) to 5 (the cells have the most cancerous appearance).

---

*Published: January 10, 2009.*

The sum of the two grades is the Gleason score. The lowest possible score is 2, which rarely occurs; the highest is 10. Scores of 2 to 4 are considered low grade; 5 through 7, intermediate grade; and 8 through 10, high grade.

High scores tend to suggest a worse prognosis than lower scores because the more deranged, high-scoring cells usually grow faster than the more normal-appearing ones.

Prognosis also depends on further refinements. In one example, a score of 7 can come in two ways: 4 plus 3 or 3 plus 4. With 4 plus 3, cancer cells in the most predominant category appear more aggressive than those in the second, suggesting a more serious threat than a 3-plus-4 score, in which cells in the most predominant group appear only moderately aggressive.

Donald Floyd Gleason was born on Nov. 20, 1920, in Spencer, Iowa, and grew up in Litchfield, Minn., where his father, Fred, ran a hardware store and his mother, Ethel, was a teacher.

Dr. Gleason earned his undergraduate, medical and Ph.D. degrees from the University of Minnesota. After an internship at the University of Maryland, Baltimore, as a lieutenant in the Army Medical Corps, he trained as a pathologist at the Minneapolis VA hospital. He became the hospital's chief of anatomic pathology and laboratories and retired in 1986.

Dr. Gleason is survived by his wife, Nancy; three daughters, Donna O'Neill of Annandale, Va., Sue Anderson of Burnsville, Minn., and Ginger Venable of Eden Prairie, Minn.; a sister, Barbara Jarl of St. Paul; and nine grandchildren.

In 1962, Dr. George Mellinger, the hospital's chief of urology, who also led a cooperative urological research project involving 14 hospitals, asked Dr. Gleason to develop a standardized pathological testing system for prostate cancer.

Dr. Gleason wrote in a personal narrative that he was well aware of the wide variation that existed in the speed with which prostate cancer spreads, as well as in the architectural patterns seen under a microscope. Many microscopic classifications existed at the time, but pathologists had difficulty applying them and often devised their own, thereby creating confusion in treatment and the evaluation of new therapies.

To sharpen comparisons, Dr. Gleason based his classification on a small number of changes seen in the architectural arrangement of cancer cells.

The patterns were strongly related to survival rates in the first 270 patients, he reported in 1966 in the journal Cancer Chemotherapy Reports. Extending the study to include 4,000 patients strengthened the findings.

Doctors adopted the Gleason score slowly until 1987, when seven leading experts in urology and pathology recommended that it be used uniformly in all scientific publications on prostate cancer.

The Gleason score became even more widely applied with the surge in the number of prostate cancers detected from a different test, the PSA (or prostate specific antigen) test, a blood test used for screening. As more cancers are detected, there is more reason to apply the score.

Last year, 186,320 people in the United States developed prostate cancer and 28,660 died from it, according to the American Cancer Society.

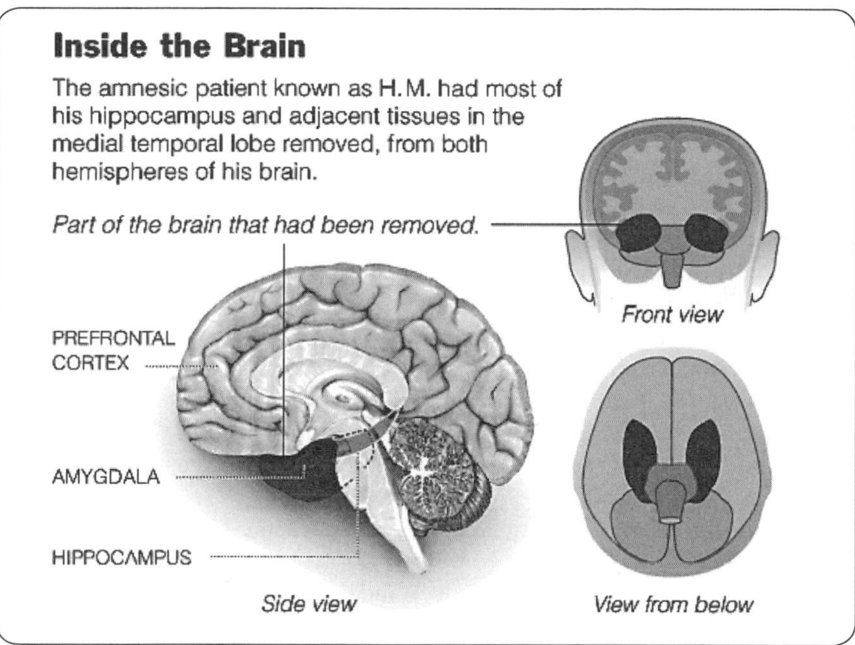

Inside the Brain
The amnesic patient known as H.M. had most of his hippocampus and adjacent tissues in the medial temporal lobe removed, from both hemispheres of his brain.
Part of the brain that had been removed.
PREFRONTAL CORTEX
AMYGDALA
HIPPOCAMPUS
Side view
Front view
View from below

The New York Times

## Selection 5.2

*An obituary is usually the most formulaic of news stories, but the next example breaks most of the rules and, in so doing, is one of the most memorable medical obituaries that you'll read. Benedict Carey, The Times behavior reporter who wrote this obituary, talks in the Q&A following this story about how he was able to track down a Nobel Prize-winning scientist to get a lead quote at the last minute and how he managed to write the obit the day of the person's death. Like the man for whom the obituary was written, the story is unusual from first to last sentence. Note the simple, yet elegant, two-sentence lede that pulls you into the story. Not until the seventh paragraph—even before we learn the name of the deceased—do we find out that he is "the most important patient in the history of brain science." Throughout the story Carey tells a fascinating science lesson about the nature of memory and researchers' efforts to study this individual's unusual condition. What distinguishes this obituary is its poetic description of the deceased as a person and as an object of intensive scientific study. Through deft writing Carey humanizes both the man and the science.*

## H. M., an Unforgettable Amnesiac, Dies at 82

By BENEDICT CAREY

He knew his name. That much he could remember.

He knew that his father's family came from Thibodaux, La., and his mother was from Ireland, and he knew about the 1929 stock market crash and World War II and life in the 1940s.

But he could remember almost nothing after that.

In 1953, he underwent an experimental brain operation in Hartford to correct a seizure disorder, only to emerge from it fundamentally and irreparably changed. He developed a syndrome neurologists call profound amnesia. He had lost the ability to form new memories.

For the next 55 years, each time he met a friend, each time he ate a meal, each time he walked in the woods, it was as if for the first time.

And for those five decades, he was recognized as the most important patient in the history of brain science. As a participant in hundreds of studies, he helped scientists understand the biology of learning, memory and physical dexterity, as well as the fragile nature of human identity.

On Tuesday evening at 5:05, Henry Gustav Molaison—known worldwide only as H. M., to protect his privacy—died of respiratory failure at a nursing home in Windsor Locks, Conn. His death was confirmed by Suzanne Corkin, a neuroscientist at the Massachusetts Institute of Technology, who had worked closely with him for decades. Henry Molaison was 82.

From the age of 27, when he embarked on a life as an object of intensive study, he lived with his parents, then with a relative and finally in an institution. His amnesia did not damage his intellect or radically change his personality. But he could not hold a job and lived, more so than any mystic, in the moment.

"Say it however you want," said Dr. Thomas Carew, a neuroscientist at the University of California, Irvine, and president of the Society for Neuroscience. "What H. M. lost, we now know, was a critical part of his identity."

At a time when neuroscience is growing exponentially, when students and money are pouring into laboratories around the world and researchers are mounting large-scale studies with powerful

---

*Published: December 4, 2008.*

brain-imaging technology, it is easy to forget how rudimentary neuroscience was in the middle of the 20th century.

When Mr. Molaison, at 9 years old, banged his head hard after being hit by a bicycle rider in his neighborhood near Hartford, scientists had no way to see inside his brain. They had no rigorous understanding of how complex functions like memory or learning functioned biologically. They could not explain why the boy had developed severe seizures after the accident, or even whether the blow to the head had anything do to with it.

Eighteen years after that bicycle accident, Mr. Molaison arrived at the office of Dr. William Beecher Scoville, a neurosurgeon at Hartford Hospital. Mr. Molaison was blacking out frequently, had devastating convulsions and could no longer repair motors to earn a living.

After exhausting other treatments, Dr. Scoville decided to surgically remove two finger-shaped slivers of tissue from Mr. Molaison's brain. The seizures abated, but the procedure—especially cutting into the hippocampus, an area deep in the brain, about level with the ears—left the patient radically changed.

Alarmed, Dr. Scoville consulted with a leading surgeon in Montreal, Dr. Wilder Penfield of McGill University, who with Dr. Brenda Milner, a psychologist, had reported on two other patients' memory deficits.

Soon Dr. Milner began taking the night train down from Canada to visit Mr. Molaison in Hartford, giving him a variety of memory tests. It was a collaboration that would forever alter scientists' understanding of learning and memory.

"He was a very gracious man, very patient, always willing to try these tasks I would give him," Dr. Milner, a professor of cognitive neuroscience at the Montreal Neurological Institute and McGill University, said in a recent interview. "And yet every time I walked in the room, it was like we'd never met."

At the time, many scientists believed that memory was widely distributed throughout the brain and not dependent on any one neural organ or region. Brain lesions, either from surgery or accidents, altered people's memory in ways that were not easily predictable. Even as Dr. Milner published her results, many researchers attributed H. M.'s deficits to other factors, like general trauma from his seizures or some unrecognized damage.

"It was hard for people to believe that it was all due" to the excisions from the surgery, Dr. Milner said.

That began to change in 1962, when Dr. Milner presented a landmark study in which she and H. M. demonstrated that a part of his memory was fully intact. In a series of trials, she had Mr. Molaison try to trace a line between two outlines of a five-point star, one inside the other, while watching his hand and the star in a mirror. The task is difficult for anyone to master at first.

Every time H. M. performed the task, it struck him as an entirely new experience. He had no memory of doing it before. Yet with practice he became proficient. "At one point he said to me, after many of these trials, 'Huh, this was easier than I thought it would be,'" Dr. Milner said.

The implications were enormous. Scientists saw that there were at least two systems in the brain for creating new memories. One, known as declarative memory, records names, faces and new experiences and stores them until they are consciously retrieved. This system depends on the function of medial temporal areas, particularly an organ called the hippocampus, now the object of intense study.

Another system, commonly known as motor learning, is subconscious and depends on other brain systems. This explains why people can jump on a bike after years away from one and take the thing for a ride, or why they can pick up a guitar that they have not played in years and still remember how to strum it.

Soon "everyone wanted an amnesic to study," Dr. Milner said, and researchers began to map out still other dimensions of memory. They saw that H. M.'s short-term memory was fine; he could hold thoughts in his head for about 20 seconds. It was holding onto them without the hippocampus that was impossible.

"The study of H. M. by Brenda Milner stands as one of the great milestones in the history of modern neuroscience," said Dr. Eric Kandel, a neuroscientist at Columbia University. "It opened the way for the study of the two memory systems in the brain, explicit and implicit, and provided the basis for everything that came later—the study of human memory and its disorders."

Living at his parents' house, and later with a relative through the 1970s, Mr. Molaison helped with the shopping, mowed the lawn, raked leaves and relaxed in front of the television. He could navigate through a day attending to mundane details—fixing a lunch, making his bed—by drawing on what he could remember from his first 27 years.

He also somehow sensed from all the scientists, students and researchers parading through his life that he was contributing to a larger endeavor, though he was uncertain about the details, said Dr. Corkin, who met Mr. Molaison while studying in Dr. Milner's laboratory and who continued to work with him until his death.

By the time he moved into a nursing home in 1980, at age 54, he had become known to Dr. Corkin's M.I.T. team in the way that Polaroid snapshots in a photo album might sketch out a life but not reveal it whole.

H. M. could recount childhood scenes: Hiking the Mohawk Trail. A road trip with his parents. Target shooting in the woods near his house.

"Gist memories, we call them," Dr. Corkin said. "He had the memories, but he couldn't place them in time exactly; he couldn't give you a narrative."

He was nonetheless a self-conscious presence, as open to a good joke and as sensitive as anyone in the room. Once, a researcher visiting with Dr. Milner and H. M. turned to her and remarked how interesting a case this patient was.

"H. M. was standing right there," Dr. Milner said, "and he kind of colored—blushed, you know—and mumbled how he didn't think he was that interesting, and moved away."

In the last years of his life, Mr. Molaison was, as always, open to visits from researchers, and Dr. Corkin said she checked on his health weekly. She also arranged for one last research program. On Tuesday, hours after Mr. Molaison's death, scientists worked through the night taking exhaustive M.R.I. scans of his brain, data that will help tease apart precisely which areas of his temporal lobes were still intact and which were damaged, and how this pattern related to his memory.

Dr. Corkin arranged, too, to have his brain preserved for future study, in the same spirit that Einstein's was, as an irreplaceable artifact of scientific history.

"He was like a family member," said Dr. Corkin, who is at work on a book on H. M., titled "A Lifetime Without Memory." "You'd think it would be impossible to have a relationship with someone who didn't recognize you, but I did."

In his way, Mr. Molaison did know his frequent visitor, she added: "He thought he knew me from high school."

Henry Gustav Molaison, born on Feb. 26, 1926, left no survivors. He left a legacy in science that cannot be erased.

## A Conversation with . . . Benedict Carey

BEHAVIOR REPORTER

© The New York Times

*Benedict Carey joined the science staff at The New York Times in 2004. Prior to that he was first a freelance and then a general health reporter for the Los Angeles Times. He began his journalism career at a shipping trade magazine in New York before joining Hippocrates, a consumer medical magazine based in San Francisco, in 1987 as a staff reporter. He graduated from the University of Colorado in 1983 with a bachelor's degree in math and later earned a master's degree in journalism at Northwestern University. The following interview was conducted on the telephone and edited for publication.*

**In the obit about H. M., what did you like best about that story?**
Oh, boy. I liked that story a lot. That may be my favorite story I've ever done. I liked best that I was doing it. This sounds selfish and egotistical. I had thought about H. M. I had read about him for so long. I felt like he was this ghostly presence, a very important one, in the study of the brain, who never got his due. He never had a coming-out party. He was never paid. He was never recognized for his contributions, which were huge.

And I thought there was a risk that no one would ever know who he was, and that his identity would be lost with the scientists. In a way, he had his identity stolen, or at least ruined or taken away in this botched surgery. Then afterwards he disappeared underneath these initials, H. M. I think there was a risk that he would die, and that would be the end of it.

So I knew that he was an old guy. I wanted to visit him, actually. That was my plan. And he died. But I had already done some legwork on this. I had already talked to some of the researchers who knew him, and I was loaded. I was ready to go. I turned around and wrote a story I'm proud of. Also the paper put it on the front page. It was just nice to be able to get a chance to do that.

**How did you arrive at the lede, which began, "He knew his name. That much he could remember"?**
Well, I went through several ledes. This was all happening very quickly, you understand. I think if I'm going to be honest, that my editor might have written that lede, Bill McDonald, who's an excellent editor. He's the editor of the obit page. We were kicking it back and forth like crazy, but I think he wrote that top, or at least those two sentences. So it's his. But I'm happy to take credit for it.

**How frequent is that occurrence, that an editor will rewrite a lede or write a substantial portion of it?**
In my case it hardly ever happens. In the case of H. M., what happened was that I wrote—well, initially the editors said, "Well, we need to write the obit, so write an obit," and the obit has a style, right, which is "William F. Buckley, brief sort of encapsulated description of who he was, died today at [his home in Stamford, Conn. He was 82]." If you look at obits, you'll see that formula. That's what they use. A lot of really great writing can be built into that formula and is here. We have very good obits.

So when I started off, I started writing it that way. That's the way they wanted it. And so it wasn't until I got back and Bill said, "Why don't we try something like this?" So he started it with that unorthodox lede, and I said, "That's great. Let's do that." So that's the way that one worked.

**How much of this obit did you write in advance of his death?**
None of it.

**So you just had the information. This was all written in a period of how much time?**
Oh, it took about a day. I started it in the morning and was done by about 4 o'clock, 5 o'clock.

**You said most of the interviews you had done in the previous week. Did you know he was dying? Is that why the timing was that way?**
No. I had no idea. What I was trying to do was to set up a story. It was a part of a series I'm doing right now. I wanted to meet him before he died. But it so happened there was a neuroscience conference in the week—I think it was the week before he died. One of the people speaking was Brenda Milner, who was the one who worked with him most closely, who did the real seminal, the most important research with him.

So I arranged to talk to Brenda. This was at the neuroscience meeting, having no idea what the health was of H. M. So I had a long conversation with her. She then presented at the meeting. I had notes from that presentation. I talked to Larry Squire at the meeting a little bit.

I talked to another memory researcher named Tom Carew, who's president of the Society for Neuroscience, about it. So I had a little bit in my pocket, and I just called back Brenda Milner that day when H. M. died. Of course, I talked at length with Suzanne Corkin, who was a student of Milner who worked with H. M. for years, really took over the care of H. M. and the studies of his memory.

**What was the biggest difficulty in putting this whole story together?**
It turned out the biggest difficulty was I needed to get a very senior person to make a big statement about how important this guy was. So I needed a Bigfoot type of person to come in here and really close the case on it. Those people are sometimes very hard to get. I was working most of the day trying to get through to a couple of researchers. I called trying to get through to Eric Kandel, who's the Nobel-winning neuroscientist at Columbia, and Kandel, at the end of the day, finally called back.

But that was a headache, because that sort of person helps you frame and organize the story. Their quotes give you a good anchor. The rest of it was written from interviews I had done with some of the main researchers just in the past week before that. Also, I knew a lot about him [H. M.]. I had read about him and about the science that was done with him and the studies and all the history. I just had to get out of my own way and write what I knew, which is what I did.

*[Note: The conversation with Benedict Carey continues at the end of Chapter 7.]*

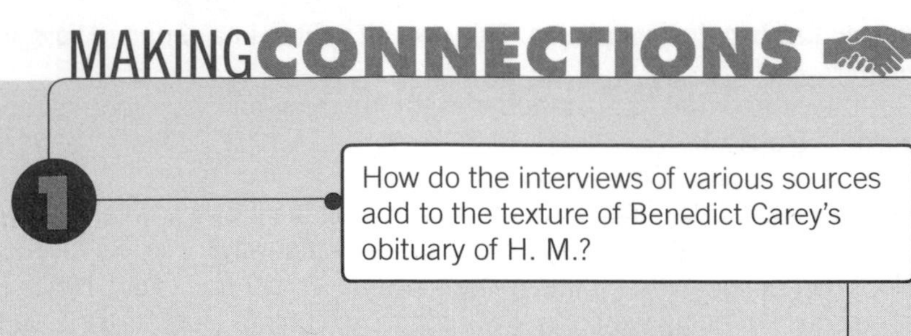


How do the interviews of various sources add to the texture of Benedict Carey's obituary of H. M.?

2) Find two obituaries about prominent medical researchers or scientists on nytimes.com and identify what you consider to be the key science lessons.

3

It's common practice for news organizations to write obituaries before a prominent individual dies. So, find a prominent scientist in your community and talk to people who know him or her to learn about that individual's unique contributions to science. After you've interviewed the individual's colleagues and friends, talk to the scientist whom you've identified to obtain a personal perspective on his or her life's work. Then write a 1,000-word obituary (minus, of course, the details about the death).

# Part II

# feature stories

ON THE HEALTH BEAT AND MOST OTHER BEATS, journalists don't use the word "feature" as much as they once did. Back when a print newspaper was most people's main news source, the line between news and features was clear: news was "X happened yesterday," and features were everything else. Today, however, anyone picking up a newspaper and many people visiting a Web site already know what happened yesterday—or this morning, or five minutes ago. They're looking to journalists for more—more sources, more perspective, more sense of how the news affects their lives. Thus, news stories, beyond the first announcements of events, often contain elements formerly identified with feature stories.

So what's left to distinguish a feature? For one thing, time. A news story becomes outdated quickly. In contrast, a feature may run days or weeks after the reporter starts working on it. A few features are so timeless that they're referred to in the newsroom as evergreens.

Features don't follow the inverted-pyramid form of traditional hard news stories. Whereas news stories usually have a direct lede that gets right to the point, a feature will often have a soft (aka delayed) lede that grabs the reader with a scene or anecdote before summarizing the story's purpose. There's no universal structure that works for every feature; instead, the writer's job is to find the form that suits the content. Features often include narrative elements like description and dialogue, and some proceed almost like fiction (but with the facts adhering strictly to reality), with a clear beginning, middle and end.

Just as news and features are not argument-proof labels, the categories of features that you'll see in this section—profiles, explanatory, perspective, historical, series and narratives—are not used by every journalist. No writer sits down and says, "OK, now I'm going to write a perspective piece"; he or she simply follows the reporting where it goes. But categories are useful for organizing a book, for studying stories in depth, and for giving you a sense of options—even if the categories overlap.

A profile (like the one on heart surgeon Dr. Michael E. DeBakey in Chapter 6) reveals a person through both narrative and explanatory elements. An explanatory story tells how a process works (like the story in Chapter 7 on how flu virus genes evolve). A perspective story (like the story about the lack of a link between autism and childhood vaccines in Chapter 8) gives the big picture. Historical stories offer background and perspective (like the history of radiology or medical grand rounds, both in Chapter 9). A series feature covers a topic in depth and appears in multiple segments. A narrative uses an almost cinematic storyline, often with an emotional appeal (like the story in Chapter 11 about a woman considering removing both her breasts even before she has a cancer diagnosis). The common elements in all features are detailed reporting and interviewing and strong, creative writing. People will read a news story, even if the writing is ordinary, because they want or need the information. But no one has to read a feature, on the health beat or any other beat. They'll read only if the focus and the writing snare them and won't let go. In the next six chapters, you'll read some of the best medical feature writing that The New York Times has to offer.

CHAPTER 6

# profiles

A PROFILE OFFERS READERS A WINDOW into the personality of the subject. What distinguishes the medical profile from profiles of political, business or sports personalities is that the reporter often wraps a biographical sketch around an important issue or scientific lesson that explains a medical process or procedure.

In the examples that follow, behavior reporter Benedict Carey and medical reporter Lawrence K. Altman tell readers about two very different people—one a patient, the other one of the world's most famous surgeons. Both pieces convey important scientific concepts that come alive through the story's protagonists.

The line between profile and narrative (see Chapter 11) can be a fine one, as profiles often contain sections written in narrative style. Sometimes the story forms merge, as you'll see in the profile of the famous heart surgeon, Dr. Michael E. DeBakey. In this riveting tale about an operation that saved DeBakey's life at age 97, the reporter uses an action-filled, chronological narrative to hook the reader.

In the other profile featured in this chapter, the reporter doesn't follow a strict chronological narrative. Instead, he starts in the present and flashes back and forth in time, giving readers a feeling for the life of his brain-injured subject through carefully chosen details, such as "the cramped two-room bungalow down a gravel road."

That kind of description helps reveal a person—as, of course do the subject's own words. Actually, however, most profiles contain fewer quotes than you might imagine. In the profile of the brain-injured man, for example, readers don't hear him speak very often. That's partly because Terry Wallis has difficulty talking, but also because the reporter illuminates the story through his own observations and the insights of the people who know Wallis best.

Because a profile obviously cannot be a full biography, you need to do enough reporting so that you can choose significant moments to include in your story. If you look back over your own life, you can identify moments when something changed. When you're researching a profile, you're looking for those same moments. In reading the profile, for instance, watch for the moment when Wallis emerges from being mute and unresponsive, or when he sees his daughter for the first time. As a writer, you don't have to tell readers that such moments are powerful. Just show them what happened, and they'll feel the power for themselves.

The story about DeBakey also uses anecdotes and key moments to reveal the man's nature: DeBakey diagnoses his own life-threatening condition, then goes on with his life and tries to avoid being hospitalized. After surgeons treat his aneurysm, DeBakey fakes being asleep so he can listen in on his doctors' conversations. Despite his fragile condition, DeBakey jumps at opportunities to lecture his treating doctors. These stories within the story lend authenticity to the profile in ways that quotes alone cannot convey—because, of course, we all reveal ourselves through our actions as much as (or more than) our words.

Action, description, talk and anecdotes give the reader a window into the subject's motivations. What prompted the 97-year-old surgeon to play possum with his doctors? How does a man emerge from 19 years of minimal consciousness and still have a zest for life? Reading these stories should give you a feel for the answers.

Finally, good profiles include a justification, a reason to read. Why should the reader care? As you read these two stories, look for the places where the writer answers that question and gives you a reason to invest your time.

## Selection 6.1

*The first story introduces you to the medical journey of 42-year-old Terry Wallis, who spent 19 years in a minimally conscious state before his recovery. As you read, look for the ways that reporter Benedict Carey reveals Wallis' personality and the realities of his new second life. The reporter's interweaving of narrative and neurology makes this story memorable and engrossing.*

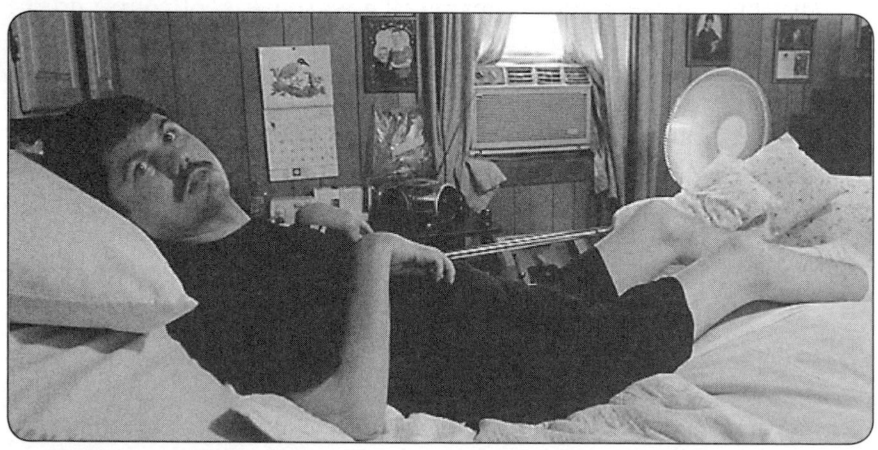

Ron Phillips for The New York Times

*Terry Wallis at his home in Arkansas.*

## Mute 19 Years, He Helps Reveal Brain's Mysteries

By BENEDICT CAREY

HARRIET, Ark., July 2—Terry Wallis spends almost all of his waking hours in bed, listening to country-western music in a cramped, two-room bungalow down a gravel road off State Highway 263.

Mr. Wallis, 42, wears an open, curious expression and speaks in a slurred but coherent voice. He volleys a visitor's pleased-to-meet-you with, "Glad to be met," and can speak haltingly of his family's plans to light fireworks at his brother's house nearby.

For his family, each word is a miracle. For 19 years—until June 11, 2003—Mr. Wallis lay mute and virtually unresponsive in a state of minimal consciousness, the result of a head injury suffered in a traffic accident. Since his abrupt recovery—his first word was "Mom," uttered at the sight of his mother—he has continued to improve, speaking more, remembering more.

But Mr. Wallis' return to the world, and the progress he has made, have also been a kind of miracle for scientists: an unprecedented opportunity to study, using advanced scanning technology, how the human brain can suddenly recover from such severe, long-lasting injury.

In a paper being published Monday, researchers are reporting that they have found strong evidence that Mr. Wallis' brain is healing itself by forming new neural connections since 2003.

The paper, appearing in The Journal of Clinical Investigation, includes a series of images of Mr. Wallis' brain, the first such pictures ever taken from a late-recovering patient.

The new findings raise the hope that doctors will eventually have the ability to determine which patients with severe brain damage have the best chance of recovering. They might also help settle disputes in cases like that of Terri Schiavo, the Florida woman who was removed from life support and died last year after a bitter national debate over patients' rights. Ms. Schiavo suffered more profound brain damage than Mr. Wallis and did not show signs of responsive awareness, according to neurologists who examined her.

"We read about these widely publicized cases of miraculous recovery every few years, but none of them—not one—has ever been followed up scientifically until now," said Dr. Nicholas Schiff, a neuroscientist at Weill Cornell Medical College in Manhattan and the senior author of the new imaging study.

An estimated 100,000 to 200,000 Americans subsist in states of partial or minimal consciousness, cut off from those around them.

---

*Published: July 4, 2006.*

On Saturday, Mr. Wallis said he felt good, but he showed no memory of the study. After prompting from his mother, he did remember the trip back from the researchers' laboratory in New York.

"Gasoline," he said, referring to a stop the airplane made to refuel. "We stopped for gasoline."

His mother, Angilee Wallis, said: "He is starting to learn things now. That right there is new."

In recent weeks, she said, he has also shown hints of self-awareness, alluding to his disabled condition for the first time.

Mrs. Wallis, 58, and her husband Jerry, 62, live with and care for their son in a white clapboard cabin, with a small concrete porch surrounded on all sides by acres of trees. Their house, between Harriet and Big Flat, is among a scattering of such hidden homes, sheds and dirt roads a couple of miles from a highway intersection anchored by two liquor stores. The nearest decent grocery store is 30 minutes away, in Mountain View, Ark.

For the Wallis family, Terry's accident, his long years of mental absence and his return have been a story of celebrity as well as recovery, of how media attention can strike like a flash flood and just as quickly dry up, leaving families to figure out what all the attention meant, if anything—and whether it was worth it.

He was a lanky 19-year-old in 1984, with a gift for elaborate pranks and engine work, when he and two friends skidded off a small bridge in a pickup, landing upside down in a dry riverbed. The family never figured out exactly what happened. The crash left their son unresponsive, breathing but immobilized, there but not there, said his father.

Terry Wallis showed no improvement in the first year, and doctors soon pronounced him to be in a persistent vegetative state, and gave him virtually no chance of recovery, his parents said.

About 52 percent of people with traumatic wounds to the head, most often from car accidents, recover some awareness in the first year after the injury, studies find; very few do so afterward. Only 15 percent of people who suffer brain damage from oxygen deprivation—like Terri Schiavo, whose heart stopped temporarily—recover some awareness within the first three months. A 1994 review of more than 700 vegetative patients found that none had done so after two years.

But at some point after his accident, probably within months, Mr. Wallis, a mechanic before his injury, entered what is called a minimally conscious state, Dr. Schiff said. The diagnosis, established formally in 2002, is given to people who are severely brain damaged but occasionally responsive. In their good moments, they can track objects with their eyes, respond to commands by blinking, grunting or making small movements. They may spend the rest of their lives in this condition, but it is a necessary intermediate step if they are ever to regain some awareness, neurologists say.

Mr. Wallis spent the second 19 years of his life at a nursing home in Mountain View, and family members who visited said they saw plenty of hints of awareness along the way. He seemed to brighten when they walked in his room. Something in his face would tighten when he was impatient or hungry.

None of which made the day he said "Mom" any less thrilling. Ms. Wallis, her voice unsteady, quickly put out the word to the extended family.

Later, the patient had another visitor, a striking blonde woman: his 19-year-old daughter, Amber, who had been 6 weeks old at the time of his accident. "I was so nervous driving over there," she said. "I was looking in the rearview mirror to check my hair, I swear, I was so worried he wouldn't recognize me."

When finally he did, she said, the first sentence he uttered was, " 'You're beautiful,' and he told me he loved me."

He was suddenly speaking; it was a transformation. He was still disabled, barely able to move or speak, but he was recognizable as Terry.

The months that followed brought a swarm of other emotions. Mr. Wallis, now considered clinically recovered but still in need of around-the-clock attention, was moved into his parents' home, shifting much of the financial burden of his care from Medicaid to them.

And the world came knocking. A camera crew from Japan arrived and spent two weeks doing daily interviews and filming. Another crew visited from England. There were talk show appearances, agents, documentary makers, forcing Mrs. Wallis to take time away from her job at a local shirt factory to help her husband, a mechanic and farmer, play host.

But the attention soon dissipated, and a fund his parents established for their son's care—the Terry Wallis Special Needs Trust—attracted few substantial contributions, they said.

Their son still needed to be fed, washed, exercised and turned in his bed every two hours, night and day. His daughter took two regular shifts a day to tend to him, and another aide began working with the family.

But in some ways it was like living with a child who never grows up or leaves home: there, out back in the trees, was his old gray Ford van, untouched since 1984; out front was an aluminum boat his father had bought for him, overturned, unused.

In 2004, Dr. Schiff contacted the family, asking if they would allow their son to be studied. He helped arrange to have the Wallises flown to New York in April of that year, and again 18 months later, for brain scanning. A research team from New York, New Jersey and New Zealand spent more than a year analyzing the results, comparing them to images from healthy brains and from another minimally conscious patient who had not recovered.

Using a novel technique, they saw evidence of new growth in the midline cerebellum, an area involved in motor control, as Mr. Wallis gained strength and range in his limbs. Another area of new growth, located along the back of the brain, is believed by some experts to be a central switching center for conscious awareness.

The daily exercises, the interactions with his parents, his regular dose of antidepressant medication: any or all of these might have spurred brain cells to grow more connections, the researchers said.

"The big missed opportunity is that we didn't know this guy would spontaneously emerge, and we didn't get to monitor him before then" to find out what preceded it, Dr. Schiff said.

To answer that kind of question in a systematic way, researchers will need to follow more minimally conscious patients for longer periods, experts say. But there is no national system to track such patients, they say, no central database like that which exists for other diseases.

"We don't see these people. They exist outside of our gaze. We don't even know where they live," said Dr. Joseph Fins, chief of the medical ethics division of New York Presbyterian Hospital-Weill Cornell Medical Center.

Mr. Wallis, it was clear over the weekend, continues to live for the day. He has a granddaughter now, Amber's child, Victoria, and the 2-year-old does not seem bothered by the pale man with the dark mustache and the inward-turned arms. He does not feel any physical pain, he told his parents, and he has no real sense of time. He also said recently that he was "proud" to be alive.

"It is good to know all that," said his father, sitting on the porch on Saturday evening. "It's good to hear him say that, because if he didn't say so, you'd just have no way to know."

## Selection 6.2

*At home one day in 2005, Dr. Michael DeBakey experienced a sharp pain in his chest and back that he diagnosed as a dissecting aortic aneurysm. That means the aorta, the main artery leading from the heart, was ballooning. Without surgery, the aneurysm would kill him. The irony was that DeBakey had devised the very operation needed to save his life. In telling the story, medical reporter Lawrence K. Altman takes us through the medical and ethical maze that eventually led cardiovascular surgeons to operate. Along the story's path, the reporter shares medical lessons about how the procedure works and how doctors deliberate over thorny questions like whether to operate on a 97-year-old man with a condition often fatal to people half his age. Most striking is the vivid portrait of DeBakey who, by his very reputation, so intimidated anesthesiologists that at first they refused to participate in his operation for fear that they would "become known as the doctors who killed him."*

## Surgery on a Surgeon

Surgeons operated in February on Dr. Michael E. DeBakey, repairing an aortic aneurysm using techniques that he had pioneered.

**The Problem**

An aneurysm, or a ballooning, developed in Dr. DeBakey's aorta, the main artery leading from the heart. The wall of the aorta weakened and tore, allowing blood to seep into the inside layers of the artery, a problem that can lead to sudden death.

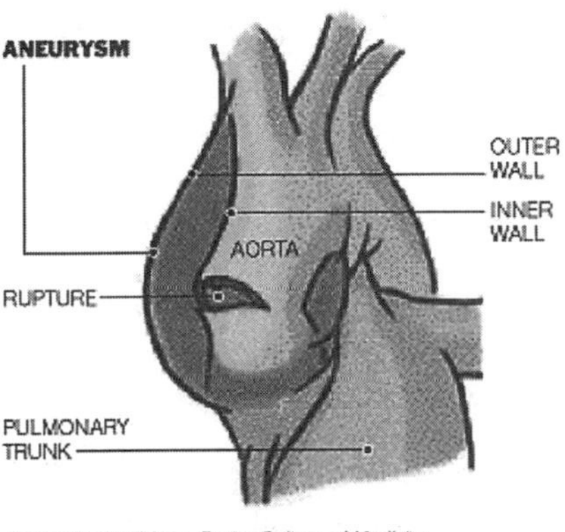


**The Repair**

A Dacron graft, 6 to 8 inches long, was used to replace the damaged section of the aorta.

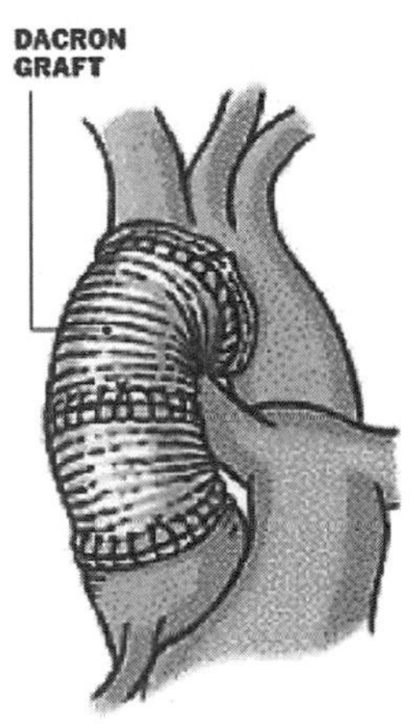


*Source: Scott Weldon, Baylor College of Medicine*

The New York Times

# The Doctor's World
# The Man on the Table Devised the Surgery

By LAWRENCE K. ALTMAN

In late afternoon last Dec. 31, Dr. Michael E. DeBakey, then 97, was alone at home in Houston in his study preparing a lecture when a sharp pain ripped through his upper chest and between his shoulder blades, then moved into his neck.

Dr. DeBakey, one of the most influential heart surgeons in history, assumed his heart would stop in a few seconds.

"It never occurred to me to call 911 or my physician," Dr. DeBakey said, adding: "As foolish as it may appear, you are, in a sense, a prisoner of the pain, which was intolerable. You're thinking, What could I do to relieve myself of it. If it becomes intense enough, you're perfectly willing to accept cardiac arrest as a possible way of getting rid of the pain."

---

*Published: December 25, 2006.*

But when his heart kept beating, Dr. DeBakey suspected that he was not having a heart attack. As he sat alone, he decided that a ballooning had probably weakened the aorta, the main artery leading from the heart, and that the inner lining of the artery had torn, known as a dissecting aortic aneurysm.

No one in the world was more qualified to make that diagnosis than Dr. DeBakey because, as a younger man, he devised the operation to repair such torn aortas, a condition virtually always fatal. The operation has been performed at least 10,000 times around the world and is among the most demanding for surgeons and patients.

Over the past 60 years, Dr. DeBakey has changed the way heart surgery is performed. He was one of the first to perform coronary bypass operations. He trained generations of surgeons at the Baylor College of Medicine; operated on more than 60,000 patients; and in 1996 was summoned to Moscow by Boris Yeltsin, then the president of Russia, to aid in his quintuple heart bypass operation.

Now Dr. DeBakey is making history in a different way—as a patient. He was released from Methodist Hospital in Houston in September and is back at work. At 98, he is the oldest survivor of his own operation, proving that a healthy man of his age could endure it.

"He's probably right out there at the cutting edge of a whole generation of people in their 90s who are going to survive" after such medical ordeals, one of his doctors, Dr. James L. Pool, said.

But beyond the medical advances, Dr. DeBakey's story is emblematic of the difficulties that often accompany care at the end of life. It is a story of debates over how far to go in treating someone so old, late-night disputes among specialists about what the patient would want, and risky decisions that, while still being argued over, clearly saved Dr. DeBakey's life.

It is also a story of Dr. DeBakey himself, a strong-willed pioneer who at one point was willing to die, concedes he was at times in denial about how sick he was and is now plowing into life with as much zest and verve as ever.

But Dr. DeBakey's rescue almost never happened.

He refused to be admitted to a hospital until late January. As his health deteriorated and he became unresponsive in the hospital in early February, his surgical partner of 40 years, Dr. George P. Noon, decided an operation was the only way to save his life. But the hospital's anesthesiologists refused to put Dr. DeBakey to sleep because such an operation had never been performed on someone his age and in his condition. Also, they said Dr. DeBakey had signed a directive that forbade surgery.

As the hospital's ethics committee debated in a late-night emergency meeting on the 12th floor of Methodist Hospital, Dr. DeBakey's wife, Katrin, barged in to demand that the operation begin immediately.

In the end, the ethics committee approved the operation; an anesthesiology colleague of Dr. DeBakey's, who now works at a different hospital, agreed to put him to sleep; and the seven-hour operation began shortly before midnight on Feb. 9. "It is a miracle," Dr. DeBakey said as he sat eating dinner in a Houston restaurant recently. "I really should not be here."

The costs of Dr. DeBakey's care easily exceeded $1 million. Methodist Hospital and his doctors say they have not charged Dr. DeBakey. His hospitalizations were under pseudonyms to help protect his privacy, which could make collecting insurance difficult. Methodist Hospital declined to say what the costs were or discuss the case further. Dr. DeBakey says he thinks the hospital should not have been secretive about his illness.

Dr. DeBakey's doctors acknowledge that he got an unusually high level of care. But they said that they always tried to abide by a family's wishes and that they would perform the procedure on any patient regardless of age, if the patient's overall health was otherwise good.

Dr. DeBakey agreed to talk, and permitted his doctors to talk, because of a professional relationship of decades with this reporter, who is also a physician, and because he wanted to set the record straight for the public about what happened and explain how a man nearly 100 years old could survive.

## A Preliminary Diagnosis

As Dr. DeBakey lay on the couch alone that night, last New Year's Eve, he reasoned that a heart attack was unlikely because periodic checkups had never indicated he was at risk. An aortic dissection was more likely because of the pain, even though there was no hint of that problem in a routine echocardiogram a few weeks earlier.

Mrs. DeBakey and their daughter, Olga, had left for the beach in Galveston, but turned back because of heavy traffic. They arrived home to find Dr. DeBakey lying on the couch. Not wanting to alarm them, he lied and said he had fallen asleep and awakened with a pulled muscle.

"I did not want Katrin to be aware of my self-diagnosis because, in a sense, I would be telling her that I am going to die soon," he said.

An anxious Mrs. DeBakey called two of her husband's colleagues: Dr. Mohammed Attar, his longtime physician, and Dr. Matthias Loebe, who was covering for Dr. Noon. They came to the house quickly and became concerned because Dr. DeBakey had been in excellent health. After listening to him give a more frank account of his pain, they shared his suspicion of an aortic dissection.

Dr. DeBakey and his doctors agreed that for a firm diagnosis he would need a CT scan and other imaging tests, but he delayed them until Jan. 3.

The tests showed that Dr. DeBakey had a type 2 dissecting aortic aneurysm, according to a standard classification system he himself devised years earlier. Rarely did anyone survive that without surgery.

Still, Dr. DeBakey says that he refused admission to Methodist Hospital, in part because he did not want to be confined and he "was hopeful that this was not as bad as I first thought." He feared the operation that he had developed to treat this condition might, at his age, leave him mentally or physically crippled. "I'd rather die," he said.

Over the years, he had performed anatomically perfect operations on some patients who nevertheless died or survived with major complications. "I was trying to avoid all that," he said.

Instead, he gambled on long odds that his damaged aorta would heal on its own. He chose to receive care at home. For more than three weeks, doctors made frequent house calls to make sure his blood pressure was low enough to prevent the aorta from rupturing. Around the clock, nurses monitored his food and drink. Periodically, he went to Methodist Hospital for imaging tests to measure the aneurysm's size.

On Jan. 6, he insisted on giving the lecture he had been preparing on New Year's Eve to the Academy of Medicine, Engineering and Science of Texas, of which he is a founding member. The audience in Houston included Nobel Prize winners and Senator Kay Bailey Hutchison.

Mrs. DeBakey stationed people around the podium to catch her husband if he slumped. Dr. DeBakey looked gray and spoke softly, but finished without incident. Then he listened to another lecture—which, by coincidence, was about the lethal dangers of dissecting aneurysms.

Dr. DeBakey, a master politician, said he could not pass up a chance to chat with the senator. He attended the academy luncheon and then went home.

In providing the extraordinary home care, the doctors were respecting the wishes of Dr. DeBakey and their actions reflected their awe of his power.

"People are very scared of him around here," said Dr. Loebe, the heart surgeon who came to Dr. DeBakey's home on New Year's Eve. "He is the authority. It is very difficult to stand up and tell him what to do."

But as time went on, the doctors could not adequately control Dr. DeBakey's blood pressure. His nutrition was poor. He became short of breath. His kidneys failed. Fluid collected in the pericardial sac covering his heart, suggesting the aneurysm was leaking.

Dr. DeBakey now says that he was in denial. He did not admit to himself that he was getting worse. But on Jan. 23, he yielded and was admitted to the hospital.

Tests showed that the aneurysm was enlarging dangerously; the diameter increased to 6.6 centimeters on Jan. 28, up from

5.2 centimeters on Jan. 3. Dr. Noon said that when he and other doctors showed Dr. DeBakey the scans and recommended surgery, Dr. DeBakey said he would re-evaluate the situation in a few days.

By Feb. 9, with the aneurysm up to 7.5 centimeters and Dr. DeBakey unresponsive and near death, a decision had to be made.

"If we didn't operate on him that day that was it, he was gone for sure," Dr. Noon said.

At that point, Dr. DeBakey was unable to speak for himself. The surgeons gathered and decided they should proceed, despite the dangers. "We were doing what we thought was right," Dr. Noon said, adding that "nothing made him a hopeless candidate for the operation except for being 97." All family members agreed to the operation.

Dr. Bobby R. Alford, one of Dr. DeBakey's physicians and a successor as chancellor of Baylor College of Medicine, said the doctors had qualms. "We could have walked away," he said.

He and Dr. Noon discussed the decision several times. "We recognized the condemnation that could occur," Dr. Alford said. "The whole surgical world would come down on us for doing something stupid, which it might have seemed to people who were not there."

Surgery would be enormously risky and unlikely to offer clear-cut results—either a full recovery or death, Dr. Noon and his colleagues told Mrs. DeBakey, Olga, sons from a first marriage, and Dr. DeBakey's sisters, Lois and Selma. The doctors said Dr. DeBakey might develop new ailments and need dialysis and a tracheostomy to help his breathing. They said the family's decision could inflict prolonged suffering for all involved.

Olga and she "prayed a lot," said Mrs. DeBakey, who is from Germany. "We had a healer in Europe who advised us that he will come through it. That helped us."

Then things got more complicated.

## A Refusal to Treat

At that point the Methodist Hospital anesthesiologists adamantly refused to accept Dr. DeBakey as a patient. They cited a standard form he had signed directing that he not be resuscitated if his heart stopped and a note in the chart saying he did not want surgery for the aortic dissection and aneurysm. They were concerned about his age and precarious physical condition.

Dr. Alford, the 72-year-old chancellor, said he was stunned by the refusal, an action he had never seen or heard about in his career.

Dr. Noon said none of the anesthesiologists had been involved in Dr. DeBakey's care, yet they made a decision based on grapevine information without reading his medical records. So he insisted that the anesthesiologists state their objections directly to the DeBakey family.

Mrs. DeBakey said the anesthesiologists feared that Dr. DeBakey would die on the operating table and did not want to become known as the doctors who killed him. Dr. Joseph J. Naples, the hospital's chief anesthesiologist, did not return repeated telephone calls to his office for comment.

Around 7 p.m., Mrs. DeBakey called Dr. Salwa A. Shenaq, an anesthesiologist friend who had worked with Dr. DeBakey for 22 years at Methodist Hospital and who now works at the nearby Michael E. DeBakey Veterans Affairs Medical Center.

Dr. Shenaq rushed from home. When she arrived, she said, Dr. Naples told her that he and his staff would not administer anesthesia to Dr. DeBakey. She said that a medical staff officer, whom she declined to name, warned her that she could be charged with assault if she touched Dr. DeBakey. The officer also told Dr. Shenaq that she could not give Dr. DeBakey anesthesia because she did not have Methodist Hospital privileges. She made it clear that she did, she said.

Administrators, lawyers and doctors discussed the situation, in particular the ambiguities of Dr. DeBakey's wishes. Yes, Dr. Pool had written on his chart that Dr. DeBakey said he did not want surgery for a dissection. But Dr. Noon and the family thought the note in the chart no longer applied because Dr. DeBakey's condition had so deteriorated and his only hope was his own procedure.

"They were going back and forth," Dr. Shenaq said. "One time, they told me go ahead. Then, no, we cannot go ahead."

To fulfill its legal responsibilities, Methodist Hospital summoned members of its ethics committee, who arrived in an hour. They met with Dr. DeBakey's doctors in a private dining room a few yards from Dr. DeBakey's room, according to five of his doctors who were present.

Their patient was a man who had always been in command. Now an unresponsive Dr. DeBakey had no control over his own destiny.

The ethics committee representatives wanted to follow Texas law, which, in part, requires assurance that doctors respect patient and family wishes.

Each of Dr. DeBakey's doctors had worked with him for more than 20 years. One, Dr. Pool, said they felt they knew Dr. DeBakey well enough to answer another crucial question from the ethics committee: As his physicians, what did they believe he would choose for himself in such a dire circumstance if he had the ability to make that decision?

Dr. Noon said that Dr. DeBakey had told him it was time for nature to take its course, but also told him that the doctors had "to do what we need to do." Members of Dr. DeBakey's medical team said they interpreted the statements differently. Some thought he meant that they should do watchful waiting, acting only if conditions warranted; others thought it meant he wanted to die.

The question was whether the operation would counter Dr. DeBakey's wishes expressed in his signed "do not resuscitate" order. Some said that everything Dr. DeBakey did was for his family. And the family wanted the operation.

After the committee members had met for an hour, Mrs. DeBakey could stand it no longer. She charged into the room.

"My husband's going to die before we even get a chance to do anything—let's get to work," she said she told them.

The discussion ended. The majority ruled in a consensus without a formal vote. No minutes were kept, the doctors said.

"Boy, when that meeting was over, it was single focus—the best operation, the best post-operative care, the best recovery we could give him," Dr. Pool said.

## The Operation

As the ethics committee meeting ended about 11 p.m. on Feb. 9, the doctors rushed to start Dr. DeBakey's anesthesia.

The operation was to last seven hours.

For part of that time, Dr. DeBakey's body was cooled to protect his brain and other organs. His heart was stilled while a heart-lung bypass machine pumped oxygen-rich blood through his body. The surgeons replaced the damaged portion of Dr. DeBakey's aorta with a six- to eight-inch graft made of Dacron, similar to material used in shirts. The graft was the type that Dr. DeBakey devised in the 1950s.

Afterward, Dr. DeBakey was taken to an intensive care unit.

Some doctors were waiting for Dr. DeBakey to die during the operation or soon thereafter, Dr. Noon said. "But he just got better."

As feared, however, his recovery was stormy.

Surgeons had to cut separate holes into the trachea in his neck and stomach to help him breathe and eat. He needed dialysis because of kidney failure. He was on a mechanical ventilator for about six weeks because he was too weak to breathe on his own. He developed infections. His blood pressure often fell too low when aides lifted him to a sitting position. Muscle weakness left him unable to stand.

For a month, Dr. DeBakey was in the windowless intensive care unit, sometimes delirious, sometimes unresponsive, depending in part on his medications. The doctors were concerned that he had suffered severe, permanent brain damage. To allow him to tell day from night and lift his spirits, the hospital converted a private suite into an intensive care unit.

Some help came from unexpected places. On Sunday, April 2, Dr. William W. Lunn, the team's lung specialist, took his oldest daughter, Elizabeth, 8, with him when he made rounds at the hospital and told her that a patient was feeling blue. While waiting, Elizabeth drew a cheery picture of a rainbow, butterflies, trees and grass and asked her father to give it to the patient. He did.

"You should have seen Dr. DeBakey's eyes brighten," Dr. Lunn said. Dr. DeBakey asked to see Elizabeth, held her hand and thanked her.

"At that point, I knew he was going to be O.K.," Dr. Lunn said.

Dr. DeBakey was discharged on May 16. But on June 2, he was back in the hospital.

"He actually scared us because his blood pressure and heart rate were too high, he was gasping for breath" and he had fluid in his lungs, Dr. Lunn said.

But once the blood pressure was controlled with medicine, Dr. DeBakey began to recover well.

## The Aftermath

At times, Dr. DeBakey says he played possum with the medical team, pretending to be asleep when he was listening to conversations.

On Aug. 21, when Dr. Loebe asked Dr. DeBakey to wake up, and he did not, Dr. Loebe announced that he had found an old roller pump that Dr. DeBakey devised in the 1930s to transfuse blood. Dr. DeBakey immediately opened his eyes. Then he gave the doctors a short lecture about how he had improved it over existing pumps.

As he recovered and Dr. DeBakey learned what had happened, he told his doctors he was happy they had operated on him. The doctors say they were relieved because they had feared he regretted their decision.

"If they hadn't done it, I'd be dead," he said.

The doctors and family had rolled the dice and won.

Dr. DeBakey does not remember signing an order saying not to resuscitate him and now thinks the doctors did the right thing. Doctors, he said, should be able to make decisions in such cases, without committees.

Throughout, Dr. DeBakey's mental recovery was far ahead of his physical response.

When Dr. DeBakey first became aware of his post-operative condition, he said he "felt limp as a rag" and feared he was a quadriplegic. Kenneth Miller and other physical therapists have helped Dr. DeBakey strengthen his withered muscles.

"There were times where he needed a good bit of encouragement to participate," Mr. Miller said. "But once he saw the progress, he was fully committed to what we were doing."

Now he walks increasingly long distances without support. But his main means of locomotion is a motorized scooter. He races it around corridors, sometimes trailed by quick-stepping doctors of all ages.

Dr. DeBakey said he hoped to regain the stamina to resume traveling, though not at his former pace.

Dr. William L. Winters Jr., a cardiologist on Dr. DeBakey's team, said: "I am impressed with what the body and mind can do when they work together. He absolutely has the desire to get back to where he was before. I think he'll come close."

Already, Dr. DeBakey is back working nearly a full day.

"I feel very good," he said Friday. "I'm getting back into the swing of things."

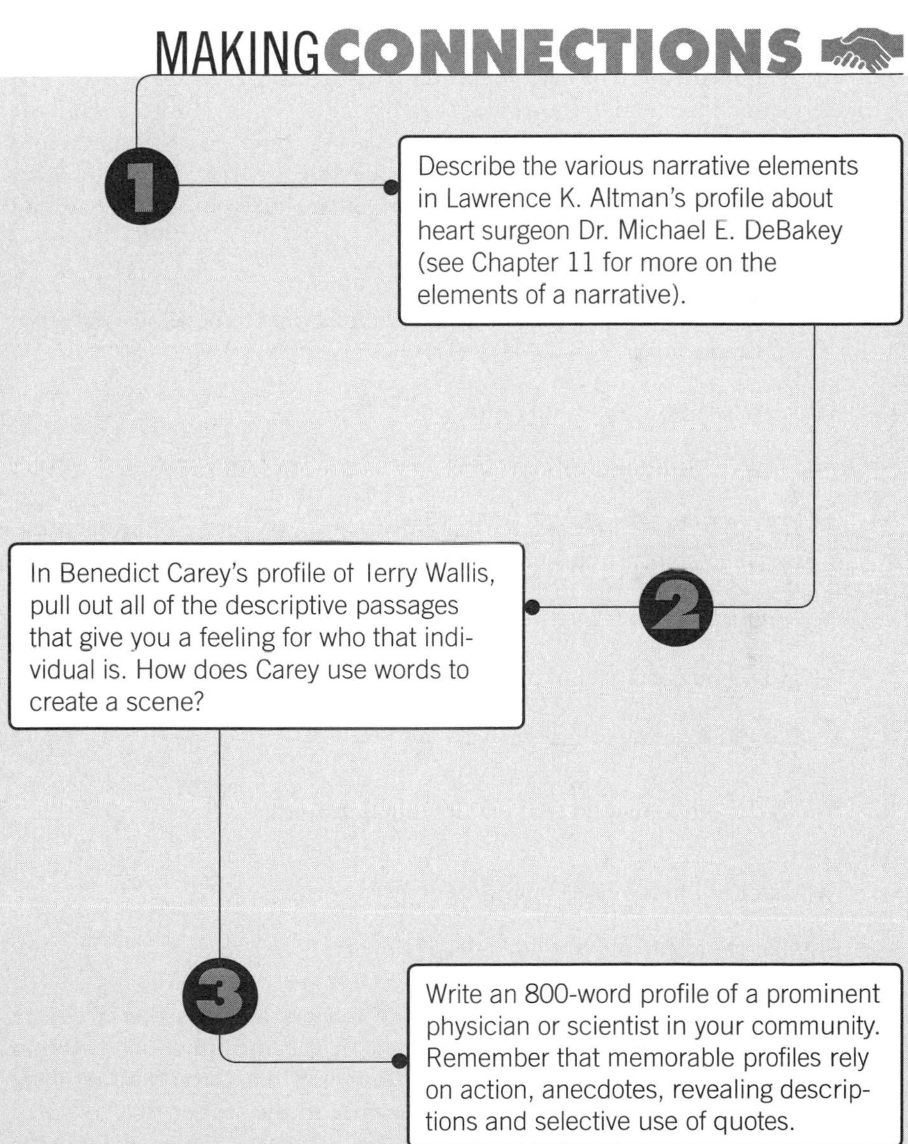

MAKING CONNECTIONS
1
Describe the various narrative elements in Lawrence K. Altman's profile about heart surgeon Dr. Michael E. DeBakey (see Chapter 11 for more on the elements of a narrative).
2
In Benedict Carey's profile of Terry Wallis, pull out all of the descriptive passages that give you a feeling for who that individual is. How does Carey use words to create a scene?
3
Write an 800-word profile of a prominent physician or scientist in your community. Remember that memorable profiles rely on action, anecdotes, revealing descriptions and selective use of quotes.

CHAPTER 7

# explanatory stories

PEOPLE READ MEDICAL STORIES TO FIND WAYS to improve their health, protect themselves from disease and learn more about science and medicine. The health reporter tries to inform readers in ways that readers can understand. Reporters act as a bridge between consumers and the medical and scientific communities by translating complex information into simple terms. Medical reporters explain how things work. In this chapter you'll read stories from The New York Times that clearly and simply explain all kinds of complex processes:

— How researchers are targeting the influenza virus to develop a universal flu vaccine.

— How viruses evolve and reproduce.

— How in vitro fertilization works and how it can lead to multiple births.

— How the brain processes visual information so that a blind man can perceive objects in his path.

— Where sarcasm is interpreted in the brain.

— How your personal narrative can determine your mental health.

— How restricting calories can extend life.

You'll also find answers to the following questions:

— Can hot liquids ease symptoms of a cold or flu?

— Can chocolate disrupt your sleep?

In all of these stories reporters educate readers in ways that are both entertaining and understandable. As noted in the introduction, before a reporter can communicate to readers the "how" of the story, she first must understand how the science works. The science in the stories that follow is sometimes simple and sometimes complex. Good medical reporters make the complex seem simple by deciphering scientific code for readers.

## Selection 7.1

*The following story by Times business and biotechnology reporter Andrew Pollack focuses on the search for a flu vaccine to protect against various strains of influenza. As Pollack explains, a universal flu vaccine is needed because influenza virus mutates so rapidly that no vaccination for a particular strain protects for long. As a result, the flu vaccine that you get in the fall won't necessarily protect you against the new strain that develops the following year. To write a good explanatory feature, you have to write science lessons that are both accurate and easy to understand. A science lesson gives readers a concise explanation of how a process or procedure works. Often reporters begin, as Pollack does here, by comparing something new with something that will be familiar to readers. As his story continues, look for two science lessons—one lesson explaining how a particular protein makes devising a universal vaccine difficult, and the second describing another protein that might make a universal vaccine work.*

## A Long Search for a Universal Flu Vaccine

By ANDREW POLLACK

Two shots of measles vaccine given during childhood protect a person for life. Four shots of polio vaccine do the same. But flu shots must be taken every year. And even so, they provide less than complete protection.

The reason is that the influenza virus mutates much more rapidly than most other viruses. A person who develops immunity to one strain of the virus is not well protected from a different strain.

That is shaping up to be a major problem as the world prepares for a possible pandemic this fall from the new strain of swine flu. It is impossible to know how many people might die before a vaccine matched to that strain can be manufactured.

But scientists and vaccine manufacturers are hard at work on a so-called universal flu vaccine that would work against all types of flu. The goal is to provide protection for years, if not a whole lifetime, against all seasonal flu strains and pandemic strains, making flu inoculation much more like that for measles and polio.

"The universal would completely change the way flu vaccination would be done," said Sarah C. Gilbert, a vaccine expert at the University of Oxford. "The sooner we have a universal vaccine the better because we can stop worrying about what the next pandemic will be."

Such a one-shot-fits-all vaccine would also end the guessing game that now occurs at the beginning of each year as scientists decide which strains should be included in the seasonal vaccine for the following winter. If they guess wrong, the vaccine is less effective.

---

*Published: May 19, 2009.*

And it would make flu immunization practical for countries that now cannot afford a yearly effort. Seasonal flu is estimated to contribute to an average of 36,000 deaths in the United States and as many as half a million worldwide each year.

Unfortunately, a universal vaccine will not be ready soon enough to combat a possible pandemic from the new strain of swine flu that has already sickened thousands of people. The most advanced of the vaccines have been tested only in small clinical trials. It is likely to take several more years to show if the vaccines really work.

Indeed, the universal vaccines developed so far do not totally prevent infection, as the strain-specific vaccines can do. Rather, they limit severity and spread of the disease. Some experts say that would be sufficient, but others have their doubts.

"It wouldn't replace the seasonal flu vaccine," said Dr. Robert Belshe, director of the center for vaccine development at Saint Louis University. "I think it would be considered a supplement to it."

Some experts say booster shots might still be needed every 10 years or so. It is also not clear if the vaccines would be able to provide protection against all strains, including animal-derived viruses like the new swine flu. Most of the universal vaccines under development do not even try to provide protection against influenza type B. They focus on type A, which tends to cause more severe disease and pandemics.

When someone is vaccinated or infected, the immune system makes antibodies that mostly attack a protein on the surface of the virus called hemagglutinin. But that protein is the fastest-changing part of the virus, so antibodies to one strain might not recognize another.

A universal vaccine would have to spur an immune system attack on part of the influenza virus that does not vary from strain to strain.

If that were easy to do, skeptics say, the immune system would have figured it out and people would have lasting protection. Vaccine researchers counter that some people might have immunity lasting at least a few years. And a vaccine can teach the immune system to do things it might not be able to do on its own.

"I don't see any reason it should be impossible," said Suzanne Epstein, a researcher at the Food and Drug Administration. "It works quite well in animals."

The big problem is that most of the flu virus proteins that do not vary much are on the inside of the virus, out of reach of antibodies. But there is one internal protein, called M2, that protrudes a bit from the virus. This external piece is not much of a target for antibodies, but it is the main focus of universal vaccine research.

"The trick is you've got to have a system that will raise a robust immune response against this puny little protein that's not present in any abundance," said Alan Shaw, president of VaxInnate, a small company trying to develop a universal vaccine that combines the external part of M2 with a bacterial protein that stimulates the immune system.

VaxInnate, Merck and Acambis, which is owned by Sanofi-Aventis, have each run a small test of their M2 vaccines on healthy volunteers. Vaccinated people do make antibodies to M2. But those antibodies do not totally prevent infection. It will take much larger tests to see if vaccines actually work to ameliorate disease during a real flu season.

Another issue is that the M2 protein in animal influenza viruses can be somewhat different from that in human viruses. That raises questions about how well an M2 vaccine might work, say, against the new swine flu, which is known formally as H1N1.

"The new H1N1 virus could throw a little bit of a wrench into things," said Andrew Pekosz, an associate professor of molecular microbiology and immunology at Johns Hopkins University.

Earlier this year, two teams of researchers reported independently that there might be another nonvarying region on the outside of the virus. It is in the stick of the lollipop-shaped hemagglutinin protein rather than the constantly changing head.

One of the groups showed that antibodies isolated from human blood that bound to this part of the stick protected mice against many strains of flu, including the 1918 pandemic Spanish flu and the H5N1 bird flu.

But experts say it will be very difficult to isolate this part of the protein from the virus to use in a vaccine, or to manufacture it using genetic engineering.

"My first thought was, 'Oh, you have to make the vaccine,'" said Dr. Hildegund C. J. Ertl, a universal vaccine researcher at the Wistar Institute in Philadelphia who was not involved in the discovery. "But then when I looked at the sequence, it wasn't straightforward at all."

An alternative would be to use the antibodies themselves as a medicine, though antibodies are expensive to manufacture and time-consuming to infuse into patients.

With constant regions outside the virus hard to find, some efforts aim at nonchanging proteins inside the virus, like one called nucleoprotein. Antibodies cannot get at these proteins to prevent an infection. So the idea is to spur other soldiers of the immune system called T cells to quickly kill the infected cells before they could make new viruses. That would limit disease severity.

Dr. Epstein of the F.D.A. said a vaccine based on a nucleoprotein from a human H1N1 virus was able to protect animals from a lethal dose of the H5N1 bird flu, the virus which stoked pandemic fears a few years ago. Oxford University has tested a T cell vaccine in 28 healthy adults and found it did increase T cell responses.

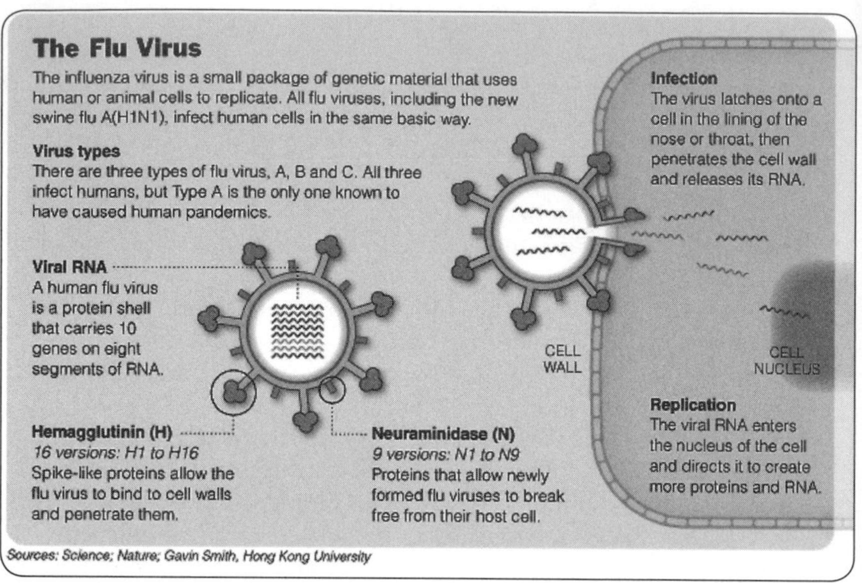

The Flu Virus
The influenza virus is a small package of genetic material that uses human or animal cells to replicate. All flu viruses, including the new swine flu A(H1N1), infect human cells in the same basic way.
Virus types
There are three types of flu virus, A, B and C. All three infect humans, but Type A is the only one known to have caused human pandemics.
Viral RNA
A human flu virus is a protein shell that carries 10 genes on eight segments of RNA.
Hemagglutinin (H)
16 versions: H1 to H16
Spike-like proteins allow the flu virus to bind to cell walls and penetrate them.
Neuraminidase (N)
9 versions: N1 to N9
Proteins that allow newly formed flu viruses to break free from their host cell.
CELL WALL
CELL NUCLEUS
Infection
The virus latches onto a cell in the lining of the nose or throat, then penetrates the cell wall and releases its RNA.
Replication
The viral RNA enters the nucleus of the cell and directs it to create more proteins and RNA.
Sources: Science; Nature; Gavin Smith, Hong Kong University


Ultimately, the best results might come from combining the techniques. Dynavax, a California biotechnology company, hopes to begin trials next year of a vaccine designed to spur antibodies against M2 and T cells against nucleoprotein.

Dr. Epstein said expectations for a universal vaccine must be realistic. "It's not intended to totally block infection," she said. "But what it can do is greatly reduce disease and spread and symptoms."

## Selection 7.2

*In the next story, reporter Carl Zimmer presents a series of science lessons in which he explains how viruses reassort their genetic codes as they travel among humans, pigs and birds. The 2009 swine flu outbreak is his peg, but the real story is how viruses evolve. The 2009 swine flu resulted from what scientists called a triple reassortment with genes from all three species. Zimmer's writing is so fluid that the casual reader might not appreciate the rigorous reporting; he quotes seven sources in this 1,300-word story. Extensive reporting and interviewing lend depth to any story. Reporters may no longer wear out their shoe leather as they pound the pavement, but the best science reporters phone and e-mail multiple sources, read the original scientific studies and do as much historical research as deadlines permit. Then the reporter words the story to read as effortlessly as possible, so that readers don't have to work the way he did in obtaining information. Explanatory writing is most effective when it's simple. Note the power of this sentence: "The sheer number of viruses on Earth is beyond our ability to imagine."*

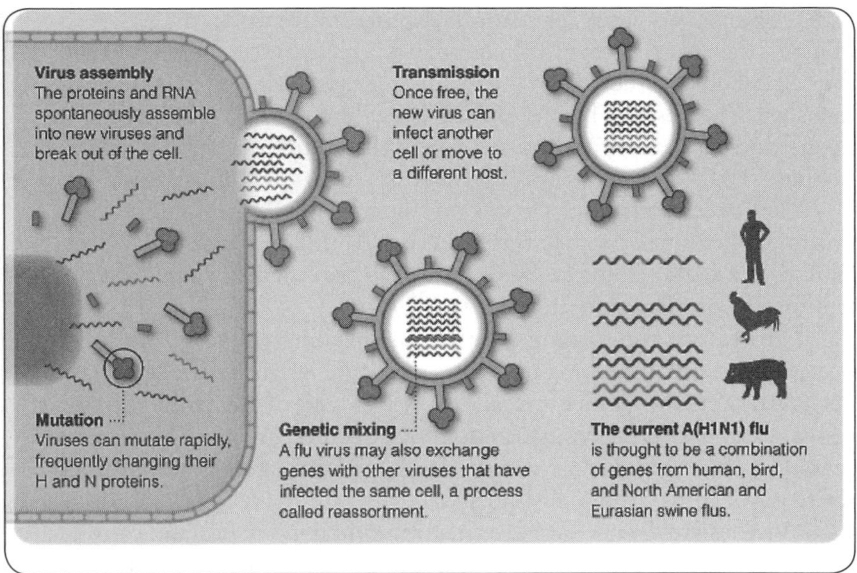

Virus assembly
The proteins and RNA spontaneously assemble into new viruses and break out of the cell.
Transmission
Once free, the new virus can infect another cell or move to a different host.
Mutation
Viruses can mutate rapidly, frequently changing their H and N proteins.
Genetic mixing
A flu virus may also exchange genes with other viruses that have infected the same cell, a process called reassortment.
The current A(H1N1) flu
is thought to be a combination of genes from human, bird, and North American and Eurasian swine flus.


The New York Times

## 10 Genes, Furiously Evolving

By CARL ZIMMER

Evolutionary biology may sometimes seem like an arcane academic pursuit, but just try telling that to Gavin Smith, a virologist at Hong Kong University. For the past week, Dr. Smith and six other experts on influenza in Hong Kong, Arizona, California and Britain have been furiously analyzing the new swine flu to figure out how and when it evolved.

The first viruses from the outbreak were isolated late last month, but Dr. Smith and his colleagues report on their Web site that the most recent common ancestor of the new viruses existed 6 to 11 months ago. "It could just have been going under the radar," Dr. Smith said.

The current outbreak shows how complex and mysterious the evolution of viruses is. That complexity and mystery are all the more remarkable because a virus is life reduced to its essentials. A human influenza virus, for example, is a protein shell measuring about five-millionths of an inch across, with 10 genes inside. (We have about 20,000.)

Some viruses use DNA, like we do, to encode their genes. Others, like the influenza virus, use single-strand RNA. But viruses all have one thing in common, said Roland Wolkowicz, a molecular virologist at San Diego State University: they all reproduce by disintegrating and then reforming.

---

*Published: May 5, 2009.*

A human flu virus, for example, latches onto a cell in the lining of the nose or throat. It manipulates a receptor on the cell so that the cell engulfs it, whereupon the virus's genes are released from its protein shell. The host cell begins making genes and proteins that spontaneously assemble into new viruses. "No other entity out there is able to do that," Dr. Wolkowicz said. "To me, this is what defines a virus."

The sheer number of viruses on Earth is beyond our ability to imagine. "In a small drop of water there are a billion viruses," Dr. Wolkowicz said. Virologists have estimated that there are a million trillion trillion viruses in the world's oceans.

Viruses are also turning out to be astonishingly diverse. Shannon Williamson of the J. Craig Venter Institute in Rockville, Md., has been analyzing the genes of ocean viruses. A tank of 100 to 200 liters of sea water may hold 100,000 genetically distinct viruses. "We're just scratching the surface of virus diversity," Dr. Williamson said. "I think we're going to be continually surprised."

Viruses are diverse because they can mutate very fast and can mix genes. They sometimes pick up genes from their hosts, and they can swap genes with other viruses. Some viruses, including flu viruses, carry out a kind of mixing known as reassortment. If two different flu viruses infect the same cell, the new copies of their genes get jumbled up as new viruses are assembled.

Viruses were probably infecting the earliest primordial microbes. "I believe viruses have been around forever," Dr. Wolkowicz said.

As new hosts have evolved, some viruses have adapted to them. Birds, for example, became the main host for influenza viruses. Many birds infected with flu viruses do not get sick. The viruses replicate in the gut and are shed with the birds' droppings.

A quarter of birds typically carry two or more strains of flu at the same time, allowing the viruses to mix their genes into a genetic blur. "Birds are constantly mixing up the constellation of these viruses," said David Spiro of the J. Craig Venter Institute.

From birds, flu viruses have moved to animals, including pigs, horses and humans. Other viruses, like H.I.V. and SARS, have also managed to jump into our species, but many others have failed. "It's a very rare event when a virus creates a new epidemic in another species," said Colin Parrish of Cornell University. In Southeast Asia, for example, a strain of bird flu has killed hundreds of people in recent years, but it cannot seem to move easily from human to human.

Only a few strains of influenza have managed to become true human viruses in the past century. To make the transition, the viruses have to adapt to their new host. Their gene-building enzymes have evolved to run at top speed at human body temperature, for example, which is a few degrees cooler than a bird's.

Influenza viruses also moved from bird guts to human airways. That shift also required flu viruses to spread in a new way: in the droplets we release in our coughs and sneezes.

"If the virus settles down on the floor, then it's gone," said Peter Palese, chairman of microbiology at Mount Sinai School of Medicine. Winter is flu season in the United States, probably because dry air enables the virus-laden droplets to float longer.

Up to a fifth of all Americans become infected each flu season, and 36,000 die. During that time, the flu virus continues to evolve. The surface proteins change shape, allowing the viruses to evade the immune systems and resist antiflu drugs.

Dr. Spiro and his colleagues have also discovered that human flu viruses experience a lot of reassortment each season. "Reassortment may be the major player in generating new seasonal viruses," Dr. Spiro said.

From time to time, a new kind of flu emerges that causes far more suffering than the typical swarm of seasonal flu viruses. In 1918, for example, the so-called Spanish flu caused an estimated 50 million deaths. In later years, some of the descendants of that strain picked up genes from bird flu viruses.

Sometimes reassortments led to new pandemics. It is possible that reassortment enables flu viruses to escape the immune system so well that they can make people sicker and spread faster to new hosts.

Reassortment also played a big role in the emergence of the current swine flu. Its genes come from several ancestors, which mainly infected pigs.

Scientists first isolated flu viruses from pigs in 1930, and their genetic sequence suggests that they descend from the Spanish flu of 1918. Once pigs picked up the flu from humans, that so-called classic strain was the only one found in pigs for decades. But in the 1970s a swine flu strain emerged in Europe that had some genes from a bird flu strain. A different pig-bird mix arose in the United States.

In the late 1990s, American scientists discovered a triple reassortant that mixed genes from classic swine flu with genes from bird viruses and human viruses. All three viruses—the triple reassortant, and the American and European pig-bird blends—contributed genes to the latest strain.

It is possible that the special biology of pigs helped foster all this mixing. Bird flu and human flu viruses can slip into pig cells, each using different receptors to gain access. "We call the pig a mixing vessel because it can replicate both avian and mammalian influenza virus at the same time," said Juergen Richt of Kansas State University. "The mixing of these genes can happen much easier in the pig than in any other species."

Fortunately, the new swine virus seems to behave like seasonal flu in terms of severity, not like the 1918 Spanish flu. "Right now it doesn't have what it takes to be a killer virus," Dr. Palese said. But could it? Dr. Palese said it was highly unlikely.

If the swine flu peters out in the next few weeks, virus trackers will still pay close attention to it over the next few months. As flu season ends in the Northern Hemisphere, the virus may be able to thrive in the southern winter or perhaps linger in the tropics, only to return to the north next fall. It will no doubt change along the way as its genes mutate, and it may pick up new genes.

The scientists will be watching that evolutionary journey with a mixture of concern and respect. "Viruses are incredibly adaptable," Dr. Spiro said. "They have managed to exploit our modern culture and spread around the world."

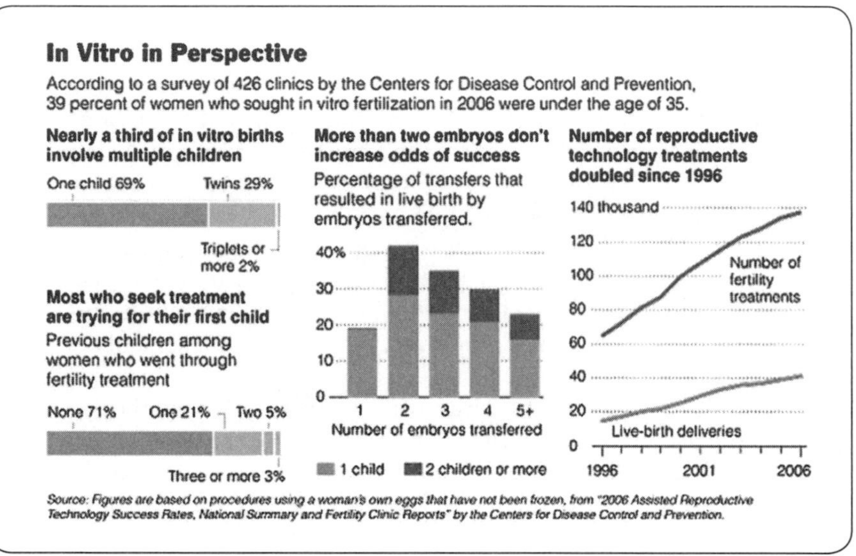
In Vitro in Perspective
According to a survey of 426 clinics by the Centers for Disease Control and Prevention, 39 percent of women who sought in vitro fertilization in 2006 were under the age of 35.
Nearly a third of in vitro births involve multiple children
One child 69%
Twins 29%
Triplets or more 2%
Most who seek treatment are trying for their first child
Previous children among women who went through fertility treatment
None 71%
One 21%
Two 5%
Three or more 3%
More than two embryos don't increase odds of success
Percentage of transfers that resulted in live birth by embryos transferred.
40%
30
20
10
0
1
2
3
4
5+
Number of embryos transferred
1 child
2 children or more
Number of reproductive technology treatments doubled since 1996
140 thousand
120
100
80
60
40
20
0
Number of fertility treatments
Live-birth deliveries
1996
2001
2006
Source: Figures are based on procedures using a woman's own eggs that have not been frozen, from "2006 Assisted Reproductive Technology Success Rates, National Summary and Fertility Clinic Reports" by the Centers for Disease Control and Prevention.

The New York Times

## Selection 7.3

*The birth of octuplets to a Southern California mother in 2009 focused attention on in vitro fertilization, in which a mother's eggs are harvested, fertilized in a laboratory with sperm and implanted in the mother's uterus. The controversy in this case stemmed from the number of embryos. Stephanie Saul reports that Nadya Suleman's doctor implanted six embryos, two of which divided into twins, resulting in eight babies for a woman who already had six children. The task for the reporter in this story is to explain how in vitro fertilization works (the science lesson) and why some mothers might pressure doctors into implanting more than one embryo, increasing the chance of multiple births. To cover this story, the reporter has to address the medical, ethical, social and economic implications of multiple embryo transfers. Notice how this story and many other medical stories use professional associations as sources (here, the American Society for Reproductive Medicine). Associations can be a great place to start your reporting because they can provide background information and have media affairs specialists to help you find doctors willing to be interviewed. But as you'll also see from this story, professional associations have no regulatory powers and can't force members to adhere to their guidelines. So there can be a difference between what associations recommend and what their members actually do.*

## Birth of Octuplets Puts Focus on Fertility Clinics

By STEPHANIE SAUL

MONTEBELLO, Calif.—Pictures of children, his trophies, decorate Dr. Tien C. Chiu's office.

Three smiling siblings, he says, were the first Japanese-American triplets conceived in a laboratory, while the robust-looking quadruplets were born after sperm was injected into their mother's eggs with a needle.

To the couples who turned to Dr. Chiu to have families, the babies were special gifts. To the government and fertility industry, though, such large multiple births have begun to look like breakdowns in the system. The issue has taken on renewed scrutiny since a California woman, Nadya Suleman, who already had six children conceived through in vitro procedures, gave birth to octuplets near here last month.

Nearly a third of in vitro births involve twins or more. The government, along with professional associations, have been pushing fertility doctors to reduce that number, citing the disastrous health consequences that sometimes come with multiple births—infant mortality, low birth weights, long-term disabilities and thousands of dollars' worth of medical care.

The American Society for Reproductive Medicine, the association of fertility doctors, even adopted guidelines in 2008 encouraging the transfer of only one embryo for women under 35, and no more than two, except in extraordinary circumstances. The guidelines allow more for older women, up to a maximum of five.

But unlike some other countries, the United States has no laws to enforce those guidelines. The Centers for Disease Control and Prevention has a surveillance system that collects data on fertility clinics, but reporting is voluntary and there are no government sanctions for not reporting.

As a result, experts say many doctors are still implanting too many embryos to increase the chance of pregnancy. Only 11 percent of in vitro procedures in the United States involve single embryos, according to 2006 data from the C.D.C.

---

*Published: February 12, 2009.*

But the 2008 guidelines say that in many cases, it is healthier to implant only one embryo, even if it means the process has to be repeated, because of the risk of multiple births. In the case of Ms. Suleman, the California Medical Board said it was investigating her fertility doctor, Michael M. Kamrava, to determine whether accepted standards of medical practice had been violated. In an interview with NBC News, Ms. Suleman, 33, said that Dr. Kamrava had implanted six embryos, and that two of them had divided into twins, resulting in eight babies.

"She wanted to have many, many babies," said Dr. Chiu, who added that he had formerly treated Ms. Suleman but declined to give details.

Efforts to reduce the multiple birth rate are also sources of tension in the industry.

One cycle of in vitro fertilization costs about $12,000. Women who are not successful the first time often try again and again, which can push the cost of having a baby to more than $100,000. Because the technology is often not covered by insurance, doctors say they are constantly urged by patients to implant extra embryos.

One woman, a nurse who could afford only one try at in vitro, pressured Dr. Chiu to transfer eight embryos. "I said under one condition," Dr. Chiu remembered. "I made her sign an agreement that she would do selective reduction." That agreement, to remove some of the embryos if they lived, was very likely unenforceable. But in the end it worked out. Only one embryo survived, and the woman gave birth to a healthy child, he said.

Dr. Chiu said that a situation in which he would implant eight embryos would be a rarity, adding, "I don't think any doctor would try to make a multiple pregnancy."

Ms. Suleman now has 14 children born through in vitro fertilization. In the NBC interview, she identified the clinic where she received her treatment as the West Coast IVF Clinic in Beverly Hills, Calif., which Dr. Kamrava runs. Dr. Kamrava did not return telephone calls seeking comment.

Ms. Suleman said in the interview that she was aware of the risks of multiple births, but that she wanted to use all the embryos available to her.

The treatment involves removing eggs from a woman's ovaries, combining them with sperm in a laboratory, and implanting the resulting embryos in the woman's uterus. (In some cases the eggs come from a donor.) The number of embryos implanted is often a judgment call and can make a big difference in a pregnancy's outcome.

"Every single decision we make about embryo transfers is a tough one, because we don't have a crystal ball," said Dr. Jeffrey M. Steinberg, who runs the Fertility Institutes, a group of fertility clinics based in Southern California.

The industry has doubled in size in the decade since the C.D.C. started collecting data in 1996. That year, 64,681 procedures were performed in 330 clinics. At last count, the number of procedures was up to 134,260 and there were more than 483 clinics across the country. More than 50,000 children a year are born as a result of in vitro fertilization in the United States. Nationwide, it is a more than $1 billion business.

The percentage of births involving triplets or more declined to 2 percent in 2006, from 7 percent in 1996. The American Society for Reproductive Medicine points to that decline as among its successes.

Dr. Daniel A. Potter, medical director of Huntington Reproductive Center, also in Southern California, said the onus remained on the doctor, regardless of the patient's wishes.

"If someone came in and wanted to transfer six embryos in a situation like we're talking about, we have an obligation to protect the patient and not let the patient do things that are unreasonable," Dr. Potter said.

Dr. David Hill, an embryologist who directs the laboratory at the ART Reproductive Center, an in vitro clinic in Beverly Hills, said that the United States had retained a laissez-faire stance toward in vitro procedures, instead of regulating the process as some other countries do.

But comparing the United States industry with Europe's, for example, may be unfair because some countries cap costs for in vitro fertilization or require coverage by health programs, removing the financial incentive by women to push for pregnancy on the first try.

"The point is, there was greater pressure for U.S. clinics to deliver, no pun intended, on the first try," Dr. Hill said, "so they would put back more embryos, and hopefully one of them would take."

More recently, methods of producing and selecting embryos have improved, removing some of the incentive to implant a high number. Success rates are higher when two or more embryos are implanted, but recent statistics suggest that the likelihood of having a child is better with two embryos than with three.

Even so, when patients hear the pros and cons, they often push to have multiple embryos implanted, Dr. Hill said. "I can't tell you how many patients will come in, and when we explain the risks of twins, they say, 'Hey, bring it on.' They're desperate to get a family going."

Part of the reason doctors might acquiesce to a patient's wish could be the fierce competition in the industry. California has more doctors performing in vitro fertilization than any other state, with many concentrated in the Los Angeles area.

The competition means that sales pitches are not unusual.

The Huntington Reproductive Center offers a refund for some women. No pregnancy? You get 90 percent of your money back.

Want to predict the sex of your baby? That is 99.99 percent guaranteed at the Fertility Institutes.

Dr. Kamrava, Ms. Suleman's doctor, had previously raised eyebrows in the industry by advocating a procedure called SEED—subendometrial embryo delivery, in which he said he could increase pregnancy rates by using a plastic tube to insert embryos under the lining of the uterus for maturation, rather than in the uterus. The procedure's value was never scientifically proven, according to Dr. Potter.

Several Southern California doctors disclosed embryo transfer rates significantly higher than the national norm, according to the C.D.C. data. A look at Dr. Kamrava's statistics in 2006, for example, might have raised red flags.

They revealed that Dr. Kamrava's clinic had one of the nation's highest rates of embryo transfer in younger women—3.5 versus a national average of 2.3. Such high embryo-transfer rates are sometimes an indication that a doctor is being too aggressive in trying to raise the number of pregnancies. In Dr. Kamrava's case, however, those numbers were among the lowest in the nation. Of 56 procedures performed by his clinic in 2006, only two resulted in women giving birth, one to a single baby and the other to twins.

The twins may have been the set born to Ms. Suleman that year.

*Margot Williams contributed reporting from New York.*

## Selection 7.4

*If you're looking for a story idea, scan scientific journals. Every week hundreds of articles appear in journals worldwide. Some journals promote their studies. Others do not. Aggregation sites like EurekAlert.org and Newswise.com offer search engines that help reporters find a particular study, but it takes a sharp reporter like Benedict Carey to know a good story when he sees it. This story began with a two-page article from the journal Current Biology reporting on a blind man who navigated an obstacle course using his brain's subcortical system. Because Carey understands that surprise is a big attraction for readers, he knew that this research stood out. "It's so interesting and so strange and also reveals something about the brain that is not obvious," says Carey in an interview for this book. In the story Carey explains the anatomy and physiology that allowed the blind man to perceive obstacles through so-called blindsight. Carey's science lessons (and there are several of them) are notable for the way he takes complicated physiological processes and simplifies them.*

## Blind, Yet Seeing: The Brain's Subconscious Visual Sense

By BENEDICT CAREY

The man, a doctor left blind by two successive strokes, refused to take part in the experiment. He could not see anything, he said, and had no interest in navigating an obstacle course—a cluttered hallway—for the benefit of science. Why bother?

When he finally tried it, though, something remarkable happened. He zigzagged down the hall, sidestepping a garbage can, a tripod, a stack of paper and several boxes as if he could see everything clearly. A researcher shadowed him in case he stumbled.

"You just had to see it to believe it," said Beatrice de Gelder, a neuroscientist at Harvard and Tilburg University in the Netherlands, who with an international team of brain researchers reported on the patient on Monday in the journal Current Biology. A video is online at www.beatricedegelder.com/books.html.

The study, which included extensive brain imaging, is the most dramatic demonstration to date of so-called blindsight, the native ability to sense things using the brain's primitive, subcortical—and entirely subconscious—visual system.

Scientists have previously reported cases of blindsight in people with partial damage to their visual lobes. The new report is the first to show it in a person whose visual lobes—one in each hemisphere, under the skull at the back of the head—were completely destroyed. The finding suggests that people with similar injuries may be able to recover some crude visual sense with practice.

*This lede spans two paragraphs. Feature ledes set the stage, hook the reader and introduce a main character. This lede does all three.*

*Note that Carey does not start at the beginning of the saga, when a researcher asked the doctor to participate. Instead, he jumps right into the middle and uses conversational language to put the reader in the blind man's place.*

*Note the level of detail in the second graf that sets the scene for the reader.*

*Notice how the quote plays with what's in your mind after reading the lede. "That's impossible!" you think. And then one of the researchers answers: "You just had to see it to believe it." It's as if she's speaking to you personally, in plain (not scientific) language. The subliminal message: This is going to be a fascinating story, and the writer will help you understand.*

*To really make the story unforgettable, Carey includes an online link to video of the blind man walking the obstacle course. The video is crucial, according to Carey, because the first thing you want to do is to see it.*

*Whenever a reporter introduces a new concept or word (like "blindsight"), he must define that word immediately.*

*In medical stories, always assume that your reader doesn't know the anatomy. Carey tells us where the visual lobes are located and why blindsight in this individual has so much scientific significance. This is the first science lesson that Carey gives his readers.*

---

*Published: December 23, 2008.*

*Excellent shoe-leather journalism in tracking down the scientist who, with two colleagues, first reported blindsight in 1973.*

"It's a very rigorously done report and the first demonstration of this in someone with apparent total absence of a striate cortex, the visual processing region," said Dr. Richard Held, an emeritus professor of cognitive and brain science at the Massachusetts Institute of Technology, who with Ernst Pöppel and Douglas Frost wrote the first published account of blindsight in a person, in 1973.

*Simple explanation of a complex physiologic process. This is Carey's second science lesson.*

The man in the new study, an African living in Switzerland at the time, suffered the two strokes in his 50s, weeks apart, and was profoundly blind by any of the usual measures. Unlike people suffering from eye injuries, or congenital blindness in which the visual system develops abnormally, his brain was otherwise healthy, as were his eyes, so he had the necessary tools to process subconscious vision. What he lacked were the circuits that cobble together a clear, conscious picture.

*Carey anticipates a question from readers that perhaps the man navigated by auditory cues. He apparently did not.*

The research team took brain scans and magnetic resonance images to see the damage, finding no evidence of visual activity in the cortex. They also found no evidence that the patient was navigating by echolocation, the way that bats do. Both the patient, T. N., and the researcher shadowing him walked the course in silence.

The man himself was as dumbfounded as anyone that he was able to navigate the obstacle course.

"The more educated people are," Dr. de Gelder said, "in my experience, the less likely they are to believe they have these resources that they are not aware of to avoid obstacles. And this was a very educated person."

Scientists have long known that the brain digests what comes through the eyes using two sets of circuits. Cells in the retina project not only to the visual cortex—the destroyed regions in this man—but also to subcortical areas, which in T.N. were intact. These include the superior colliculus, which is crucial in eye movements and may have other sensory functions; and, probably, circuits running through the amygdala, which registers emotion.

*The reporter takes a complicated physiological process and simplifies it. Each time he introduces a new area of anatomy, superior colliculus, for example, he defines it. He references the amygdala and tells us its function. This is good explanatory journalism. This is also Carey's third and most important science lesson, the one that explains how the blind man can perceive objects in his path.*

In an earlier experiment, one of the authors of the new paper, Dr. Alan Pegna of Geneva University Hospitals, found that the same African doctor had emotional blindsight. When presented with images of fearful faces, he cringed subconsciously in the same way that almost everyone does, even though he could not consciously see the faces. The subcortical, primitive visual system apparently registers not only solid objects but also strong social signals.

*Fascinating detail.*

Dr. Held, the M.I.T. neuroscientist, said that in lower mammals these midbrain systems appeared to play a much larger role in perception. In a study of rats published in the journal Science last Friday, researchers demonstrated that cells deep in the brain were in fact specialized to register certain qualities of the environment.

*When a reporter brings back a character who has been missing from the story for several paragraphs, he needs to briefly re-identify that character.*

They include place cells, which fire when an animal passes a certain landmark, and head-direction cells, which track which way the face is pointing. But the new study also found strong evidence of what the scientists, from the Norwegian University of Science and Technology in Trondheim, called "border cells," which fire when an animal is close to a wall or boundary of some kind.

*Carey introduces new scientific terms and again immediately defines them or tells us their function.*

All of these types of neurons, which exist in some form in humans, may too have assisted T.N. in his navigation of the obstacle course.

*For any new scientific finding, the medical reporter should seek and report the possible significance of that finding.*

In time, and with practice, people with brain injuries may learn to lean more heavily on such subconscious or semiconscious systems, and perhaps even begin to construct some conscious vision from them.

"It's not clear how sharp it would be," Dr. Held said. "Probably a vague, low-resolution spatial sense. But it might allow them to move around more independently."

## Selection 7.5

*An explanatory piece not only can inform, it also can entertain. If you don't find the next story amusing, you may want to get an M.R.I. of your right parahippocampal gyrus. Dan Hurley sandwiches a lot of neuroscience between an amusing lede and an equally amusing tag. Note how Hurley avoids clichés as he plays with words and with his readers' minds.*

### The Science of Sarcasm (Not That You Care)

By DAN HURLEY

There was nothing very interesting in Katherine P. Rankin's study of sarcasm—at least, nothing worth your important time. All she did was use an M.R.I. to find the place in the brain where the ability to detect sarcasm resides. But then, you probably already knew it was in the right parahippocampal gyrus.

What you may not have realized is that perceiving sarcasm, the smirking put-down that buries its barb by stating the opposite, requires a nifty mental trick that lies at the heart of social relations: figuring out what others are thinking. Those who lose the ability, whether through a head injury or the frontotemporal dementias afflicting the patients in Dr. Rankin's study, just do not get it when someone says during a hurricane, "Nice weather we're having."

*Published: June 3, 2008.*

"A lot of the social cognition we take for granted and learn through childhood, the ability to appreciate that someone else is being ironic or sarcastic or angry—the so-called theory of mind that allows us to get inside someone else's head—is characteristically lost very early in the course of frontotemporal dementia," said Dr. Bradley F. Boeve, a behavioral neurologist at the Mayo Clinic in Rochester, Minn.

"It's very disturbing for family members, but neurologists haven't had good tools for measuring it," he went on. "That's why I found this study by Kate Rankin and her group so fascinating."

Dr. Rankin, a neuropsychologist and assistant professor in the Memory and Aging Center at the University of California, San Francisco, used an innovative test developed in 2002, the Awareness of Social Inference Test, or Tasit. It incorporates videotaped examples of exchanges in which a person's words seem straightforward enough on paper, but are delivered in a sarcastic style so ridiculously obvious to the able-brained that they seem lifted from a sitcom.

"I was testing people's ability to detect sarcasm based entirely on paralinguistic cues, the manner of expression," Dr. Rankin said.

In one videotaped exchange, a man walks into the room of a colleague named Ruth to tell her that he cannot take a class of hers that he had previously promised to take. "Don't be silly, you shouldn't feel bad about it," she replies, hitting the kind of high and low registers of a voice usually reserved for talking to toddlers. "I know you're busy—it probably wasn't fair to expect you to squeeze it in," she says, her lips curled in derision.

Although people with mild Alzheimer's disease perceived the sarcasm as well as anyone, it went over the heads of many of those with semantic dementia, a progressive brain disease in which people forget words and their meanings.

"You would think that because they lose language, they would pay close attention to the paralinguistic elements of the communication," Dr. Rankin said.

To her surprise, though, the magnetic resonance scans revealed that the part of the brain lost among those who failed to perceive sarcasm was not in the left hemisphere of the brain, which specializes in language and social interactions, but in a part of the right hemisphere previously identified as important only to detecting contextual background changes in visual tests.

"The right parahippocampal gyrus must be involved in detecting more than just visual context—it perceives social context as well," Dr. Rankin said.

The discovery fits with an increasingly nuanced view of the right hemisphere's role, said Dr. Anjan Chatterjee, an associate professor in the Center for Cognitive Neuroscience at the University of Pennsylvania.

"The left hemisphere does language in the narrow sense, understanding of individual words and sentences," Dr. Chatterjee said. "But it's now thought that the appreciation of humor and language that is not literal, puns and jokes, requires the right hemisphere."

Dr. Boeve, at the Mayo Clinic, said that beyond the curiosity factor of mapping the cognitive tasks of the brain's ridges and furrows, the study offered hope that a test like Tasit could help in the diagnosis of frontotemporal dementia.

"These people normally do perfectly well on traditional neuropsychological tests early in the course of their disease," he said. "The family will say the person has changed dramatically, but even neurologists will often just shrug them off as having a midlife crisis."

Short of giving such a test, he said, the best way to diagnose such problems is by talking with family members about how the person has changed over time.

After a presentation of her findings at the American Academy of Neurology's annual meeting in April, Dr. Rankin was asked whether even those with intact brains might have differences in brain areas that explain how well they pick up on sarcasm.

"We all have strengths and weaknesses in our cognitive abilities, including our ability to detect social cues," she said. "There may be volume-based differences in certain regions that explain variations in all sorts of cognitive abilities."

So is it possible that Jon Stewart, who wields sarcasm like a machete on "The Daily Show," has an unusually large right parahippocampal gyrus?

"His is probably just normal," Dr. Rankin said. "The right parahippocampal gyrus is involved in detecting sarcasm, not being sarcastic."

But, she quickly added, "I bet Jon Stewart has a huge right frontal lobe; that's where the sense of humor is detected on M.R.I."

A spokesman for Mr. Stewart said he would have no comment—not that a big-shot television star like Jon Stewart would care about the size of his neuroanatomy.

## Selection 7.6

*Writing an explanatory piece on a psychological topic is especially difficult because mental processes don't lend themselves to easy storytelling. In the next article Benedict Carey tackles the complex relationship between self-perception and psychological change. Carey describes what researchers are learning about how one's personal narrative can both determine and signal personal growth. To explain the process, Carey uses the metaphor of a screenplay. Metaphors and similes are useful devices that can help make abstract concepts concrete. Also, note how Carey integrates a variety of sources and source materials (interviews with experts, a conference presentation, a journal report, an older experiment and even a Joan Didion play) to make his points. We challenge anyone to read this piece and not start reassessing his or her own life story.*

## This Is Your Life (and How You Tell It)

By BENEDICT CAREY

For more than a century, researchers have been trying to work out the raw ingredients that account for personality, the sweetness and neuroses that make Anna Anna, the sluggishness and sensitivity that make Andrew Andrew. They have largely ignored the first-person explanation—the life story that people themselves tell about who they are, and why.

Stories are stories, after all. The attractive stranger at the airport bar hears one version, the parole officer another, and the P.T.A. board gets something entirely different. Moreover, the tone, the lessons, even the facts in a life story can all shift in the changing light of a person's mood, its major notes turning minor, its depths appearing shallow.

Yet in the past decade or so a handful of psychologists have argued that the quicksilver elements of personal narrative belong in any three-dimensional picture of personality. And a burst of new findings is now helping them make the case. Generous, civic-minded adults from diverse backgrounds tell life stories with very similar and telling features, studies find; so likewise do people who have overcome mental distress through psychotherapy.

Every American may be working on a screenplay, but we are also continually updating a treatment of our own life—and the way in which we visualize each scene not only shapes how we think about ourselves, but how we behave, new studies find. By better understanding how life stories are built, this work suggests, people may be able to alter their own narrative, in small ways and perhaps large ones.

"When we first started studying life stories, people thought it was just idle curiosity—stories, isn't that cool?" said Dan P. McAdams, a professor of psychology at Northwestern and author of the 2006 book, "The Redemptive Self." "Well, we find that these narratives guide behavior in every moment, and frame not only how we see the past but how we see ourselves in the future."

Researchers have found that the human brain has a natural affinity for narrative construction. People tend to remember facts more accurately if they encounter them in a story rather than in a list,

---

*Published: May 22, 2007.*

studies find; and they rate legal arguments as more convincing when built into narrative tales rather than on legal precedent.

YouTube routines notwithstanding, most people do not begin to see themselves in the midst of a tale with a beginning, middle and eventual end until they are teenagers. "Younger kids see themselves in terms of broad, stable traits: 'I like baseball but not soccer,' " said Kate McLean, a psychologist at the University of Toronto in Mississauga. "This meaning-making capability—to talk about growth, to explain what something says about who I am—develops across adolescence."

Psychologists know what life stories look like when they are fully hatched, at least for some Americans. Over the years, Dr. McAdams and others have interviewed hundreds of men and women, most in their 30s and older.

During a standard life-story interview, people describe phases of their lives as if they were outlining chapters, from the sandlot years through adolescence and middle age. They also describe several crucial scenes in detail, including high points (the graduation speech, complete with verbal drum roll); low points (the college nervous breakdown, complete with the list of witnesses); and turning points. The entire two-hour session is recorded and transcribed.

In analyzing the texts, the researchers found strong correlations between the content of people's current lives and the stories they tell. Those with mood problems have many good memories, but these scenes are usually tainted by some dark detail. The pride of college graduation is spoiled when a friend makes a cutting remark. The wedding party was wonderful until the best man collapsed from drink. A note of disappointment seems to close each narrative phrase.

By contrast, so-called generative adults—those who score highly on tests measuring civic-mindedness, and who are likely to be energetic and involved—tend to see many of the events in their life in the reverse order, as linked by themes of redemption. They flunked sixth grade but met a wonderful counselor and made honor roll in seventh. They were laid low by divorce, only to meet a wonderful new partner. Often, too, they say they felt singled out from very early in life—protected, even as others nearby suffered.

In broad outline, the researchers report, such tales express distinctly American cultural narratives, of emancipation or atonement, of Horatio Alger advancement, of epiphany and second chances. Depending on the person, the story itself might be nuanced or simplistic, powerfully dramatic or cloyingly pious. But the point is that the narrative themes are, as much as any other trait, driving factors in people's behavior, the researchers say.

"We find that when it comes to the big choices people make—should I marry this person? should I take this job? should I move across the country?—they draw on these stories implicitly, whether they know they are working from them or not," Dr. McAdams said.

Any life story is by definition a retrospective reconstruction, at least in part an outgrowth of native temperament. Yet the research so far suggests that people's life stories are neither rigid nor wildly variable, but rather change gradually over time, in close tandem with meaningful life events.

Jonathan Adler, a researcher at Northwestern, has found that people's accounts of their experiences in psychotherapy provide clues about the nature of their recovery. In a recent study presented at the annual meeting of the Society for Personality and Social Psychology in January, Mr. Adler reported on 180 adults from the Chicago area who had recently completed a course of talk therapy. They sought treatment for things like depression, anxiety, marital problems and fear of flying, and spent months to years in therapy.

At some level, talk therapy has always been an exercise in replaying and reinterpreting each person's unique life story. Yet Mr. Adler found that in fact those former patients who scored highest on measures of well-being—who had recovered, by standard measures—told very similar tales about their experiences.

They described their problem, whether depression or an eating disorder, as coming on suddenly, as if out of nowhere. They characterized their difficulty as if it were an outside enemy, often giving it a name (the black dog, the walk of shame). And eventually they conquered it.

"The story is one of victorious battle: 'I ended therapy because I could overcome this on my own,'" Mr. Adler said. Those in the study who scored lower on measures of psychological well-being were more likely to see their moods and behavior problems as a part of their own character, rather than as a villain to be defeated. To them, therapy was part of a continuing adaptation, not a decisive battle.

The findings suggest that psychotherapy, when it is effective, gives people who are feeling helpless a sense of their own power, in effect altering their life story even as they work to disarm their own demons, Mr. Adler said.

Mental resilience relies in part on exactly this kind of autobiographical storytelling, moment to moment, when navigating life's stings and sorrows. To better understand how stories are built in real time, researchers have recently studied how people recall vivid scenes from recent memory. They find that one important factor is the perspective people take when they revisit the scene—whether in the first person, or in the third person, as if they were watching themselves in a movie.

In a 2005 study reported in the journal Psychological Science, researchers at Columbia University measured how student participants reacted to a bad memory, whether an argument or failed exam, when it was recalled in the third person. They tested levels of conscious and unconscious hostility after the recollections, using both standard questionnaires and students' essays. The investigators found that the third-person scenes were significantly less upsetting, compared with bad memories recalled in the first person.

"What our experiment showed is that this shift in perspective, having this distance from yourself, allows you to relive the experience and focus on why you're feeling upset," instead of being immersed in it, said Ethan Kross, the study's lead author. The emotional content of the memory is still felt, he said, but its sting is blunted as the brain frames its meaning, as it builds the story.

Taken together, these findings suggest a kind of give and take between life stories and individual memories, between the larger screenplay and the individual scenes. The way people replay and recast memories, day by day, deepens and reshapes their larger life story. And as it evolves, that larger story in turn colors the interpretation of the scenes.

Nic Weststrate, 23, a student living in Toronto, said he was able to reinterpret many of his most painful memories with more compassion after having come out as a gay man. He was very hard on himself, for instance, when at age 20 he misjudged a relationship with a friend who turned out to be straight.

He now sees the end of that relationship as both a painful lesson and part of a larger narrative. "I really had no meaningful story for my life then," he said, "and I think if I had been open about being gay I might not have put myself in that position, and he probably wouldn't have either."

After coming out, he said: "I saw that there were other possibilities. I would be presenting myself openly to a gay audience, and just having a coherent story about who I am made a big difference. It affects how you see the past, but it also really affects your future."

Psychologists have shown just how interpretations of memories can alter future behavior. In an experiment published in 2005, researchers had college students who described themselves as socially awkward in high school recall one of their most embarrassing moments. Half of the students reimagined the humiliation in the first person, and the other half pictured it in the third person.

Two clear differences emerged. Those who replayed the scene in the third person rated themselves as having changed significantly since high school—much more so than the first-person group did. The third-person perspective allowed people to reflect on the meaning of their social miscues, the authors suggest, and thus to perceive more psychological growth.

And their behavior changed, too. After completing the psychological questionnaires, each study participant spent time in a waiting room with another student, someone the research subject thought was taking part in the study. In fact the person was working for the research team, and secretly recorded the conversation between the pair, if any. This double agent had no idea which study participants had just relived a high school horror, and which had viewed theirs as a movie scene.

The recordings showed that members of the third-person group were much more sociable than the others. "They were more likely to initiate a conversation, after having perceived themselves as more changed," said Lisa Libby, the lead author and a psychologist at Ohio State University. She added, "We think that feeling you have changed frees you up to behave as if you have; you think, 'Wow, I've really made some progress' and it gives you some real momentum."

Dr. Libby and others have found that projecting future actions in the third person may also affect what people later do, as well. In another study, students who pictured themselves voting for president in the 2004 election, from a third-person perspective, were more likely to actually go to the polls than those imagining themselves casting votes in the first person.

The implications of these results for self-improvement, whether sticking to a diet or finishing a degree or a novel, are still unknown. Likewise, experts say, it is unclear whether such scene-making is more functional for some people, and some memories, than for others. And no one yet knows how fundamental personality factors, like neuroticism or extraversion, shape the content of life stories or their component scenes.

But the new research is giving narrative psychologists something they did not have before: a coherent story to tell. Seeing oneself as acting in a movie or a play is not merely fantasy or indulgence; it is fundamental to how people work out who it is they are, and may become.

"The idea that whoever appeared onstage would play not me but a character was central to imagining how to make the narrative: I would need to see myself from outside," the writer Joan Didion has said of "The Year of Magical Thinking," her autobiographical play about mourning the death of her husband and her daughter. "I would need to locate the dissonance between the person I thought I was and the person other people saw."

## Selection 7.7

*The search for eternal life has spawned folklore and science fiction. Now scientists are studying how organisms age, and they are looking for ways—including calorie restriction—to slow the aging process. In the next story Michael Mason surveys anti-aging research through interviews and a brief history of the field. He puts a face on the story by starting with two older rhesus monkeys—one who's calorie restricted and aging gracefully and the other who's eating a normal diet and showing his age—and describing them as if they were people. Through use of anecdotes and simply explained science lessons, Mason gives readers a window into the future. We learn about roundworms that live six times longer than normal and what that may mean for human life extension. And we read about how calorie restriction in both yeast and mice leads to activation of a gene that may have a connection to long-term survival. A similar gene is found in humans. We also meet a 6-foot-tall man who weighs 135 pounds and says he's never been healthier. Too many writers end stories with quotes—so if you're going to use one, make sure it's as good as the final quote in this story.*

## One for the Ages: A Prescription That May Extend Life

By MICHAEL MASON

How depressing, how utterly unjust, to be the one in your social circle who is aging least gracefully.

In a laboratory at the Wisconsin National Primate Research Center, Matthias is learning about time's caprice the hard way. At 28, getting on for a rhesus monkey, Matthias is losing his hair, lugging a paunch and getting a face full of wrinkles.

Yet in the cage next to his, gleefully hooting at strangers, one of Matthias's lab mates, Rudy, is the picture of monkey vitality, although he is slightly older. Thin and feisty, Rudy stops grooming his smooth coat just long enough to pirouette toward a proffered piece of fruit.

Tempted with the same treat, Matthias rises wearily and extends a frail hand. "You can really see the difference," said Dr. Ricki Colman, an associate scientist at the center who cares for the animals.

What a visitor cannot see may be even more interesting. As a result of a simple lifestyle intervention, Rudy and primates like him seem poised to live very long, very vital lives.

This approach, called calorie restriction, involves eating about 30 percent fewer calories than normal while still getting adequate amounts of vitamins, minerals and other nutrients. Aside from direct genetic manipulation, calorie restriction is the only strategy known to extend life consistently in a variety of animal species.

How this drastic diet affects the body has been the subject of intense research. Recently, the effort has begun to bear fruit, producing a steady stream of studies indicating that the rate of aging is plastic, not fixed, and that it can be manipulated.

In the last year, calorie-restricted diets have been shown in various animals to affect molecular pathways likely to be involved in the

*Published: October 31, 2006.*

progression of Alzheimer's disease, diabetes, heart disease, Parkinson's disease and cancer. Earlier this year, researchers studying dietary effects on humans went so far as to claim that calorie restriction may be more effective than exercise at preventing age-related diseases.

Monkeys like Rudy seem to be proving the thesis. Recent tests show that the animals on restricted diets, including Canto and Eeyore, two other rhesus monkeys at the primate research center, are in indisputably better health as they near old age than Matthias and other normally fed lab mates like Owen and Johann. The average lifespan for laboratory monkeys is 27.

The findings cast doubt on long-held scientific and cultural beliefs regarding the inevitability of the body's decline. They also suggest that other interventions, which include new drugs, may retard aging even if the diet itself should prove ineffective in humans. One leading candidate, a newly synthesized form of resveratrol—an antioxidant present in large amounts in red wine—is already being tested in patients. It may eventually be the first of a new class of anti-aging drugs. Extrapolating from recent animal findings, Dr. Richard A. Miller, a pathologist at the University of Michigan, estimated that a pill mimicking the effects of calorie restriction might increase human life span to about 112 healthy years, with the occasional senior living until 140, though some experts view that projection as overly optimistic.

According to a report by the Rand Corporation, such a drug would be among the most cost-effective breakthroughs possible in medicine, providing Americans more healthy years at less expense (an estimated $8,800 a year) than new cancer vaccines or stroke treatments.

"The effects are global, so calorie restriction has the potential to help us identify anti-aging mechanisms throughout the body," said Richard Weindruch, a gerontologist at the University of Wisconsin who directs research on the monkeys.

Many scientists regard the study of life extension, once just a reliable plotline in science fiction, as a national priority. The number of Americans 65 and older will double in the next 25 years to about 72 million, according to government census data. By then, seniors will account for nearly 20 percent of the population, up from just 12 percent in 2003.

Earlier this year, four prominent gerontologists, among them Dr. Miller, published a paper calling for the government to spend $3 billion annually in pursuit of a modest goal: delaying the onset of age-related diseases by seven years.

Doing so, the authors asserted, would lay the foundation for a healthier and wealthier country, a so-called longevity dividend.

"The demographic wave entering their 60s is enormous, and that is likely to greatly increase the prevalence of diseases like diabetes and heart disease," said Dr. S. Jay Olshansky, an epidemiologist at the University of Illinois at Chicago, and one of the paper's authors. "The simplest way to positively affect them all is to slow down aging."

Science, of course, is still a long way from doing anything of the sort. Aging is a complicated phenomenon, the intersection of an array of biological processes set in motion by genetics, lifestyle, even evolution itself.

Still, in laboratories around the world, scientists are becoming adept at breeding animal Methuselahs, extraordinarily long lived and healthy worms, fish, mice and flies.

In 1935, Dr. Clive McCay, a nutritionist at Cornell University, discovered that mice that were fed 30 percent fewer calories lived about 40 percent longer than their free-grazing laboratory mates. The dieting mice were also more physically active and far less prone to the diseases of advanced age.

Dr. McCay's experiment has been successfully duplicated in a variety of species. In almost every instance, the subjects on low-calorie diets have proven to be not just longer lived, but also more resistant to age-related ailments.

"In mice, calorie restriction doesn't just extend life span," said Leonard P. Guarente, professor of biology at the Massachusetts Institute of Technology. "It mitigates many diseases of aging: cancer, cardiovascular disease, neurodegenerative disease. The gain is just enormous."

For years, scientists financed by the National Institute on Aging have closely monitored rhesus monkeys on restricted and normal-calorie diets. At the University of Wisconsin, where 50 animals survive from the original group of 76, the differences are just now becoming apparent in the older animals.

Those on normal diets, like Matthias, are beginning to show signs of advancing age similar to those seen in humans. Three of them, for instance, have developed diabetes, and a fourth has died of the disease. Five have died of cancer.

But Rudy and his colleagues on low-calorie meal plans are faring better. None have diabetes, and only three have died of cancer. It is too early to know if they will outlive their lab mates, but the dieters here and at the other labs also have lower blood pressure and lower blood levels of certain dangerous fats, glucose and insulin.

"The preliminary indicators are that we're looking at a robust life extension in the restricted animals," Dr. Weindruch said.

Despite widespread scientific enthusiasm, the evidence that calorie restriction works in humans is indirect at best. The practice was popularized in diet books by Dr. Roy Walford, a legendary pathologist at the University of California, Los Angeles, who spent much of the last 30 years of his life following a calorie-restricted regimen. He died of Lou Gehrig's disease in 2004 at 79.

Largely as a result of his advocacy, several thousand people are now on calorie-restricted diets in the United States, says Brian M. Delaney, president of the Calorie Restriction Society.

Mike Linksvayer, a 36-year-old chief technology officer at a San Francisco nonprofit group, embarked on just such a diet six years ago. On an average day, he eats an apple or some cereal for breakfast, followed by a small vegan dish at lunch. Dinner is whatever his wife has cooked, excluding bread, rice, sugar and whatever else Mr. Linksvayer deems unhealthy (this often includes the entrée). On weekends, he occasionally fasts.

Mr. Linksvayer, 6 feet tall and 135 pounds, estimated that he gets by on about 2,000 to 2,100 calories a day, a low number for men of his age and activity level, and his blood pressure is a remarkably low 112 over 63. He said he has never been in better health.

"I don't really get sick," he said. "Mostly I do the diet to be healthier, but if it helps me live longer, hey, I'll take that, too."

Researchers at Washington University in St. Louis have been tracking the health of small groups of calorie-restricted dieters. Earlier this year, they reported that the dieters had better-functioning hearts and fewer signs of inflammation, which is a precursor to clogged arteries, than similar subjects on regular diets.

In previous studies, people in calorie-restricted groups were shown to have lower levels of LDL, the so-called bad cholesterol, and triglycerides. They also showed higher levels of HDL, the so-called good cholesterol, virtually no arterial blockage and, like Mr. Linksvayer, remarkably low blood pressure.

"Calorie restriction has a powerful, protective effect against diseases associated with aging," said Dr. John O. Holloszy, a Washington University professor of medicine. "We don't know how long each individual will end up living, but they certainly have a longer life expectancy than average."

Researchers at Louisiana State University reported in April in The Journal of the American Medical Association that patients on an experimental low-calorie diet had lower insulin levels and body temperatures, both possible markers of longevity, and fewer signs of the chromosomal damage typically associated with aging.

These studies and others have led many scientists to believe they have stumbled onto a central determinant of natural life span. Animals on restricted diets seem particularly resistant to environmental stresses like oxidation and heat, perhaps even radiation. "It is a very deep, very important function," Dr. Miller said. Experts theorize that limited access to energy alarms the body, so to speak, activating a cascade of biochemical signals that tell each cell to direct energy away from reproductive functions, toward repair and maintenance. The calorie-restricted organism is stronger, according to this hypothesis, because individual cells are more efficiently repairing mutations, using energy, defending themselves and mopping up harmful byproducts like free radicals.

"The stressed cell is really pulling out all the stops" to preserve itself, said Dr. Cynthia Kenyon, a molecular biologist at the University of California, San Francisco. "This system could have evolved as a way of letting animals take a timeout from reproduction when times are harsh."

But many experts are unsettled by the prospect, however unlikely, of Americans adopting a draconian diet in hopes of living longer. Even the current epidemiological data, they note, do not consistently show that those who are thinnest live longest. After analyzing decades of national mortality statistics, federal researchers reported last year that exceptional thinness, a logical consequence of calorie restriction, was associated with an increased risk of death. This controversial study did not attempt to assess the number of calories the subjects had been consuming, or the quality of their diets, which may have had an effect on mortality rates.

Despite the initially promising results from studies of primates, some scientists doubt that calorie restriction can ever work effectively in humans. A mathematical model published last year by researchers at University of California, Los Angeles, and University of California, Irvine, predicted that the maximum life span gain from calorie restriction for humans would be just 7 percent. A more likely figure, the authors said, was 2 percent.

"Calorie restriction is doomed to fail, and will make people miserable in the process of attempting it," said Dr. Jay Phelan, an evolutionary biologist at the University of California, Los Angeles, and a co-author of the paper. "We do see benefits, but not an increase in life span."

Mice who must scratch for food for a couple of years would be analogous, in terms of natural selection, to humans who must survive 20-year famines, Dr. Phelan said. But nature seldom demands that humans endure such conditions.

Besides, he added, there is virtually no chance Americans will adopt such a severe menu plan in great numbers.

"Have you ever tried to go without food for a day?" Dr. Phelan asked. "I did it once, because I was curious about what the mice in my lab experienced, and I couldn't even function at the end of the day."

Even researchers who believe calorie restriction can extend life in humans concede that few Americans are likely to stick to such a restrained diet over a long period. The aging of the body is the aging of its cells, researchers like to say. While cell death is hardwired into every organism's DNA, much of the infirmity that comes with advancing years is from an accumulation of molecular insults that, experts contend, may to some degree be prevented, even reversed.

"The goal is not just to make people live longer," said Dr. David A. Sinclair, a molecular biologist at Harvard. "It's to see eventually that an 80-year-old feels like a 50-year-old does today."

In a series of studies, Dr. Kenyon, of the University of California, San Francisco, has created mutant roundworms that live six times longer than normal, largely because of a mutation in a single gene called daf-2. The gene encodes a receptor on the surface of cells similar to a receptor in humans that responds to two important hormones, insulin and the insulin-like growth factor 1 or IGF-1.

Insulin is necessary for the body to transport glucose into cells to fuel their operations. Dr. Kenyon and other researchers suggest that worm cells with mutated receptors may be "tricked" into sensing that nutrients are not available, even when they are. With its maintenance machinery thereby turned on high, each worm cell lives far longer—and so does the worm.

Many experts are now convinced that the energy-signaling pathways that employ insulin and IGF-1 are very involved in fixing an organism's life span. Some researchers have even described Type 2 diabetes, which is marked by insensitivity to the hormone insulin, as simply an accelerated form of aging.

In yeast, scientists have discovered a gene similar to daf-2 called SIR2, that also helps to coordinate the cell's defensive response once activated by calorie restriction or another external stressor. The genes encode proteins called sirtuins, which are found in both plants and animals.

A mammalian version of the SIR2 gene, called SIRT1, has been shown to regulate a number of processes necessary for long-term survival in calorie-restricted mice.

Scientists are now trying to develop synthetic compounds that affect the genes daf-2 and SIRT1.

Several candidate drugs designed to prevent age-related diseases, particularly diabetes, are on the drawing boards at biotech companies. Sirtris Pharmaceuticals, in Boston, already has begun testing a new drug in patients with Type 2 diabetes that acts on SIRT1 to improve the functioning of mitochondria, the cell's energy factories.

While an anti-aging pill may be the next big blockbuster, some ethicists believe that the all-out determination to extend life span is veined with arrogance. As appointments with death are postponed, says Dr. Leon R. Kass, former chairman of the President's Council on Bioethics, human lives may become less engaging, less meaningful, even less beautiful.

"Mortality makes life matter," Dr. Kass recently wrote. "Immortality is a kind of oblivion—like death itself."

That man's time on this planet is limited, and rightfully so, is a cultural belief deeply held by many. But whether an increasing life span affords greater opportunity to find meaning or distracts from the pursuit, the prospect has become too great a temptation to ignore—least of all, for scientists.

"It's a just big waste of talent and wisdom to have people die in their 60s and 70s," said Dr. Sinclair of Harvard.

## Selection 7.8

*You don't have to write a long article to explain a medical or health concept. In a regular feature called Really? in Tuesday's Science Times, Anahad O'Connor takes a health claim and, in fewer than 250 words, shares scientists' best take on where the truth lies. In the feature on hot liquids easing cold symptoms, O'Connor boils down the explanation to just one sentence: "Chicken soup also contains cold-fighting compounds that help dissolve mucus in the lungs and suppress inflammation." In the second story, the explanation for why chocolate can keep you awake is equally simple. Readers like simplicity, and they especially like "the bottom line," the payoff for this popular feature.*

### REALLY?
### The Claim: Hot Liquids Can Ease Symptoms of a Cold or Flu

By ANAHAD O'CONNOR

#### The Facts

Like ice for a burn or a lozenge for a cough, a cup of hot tea is an age-old balm for sniffles, sneezing and stuffiness.

Hot liquids, it is said, help loosen secretions in the chest and sinuses, making them easier to expel and ultimately clearing up congestion.

The fluids are also meant to reverse dehydration.

But only recently have scientists examined whether the effect is real. In December, researchers at the Common Cold Center at Cardiff University in Britain looked at whether hot beverages relieved the symptoms of 30 people suffering from the flu or common cold any better than drinks at room temperature. They found that the contrast was marked.

"The hot drink provided immediate and sustained relief from symptoms of runny nose, cough, sneezing, sore throat, chilliness and tiredness," they reported, "whereas the same drink at room temperature only provided relief from symptoms of runny nose, cough and sneezing."

---

*Published: January 27, 2009.*

While this was the first study to look specifically at the effects of hot drinks on cold and flu symptoms, others have looked at hot foods like chicken soup and had similar results.

Chicken soup also contains cold-fighting compounds that help dissolve mucus in the lungs and suppress inflammation.

### The Bottom Line

Research confirms that a hot beverage can reduce congestion and other cold and flu symptoms.

## Selection 7.9

## REALLY? The Claim: Chocolate Can Be Disruptive to Sleep

By ANAHAD O'CONNOR

### The Facts

Chocolate can stir affection and awaken the taste buds, but some people wonder if it can have a less pleasant side effect: keeping them up at night.

Chocolate contains caffeine, as many people know, but in varying amounts depending on the type. A 1.5-ounce Hershey's milk chocolate bar, for example, contains nine milligrams, about three times as much caffeine as a cup of decaffeinated coffee. But a dark chocolate Hershey's candy bar has far more: about 30 milligrams. That is the same as a cup of instant tea, and slightly less than a typical cup of brewed tea, about 40 milligrams.

In other words, a dark chocolate dessert, eaten late enough, might leave you counting plenty of sheep.

And chocolate has other stimulants. One is theobromine, the compound that makes chocolate dangerous to dogs and cats because they metabolize it so slowly. Theobromine, which increases heart rate and causes sleeplessness, is found in small amounts in chocolate, especially dark. The National Sleep Foundation recommends avoiding chocolate—as well as coffee, tea and soft drinks—before bedtime.

But there is an alternative. White chocolate does not contain any theobromine, and little if any caffeine.

### The Bottom Line

Eating chocolate at night can potentially keep you awake.

---

*Published: January 13, 2009.*

## A Conversation with . . . Benedict Carey

BEHAVIOR REPORTER (continued from chapter 5)

**What is your background in the field in which you report?**
My background is entirely as a reporter and journalist. I studied physics and math in college [University of Colorado] and then covered for years general medical topics. I wrote about all sorts of things: cardiology and genetics and also some psychology and some psychiatry. I began to specialize in mental health issues about eight years ago when I was a health reporter at the L.A. Times and have specialized in mental health since then.

**How would you define your beat?**
I have three areas to my beat. One is psychiatry. The other is social psychology, or everyday psychology. And the third is brain science.

Psychiatry, a lot of that coverage is about drug treatments and drug trials and controversies over schizophrenia treatment, over bipolar diagnosis in kids, very controversial area, about the DSM [Diagnostic and Statistical Manual], the guidebook of mental disorders, a very influential book.

Social psychology, or everyday psychology, is this world of lab experiments to try to elucidate the patterns in everyday, normal behavior, not abnormal or pathological behavior. That is a very interesting world of how we tell secrets and the role of revenge and denial and betrayal, but [it] also can involve sociological studies which might bear on a certain issue, anthropology, ethnography, all the soft social sciences which can help illuminate normal, everyday behaviors.

The brain science stuff is everything from the findings from mouse models, from primates, the very hard neuroscience, the molecular findings to do with memory, to do with pathology, the hard lab findings that are coming out all the time now. That also includes the brain imaging side of neuroscience.

**What's the most interesting part of your beat?**
It's all interesting. There's so little that's certain about the brain. Behavior is very hard to predict. People are so different. The whole language in talking about behavior is loaded with moral presumptions. People argue how much of a science are all these things, like psychiatry and psychology. Well, they're trying to find their way as sciences.

I find very exciting some of the new brain science. This is a young science. So some of the basic findings are fundamental ones. That's exciting to be around, to be able to watch that happen. In psychiatry, I think that it's just a much more controversial area, and a frustrated and thwarted one right now. I would like to tell more happy stories in psychiatry. There aren't that many of them.

Social psychology is interesting stuff, too. [The] writing I do in social psychology is to put together findings from a variety of sciences. One of the most exciting areas now is in the crossover sciences. You now have people who are mathematicians and even physicists coming in big numbers into the behavioral sciences and really adding a lot, and updating and enlivening some of the more moribund areas of research.

A good example is evolutionary psychology, which sort of plateaued. There wasn't much happening. Now there's a whole group that's looking at applying game theory to evolution. They have findings applicable to a whole bunch of different behaviors. They're just not limited to looking at reproduction and murder and really have advanced evolutionary psychology a lot.

Physicists are also coming into the imaging world, like brain imaging, which also hit a wall, where the findings were no longer particularly interesting. Now, with advanced techniques they're beginning to map out circuits and sketch out some of the more subterranean things that are happening in the brain.

**How do you work out your story assignments with Times editors? Do you pitch them the stories? Do they suggest them to you? Who determines story length?**

I come up with most of the stories. I usually decide if something is newsworthy, if it appears to be a news story, like a publication of a study. The editors might see something that I missed, and they'll tap me on the shoulder and say, "Hey, what about this?" Then we'll talk about whether that's a story and how long it is. So those are pretty straightforward negotiations about how important is this story, what kind of story is it, where is it going to appear?

If it's a huge government study which finds an entire class of psychiatric drugs is not working very well—that's a real example—then that is a pretty good-sized story, certainly a news story, perhaps a front-page story. It's also a story that has some history and some scientific background to tell. So, with all those in mind, you, with the editor, talk about length, in that case maybe 1,200 words.

A smaller study, let's say a finding that people who are reminded of some of their moral failures are more likely to wash their hands than people who aren't—this is another real study that was published in Science—that's an interesting finding, lower importance, placement being much lower in the paper. But those things are negotiated right up front. How long is this going to be? Where should it go and should it go at all?

**How has the online world, nytimes.com, affected your reporting, both in terms of frequency of meeting rolling deadlines and also the way you write?**

It's affected both things a little bit. Of course, the rolling deadlines mean that you have to finish stories faster. But the understanding is that the bar is a little bit lower, meaning that the length doesn't have to be as long. And you're still working on the story. So you can build the story through the day, even though you had to file it online [at], say, 1 or 2 o'clock.

**Has writing for online publication changed your style of writing?**
My style is my style. I try to write as clearly as possible, as sparely as possible, as engagingly as possible. That's it. I don't change that.

The other difference, though, is that there are podcasts and photographs, and you can record sources. All those things have added a layer of work for us. We very often not only write a story, we might be interviewed about the story. We might post a short, edited interview with a source. We might even answer questions from readers on a story. So the online world has a lot more possibilities, and we try to enlarge the story from just the print one. That means we have to work more on a single story.

**Are these online sidebars initiated by you or by one of the online editors or producers?**
Usually someone else says, "Let's do a podcast on this" or "Why don't you think about recording your interview?" We're all at various stages of transitioning to this bigger, multimedia platform. We also have begun to link in our stories. If you read the story online, you'll have a bunch of links to original material, original sources, whether it's studies or Web sites or whatever. That's another thing that adds to the work.

**When you explain the science behind the story, who is your intended reader?**
I don't know that I always hit this mark, but I'm aiming for somebody who is a general reader, who doesn't necessarily know anything about neuroscience. It should be fairly straightforward and not exclude people.

**Is there a general education level you're shooting for?**
No, I don't really think of it that way. Explain it like you would be explaining it to somebody in a bar or somebody around the kitchen table or somebody standing on the corner. Try and keep it as straightforward as you can, using fairly straightforward language, not jargon, and leave out the confusing parts if you can.

**What's the most fun about your job?**
It's no one thing. I mean it's just everything. Getting people to read your stories is pretty fun. Being able to talk to really interesting leading figures and scientists is another. Being able to think for yourself and turn science, which might be ignored, into something that's interesting is fun. So it's all of it.

# MAKING CONNECTIONS

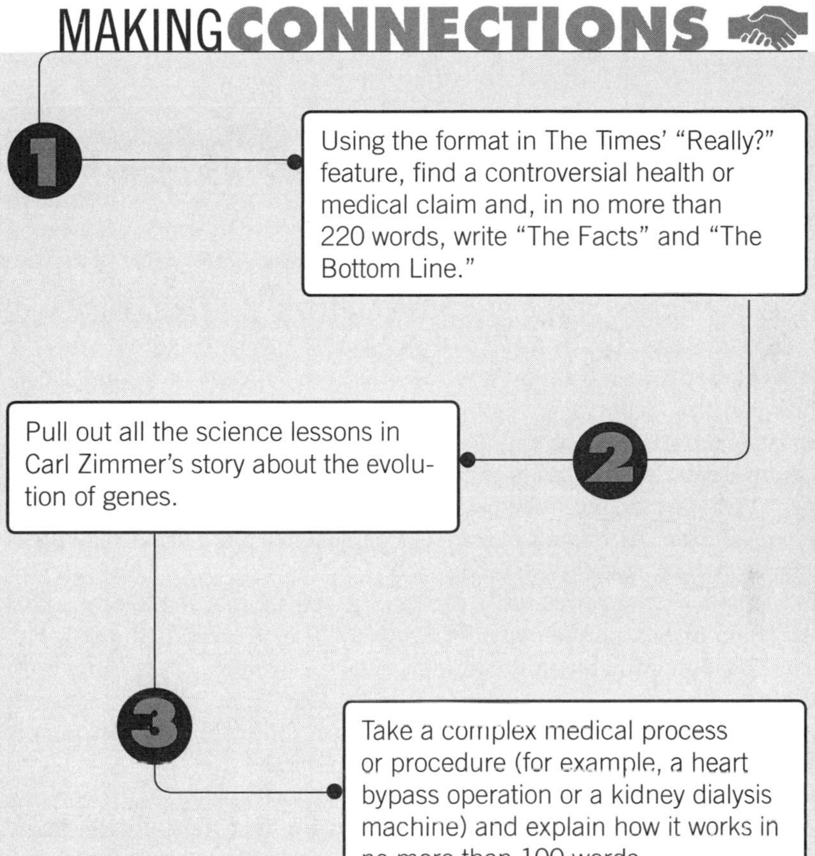

1. Using the format in The Times' "Really?" feature, find a controversial health or medical claim and, in no more than 220 words, write "The Facts" and "The Bottom Line."

2. Pull out all the science lessons in Carl Zimmer's story about the evolution of genes.

3. Take a complex medical process or procedure (for example, a heart bypass operation or a kidney dialysis machine) and explain how it works in no more than 100 words.

CHAPTER 8

# perspective stories

A PERSPECTIVE PIECE PROVIDES THE READER with insight into how a particular topic in the news fits into the bigger picture. A perspective story can take almost any form and can appear as a feature, a column or even a blog. A perspective story has much in common with explanatory and narrative reports. Like an explanatory story (see Chapter 7), a perspective piece shows how a particular issue or problem evolved. Like a narrative (see Chapter 11), a perspective story may begin with a complication and at least hint at a resolution. Also like a narrative, a perspective piece usually involves characters to whom readers can relate.

To research a perspective story, the reporter taps into a stable of medical experts, some of whom she consults regularly. For precision, the reporter references the best available epidemiologic data; for breadth, she reviews both recent and more distant history. The result is a story that relies on research data and expert opinion to correct misinformation about subjects that, in this chapter, range from cancer to teen sex to sudden death.

Scientific data is dry. To hook the reader, the reporter often focuses on one or more individuals through whose experiences the reporter tells the story. Unlike in a profile or narrative, the individual is not the focus but rather a vehicle to carry readers into and through the story. The topic, not the characters, drives the story.

## Selection 8.1

*The next story details the gap between perception and reality about medical advances in the battle to treat cancer. The main theme in medical reporter Gina Kolata's story is that in the past 40 years, despite millions of dollars of research, deaths from cancer have barely edged downward.*

*The measured pace and cautious tone of this story differ markedly from a controversial piece on cancer research that Kolata wrote for The Times in 1998.[1] That story concerned two new drugs that eradicated cancers in mice, not people, but that distinction escaped many readers, especially because of a prominently featured quote from Nobel laureate James Watson saying that he expected to see a cure for cancer in two years. The story, which appeared on the front page of the Sunday New York Times, provoked a media frenzy—cover stories in Time and Newsweek and lead stories on all three major broadcast networks.*[2] *Then, four days after the story's publication, Watson denied making the statement.*[3]

*Kolata still says she quoted him correctly, but she acknowledges that she would write the story far differently today. For one thing, she says she is much more skeptical now when researchers, even respected ones, make major unexpected statements. (For more from Kolata on this topic, see the interview at the end of Chapter 10.)*

*In the same way that one quotation can overwhelm a story, Kolata says she believes that an anecdotal lede can also put readers on the wrong track. In the 2009 cancer story that follows, Kolata avoids what she calls the "tyranny of the anecdote." She could have begun by introducing readers to a person whose downward cancer course illustrated the story's point. That's often an effective technique, but it's not the only way to start a story, and some reporters use the anecdotal lede so often that it verges on cliché. Instead, Kolata presents the historical perspective illustrated in The Times graphic below.*

*"I think anecdotes, especially anecdotes of people with cancer, can be so powerful and so overwhelming that it can be hard to tell a story," Kolata*

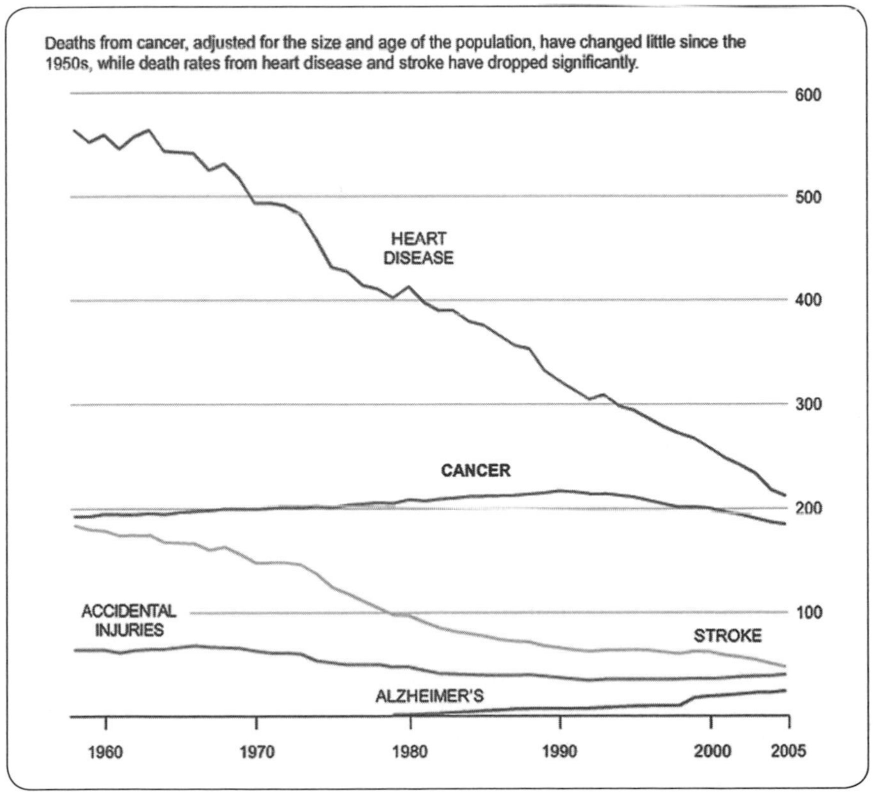
Deaths from cancer, adjusted for the size and age of the population, have changed little since the 1950s, while death rates from heart disease and stroke have dropped significantly.
600
500
400
300
200
100
HEART DISEASE
CANCER
ACCIDENTAL INJURIES
STROKE
ALZHEIMER'S
1960
1970
1980
1990
2000
2005

The New York Times

*says. "I thought the way to start would be to say, 'Here's what's really going on,' and then move onto the person rather than start with the person because it's too emotional."*

*If Kolata had started this story with the cancer patient, the reader would have missed her point. "You're already up there saying, 'Oh no, maybe if she caught it earlier,' so you're on the wrong track emotionally to read that story," she says. Instead, she tracks the history of cancer treatment and lays out in detail how the war on cancer has failed to deliver on its promise. To make the case, she relies on epidemiologic data and contrasts that with a New York Times/CBS News poll about people's perceptions on progress in treating cancer. Only after she puts the relative lack of progress in cancer treatment in perspective does Kolata introduce readers to the 61-year-old woman whose breast cancer has spread despite aggressive treatment.*

## FORTY YEARS' WAR
## Advances Elusive in the Drive to Cure Cancer

By GINA KOLATA

In 1971, flush with the nation's success in putting a man on the Moon, President Richard M. Nixon announced a new goal. Cancer would be cured by 1976, the bicentennial.

When 1976 came and went, the date for a cure, or at least substantial progress, kept being put off. It was going to happen by 2000, then by 2015.

Now, President Barack Obama, discussing his plans for health care, has vowed to find "a cure" for cancer in our time and said that, as part of the economic stimulus package, he would increase federal money for cancer research by a third for the next two years.

Cancer has always been an expensive priority. Since the war on cancer began, the National Cancer Institute, the federal government's main cancer research entity, with 4,000 employees, has alone spent $105 billion. And other government agencies, universities, drug companies and philanthropies have chipped in uncounted billions more.

Yet the death rate for cancer, adjusted for the size and age of the population, dropped only 5 percent from 1950 to 2005. In contrast, the death rate for heart disease dropped 64 percent in that time, and for flu and pneumonia, it fell 58 percent.

Still, the perception, fed by the medical profession and its marketers, and by popular sentiment, is that cancer can almost always be prevented. If that fails, it can usually be treated, even beaten.

The good news is that many whose cancer has not spread do well, as they have in the past. In some cases, like early breast cancer,

---

*Published: April 23, 2009.*

drugs introduced in the past decade have made an already good prognosis even better. And a few rare cancers, like chronic myeloid leukemia, can be controlled for years with new drugs. Cancer treatments today tend to be less harsh. Surgery is less disfiguring, chemotherapy less disabling.

But difficulties arise when cancer spreads, and, often, it has by the time of diagnosis. That is true for the most common cancers as well as rarer ones.

With breast cancer, for example, only 20 percent with metastatic disease—cancer that has spread outside the breast, like to bones, brain, lungs or liver—live five years or more, barely changed since the war on cancer began.

With colorectal cancer, only 10 percent with metastatic disease survive five years. That number, too, has hardly changed over the past four decades. The number has long been about 30 percent for metastatic prostate cancer, and in the single digits for lung cancer.

As for prevention, progress has been agonizingly slow. Only a very few things—stopping smoking, for example—make a difference. And despite marketing claims to the contrary, rigorous studies of prevention methods like high-fiber or low-fat diets, or vitamins or selenium, have failed to find an effect.

What has happened? Is cancer just an impossibly hard problem? Or is the United States, the only country to invest so much in cancer research, making fundamental mistakes in the way it fights the cancer war?

Researchers say the answer is yes on both counts. Cancer is hard—it is not one disease or, if it is, no one has figured out the weak link in cancer cells that would lead to a cure. Instead, cancer investigators say, the more they study cancer, the more complex it seems. Many are buoyed by recent progress in cancer molecular biology, but confess they have a long way to go.

There also are unnecessary roadblocks. Research lurches from fad to fad—cancer viruses, immunology, genomics. Advocacy groups have lobbied and directed research in ways that have not always advanced science.

And for all the money poured into cancer research, there has never been enough for innovative studies, the kind that can fundamentally change the way scientists understand cancer or doctors treat it. Such studies are risky, less likely to work than ones that are more incremental. The result is that, with limited money, innovative projects often lose out to more reliably successful projects that aim to tweak treatments, perhaps extending life by only weeks.

"Actually, that is the biggest threat," said Dr. Robert C. Young, chancellor of the Fox Chase Cancer Center in Philadelphia. "Every organization says, 'Oh, we want to fund high-risk research.' And I think they mean it. But as a matter of fact, they don't do it."

A recent New York Times/CBS News poll found the public divided about progress. Older people, more likely to have friends or relatives who had died of cancer, were more dubious—just 26 percent said a lot of progress had been made. The figure was 40 percent for middle-aged people, who may be more likely to know people who, with increased screening, had received a cancer diagnosis and seemed fine.

Yet the grim facts about cancer can be lost among the positive messages from the news media, advocacy groups and medical centers, and even labels on foods and supplements, hinting that they can fight or prevent cancer. The words tend to be carefully couched, but their impression is unmistakable and welcomed: cancer is preventable if you just eat right and exercise. If you are screened regularly, cancers can be caught early and almost certainly will be cured. If by some awful luck, your cancer is potentially deadly, miraculous new treatments and more in the pipeline could cure you or turn your cancer into a manageable disease.

Unfortunately, as many with cancer have learned, the picture is not always so glowing.

Phyllis Kutt, 61, a retired teacher in Cambridge, Mass., believed the advertisements and public service announcements. She thought she would never get cancer—she is a vegetarian, she exercises, she is not overweight, she does not smoke. And only two people in her extended family ever had cancer.

Then, in May 2006, Ms. Kutt's mammogram showed a foggy spot. The radiologist decided it was insignificant, but six months later, her internist found a walnut-sized lump in her right breast close to her armpit. It was the area that had been foggy on the mammogram.

"I was in real shock," Ms. Kutt said. "How could this be happening to me?"

Still, it looked as if she would be fine. There was no sign of cancer in her lymph nodes, and her surgeon removed the tumor.

Ms. Kutt, her husband and her oncologist were worried, though, and decided on aggressive treatment—four months of chemotherapy followed by 33 rounds of radiation. When it ended, she thought she was finished with cancer.

"My doctors never used the word 'cure' and I bless them for that," Ms. Kutt said. "But they do celebrate the end of chemo and they celebrate the end of radiation."

Last May the cancer came back, as a string of tiny lumps under her arm and a lump on her bicep. CT scans revealed she also had tumors in her lungs.

But cancer is curable, she thought. There are amazing new treatments. She found out otherwise.

It turns out that, with few exceptions, mostly childhood cancers and testicular cancer, there is no cure once a cancer has spread. The best that can be done is to keep it at bay for a while.

Last June, Ms. Kutt started a new regimen—three weeks of chemotherapy, followed by a week off. She is also taking a new drug, Avastin.

"I am still on that and will be forever until the cancer progresses and I change to other drugs or some new drugs are developed, or I die," she said.

The hardest part is explaining to friends and family.

"People will say to me, 'So when is your treatment going to be over?' " Ms. Kutt said. "That's the perception. You get treated. You're done. You're cured."

"I think some of my family members still believe that," she added. "Even though I told them, they forget. I get cards from my nieces, 'How are you doing? You'll be done soon, right?'"

Dr. Leonard Saltz, a colon cancer specialist at Memorial Sloan-Kettering Cancer Center, deals with misperceptions all the time. "People too often come to us expecting that the newest drugs can cure widespread metastatic cancer," Dr. Saltz said. "They are often shocked to find that the latest technology is not a cure."

One reason for the misunderstanding, he said, is the words that cancer researchers and drug companies often use. "Sometimes by accident, sometimes deliberately, sometimes with the best intentions, sometimes not, we may paint a picture that is overly rosy," he said.

For example, a study may state that a treatment offers a "significant survival advantage" or a "highly significant survival advantage." Too often, Dr. Saltz says, the word "significant" is mistaken to mean "substantial," and "improved survival" is often interpreted as "cure."

Yet in this context, "significant" means "statistically significant," a technical way of saying there is a difference between two groups of patients that is unlikely to have occurred by chance. But the difference could mean simply surviving for a few more weeks or days.

Then there is "progression-free survival," which doctors, researchers and companies use to mean the amount of time from the start of treatment until the tumor starts growing again. It does not mean that a patient lives longer, only that the cancer is controlled longer, perhaps for weeks or, at best, months. A better term would be "progression-free interval," Dr. Saltz said. "You don't need the word 'survival' in there."

As a doctor who tries to be honest with patients, Dr. Saltz says he sees the allure of illusions.

"It would be very hard and insensitive to say, 'All I've got is a drug that will cost $10,000 a month and give you an average survival benefit of a month or two,'" he said. "The details are very, very tough to deal with."

That does not help Ms. Kutt, who chafes at the way breast cancer is presented—the pink ribbons, the celebration of survivors, the emphasis on early detection, as though that will insure you will never get an incurable cancer.

She knows she frightens people with her bald head, so obviously a cancer patient. When someone is on crutches with a broken ankle, strangers offer condolences and ask about the injury. But people avert their eyes when they see Ms. Kutt. Only once, she said, did a stranger approach, and that was a woman who also had breast cancer.

And in her online discussion group of women with metastatic disease, some said they had been asked to leave breast cancer support groups. Members whose cancer had not spread considered themselves survivors, and those whose cancer had spread were too grim a reminder of what could happen.

"It's fear," Ms. Kutt said. "You're part of the death group."

## Selection 8.2

*The next story by health columnist and blogger Tara Parker-Pope starts with a question—not a technique recommended for news or most feature stories, but permissible in a column. As the main writer for both the Well column and the Well blog, Parker-Pope says she tries to present "actionable consumer health information" for the reader. Parker-Pope questions the commonly held view that teenagers are engaging in more sex than in the past. She pokes holes in that misconception through survey data and quotes from expert sources. Parker-Pope parses data from the National Center for Health Statistics by presenting evidence that the increase in births by 15- to 19-year-olds probably "reflects changing patterns in contraceptive use rather than a major change in sexual behavior." In other words, teenagers aren't engaging in more sex, just sex without contraceptives. She adds that the rate of teenage childbearing is much lower now than in the late 1950s. She anticipates the reader's next question by noting that the drop can't be explained by the greater availability of abortions since teenage abortion rates have also decreased. The author fashions an excellent perspective piece by doing two tasks well. She reviews the relevant data, and she anticipates readers' possible criticisms and responds to them.*

### Well

### The Myth of Rampant Teenage Promiscuity

By TARA PARKER-POPE

Have American teenagers gone wild?

Parents have worried for generations about changing moral values and risky behavior among young people, and the latest news seems particularly worrisome.

---

*Published: January 27, 2009.*

It came from the National Center for Health Statistics, which reported this month that births to 15- to 19-year-olds had risen for the first time in more than a decade.

And that is not the only alarm being sounded. The talk show host Tyra Banks declared a teen sex crisis last fall after her show surveyed girls about sexual behavior. A few years ago, Oprah Winfrey warned parents of a teenage oral-sex epidemic.

The news is troubling, but it's also misleading. While some young people are clearly engaging in risky sexual behavior, a vast majority are not. The reality is that in many ways, today's teenagers are more conservative about sex than previous generations.

Today, fewer than half of all high school students have had sex: 47.8 percent as of 2007, according to the National Youth Risk Behavior Survey, down from 54.1 percent in 1991.

A less recent report suggests that teenagers are also waiting longer to have sex than they did in the past. A 2002 report from the Department of Health and Human Services found that 30 percent of 15- to 17-year-old girls had experienced sex, down from 38 percent in 1995. During the same period, the percentage of sexually experienced boys in that age group dropped to 31 percent from 43 percent.

The rates also went down among younger teenagers. In 1995, about 20 percent said they had had sex before age 15, but by 2002 those numbers had dropped to 13 percent of girls and 15 percent of boys.

"There's no doubt that the public perception is that things are getting worse, and that kids are having sex younger and are much wilder than they ever were," said Kathleen A. Bogle, an assistant professor of sociology and criminal justice at La Salle University. "But when you look at the data, that's not the case."

One reason people misconstrue teenage sexual behavior is that the system of dating and relationships has changed significantly. In the first half of the 20th century, dating was planned and structured—and a date might or might not lead to a physical relationship. In recent decades, that pattern has largely been replaced by casual gatherings of teenagers.

In that setting, teenagers often say they "fool around," and in a reversal of the old pattern, such an encounter may or may not lead to regular dating. The shift began around the late 1960s, said Dr. Bogle, who explored the trend in her book "Hooking Up: Sex, Dating and Relationships on Campus" (N.Y.U. Press, 2008).

The latest rise in teenage pregnancy rates is cause for concern. But it very likely reflects changing patterns in contraceptive use rather than a major change in sexual behavior. The reality is that the rate of teenage childbearing has fallen steeply since the late 1950s. The declines aren't explained by the increasing availability of abortions: teenage abortion rates have also dropped.

"There is a group of kids who engage in sexual behavior, but it's not really significantly different than previous generations," said Maria Kefalas, an associate professor of sociology at St. Joseph's University in Philadelphia and co-author of "Promises I Can Keep: Why Poor Women Put Motherhood Before Marriage" (University of California Press, 2005). "This creeping up of teen pregnancy is not because so many more kids are having sex, but most likely because more kids aren't using contraception."

As for that supposed epidemic of oral sex, especially among younger teenagers: national statistics on the behavior have only recently been collected, and they are not as alarming as some reports would have you believe. About 16 percent of teenagers say they have had oral sex but haven't yet had intercourse. Researchers say children's more relaxed attitude about oral sex probably reflects a similar change among adults since the 1950s. In addition, some teenagers may view oral sex as "safer," since unplanned pregnancy is not an issue.

Health researchers say parents who fret about teenage sex often fail to focus on the important lessons they can learn from the kids who aren't having sex. Teenagers with more parental supervision, who come from two-parent households and who are doing well in school are more likely to delay sex until their late teens or beyond.

"For teens, sex requires time and lack of supervision," Dr. Kefalas said. "What's really important for us to pay attention to, as researchers and as parents, are the characteristics of the kids who become pregnant and those who get sexually transmitted diseases.

"This whole moral panic thing misses the point, because research suggests kids who don't use contraception tend to be kids who are feeling lost and disconnected and not doing well."

Although the data is clear, health researchers say it is often hard to convince adults that most teenagers have healthy attitudes about sex.

"I give presentations nationwide where I'm showing people that the virginity rate in college is higher than you think and the number of partners is lower than you think and hooking up more often than not does not mean intercourse," Dr. Bogle said. "But so many people think we're morally in trouble, in a downward spiral and teens are out of control. It's very difficult to convince people otherwise."

## Selection 8.3

*Having regularly covered drug safety as The Times public health reporter, Gardiner Harris knows the subject, sources and history. He relies on all three to report the next story on how antibiotic and other drug manufacturing has left the U.S. Often newspaper stories go on to become longer magazine pieces, but this one went the other way. Gardiner decided to write it after touching on the issue in a much longer article, "The Safety Gap," that appeared in The New York Times Magazine in October 2008. "It was a story that I had done a lot of reporting on, and I just wanted it to find a place in the newspaper," Harris says. The angle of the story—that in the event of a future medical emergency the United States will be totally dependent on pharmaceuticals from other countries, especially China and India—makes this subject noteworthy.*

*His use of an anecdote in his first sentence hooks the reader. In the fifth and sixth paragraphs, Harris lays out the essence of the story to follow. Harris makes his case by providing plenty of details, like the percentage of American pharmaceutical plants mentioned in generic drug applications to the Food and Drug Administration. He tells us what percentage of plants mentioned in the applications were from China and India. He also gives specific examples of drugs manufactured almost exclusively abroad and ends the story with a powerful quote that ties the bow on a scary package for anyone concerned about public health preparedness in the United States.*

## Drug Making's Move Abroad Stirs Concerns

By GARDINER HARRIS

WASHINGTON—In 2004, when Bristol-Myers Squibb said it would close its factory in East Syracuse, N.Y.—the last plant in the United States to manufacture the key ingredients for crucial antibiotics like penicillin—few people worried about the consequences for national security.

"The focus at the time was primarily on job losses in Syracuse," said Rebecca Goldsmith, a company spokeswoman.

But now experts and lawmakers are growing more and more concerned that the nation is far too reliant on medicine from abroad, and they are calling for a law that would require that certain drugs be made or stockpiled in the United States.

"The lack of regulation around outsourcing is a blind spot that leaves room for supply disruptions, counterfeit medicines, even bioterrorism," said Senator Sherrod Brown, Democrat of Ohio, who has held hearings on the issue.

Decades ago, most pills consumed in the United States were made here. But like other manufacturing operations, drug plants have been moving to Asia because labor, construction, regulatory and environmental costs are lower there.

The critical ingredients for most antibiotics are now made almost exclusively in China and India. The same is true for dozens of other crucial medicines, including the popular allergy medicine prednisone; metformin, for diabetes; and amlodipine, for high blood pressure.

---

*Published: January 20, 2009.*

Of the 1,154 pharmaceutical plants mentioned in generic drug applications to the Food and Drug Administration in 2007, only 13 percent were in the United States. Forty-three percent were in China, and 39 percent were in India.

Some of these medicines are lifesaving, and health care in the United States depends on them. Half of all Americans take a prescription medicine every day.

Penicillin, a crucial building block for two classes of antibiotics, tells the story of the shifting pharmaceutical marketplace. Industrial-scale production of penicillin was developed by an American military research group in World War II, and nearly every major drug manufacturer once made it in plants scattered throughout the country.

But beginning in the 1980s, the Chinese government invested huge sums in penicillin fermenters, "disrupting prices around the globe and forcing most Western producers from the market," said Enrico Polastro, a Belgian drug industry consultant who is an expert in antibiotics.

Part of the reason these plants went overseas is that the F.D.A. inspects domestic plants far more often than foreign ones, making production more expensive in the United States.

"U.S. companies are more regulated and are under more scrutiny than foreign producers, particularly those from emerging countries. And that's just totally backwards," said Joe Acker, president of the Synthetic Organic Chemical Manufacturers Association. "We need a level playing field."

The Bush administration spent more than $50 billion after the 2001 anthrax attacks to protect the country from bioterrorism attacks and flu pandemics; some of that money went to increase domestic manufacturing capacity for flu vaccines.

Even so, officials have said that during a pandemic the United States would not be able to rely on vaccines manufactured largely in Europe because of possible border closures and supply shortages. And the situation is similar with antibiotics like penicillin; researchers have found that during the 1918 flu pandemic, most victims died of bacterial infections, not viral ones.

The Centers for Disease Control and Prevention has a stockpile of medicines with enough antibiotics to treat 40 million people. If more are needed, however, the nation lacks the plants to produce them. A penicillin fermenter would take two years to build from scratch, Mr. Polastro said.

Dr. Yusuf K. Hamied, chairman of Cipla, one of the world's most important suppliers of pharmaceutical ingredients, says his company and others have grown increasingly dependent on Chinese suppliers. "If tomorrow China stopped supplying pharmaceutical ingredients, the worldwide pharmaceutical industry would collapse," he said.

Since drug makers often view their supply chains as trade secrets, the true source of a drug's ingredients can be difficult or impossible to discover. The F.D.A. has a public listing of drug suppliers, called drug master files. But the listing is neither up to date nor entirely reliable, because drug makers are not required to disclose supplier information.

One federal database lists nearly 3,000 overseas drug plants that export to the United States; the other lists 6,800 plants. Nobody knows which is right.

Drug labels often claim that the pills are manufactured in the United States, but the listed plants are often the sites where foreign-made drug powders are pounded into pills and packaged.

"Pharmaceutical companies do not like to reveal where their sources are," for fear that competitors will steal their suppliers, Mr. Polastro said.

China's position as the pre-eminent supplier of medicines is a result of government policy, said Guy Villax, the chief executive of Hovione, a maker of crucial drug ingredients with plants in Portugal and China.

The regional government in Shanghai has promised to pay local drug makers about $15,000 for any drug approval they garner from the F.D.A. and about $5,000 for any approval from European regulators, according to a document Mr. Villax provided.

"This shows that there has been a government plan in China to become a pharmaceutical industry leader," Mr. Villax said.

The world's growing dependence on Chinese drug manufacturers became apparent in the heparin scare. A year ago, Baxter International and APP Pharmaceuticals split the domestic market for heparin, an anticlotting drug needed for surgery and dialysis.

When federal drug regulators discovered that Baxter's product had been contaminated by Chinese suppliers, the F.D.A. banned Baxter's product and turned almost exclusively to the one from APP. But APP also got its product from China.

So for now, like it or not, China has the upper hand. As Mr. Polastro put it, "If China ever got very upset with President Obama, it could be a big problem."

## Selection 8.4

*The death of television newsman Tim Russert in 2008 raised concerns among many middle-aged and older people that they too could die from a sudden heart attack. Russert had no known heart disease symptoms, but he carried risk factors because he was overweight and had high blood pressure, for which he was taking medication. In the next story medical reporter Denise Grady reviews what was known about Russert's medical condition and puts his risk for sudden death in perspective. She sets up her story with a lede that helps readers identify with Russert. Grady then references dozens of e-mails from readers who insisted "that something must have been missed" to explain Russert's sudden death. In response, Grady talks to experts who concede that they can't identify higher short-term risk in all people. The bottom line, she tells us, is that doctors can't predict who is going to die suddenly from a heart attack—not very reassuring, but definitely a perspective worth knowing.*

## Second Opinion
## From a Prominent Death, Some Painful Truths

By DENISE GRADY

Apart from its sadness, Tim Russert's death this month at 58 was deeply unsettling to many people who, like him, had been earnestly following their doctors' advice on drugs, diet and exercise in hopes of avoiding a heart attack.

Mr. Russert, the moderator of "Meet the Press" on NBC News, took blood pressure and cholesterol pills and aspirin, rode an exercise bike, had yearly stress tests and other exams and was dutifully trying to lose weight. But he died of a heart attack anyway.

An article in The New York Times last week about his medical care led to e-mail from dozens of readers insisting that something must have been missed, that if only he had been given this test or that, his doctors would have realized how sick he was and prescribed more medicine or recommended bypass surgery.

Clearly, there was sorrow for Mr. Russert's passing, but also nervous indignation. Many people are in the same boat he was in, struggling with weight, blood pressure and other risk factors—16 million Americans have coronary artery disease—and his death threatened the collective sense of well-being. People are not supposed to die this way anymore, especially not smart, well-educated professionals under the care of doctors.

Mr. Russert's fate underlines some painful truths. A doctor's care is not a protective bubble, and cardiology is not the exact science that many people wish it to be. A person's risk of a heart attack can only be estimated, and although drugs, diet and exercise may lower that risk, they cannot eliminate it entirely. True, the death rate from heart disease has declined, but it is still the leading cause of death in the United States, killing 650,000 people a year. About 300,000 die suddenly, and about half, like Mr. Russert, have no symptoms.

---

*Published: June 24, 2008.*

Cardiologists say that although they can identify people who have heart disease or risk factors for it, they are not so good at figuring out which are in real danger of having an attack soon, say in the next year or so. If those patients could be pinpointed, doctors say, they would feel justified in treating them aggressively with drugs and, possibly, surgery.

"It's the real dilemma we have in cardiology today," said Dr. Sidney Smith, a professor of medicine at the University of North Carolina and a past president of the American Heart Association. "Is it possible to identify the group at higher short-term risk?"

What killed Mr. Russert was a plaque rupture. A fatty, pimple-like lesion in a coronary artery burst, and a blood clot formed that closed the vessel and cut off circulation to part of the heart muscle. It was a typical heart attack, or myocardial infarction, an event that occurs 1.2 million times a year in the United States, killing 456,000 people.

In Mr. Russert's case, the heart attack led to a second catastrophe, an abnormal heart rhythm that caused cardiac arrest and quickly killed him. An electric shock from a defibrillator might have restarted his heart if it had been given promptly when he collapsed at his desk. But it was apparently delayed.

Dr. Smith and other cardiologists say the main problem is that there is no way to figure out who has "vulnerable plaques," those prone to rupture. Researchers are trying to find biomarkers, substances in the blood that can show the presence of these dangerous, ticking time-bomb plaques. So far, no biomarker has proved very accurate.

Mr. Russert's heart disease was a mixed picture. Some factors looked favorable. There was no family history of heart attacks. Though he had high blood pressure, drugs lowered it pretty well, said his internist, Dr. Michael A. Newman. His total cholesterol was not high, nor was his LDL, the bad type of cholesterol, or his C-reactive protein, a measure of inflammation that is thought to contribute to plaque rupture. He did not smoke. At his last physical, in April, he passed a stress test, and his heart function was good. Dr. Newman estimated his risk of a heart attack in the next 10 years at 5 percent, based on a widely used calculator.

On the negative side, Mr. Russert had low HDL, the protective cholesterol, and high triglycerides. He was quite overweight; a waist more than 40 inches in men increases heart risk. A CT scan of his coronary arteries in 1998 gave a calcium score of 210, indicating artery disease—healthy arteries do not have calcium deposits—and a moderate to high risk of a heart attack. An echocardiogram in April found that the main heart pumping chamber had thickened, his ability to exercise had decreased slightly, and his blood pressure had increased a bit. Dr. Newman and his cardiologist, Dr. George Bren, changed his blood pressure medicines, and the pressure lowered to 120/80, Dr. Newman said.

Another blood test, for a substance called apoB, might have been a better measure of risk than LDL, some doctors say. Others disagree.

Some doctors say people like Mr. Russert, with no symptoms but risk factors like a thickened heart, should have angiograms, in which a catheter is threaded into the coronary arteries, dye is injected, and X-rays are taken to look for blockages. Some advocate less invasive CT angiograms. Both types of angiogram can identify plaque deposits, and if extensive disease or blockages at critical points are found, a bypass is usually recommended. But the tests still cannot tell if plaques are likely to rupture, Dr. Smith and other cardiologists say. And Mr. Russert's doctors did not think that an angiogram was needed.

An autopsy found, in addition to the plaque rupture, extensive disease in Mr. Russert's coronary arteries, enough to surprise his doctors, they said. Had they found it before, Dr Newman said, a bypass would have been recommended. Dr. Bren differed, saying many cardiologists would still not have advised surgery.

Given all the uncertainties, what's a patient to do?

"You want to be sure your blood pressure and lipids are controlled, that you're not smoking, and you have the right waist circumference," Dr. Smith said.

Statins can reduce the risk of dying from a heart attack by 30 percent, he said.

"But what about the other 70 percent?" Dr. Smith asked. "There are other things we need to understand. There's tremendous promise, but miles to go before we sleep."

## Selection 8.5

*In the next story Dr. Lawrence K. Altman reviews how journals miss flawed research. Since this piece is identified as a column and is written by a veteran physician journalist with considerable medical experience, the writer can rely less on sources than the average reporter. Altman provides a peek behind the curtain, an inside view that few outside the scientific world have. He provides perspective by telling readers how the peer review process works and how outright fraud or poorly designed studies can find their way to publication. The young reporter can find the same facts as Altman but may have difficulty writing with the conviction of a 40-year reporting veteran. Still, the young medical reporter can approach sources with a critical eye. "Question the reasoning, question the statements," Altman says in an interview for this book. "In all types of journalism you should have a degree of healthy skepticism not to accept something as a fait accompli."*

## The Doctor's World
# For Science's Gatekeepers, a Credibility Gap

By LAWRENCE K. ALTMAN, M.D.

Recent disclosures of fraudulent or flawed studies in medical and scientific journals have called into question as never before the merits of their peer-review system.

The system is based on journals inviting independent experts to critique submitted manuscripts. The stated aim is to weed out sloppy and bad research, ensuring the integrity of what it has published.

Because findings published in peer-reviewed journals affect patient care, public policy and the authors' academic promotions, journal editors contend that new scientific information should be published in a peer-reviewed journal before it is presented to doctors and the public.

That message, however, has created a widespread misimpression that passing peer review is the scientific equivalent of the Good Housekeeping seal of approval.

Virtually every major scientific and medical journal has been humbled recently by publishing findings that are later discredited. The flurry of episodes has led many people to ask why authors, editors and independent expert reviewers all failed to detect the problems before publication.

The publication process is complex. Many factors can allow error, even fraud, to slip through. They include economic pressures for journals to avoid investigating suspected errors; the desire to avoid displeasing the authors and the experts who review manuscripts; and the fear that angry scientists will withhold the manuscripts that are the lifeline of the journals, putting them out of business. By promoting the sanctity of peer review and using it to justify a number of their actions in recent years, journals have added to their enormous power.

The release of news about scientific and medical findings is among the most tightly managed in country. Journals control when the public learns about findings from taxpayer-supported research by setting dates when the research can be published. They also impose severe restrictions on what authors can say publicly, even before they submit a manuscript, and they have penalized authors for infractions by refusing to publish their papers. Exceptions are made for scientific meetings and health emergencies.

But many authors have still withheld information for fear that journals would pull their papers for an infraction. Increasingly, journals and authors' institutions also send out news releases ahead of time

*Published: May 2, 2006.*

about a peer-reviewed discovery so that reports from news organizations coincide with a journal's date of issue.

A barrage of news reports can follow. But often the news release is sent without the full paper, so reports may be based only on the spin created by a journal or an institution.

Journal editors say publicity about corrections and retractions distorts and erodes confidence in science, which is an honorable business. Editors also say they are gatekeepers, not detectives, and that even though peer review is not intended to detect fraud, it catches flawed research and improves the quality of the thousands of published papers.

However, even the system's most ardent supporters acknowledge that peer review does not eliminate mediocre and inferior papers and has never passed the very test for which it is used. Studies have found that journals publish findings based on sloppy statistics. If peer review were a drug, it would never be marketed, say critics, including journal editors.

None of the recent flawed studies have been as humiliating as an article in 1972 in the journal Pediatrics that labeled sudden infant death syndrome a hereditary disorder, when, in the case examined, the real cause was murder.

Twenty-three years later, the mother was convicted of smothering her five children. Scientific naïveté surely contributed to the false conclusion, but a forensic pathologist was not one of the reviewers. The faulty research in part prompted the National Institutes of Health to spend millions of dollars on a wrong line of research.

Fraud, flawed articles and corrections have haunted general interest news organizations. But such problems are far more embarrassing for scientific journals because of their claims for the superiority of their system of editing.

A widespread belief among nonscientists is that journal editors and their reviewers check authors' research firsthand and even repeat the research. In fact, journal editors do not routinely examine authors' scientific notebooks. Instead, they rely on peer reviewers' criticisms, which are based on the information submitted by the authors.

While editors and reviewers may ask authors for more information, journals and their invited experts examine raw data only under the most unusual circumstances.

In that respect, journal editors are like newspaper editors, who check the content of reporters' copy for facts and internal inconsistencies but generally not their notes. Still, journal editors have refused to call peer review what many others say it is—a form of vetting or technical editing.

In spot checks, many scientists and nonscientists said they believed that editors decided what to publish by counting reviewers' votes. But journal editors say that they are not tally clerks and that decisions to publish are theirs, not the reviewers'.

Editors say they have accepted a number of papers that reviewers have harshly criticized as unworthy of publication and have rejected many that received high plaudits.

Many nonscientists perceive reviewers to be impartial. But the reviewers, called independent experts, in fact are often competitors of the authors of the papers they scrutinize, raising potential conflicts of interest.

Except when gaffes are publicized, there is little scrutiny of the quality of what journals publish.

Journals have rejected calls to make the process scientific by conducting random audits like those used to monitor quality control in medicine. The costs and the potential for creating distrust are the most commonly cited reasons for not auditing.

In defending themselves, journal editors often shift blame to the authors and excuse themselves and their peer reviewers.

Journals seldom investigate frauds that they have published, contending that they are not investigative bodies and that they could not afford the costs. Instead, the journals say that the investigations are up to the accused authors' employers and agencies that financed the research.

Editors also insist that science corrects its errors. But corrections often require whistle-blowers or prodding by lawyers. Editors at The New England Journal of Medicine said they would not have learned about a problem that led them to publish two letters of concern about omission of data concerning the arthritis drug Vioxx unless lawyers for the drug's manufacturer, Merck, had asked them questions in depositions. Fraud has also slipped through in part because editors have long been loath to question the authors.

"A request from an editor for primary data to support the honesty of an author's findings in a manuscript under review would probably poison the air and make civil discourse between authors and editors even more difficult than it is now," Dr. Arnold S. Relman wrote in 1983. At the time, he was editor of The New England Journal of Medicine, and it had published a fraudulent paper.

Fraud is a substantial problem, and the attitude toward it has changed little over the years, other editors say. Some journals fail to retract known cases of fraud for fear of lawsuits.

Journals have no widely accepted way to retract papers, said Donald Kennedy, editor in chief of Science, after the it retracted two papers by the South Korean researcher Dr. Hwang Woo Suk, who fabricated evidence that he had cloned human cells.

In the April 18 issue of Annals of Internal Medicine, its editor, Dr. Harold C. Sox, wrote about lessons learned after the journal retracted an article on menopause by Dr. Eric Poehlman of the University of Vermont.

When an author is found to have fabricated data in one paper, scientists rarely examine all of that author's publications, so the scientific literature may be more polluted than believed, Dr. Sox said.

Dr. Sox and other scientists have documented that invalid work is not effectively purged from the scientific literature because the authors of new papers continue to cite retracted ones.

When journals try to retract discredited papers, Dr. Sox said, the process is slow, and the system used to inform readers faulty. Authors often use euphemisms instead of the words "fabrication" or "research misconduct," and finding published retractions can be costly because some affected journals charge readers a fee to visit their Web sites to learn about them, Dr. Sox said.

Despite its flaws, scientists favor the system in part because they need to publish or perish. The institutions where the scientists work and the private and government agencies that pay for their grants seek publicity in their eagerness to show financial backers results for their efforts.

The public and many scientists tend to overlook the journals' economic benefits that stem from linking their embargo policies to peer review. Some journals are owned by private for-profit companies, while others are owned by professional societies that rely on income from the journals. The costs of running journals are low because authors and reviewers are generally not paid.

A few journals that not long ago measured profits in the tens of thousands of dollars a year now make millions, according to at least three editors who agreed to discuss finances only if granted anonymity, because they were not authorized to speak about finances.

Any influential system that profits from taxpayer-financed research should be held publicly accountable for how the revenues are spent. Journals generally decline to disclose such data.

Although editors of some journals say they demand statements from their editing staff members that they have no financial conflicts of interest, there is no way to be sure. At least one editor of a leading American journal had to resign because of conflicts of interest with industry.

Journals have devolved into information-laundering operations for the pharmaceutical industry, say Dr. Richard Smith, the former editor of BMJ, the British medical journal, and Dr. Richard Horton, the editor of The Lancet, also based in Britain.

The journals rely on revenues from industry advertisements. But because journals also profit handsomely by selling drug companies reprints of articles reporting findings from large clinical trials involving their products, editors may "face a frighteningly stark conflict of interest" in deciding whether to publish such a study, Dr. Smith said.

## Selection 8.6

*Perhaps no recent issue in medicine has been more charged than allegations of a link between thimerosal—a mercury-containing preservative once routinely used in childhood vaccines—and autism. In the next story Gardiner Harris and Anahad O'Connor put the topic in perspective. Although reporters who cover other subjects, such as a hotly contested election, must be careful to provide balance and not take sides, Harris says those rules don't apply to a science story when the preponderance of scientific opinion weighs much more heavily on one side. Harris says the report that follows was a landmark story because, until its publication in The New York Times, many media organizations were airing the claim that thimerosal might be responsible for an increase in the incidence of autism. "After our story came out, those other more credulous pieces in other media really stopped for many years," Harris says.*

*Note how Harris and O'Connor provide documentation to make their case. They cite five well-respected scientific organizations and five major studies, all of which dismiss the notion that thimerosal leads to autism. The reporters acknowledge the one researcher who says he's found a link, but they quote scientists who say that the researcher's studies relied on flawed methodology. With this story, Harris and O'Connor took on a well-organized and vocal group of parents, many of whom are convinced that vaccines with thimerosal caused their children's autism. But the reporters have done their homework, researched the studies and know the science. That's the recipe for reporting a perspective piece on a red-hot topic.*

## On Autism's Cause, It's Parents vs. Research

By GARDINER HARRIS AND ANAHAD O'CONNOR

Kristen Ehresmann, a Minnesota Department of Health official, had just told a State Senate hearing that vaccines with microscopic amounts of mercury were safe. Libby Rupp, a mother of a 3-year-old girl with autism, was incredulous.

"How did my daughter get so much mercury in her?" Ms. Rupp asked Ms. Ehresmann after her testimony.

"Fish?" Ms. Ehresmann suggested.

"She never eats it," Ms. Rupp answered.

"Do you drink tap water?"

"It's all filtered."

"Well, do you breathe the air?" Patricia Segal-Freeman, a colleague of Ms. Ehresmann at the Health Department, asked, with a resigned smile. Several parents looked angrily at Ms. Ehresmann, who left.

Ms. Rupp remained, shaking with anger. That anyone could defend mercury in vaccines, she said, "makes my blood boil."

---

*Published: June 25, 2005.*

### Autism and Vaccinations

In 2003, the Institute of Medicine, an arm of the National Academy of Sciences, reviewed research into autism and thimerosal, a mercury-based preservative once routinely used in childhood vaccines. The Institute's 2004 report rejected a link between vaccines and autism. It was based on more than 200 studies, including those shown here.

| RESEARCHERS | **Anders Hviid, et al.** | **Dr. Thomas Verstraeten, et al.** | **Dr. Kreesten Meldgaard Madsen, et al.** |
|---|---|---|---|
| WHERE PUBLISHED | Journal of the American Medical Association | Pediatrics | Pediatrics |
| DESCRIPTION | Assessed outcomes for 467,450 Danish children who received thimerosal vaccines from 1990 to1996. Autism incidence increased after thimerosal was eliminated in 1992. | Analyzed vaccine histories in H.M.O. databases to determine any link between mercury content and autism in 125,000 children born from 1991 to1999. No associations between thimerosal and autism were found. | Studied Danish children whose condition was diagnosed as autism from 1971 to 2000. Autism began to increase in 1991 and continued to rise after the discontinuation of thimerosal. |
| DID RESEARCH FIND A LINK BETWEEN AUTISM AND THIMEROSAL? | NO | NO | NO |

Public health officials like Ms. Ehresmann, who herself has a son with autism, have been trying for years to convince parents like Ms. Rupp that there is no link between thimerosal—a mercury-containing preservative once used routinely in vaccines—and autism.

They have failed.

The Centers for Disease Control and Prevention, the Food and Drug Administration, the Institute of Medicine, the World Health Organization and the American Academy of Pediatrics have all largely dismissed the notion that thimerosal causes or contributes to autism. Five major studies have found no link.

Yet despite all evidence to the contrary, the number of parents who blame thimerosal for their children's autism has only increased. And in recent months, these parents have used their numbers, their passion and their organizing skills to become a potent national force. The issue has become one of the most fractious and divisive in pediatric medicine.

"This is like nothing I've ever seen before," Dr. Melinda Wharton, deputy director of the National Immunization Program, told a gathering of immunization officials in Washington in March. "It's an era where it appears that science isn't enough."

Parents have filed more than 4,800 lawsuits—200 from February to April alone—pushed for state and federal legislation banning thimerosal and taken out full-page advertisements in major newspapers. They have also gained the support of politicians, including Senator Joseph I. Lieberman, Democrat of Connecticut, and Representatives Dan Burton, Republican of Indiana, and Dave Weldon, Republican of Florida. And Robert F. Kennedy Jr. wrote an article in the June 16 issue of Rolling Stone magazine arguing that most studies of the issue

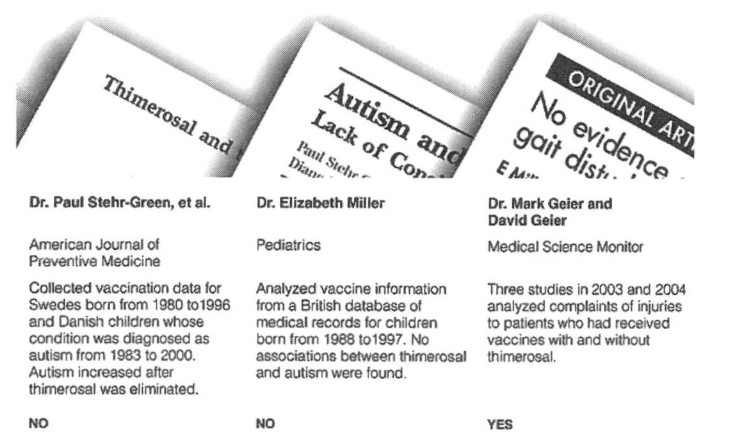

Thimerosal and
Autism and
No evidence
Dr. Paul Stehr-Green, et al.
American Journal of Preventive Medicine
Collected vaccination data for Swedes born from 1980 to1996 and Danish children whose condition was diagnosed as autism from 1983 to 2000. Autism increased after thimerosal was eliminated.
NO
Dr. Elizabeth Miller
Pediatrics
Analyzed vaccine information from a British database of medical records for children born from 1988 to1997. No associations between thimerosal and autism were found.
NO
Dr. Mark Geier and David Geier
Medical Science Monitor
Three studies in 2003 and 2004 analyzed complaints of injuries to patients who had received vaccines with and without thimerosal.
YES


The New York Times

are flawed and that public health officials are conspiring with drug makers to cover up the damage caused by thimerosal.

"We're not looking like a fringe group anymore," said Becky Lourey, a Minnesota state senator and a sponsor of a proposed thimerosal ban. Such a ban passed the New York State Legislature this week.

But scientists and public health officials say they are alarmed by the surge of attention to an idea without scientific merit. The anti-thimerosal campaign, they say, is causing some parents to stay away from vaccines, placing their children at risk for illnesses like measles and polio.

"It's really terrifying, the scientific illiteracy that supports these suspicions," said Dr. Marie McCormick, chairwoman of an Institute of Medicine panel that examined the controversy in February 2004.

Experts say they are also concerned about a raft of unproven, costly and potentially harmful treatments—including strict diets, supplements and a detoxifying technique called chelation—that are being sold for tens of thousands of dollars to desperate parents of autistic children as a cure for "mercury poisoning."

In one case, a doctor forced children to sit in a 160-degree sauna, swallow 60 to 70 supplements a day and have so much blood drawn that one child passed out.

Hundreds of doctors list their names on a Web site endorsing chelation to treat autism, even though experts say that no evidence supports its use with that disorder. The treatment carries risks of liver and kidney damage, skin rashes and nutritional deficiencies, they say.

In recent months, the fight over thimerosal has become even more bitter. In response to a barrage of threatening letters and phone calls, the Centers for Disease Control has increased security and instructed employees on safety issues, including how to respond if pies are thrown in their faces. One vaccine expert at the centers wrote in an internal e-mail message that she felt safer working at a malaria field station in Kenya than she did at the agency's offices in Atlanta.

## An Alarm Is Sounded

Thimerosal was for decades the favored preservative for use in vaccines. By weight, it is about 50 percent ethyl mercury, a form of mercury most scientists consider to be less toxic than methyl mercury, the type found in fish. The amount of ethyl mercury included in each childhood vaccine was once roughly equal to the amount of methyl mercury found in the average tuna sandwich.

In 1999, a Food and Drug Administration scientist added up all the mercury that American infants got with a full immunization schedule and concluded that the amount exceeded a government guideline. Some health authorities counseled no action, because there was no evidence that thimerosal at the doses given was harmful and removing it might cause alarm. Others were not so certain that thimerosal was harmless.

In July 1999, the American Academy of Pediatrics and the Public Health Service released a joint statement urging vaccine makers to remove thimerosal as quickly as possible. By 2001, no vaccine routinely administered to children in the United States had more than half of a microgram of mercury—about what is found in an infant's daily supply of breast milk.

Despite the change, government agencies say that vaccines with thimerosal are just as safe as those without, and adult flu vaccines still contain the preservative.

But the 1999 advisory alarmed many parents whose children suffered from autism, a lifelong disorder marked by repetitive, sometimes self-destructive behaviors and an inability to form social relationships. In 10 to 25 percent of cases, autism seems to descend on young children seemingly overnight, sometime between their first and second birthdays.

Diagnoses of autism have risen sharply in recent years, from roughly 1 case for every 10,000 births in the 1980's to 1 in 166 births in 2003.

Most scientists believe that the illness is influenced strongly by genetics but that some unknown environmental factor may also play a role.

Dr. Tom Insel, director of the National Institute for Mental Health, said: "Is it cellphones? Ultrasound? Diet sodas? Every parent has a theory. At this point, we just don't know."

In 2000, a group of parents joined together to found SafeMinds, one of several organizations that argue that thimerosal is that environmental culprit. Their cause has been championed by politicians like Mr. Burton.

"My grandson received nine shots in one day, seven of which contained thimerosal, which is 50 percent mercury as you know, and he became autistic a short time later," he said in an interview.

In a series of House hearings held from 2000 through 2004, Mr. Burton called the leading experts who assert that vaccines cause autism to testify. They included a chemistry professor at the University of Kentucky who says that dental fillings cause or exacerbate autism and other diseases and a doctor from Baton Rouge, La., who says that God spoke to her through an 87-year-old priest and told her that vaccines caused autism.

Also testifying were Dr. Mark Geier and his son, David Geier, the experts whose work is most frequently cited by parents.

## Trying to Build a Case

Dr. Geier has called the use of thimerosal in vaccines the world's "greatest catastrophe that's ever happened, regardless of cause."

He and his son live and work in a two-story house in suburban Maryland. Past the kitchen and down the stairs is a room with cast-off, unplugged laboratory equipment, wall-to-wall carpeting and faux wood paneling that Dr. Geier calls "a world-class lab—every bit as good as anything at N.I.H."

Dr. Geier has been examining issues of vaccine safety since at least 1971, when he was a lab assistant at the National Institutes of Health, or N.I.H. His résumé lists scores of publications, many of which suggest that vaccines cause injury or disease.

He has also testified in more than 90 vaccine cases, he said, although a judge in a vaccine case in 2003 ruled that Dr. Geier was "a professional witness in areas for which he has no training, expertise and experience."

In other cases, judges have called Dr. Geier's testimony "intellectually dishonest," "not reliable" and "wholly unqualified."

The six published studies by Dr. Geier and David Geier on the relationship between autism and thimerosal are largely based on complaints sent to the disease control centers by people who suspect that their children were harmed by vaccines.

In the first study, the Geiers compared the number of complaints associated with a thimerosal-containing vaccine, given from 1992 to 2000, with the complaints that resulted from a thimerosal-free version given from 1997 to 2000. The more thimerosal a child received, they concluded, the more likely an autism complaint was filed. Four other studies used similar methods and came to similar conclusions.

Dr. Geier said in an interview that the link between thimerosal and autism was clear.

Public health officials, he said, are "just trying to cover it up."

## Assessing the Studies

Scientists say that the Geiers' studies are tainted by faulty methodology.

"The problem with the Geiers' research is that they start with the answers and work backwards," said Dr. Steven Black, director of the Kaiser Permanente Vaccine Study Center in Oakland, Calif. "They are doing voodoo science."

Dr. Julie L. Gerberding, the director of the disease control centers, said the agency was not withholding information about any potentially damaging effects of thimerosal.

"There's certainly not a conspiracy here," she said. "And we would never consider not acknowledging information or evidence that would have a bearing on children's health."

In 2003, spurred by parents' demands, the C.D.C. asked the Institute of Medicine, an arm of the National Academy of Sciences and the nation's most prestigious medical advisory group, to review the evidence on thimerosal and autism.

In a report last year, a panel convened by the institute dismissed the Geiers' work as having such serious flaws that their studies were "uninterpretable." Some of the Geiers' mathematical formulas, the committee found, "provided no information," and the Geiers used basic scientific terms like "attributable risk" incorrectly.

In contrast, the committee found five studies that examined hundreds of thousands of health records of children in the United States, Britain, Denmark and Sweden to be persuasive.

A study by the World Health Organization, for example, examined the health records of 109,863 children born in Britain from 1988 to 1997 and found that children who had received the most thimerosal in vaccines had the lowest incidence of developmental problems like autism.

Another study examined the records of 467,450 Danish children born from 1990 to 1996. It found that after 1992, when the country's only thimerosal-containing vaccine was replaced by one free of the preservative, autism rates rose rather than fell.

In one of the most comprehensive studies, a 2003 report by C.D.C. scientists examined the medical records of more than 125,000 children born in the United States from 1991 to 1999. It found no difference in autism rates among children exposed to various amounts of thimerosal.

Parent groups, led by SafeMinds, replied that documents obtained from the disease control centers showed that early versions of the study had found a link between thimerosal and autism.

But C.D.C. researchers said that it was not unusual for studies to evolve as more data and controls were added. The early versions of the study, they said, failed to control for factors like low birth weight, which increases the risk of developmental delays.

The Institute of Medicine said that it saw "nothing inherently troubling" with the C.D.C.'s adjustments and concluded that thimerosal did not cause autism. Further studies, the institute said, would not be "useful."

## Threats and Conspiracy Talk

Since the report's release, scientists and health officials have been bombarded with hostile e-mail messages and phone calls. Dr. McCormick, the chairwoman of the institute's panel, said she had received threatening mail claiming that she was part of a conspiracy. Harvard University has increased security at her office, she said.

An e-mail message to the C.D.C. on Nov. 28 stated, "Forgiveness is between them and God. It is my job to arrange a meeting," according to records obtained by The New York Times after the filing of an open records request.

Another e-mail message, sent to the C.D.C. on Aug. 20, said, "I'd like to know how you people sleep straight in bed at night knowing all the lies you tell & the lives you know full well you destroy with the poisons you push & protect with your lies." Lyn Redwood of SafeMinds said that such e-mail messages did not represent her organization or other advocacy groups.

In response to the threats, C.D.C. officials have contacted the Federal Bureau of Investigation and heightened security at the disease control centers. Some officials said that the threats had led them to look for other jobs.

In "Evidence of Harm," a book published earlier this year that is sympathetic to the notion that thimerosal causes autism, the author, David Kirby, wrote that the thimerosal theory would stand or fall within the next year or two.

Because autism is usually diagnosed sometime between a child's third and fourth birthdays and thimerosal was largely removed from childhood vaccines in 2001, the incidence of autism should fall this year, he said.

No such decline followed thimerosal's removal from vaccines during the 1990's in Denmark, Sweden or Canada, researchers say.

But the debate over autism and vaccines is not likely to end soon.

"It doesn't seem to matter what the studies and the data show," said Ms. Ehresmann, the Minnesota immunization official. "And that's really scary for us because if science doesn't count, how do we make decisions? How do we communicate with parents?"

# MAKING CONNECTIONS

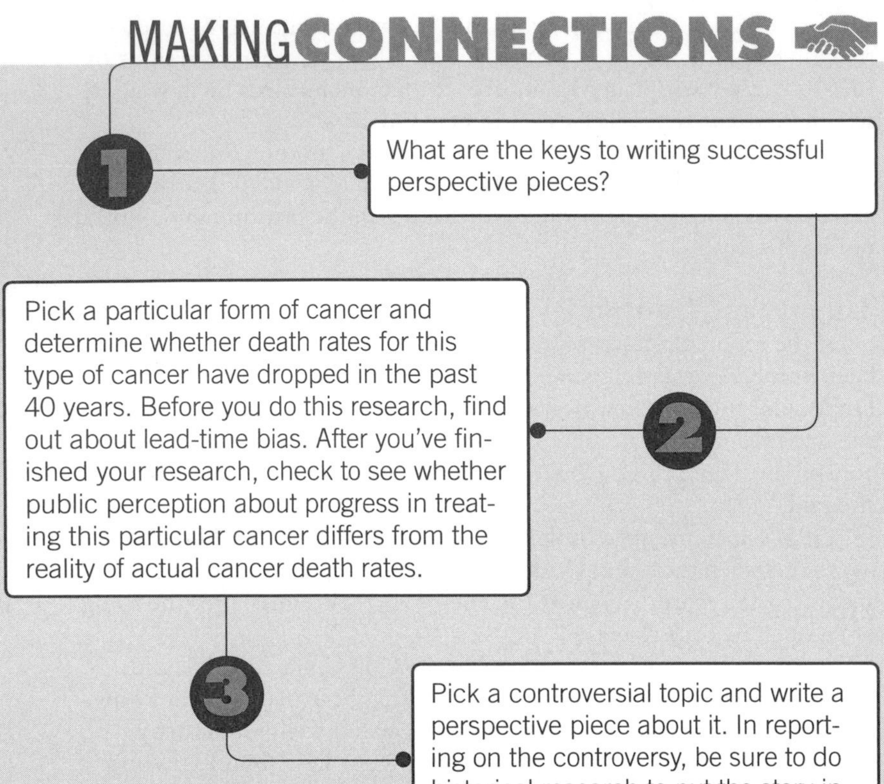

1
What are the keys to writing successful perspective pieces?
2
Pick a particular form of cancer and determine whether death rates for this type of cancer have dropped in the past 40 years. Before you do this research, find out about lead-time bias. After you've finished your research, check to see whether public perception about progress in treating this particular cancer differs from the reality of actual cancer death rates.
3
Pick a controversial topic and write a perspective piece about it. In reporting on the controversy, be sure to do historical research to put the story in perspective.

CHAPTER 9

# historical stories

HISTORICAL ARTICLES GIVE READERS the long view on medical and health topics. The spark for the story can come from a current news item or the anniversary of an important medical milestone or event. As cases of swine flu appeared in 2009, for example, readers' interest in the so-called Spanish influenza pandemic of 1918–1919 increased. The awarding of a Nobel Prize might prompt a story on the winner's area of scientific achievement, while the discovery of a new treatment for an old disease could spur a reporter to take a look back.

In The New York Times, historical features typically appear in the Tuesday Science Times section. For the reporter, researching a history piece includes poring over archives, interviewing sources with various points of view and, sometimes, as in the two pieces in this chapter, drawing from personal experience.

The New York Times

***LEAD COCOON*** *Dr. William S. Altman practiced radiology at home.*

## Selection 9.1

*The next story by medical reporter Dr. Lawrence K. Altman takes the unusual approach of combining a profile of his father, a radiologist, with a reflection on more than 110 years of radiologic history. Although he doesn't mention it in the story, Altman says his 70th birthday and the timing of the article's publication on Father's Day led to the idea. He wanted to write about changes in the field of radiology since 1895, when Wilhelm K. Roentgen discovered X-rays, and he realized that a first-person account "allowed me to provide insight that somebody who didn't have that upbringing or didn't come from a medical family" would not have.*

*Altman's weaving of history with personal observations gives the story authenticity. Colorful family anecdotes enliven what could otherwise be a dry account. Note Altman's short sentences and wonderful turns of phrase, like the one in the lede. Also note his attention to detail, the hallmark of a good reporter. We learn exactly where his father stored radium, what protective gear he wore, what his machines looked like, and what life in a house that doubled as a doctor's office felt like, sounded like and even smelled like to a boy growing up. The final detail in the story, the most telling, explains why Altman chose to be a medical journalist.*

### The Doctor's World
### Radiology Was Young, and So Was I

By LAWRENCE K. ALTMAN, M.D.

Some people are born with silver spoons in their mouths. I grew up in a lead cocoon.

My father, Dr. William S. Altman, known as Sol, was a radiologist, and his office and its X-ray machines occupied the first floor of our house in Quincy, Mass. To protect his staff members, his patients and our family from scatter radiation, he lined many walls, floors and doors with lead sheets. We learned to open and close those heavy doors carefully to avoid jamming a finger.

Whether for convenience or frugality, many doctors, even in a technically oriented field like radiology, practiced in a home office until shortly after World War II.

As I turn 70 today, I am reminded of this piece of Americana that has largely disappeared. Into the 1970s, X-rays helped detect many diseases, but changed the course of few.

Radiology has made major advances since Wilhelm K. Roentgen discovered X-rays in 1895 in Germany, providing the first opportunity to see inside a body without opening it up.

---

*Published: June 19, 2007.*

CT scans take radiographic slices of the body in details Roentgen could not have imagined. Interventional radiologists perform surgery guided by X-ray images to stop bleeding from the intestines, prevent some strokes and treat other problems. Use of radium furthered development of other radioactive isotopes that produce images to detect thyroid and other glandular abnormalities.

These and other imaging techniques not based on radiation, like ultrasound and magnetic resonance imaging, now spare many patients exploratory operations and improve the precision of surgery.

My father was a man of enormous patience and a wonderful sense of humor who liked dealing with people. All of that contributed to an excellent bedside manner. In the early 1930s, after a year in general medicine, he became one of the first trained radiologists in this country. He changed fields in part because of a love of tinkering that he learned from his own father, who was an electrician.

Fully respecting the hazards of radiation, he always wore cumbersome but protective lead aprons and gloves while working, unlike some colleagues, who later succumbed to leukemia and other blood ailments. He lived to 83; those who died younger included general practitioners who took X-rays in their offices.

My father, like many radiologists, split the day between home and hospital offices.

Occasionally he wrote scientific articles and reviews. Twice a week he volunteered to teach at Tufts University, where he and I attended medical school, and to join colleagues who shared X-rays of their most perplexing or interesting cases.

Routine use of X-rays caught on slowly in this country. In important ways, American radiology was a specialty imported from Germany. In bringing their expertise and equipment, German and Austrian refugee radiologists made Boston an early national leader in the field.

The name of one, Dr. Richard Schatzki, is now attached to a circular narrowing of the esophagus—a Schatzki ring—that causes food to stick in the gullet of many patients.

In time, American leaders emerged, and they joined the conferences when visiting Boston. One, Dr. Henry S. Kaplan, cured a case of Hodgkin's disease with radiation at Stanford, and I studied with him there as a visiting medical student.

Radiologists were said to work regular hours, but that was a myth. Often a middle-of-the-night call from the hospital would summon my father to look at the X-rays of accident victims and patients needing emergency surgery. He considered the trips a normal part of his job.

While emergency X-rays were performed at the local hospital, office practices handled elective cases. Some patients rang the office bell because they wanted an X-ray and expected it on demand, even in the middle of the night. My father explained calmly that radiologists never accepted a patient without a doctor's referral.

The office telephone also rang in our living quarters because doctors and patients called at all hours to make appointments. My mother (Esther), my sister (Dorothy) or I would record an agreed-upon time in the appointment book and pass on to the patient instructions like not eating or drinking from midnight before the day of the requested procedure.

Radiologists sometimes made house calls, usually for patients bedridden with a fractured hip. Dad's "black bag" was a portable X-ray machine the size of a large suitcase and heavy. Use of portable X-rays was limited, because the radiation exposure time was long and the quality of the films seldom matched those taken in an office.

The first-floor waiting room was paneled in knotty pine. Magazines were piled on stands next to the chairs. To preserve the quiet atmosphere, my father would not let me take up the trumpet or drums. (He encouraged me to take piano and clarinet lessons, but the sour notes I produced upstairs could not have sounded any better.)

Two rooms were for diagnostic X-rays, mostly of bones, lungs, kidneys and bowels. Mammograms were rarely performed in those days. Fluoroscopy—the use of X-rays and a fluorescent screen to produce images of the body's internal structures, such as the stomach and intestines—was a standard procedure, performed in the dark. To see better, fluoroscopists wore red goggles; because it took time to adapt vision from light to dark, they would often wear them for about a half-hour beforehand. When my father went from the home office to the hospital to do fluoroscopies, my mother often drove him.

Dad also performed special procedures. The one he hated most was a pneumoencephalogram, in which he had to insert a needle in a patient's lower back, remove spinal fluid and inject air. That procedure could outline the ventricles in the brain on X-rays. But the patient invariably suffered an excruciating headache, and only the rare patient would agree to any additional test. Now the accuracy of CT and M.R.I. scans have made pneumoencephalograms a relic of the past, as they have a number of other once-routine procedures.

A third room was for a different form of X-ray—radiation therapy. Sometimes it was curative. But mostly it provided symptomatic relief and palliation, particularly in cancer, making radiologists known as "the cancer doctors."

Before the introduction of steroid drugs, a small blast or two of radiation often was given for a few benign conditions. One was bursitis in the shoulder; radiation quickly relieved the pain and, with exercises, allowed restoration of full shoulder motion. Now radiation is rarely given for noncancerous ailments.

Dad also used radium to treat cancers, mostly those of the cervix and uterus. He stored the radium in a lead-lined case in a safe in the cellar.

Today, we would call such treatments palliative, though they were not regarded that way in an era when most cancers were detected in their late stages. In my youth, chemotherapy was in its infancy, and people spoke about cancer in euphemisms. In something rarely seen today, many patients arrived with cancers that were so advanced they formed festering ulcers. Maggots even grew in a few such cancers.

X-ray films were developed in a darkened room with the type of chemical solutions used for camera film. A technician mixed fresh solutions daily, and they stank. Radiologists would give a preliminary "wet reading" after looking at the X-rays before they dried. The digital age has eliminated those steps by making X-ray film obsolete.

One convenience of a home office was that my father could go upstairs to nap. The bathroom doubled as a library, with stacks of the latest scientific journals.

After dinner with the family, Dad went down to the office, stood before a viewing box, examined each patient's dry X-ray films, and dictated reports far into the night.

I do not remember how old I was when I first joined him and peered over a shoulder at the films. But I have vivid memories of a number of patients who had large areas in their lung X-rays that appeared white, instead of the normal black, from silicosis—a serious disease that many workers acquired in the local granite quarries. In such cases, my father taught me to take a closer look because silicosis increased the risk of tuberculosis.

To the untrained eye, X-rays were mostly uninterpretable shadows. Radiologists learn to look at them in a disciplined, systematic way. For example, they scan the chest X-rays that were taken at various angles. Then they look at the lungs, heart and ribs in detail.

"The more experienced eye can take in a complex pattern of shadows and images almost at a glance and become instinctively sensitive to an abnormal contour or shadow," said Dr. Joseph T. Ferrucci Jr., the emeritus chairman of radiology at Boston University, whose radiologist father was one of my dad's colleagues.

Radiologists and other medical specialists have a different perspective on patients and their diseases. As one aphorism puts it: A physician sees a patient at the bedside and imagines the disease. A radiologist sees the disease on the film and imagines the patient.

As X-ray technology improved, my father often replaced older machines with newer, larger and more powerful ones that produced better pictures. Ultimately he had to expand the office to the point where only a rock garden was left between the front of the house and the street.

The equipment often broke down. When the X-ray repairmen came, he joined them in spreading across the floor the diagrams needed to trace the complex circuitry and pinpoint the problem. His acumen was so sharp that Harvey Picker, whose company made X-ray machines, came along. I did not inherit those interests.

My father was curious about the causes of the medical problems he saw and sought ways to prevent them. He drew out epidemiologic information by talking with patients. For example, he asked victims of automobile accidents about the model and color of the cars involved. Because so many victims said the color was dark, he bought only light-colored cars (much easier to see at night) and advised others to do likewise.

Other conversations and observations convinced him, long before the 1964 surgeon general's report, that cigarette smoking caused lung cancer. No one in our household smoked, though relatives who did died from ailments related to smoking.

My father was puzzled by why so many workers at the Fore River shipyard in Quincy developed mesotheliomas and other cancers. He tried to persuade the owners to find out why. Doctors later determined that many were from asbestos. Those anecdotes and studies kindled my interest in epidemiology.

Dad and other radiologists would be irked when referring doctors failed to communicate the specific symptoms and physical findings that led them to order a patient's X-rays. Such details help radiologists know what to look for.

The lack of precise information still is a common problem between radiologists and referring doctors. And that is a symptom of a much larger problem: lapses in communication among medical professionals and the public. It was partly to remedy such lapses, and partly to inform the public about medicine and its advances, that I chose the specialty I have pursued for four decades: medical journalism.

## Selection 9.2

*The next story ran in 2006 as the fourth of a five-part series: Medicine Then and Now. In the series Altman looks back at major events in medicine. Stories include Alfred Nobel's obtaining a patent for dynamite in 1867 and the awarding of the first Nobel Prize in Physiology or Medicine in 1901, the first international AIDS conference in 1985, the Legionnaires' disease outbreak in 1987 and advances in the treatment of heart disease and other disorders in the past 50 years.*

*In an interview for this book Altman says even doctors neglect medical history: "You need to know where you came from to know where you are and where you're going. I know that medical history is disdained in medical schools. It's the rare medical school that has a required course in medical history . . . or have people on the faculty who are truly knowledgeable about medical history."*

*In the next story about grand rounds, Altman reflects on a medical institution that has changed radically in the past 40 years. Some young practitioners may never have attended grand rounds, in which patients were wheeled into lecture halls to serve as teaching cases for attending physicians and doctors in training. That may be for the better, since the experience for the grand rounds patient could be impersonal and humiliating.*

*As in the first article on radiology, Altman writes in the first person, although this story is more general and less personal than the account of his radiologist father. Altman builds his story with a series of anecdotes, some from his own experience, but he is careful to explain enough so that the non-medical audience can follow along. The writing is conversational, yet snappy. "Socratic dialogue has given way to PowerPoint. These rounds [now] are often useful, but certainly not grand," Altman tells us. For someone uninitiated in the ritual of grand rounds, Altman offers a peek behind the curtain in a theater where the show is nearing the end of its run.*

## The Doctor's World
## Socratic Dialogue Gives Way to PowerPoint

By LAWRENCE K. ALTMAN, M.D.

Grand rounds are not so grand anymore.

For at least a century at many teaching and community hospitals, properly dressed doctors in ties and white coats have assembled each week, usually in an auditorium, for a master class in the art and science of medicine from the best clinicians. Before us was often a patient who sat in a chair or rested on a gurney and two doctors, one in training and the other a professor or senior doctor at the hospital. In a Socratic dialogue, they often led the audience in a step-by-step deciphering of the ailment.

But in recent years, grand rounds have become didactic lectures focusing on technical aspects of the newest biomedical research. Patients have disappeared. If a case history is presented, it is usually as a brief synopsis and the discussant rarely makes even a passing reference to it.

Now grand rounds are often led by visiting professors from distant hospitals and medical schools. Sometimes, manufacturers of drugs and devices pay the visitor an honorarium and expenses, a practice that has drawn criticism. And the Socratic dialogue has given way to PowerPoint. These rounds are often useful, but certainly not grand.

---

*Published: December 12, 2006.*

Precisely when and where grand rounds began is not known. There are many types of rounds where doctors learn from patients. For example, there are the daily working rounds as doctors walk through a hospital to visit and examine patients. In teaching rounds, more senior doctors supervise the work of residents, or house officers, at a patient's bedside or in a clinic.

Grand rounds were showcases featuring the best clinicians, and the practice thrived in an era when doctors knew little more than what they observed at the bedside. Professors often demonstrated characteristics of physical findings like an enlarged thyroid, a belly swollen with fluid or another grotesque disfigurement that the audience could see. Those with a flair for showmanship were often the best teachers, adapting the predictable structure to their needs and talents.

Grand rounds usually began with a younger doctor's reciting the medical history of a patient with an unusual disease, physical finding or symptom. Sometimes the professor knew about the case, other times he did not. The professor would then ask the patient what was wrong. The more compassionate professors gave reassurance by placing their hands on the patients.

The professor would conduct the interview much like a journalist. When did the fever begin? How high was it? Did you notice a rash? Did you have pain? Where did you feel it? What relieved it?

Each major specialty, like internal medicine and surgery, held separate grand rounds. Pediatrics had a different style. A child unable to relate the events involved in his or her medical history often sat on a parent's lap. The format promoted direct dialogue and emotional reaction between the pediatrician and the family in a way that would not come across if a doctor coldly presented the child's case.

After arriving at a diagnosis, the professor related the current state of medical knowledge to the patient's case. The emphasis was on diagnosis, treatment and the management of a patient, not on research.

In those earlier days, the patient stayed for part or all of the session, which usually lasted an hour. Sometimes doctors in the audience asked questions of the patient and professor. Humor trickled into some sessions. So did personal attacks among faculty members.

As a student at the Tufts Medical School in Boston beginning in 1958, I joined the throngs of doctors on grand rounds when Dr. Louis Weinstein spoke about infectious diseases.

Usually, the patient's pertinent information was on a blackboard. Dr. Weinstein would study the fever chart, seeking clues in the pattern to help identify a particular infection. Then he would regale the crowd with anecdotes from his vast experience in caring for patients with typhoid fever, diphtheria, polio and many other infectious diseases.

Before the Medicare and Medicaid plans were enacted in 1965, many patients treated in teaching hospitals received charity care. In those days, when costs were less of an obstacle, professors sometimes hospitalized patients a few extra days so they could be presented at grand rounds. In other cases, many patients returned after discharge in gratitude for their free care.

Even the smartest experts had to be on their toes, because younger doctors often selected a case intended to tax their brains. Another intention was to have the experts explain their thinking as they matched wits against colleagues and the illness itself.

In San Francisco in 1987, I heard a visiting expert discuss the possible reasons that a woman in her 80s, who complained of weakness and muscle spasms in her back, had a severe loss of potassium.

After the resident gave a detailed account of her illness, the discussant, Dr. Donald W. Seldin, then the chief physician at the University of Texas Southwest Medical Center in Dallas, went to a blackboard to highlight the crucial elements and list possible causes.

As he narrowed the list, Dr. Seldin suggested licorice. But he was told that the patient did not eat it. Next, Dr. Seldin asked whether the patient chewed tobacco. Yes, the resident said. Did she swallow the juice? Again, yes. Dr. Seldin then identified the culprit. The tobacco brand that she chewed contained enough licorice to account for her problem.

Over the years, I have attended grand rounds at a number of hospitals and have even led some. I have also discussed grand rounds with a number of doctors across the country and abroad who recalled some unusual ones.

Dr. Joseph E. Murray, a Nobel Prize-winning transplant surgeon in Boston, recalled a grand rounds session at what is now Brigham and Women's Hospital. Dr. Francis D. Moore, the renowned chief of surgery at Harvard, talked to a woman who had had recent gall bladder surgery. She sat in a wheelchair with her back to the audience, presumably so she could see the X-rays. Only at the end of the discussion, when Dr. Moore turned her wheelchair around, did he disclose that the patient was his wife.

An occasional grand rounds session became a lesson on decorum.

Dr. Samuel L. Katz, emeritus chairman of pediatrics at Duke, recalled his first grand rounds as a medical student, at Harvard in 1951. The expert was Dr. Oliver Cope, a leading surgeon. As Dr. Cope began talking with a patient on a gurney, he spotted one of Dr. Katz's fellow students in the audience with an open shirt and no tie.

Dr. Cope ordered the patient wheeled out of the room. He spent the rest of the hour describing the proper attire for young doctors in the presence of patients. "That made an indelible impression," said Dr. Katz, who has since kept ties handy for students who were not properly dressed.

Other grand rounds have set the stage for ruckuses.

Dr. A. Stone Freedberg, an emeritus professor at Harvard who is 98, recalled a conflict that developed over a patient who died after a lengthy illness and an unexplained fever. The discussant's list of possible causes did not include histoplasmosis, a fungal infection that occurs in many regions but that is more common in the Midwest.

Dr. Henry A. Christian, chief physician at a Harvard teaching hospital, was in the audience and asked why histoplasmosis was excluded. Because no such case had been seen at their hospital, the discussant replied. Dr. Christian pointed out that theirs was not the only hospital in the area and that the patient might have acquired histoplasmosis elsewhere.

The discussant retorted by asking whether Dr. Christian had ever seen a patient with histoplasmosis. No, Dr. Christian replied, adding that there were many ailments he had never seen but had to think about in examining patients. The discussion grew increasingly heated before another participant told them to continue their argument outside.

Grand rounds remain important in continuing medical education. But in interviews and conversation, many physicians expressed uneasiness about the lecture format and were disturbed by the lack of a focus on patient-related problems. Many younger doctors did not know that grand rounds were once conducted with patients on stage.

The critics say the switch to lectures is a sign of the time pressures that have contributed to erosions in the patient-doctor relationship and to the dehumanization of medicine. The absence of a patient case history and the impersonality of the lecture format also draw attention from the primary objective of focusing on the patient, they say.

But the classic grand rounds format may no longer be enough to teach doctors what they need to know about proper care. Exercises in solving clinical problems like the licorice case occur in many other conferences in medical schools and hospitals. Since World War II, medicine has become increasingly subspecialized. The size of hospital staffs has soared. Some department staffs list hundreds of faculty members, including some without medical degrees.

Medicine has advanced far beyond learning from bedside observations, though those remain important. Now doctors need to know about the physiological mechanisms and reasons for prescribing a drug or performing a procedure. Understanding a disease depends far more on information from scientifically rigorous trials involving a large number of patients than a professor's cumulative anecdotal experience.

Nevertheless, experiences with single cases can be important because doctors have to mold treatments for the many patients who do not match the criteria used in studies.

The lecture format may be a more efficient way to learn science, but it is hard to know for sure, because published data documenting the effectiveness of grand rounds as a teaching forum is sparse.

In an era of proliferating subspecialties, a chief aim of grand rounds is to emphasize a core body of knowledge that all physicians need to share and to keep abreast of. And the meetings serve a social function. With coffee cups and bagels or pizza in hand, doctors mingle with colleagues before and after grand rounds. For some, it is the only time they see one another during the week.

Yet attendance at grand rounds has reportedly declined in recent years. Many subspecialists prefer to attend rounds in their narrower field, and doctors who go to national and international meetings can hear much of the same information that may be later presented in lectures at grand rounds.

State licensing boards require doctors to earn a specified number of continuing medical education credits each year. While attending grand rounds qualifies, other accredited conferences often win out in the competition. So some hospitals now require doctors to attend a specified number of grand rounds each year to maintain their staff positions.

As medical educators seek ways to increase the appeal of grand rounds, they might look at being more imaginative and restoring a sense of humor.

In 1961, Dr. Roy Y. Calne, a British surgeon who was working with Dr. Moore at Harvard, achieved a milestone in his search for a drug to prevent the rejection of transplanted organs. He successfully used azathioprine to keep a dog, Lollipop, alive and healthy with normal kidney function for six months after a kidney transplant.

So Dr. Moore asked Dr. Calne, now Sir Roy, to present his findings at a grand rounds session. In his college days, Dr. Moore had been president of The Harvard Lampoon humor magazine. (For full disclosure, years later I was an officer of The Lampoon.) So after Dr. Calne summarized the case, and with Dr. Moore's approval, he invited the patient to join grand rounds.

As the door opened, Lollipop "pranced into the crowded auditorium, making friends with the distinguished professors in the front row," Dr. Calne said. After a brief pause, the surprised audience broke out in laughter.

Azathioprine later was licensed as one of a standard antirejection drug for kidney transplants and for severe rheumatoid arthritis that does not respond to standard therapy.

## A Conversation with . . . Lawrence K. Altman, M.D.

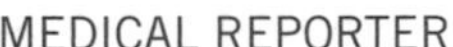

MEDICAL REPORTER

© The New York Times

*Lawrence K. Altman, M.D., has been a member of The New York Times science news staff since 1969. In addition to reporting, he writes The Doctor's World column in Science Times. Trained in internal medicine at the University of Washington, Altman worked from 1963 to 1966 with the U.S. Public Health Service's Centers for Disease Control and Prevention in Atlanta. There he was editor of its Morbidity and Mortality Weekly Report, a journal dealing with reported cases of communicable diseases around the world. Altman graduated from Tufts University School of Medicine in 1962. He graduated from Harvard in 1958 with a bachelor's degree in government. The following is an edited transcript of a telephone interview.*

**How did you get into the field of medical journalism?**

As a student in high school and college, I worked for the local paper where I grew up, the Patriot Ledger in Quincy, Massachusetts, and had an interest in journalism from that experience. I grew up in a medical family and was interested in medicine. When I went off to medical school, the publisher and the editor of the Quincy Patriot Ledger made it clear to me that the world was becoming more complicated, and journalism needed more specialists. I didn't go to medical school specifically for that purpose, but that idea was in the background. They said, "There's always the possibility you can put the two together."

The more I got through medical school and thereafter, the more I felt a need for communicating what was going on in medicine to the public. When I was editor of the Morbidity and Mortality Weekly Report, I saw the synergy between medicine and reporting on medicine.

When I finished my training, I thought I would be able to work on ideas that I had beginning in medical school, but I fell between the cracks. When I tried to get grants, there was no grant mechanism for what I wanted—to travel, to interview and to put together information on themes. So I wrote The Times, and we agreed to enter an experiment. Forty years later I'm still experimenting.

**In those 40 years, how has the way The Times covers medical topics changed?**

Well, certainly there's more space given to medicine/science today than there was when I started. There's a science section, Science Times, today that didn't exist at the time I started. The medicine/science news was largely confined within the context of the main paper, the "A" section, largely. The staff is larger, there is obviously more that's covered because there is a larger hole for the material that you can produce.

**Do you see your job as different from that of a lay medical reporter?**
In many ways the same, but in many ways different, because I can draw on the medical knowledge I have for interpretation, for anticipation of the potential significance of what I might be reporting on, or to explain the information or put it in a broader context. Certainly the background in epidemiology that I had, and clinically in infectious diseases, is an advantage in reporting because a lot of what gets covered in the news media is epidemiologically based. There's a lot of similarity between shoe-leather journalism and shoe-leather epidemiology. You go out, find out what you can and then you report it.

**What do you think is the biggest problem that medical reporters have in translating complex medical concepts and jargon?**
The ability of whoever you're interviewing—the scientist, the doctor, the health worker, whatever—to explain things that they mean in common, everyday language without the use of jargon. There are many examples where the medical or health profession speaks in jargon, assumes that everybody else knows what they're talking about. This phenomenon goes on in the medical literature. It goes on in everyday conversation. It goes on in communications with patients.

Other examples are evidence-based medicine. "Evidence-based medicine" is the most meaningless phrase I can imagine. Or "peer review." There is no standard definition. There is little agreement on who is a peer, what the extent of review is, what role the process plays in the final decision. If it's a journal, is it review from within the journal or is it external? All these terms just are used very loosely.

If it's a laboratory research or study, it's written as if you knew from the very beginning what the objective and answer would be. That isn't the way science happens. There's a lot of serendipity. There's a lot of rethinking and reanalyzing what's going on as you do the experiment. Only in retrospect do you put it together. From that point of view medical literature is written from a retrospective frame, not as an ongoing way as it would be chronicled if you were doing a day-to-day diary or covering a story for a news organization.

**When you write, is there a particular individual whom you're thinking of as your audience?**
The reader that I'm thinking of is someone who wants to understand what the topic is that I'm writing about. I try to anticipate the questions that the reader might ask and want to know. I think of the reader as sort of a patient across the desk from me, anticipating the questions that the individual would want to have answered.

**How much of your writing work is education and how much is reporting?**
It's a combination of both because you're reporting, and in the course of reporting you may be uncovering new material—either new to you, new to the reader or something new that's just being discovered. That's education. It's certainly providing information, and providing information is part of education.

You're trying to report and you're trying to inform, and I'm using "inform" in the sense of educate at the same time. It can't be a lesson. That's quite different from the way formal education is. You're a captive audience in formal education. In journalism you've got to capture somebody's attention right from the beginning, and it's not captive. The reader or the viewer or the listener is free to tune in or tune out or do something else right away if it doesn't catch their attention.

**When medical reporters read a journal article, what should be their goal?**
Aim to understand what the author or authors set out to do, what they did, how much of their original goal they achieved, and to try to put that into perspective. That involves analyzing the paper as best you can. You can't go back and do all the statistics. You have to assume that that's been done. But analyze the tables and graphs. Question the reasoning, question the statements. You may not always pick up the caveats, but you should be striving to look for those as best you can.

**As a doctor trained at the CDC's Epidemic Intelligence Service, what's your take on the issue of when to warn people about epidemics?**
That's something that public health people will have to pay more and more attention to. There's always been the need for communication to the public as part of public health.

Today the public is deeply involved. Journalism is involved. Public health officials, in that sense of the word, have to explain more to the public and are more accountable to the public, as they should be. They have to be more precise in the criteria that they use in, say, declaring an epidemic or an outbreak or informing the public of what the implications of a cluster of cases may or may not mean for them and what means of protection they should or shouldn't take.

**Do you have any advice to health professionals who would like to follow your career path?**
I'd try to encourage as many people to put medicine and journalism together as best they can. But one has to be totally realistic. The era of daily journalism is on the wane. I hope it recovers, but it's certainly a bleak forecast at the moment. Practically speaking, I'm not sure if one should be very encouraging, given the reality of the workplace. Another point—a number of people I hear from are fed up with this or that in medicine, and they want to reject whatever they are doing. What they seem to say is: "Your job sounds interesting. I want to do it." That's not a good reason to go into journalism. What outlooks there

are going to be for people who have this interest as the opportunities in daily newspapers dwindle, I don't know. I don't know what the Internet is going to provide in the long run.

**Any advice to those who want to follow a medical reporting path and who don't have a professional background?**
I'd encourage them to do it, too. I think journalism needs both. I don't think it should be a monolithic structure. I'd encourage them as well, but I'd have the exact same caveats.

**What's been the most fun part of your job over the last 40 years?**
You have to look at the fun in retrospect, because it's a lot of hard work. But I think it's being a witness, and maybe even a participant, in a number of major changes that have occurred in medicine and shared experiences with the people who have brought those changes about. Getting to know them, getting to report on them, and getting to tell the reader what has happened, why this has happened and what it might lead to.

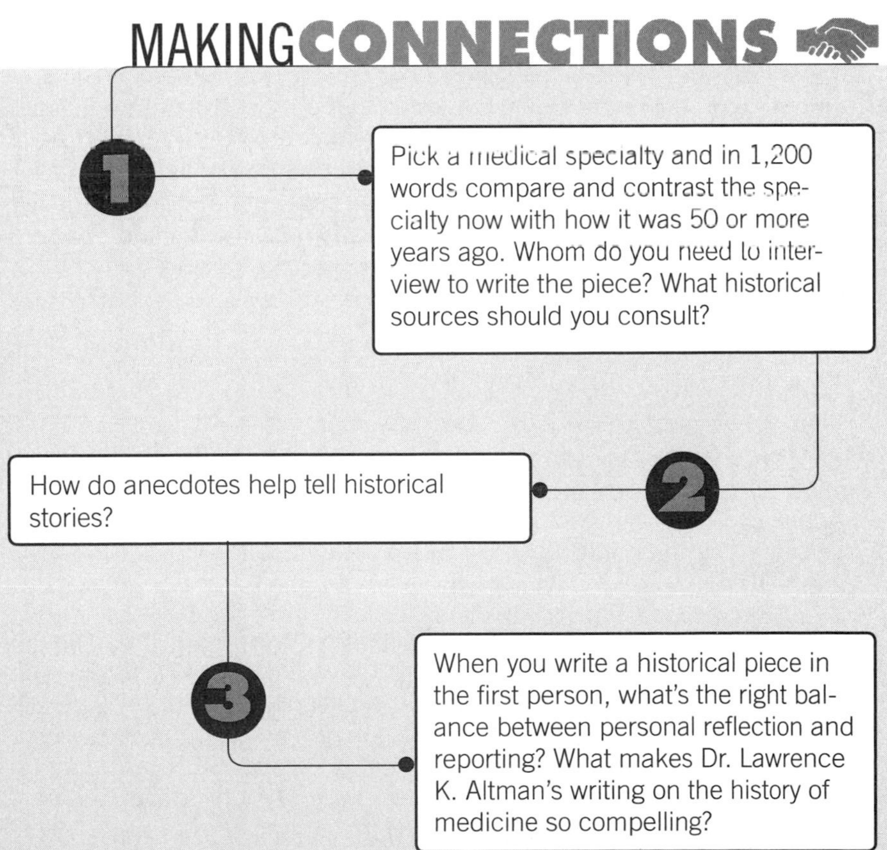

MAKING CONNECTIONS
1
Pick a medical specialty and in 1,200 words compare and contrast the specialty now with how it was 50 or more years ago. Whom do you need to interview to write the piece? What historical sources should you consult?
2
How do anecdotes help tell historical stories?
3
When you write a historical piece in the first person, what's the right balance between personal reflection and reporting? What makes Dr. Lawrence K. Altman's writing on the history of medicine so compelling?

CHAPTER 10

# series features

A STAPLE OF MEDICAL REPORTING IS THE SERIES: a number of related stories, usually three or more, that may run over the course of a week, several months, a year or even longer. Reporters like to work on a series since they can cover one topic in depth over time. Editors like series since the story installments pull in readers and showcase the news organization's reporting capabilities. A series is also an excellent platform for medical and health reporting that covers complex subjects that are best addressed one piece at a time.

In recent years The New York Times has featured a number of series covering topics like the high rate of maternal death in Africa, the 40-year war to fight cancer, troubled children, the history of medicine, and six major killers, one of which is featured in this chapter.

In a series, reporters break down a big topic by taking several slices of the pie in successive installments. For example, in the Six Killers series Times reporters examined the leading causes of illness and death in the United States: heart disease, cancer, stroke, chronic obstructive pulmonary disease, diabetes and Alzheimer's disease, in that order. As The Times pointed out, these diseases are expensive, sometimes are associated with one another and often are undertreated or treated inappropriately. One especially riveting story in this series addressed stroke, a common occurrence that can lead to death if not treated within a very short time.

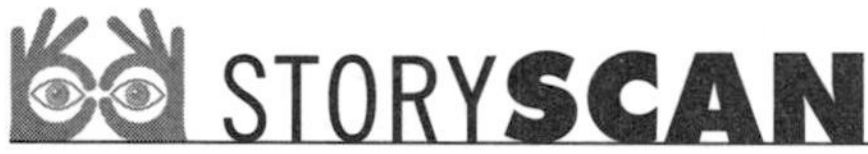


## Selection 10.1

*Medical reporter Gina Kolata uses the narrative of one individual as a jumping-off point to tell a bigger story about how the medical system copes with patients who are in the midst of a stroke. In an interview for this book, Kolata says she often divides her longer stories into what she calls "chapters." Each chapter has a ministory that moves the narrative along. "You can bring up different issues without feeling you have to waste a lot of space making it seem like you're moving smoothly from one to the next," Kolata says. "When you do chapters, it allows you to gracefully get several topics and make them readable because each one is a story in itself." In the annotated story that follows, note how Kolata uses her main character to push the story forward. Once she's hooked her readers, the reporter can step back and give the big picture. This narrative technique works especially well for medical series stories since readers can connect a face with the problem and not initially be overwhelmed by the science.*

Todd Heisler/The New York Times

*Dr. Diana Fite, an emergency medicine specialist in Houston, has completely recovered since suffering a stroke while driving.*

## Six Killers | Stroke
## Lost Chances for Survival, Before and After Stroke

By GINA KOLATA

Dr. Diana Fite, a 53-year-old emergency medicine specialist in Houston, knew her blood pressure readings had been dangerously high for five years. But she convinced herself that those measurements, about 200 over 120, did not reflect her actual blood pressure. Anyway, she was too young to take medication. She would worry about her blood pressure when she got older.

*By introducing the face for the story at the outset, the reporter draws the reader quickly into her narrative.*

Then, at 9:30 the morning of June 7, Dr. Fite was driving, steering with her right hand, holding her cellphone in her left, when, for a split second, the right side of her body felt weak. "I said: 'This is silly, it's my imagination. I've been working too hard.'"

*Kolata drills deeper into the narrative by giving voice to Dr. Fite's thoughts.*

Suddenly, her car began to swerve.

*Note the short sentence and active voice.*

*Published: May 28, 2007.*

"I realized I had no strength whatsoever in my right hand that was holding the wheel," Dr. Fite said. "And my right foot was dead. I could not get it off the gas pedal."

She dropped the cellphone, grabbed the steering wheel with her left hand, and steered the car into a parking lot. Then she used her left foot to pry her right foot off the accelerator. She pulled down the visor to look in the mirror. The right side of her face was paralyzed.

*Lots of action verbs give the story momentum. Also note the importance of detail in describing what's happening as the stroke occurs.*

With great difficulty, Dr. Fite twisted her body and grasped her cellphone.

"I called 911, but nothing would come out of my mouth," she said. Then she found that if she spoke very slowly, she could get out words. So, she recalled, "I said 'stroke' in this long, horrible voice."

*Great quote conveys the gravity of the situation.*

Dr. Fite is one of an estimated 700,000 Americans who had a stroke last year, but one of the very few who ended up at a hospital with the equipment and expertise to accurately diagnose and treat it.

*Kolata waits until graf 8 to give the story context. In a shorter story context should appear much higher.*

Stroke is the third-leading cause of death in this country, behind heart disease and cancer, killing 150,000 Americans a year, leaving many more permanently disabled, and costing the nation $62.7 billion in direct and indirect costs, according to the American Stroke Association.

*Numbers give the story weight and credibility.*

But from diagnosis to treatment to rehabilitation to preventing it altogether, a stroke is a litany of missed opportunities. Many patients with stroke symptoms are examined by emergency room doctors who are uncomfortable deciding whether the patient is really having a stroke—a blockage or rupture of a blood vessel in the brain that injures or kills brain cells—or is suffering from another condition. Doctors are therefore reluctant to give the only drug shown to make a real difference, tPA, or tissue plasminogen activator.

*"Litany of missed opportunities" says a lot in a few words.*

*The reporter introduces us to the other character in this drama, tPA. Characters don't always have to be animate.*

Many hospitals say they cannot afford to have neurologists on call to diagnose strokes, and cannot afford to have M.R.I. scanners, the most accurate way to diagnose strokes, for the emergency room.

Although tPA was shown in 1996 to prevent brain damage, and although the drug could help half of all stroke patients, only 3 percent to 4 percent receive it. Most patients, denying or failing to appreciate their symptoms, wait too long to seek help—tPA must be given within three hours. And even when patients call 911 promptly, most hospitals, often uncertain about stroke diagnoses, do not provide the drug.

*A good reporter includes key statistics.*

"I label this a national tragedy or a national embarrassment," said Dr. Mark J. Alberts, a neurology professor at the Feinberg School of Medicine at Northwestern University. "I know of no disease that is as common or as serious as stroke and where you basically have one therapy and it's only used in 3 to 4 percent of patients. That's like saying you only treat 3 to 4 percent of patients with bacterial pneumonia with antibiotics."

*This is the contextual quote from an expert that establishes the import of the story.*

And the strokes in the statistics are only the beginning. For every stroke that doctors know about, there are 5 to 10 tiny, silent strokes, said Dr. Vladimir Hachinski, the editor of the journal Stroke and a neurologist at the London Health Sciences Centre in Ontario.

*More useful data that help us understand the prevalence of strokes.*

"They are only silent because we don't ask questions," Dr. Hachinski said. "They do not involve memory, but they involve judgment, planning ahead, shifting your attention from one thing to another. And they also may involve late-life depression."

They are also warning signs that a much larger stroke may be on the way.

Most strokes would never happen if people took simple measures like controlling their blood pressure. Few do. Many say they forget to take medication; others, like Dr. Fite, decide not to. Some have no idea they need the drugs.

*Notice the smooth segue to the prevention message.*

Still, there is much more hope now, said Dr. Ralph L. Sacco, professor and chairman of neurology at the Miller School of Medicine at the University of Miami. Like most stroke neurologists, Dr. Sacco entered the field more than a decade ago, when little could be done for such patients.

*Sad commentary on how practice lags behind research, a common occurrence in medicine.*

Now, Dr. Sacco said, there is a device, an M.R.I. scanner, that greatly improves diagnosis, there is a treatment that works and there are others being tested. "Medical systems have to catch up to the research," he said.

In medicine, Dr. Sacco said, "stroke is a new frontier."

*Here's a new chapter that Kolata talked about in the introduction to this story.*

## Promise Unfulfilled

One Tuesday morning in March, Dr. Steven Warach, chief of the stroke program at the National Institute of Neurological Disorders and Stroke, met with a team from Washington Hospital Center, the largest private hospital in Washington, to review M.R.I. scans of recently admitted patients. They were joined in a teleconference by neurologists at Suburban Hospital in Bethesda, Md., the only other stroke center in the Washington and suburban Maryland area.

*That's a great line and also a nice way to introduce the patients' minihistories that follow.*

The images were mementos of suffering.

There was a 66-year-old woman with a stroke so big the scan actually showed degenerating fibers that carry nerve signals across the brain.

There was a 75-year-old who had trouble moving her right arm and right side in the recovery room after heart surgery. At first doctors thought she was just slow to wake up from the anesthesia. Now, though, it was clear she had suffered a stroke. She had lost the right half of her vision in both eyes and her right side was weak.

*Again note the importance of detail in your reporting and writing. All these minihistories are replete with key details.*

There was an 88-year-old who slumped forward at lunch, losing consciousness. When he came to, he had trouble forming words.

*A reporter needs to have a good ear to catch the drama within each scene.*

There was a middle-age man whose stroke was unforgettable. When Dr. Warach saw his initial M.R.I. scan, in his basement office at his home, he cried out in astonishment so loudly his wife ran downstairs. "I have never seen anything so severe," Dr. Warach said. None of the three arteries that supplied the man's right hemisphere were getting any blood.

Now the man lay in a coma, twitching on his left side, paralyzed on his right, breathing with the help of a ventilator. If he survived, he would have severe brain damage.

There was Michael Collins, a 49-year-old police officer who had had a stroke in his police car in Takoma Park, Md. Unlike the others, Mr. Collins seemed mostly recovered. The next few days, though, would determine whether he was among the lucky 10 percent of stroke patients who escape unscathed or whether he would always be weaker on his left side. If that happened, Mr. Collins said, he could never return to his job.

*Note the seamless transition to the chapter on Michael Collins in the story.*

"You have to be able to shoot a gun with either hand," he explained. But as time passed, Mr. Collins continued to be plagued by numbness in his left hand and on the left side of his face. He wanted to return to work—"I'm doing great," he said this month—but the Police Department insisted that he retire, telling him, he said, "it's an officer safety issue."

*The reporter followed up on this case to find out that the P.D. insisted that Collins retire.*

The rest of the patients in the stroke units at the two hospitals that day were less fortunate: almost certain to live, but also almost certain to end up with brain damage. Some would have to spend time at a rehabilitation center.

On average, said Dr. Brendan E. Conroy, medical director of the stroke recovery program at the National Rehabilitation Hospital, which is attached to the Washington Hospital Center, a third of the Washington hospital's stroke patients die, a third go home and a third come to him.

*Presenting statistics in a simple way helps to keep the reader's attention.*

Those whose balance is affected typically spend 20 days learning to deal with a walker or a cane; those who are partly blind or paralyzed must learn to care for themselves. Many functions return, Dr. Conroy said, but rehabilitation also means learning to live with a disability.

*The reporter notes 20 days, not just a couple weeks. Always be specific. Don't generalize.*

But what was perhaps saddest to the neurologists viewing the M.R.I. scans that morning was that tPA, which only recently appeared to be a triumph of medicine, had made not a whit of difference to these patients. They either had not arrived at the hospital in time or had been considered otherwise medically unsuitable to receive it.

*Here's another new chapter. Call it the history chapter on tPA.*

Few would have predicted that fate for the drug. In 1995, after 40 years of trying to find something to break up blood clots in the brain, the cause of most strokes, researchers announced that tPA worked. A large federal study showed that, without it, about one patient in five escaped serious injury. With it, one in three escaped.

The drug had a serious side effect—it could cause potentially life-threatening bleeding in the brain in about 6 percent of patients. But the clinical trial demonstrated that the drug's benefits outweighed its risks.

When the study's results were announced, Dr. James Grotta of the University of Texas Medical School at Houston expressed the researchers' elation. "Until today, stroke was an untreatable disease," Dr. Grotta said.

*History gives a story breadth and context.*

*A short sentence has much greater impact than a long sentence.*

But the expected sea change did not occur.

One problem was that patients showed up too late. Many had no choice. Strokes often occur in the morning when people are sleeping. They awake with terrifying symptoms, paralyzed on one side or unable to speak.

*The next few grafs form part of the science lesson.*

"That's the challenge—we have to ask the patient" when the stroke began, said Dr. A. Gregory Sorensen, a co-director of the Athinoula A. Martinos Center for Biomedical Imaging at Massachusetts General Hospital. "If they don't know or can't talk, we're out of luck."

Another problem is deciding whether a patient is really having a stroke. A person who has trouble forming words could just be confused. Or what about someone whose arm or leg is weak?

"A lot of things can cause weakness," Dr. Warach said. "A nerve injury can cause weakness; sometimes brain tumors can be suddenly symptomatic. Sometimes people have migraines that can completely mimic a stroke."

In fact, he said, a quarter of emergency room patients with symptoms suggestive of a stroke are not actually having one.

Most get CT scans, which are useful mostly to rule out hemorrhagic strokes, the less common type that is caused by bleeding in the brain and should not be treated with tPA. Stroke specialists can usually then decide whether the patient is having a stroke caused by a blocked blood vessel and whether it can be treated with tPA.

But most stroke patients are handled by emergency room physicians who often say they are not sure of the diagnosis and therefore hesitate to give tPA.

*Kolata explains why doctors don't give tPA as often as they should.*

Dr. Richard Burgess, a member of Dr. Warach's stroke team, explained the situation: There is no particular penalty for not giving tPA. Doctors are unlikely to be sued if the patient dies or is left with brain damage that could have been avoided. But there is a penalty for giving tPA to someone who is not having a stroke. If that patient bleeds into the brain, the drug not only caused a tragic outcome but the doctor could also be sued. Few emergency room doctors want to take that chance.

## Treatment Barriers

There is a way to diagnose strokes more accurately—with a diffusion M.R.I., a type of scan that shows water moving in the brain. During a stroke, the flow of water slows to a crawl as dead and dying cells swell. In one recent study, diffusion M.R.I. scans found five times as many strokes as CT scans, with twice the accuracy.

*More of the science lesson.*

A diffusion M.R.I. "answers the question 95 percent of the time," Dr. Sorensen said.

It seemed the perfect solution, but it was not.

Most hospitals say they cannot provide such scans to stroke patients. They would need both an M.R.I. technician and an expert to interpret the scans around the clock. They would need an M.R.I. machine near the emergency room. Most hospitals have the huge machines elsewhere, steadily booked far in advance for other patients.

It is simply not practical to demand the scans at every hospital or even every stroke center, said Dr. Edward C. Jauch, an emergency medicine doctor at the University of Cincinnati and a member of the Greater Cincinnati/Northern Kentucky Stroke Team.

*Note the many sources that Kolata has consulted.*

"If you made M.R.I. the standard of care before giving tPA, most centers would not be able to comply," Dr. Jauch said. And if it takes more time to get a scan—as it often does—it might be better to forgo it and give tPA immediately if the patient's symptoms seem unambiguous.

Doctors do not need an M.R.I. to diagnose and treat stroke, said Dr. Lee H. Schwamm, vice chairman of the department of neurology at Massachusetts General Hospital. But, Dr. Schwamm added, if the question is whether it helps, there is one reply: "By all means."

*Kolata cautions us not to get carried away with the benefits of M.R.I. scans.*

It has still not been shown, though, that M.R.I. scans actually improve outcomes. It might depend on the circumstances and the hospital, said Dr. Walter J. Koroshetz, deputy director of the National Institute of Neurological Disorders and Stroke.

But some who use M.R.I. scans, and who have studied them in research, say the system has to change. They say enough is known about the scans to advocate having them at every major medical center that will treat stroke patients.

*After presenting the problem, the reporter is now offering solutions.*

"All these problems could be solved if there was a will to do it," Dr. Sorensen said. In his opinion, it comes down to old and outdated assumptions that there is not much to be done for a stroke, to financial considerations and to a medical system that resists change. But the most significant barriers, he said, are financial.

Another approach, stroke specialists say, is to direct all patients with stroke symptoms to designated stroke centers. There, stroke patients would be treated by experienced neurologists and admitted to stroke units for additional care. For the first time, in its newly published guidelines, the American Stroke Association recommended the routing of patients to stroke centers.

*Kolata begins another chapter in her story.*

But even with such a system in place, many patients end up at hospitals that are not prepared to treat them, as Dr. Grotta discovered in Houston.

He thought he could change stroke care in Houston with the stroke center idea. The first step went well—the city's ambulance services agreed to take all patients with stroke symptoms to designated stroke centers.

Then, Dr. David E. Persse, the city's director of emergency medical services, asked every one of Houston's 25 hospitals if it wanted to be a stroke center. While seven have said yes, others have declined.

Stroke patients, unlike heart attack patients, are not moneymakers. Because of the way medical care is reimbursed, most hospitals either lose money or do little more than break even with stroke care but can often make several thousand dollars opening the arteries of a heart attack patient. And being a stroke center means finding and paying stroke specialists to be available around the clock.

*It's important in any medical story to deal with cost.*

Soon another problem emerged. As many as a third of the patients refused to let the ambulance take them to a stroke center, demanding to go to their local hospital.

"By law in Texas, we cannot take that man to another hospital against his will," Dr. Persse said. "We could be charged with assault and battery and kidnapping and unlawful imprisonment."

The Joint Commission, which accredits hospitals, recently started certifying stroke centers, requiring that the hospitals be willing to treat stroke patients aggressively. But only 322 of the 4,280 accredited hospitals in the nation qualify, and most patients and doctors have no idea whether a hospital nearby is among them. (The list is available on the site http://www.jointcommission.org/CertificationPrograms/Disease-SpecificCare/DSCOrgs/ under "primary stroke centers.") Some states, like New York, Massachusetts and Florida, do their own certifying of stroke centers.

*More numbers to drive home her points.*

*Helpful Web link.*

Nonetheless, most ambulances do not consider stroke center designations when they transport patients. And, said John Becknell, a spokesman for the National Association of Emergency Medical Technicians, national programs can be difficult because every community has its own rules for which ambulances pick up patients and where they take them.

As a result, most stroke patients have no access to the recommended care and even fewer get M.R.I.'s, a situation Dr. Warach said he found appalling.

"How can it ever be in the patient's best interest to have an inferior diagnosis?" he asked. "It borders on malpractice that given a choice between two noninvasive tests, one of which is clearly superior, the worse test is the one that is preferred."

## Averting Catastrophe

*The narrative now comes full circle as Kolata returns to Dr. Fite, the stroke patient introduced in the lede.*

In those awful moments when she realized she had had a stroke, Dr. Fite, unlike most patients, knew what to do. She told the ambulance crew to take her to Memorial Hermann Hospital, even though it was about an hour away. She knew that it was one of the Houston stroke centers, that Dr. Grotta worked there, and that its doctors had experience diagnosing strokes and giving tPA.

*Note how the reporter picks up the chronology. In a chronology the reporter can go back once, but then should always move forward in time.*

When she arrived, Dr. Grotta asked if she was sure she wanted the drug. Did she want to risk bleeding in the brain? Dr. Fite did not hesitate. The stroke, she said, "was just so devastating that I would rather die of a hemorrhage in the brain than be left completely paralyzed in my right side."

*Second mention of her "horrible voice."*

"In my horrible voice, I said, 'Yes, I want the tPA,'" Dr. Fite said.

Within 10 to 15 minutes, the drug started to dissolve the clot.

*Excellent choice of quote since few readers would know what it feels like to recover from what was a stroke in progress.*

"I had weird spasms as nerves started to work again," Dr. Fite said. "An arm would draw up real quick, a leg would tighten up. It hurt so bad I was crying because of the pain. But it was movement, and I knew something was going on."

Now, she looks back with dismay on her cavalier attitude toward high blood pressure. She knew very well how to prevent a stroke but, like many patients and despite her medical training, she found it all too easy to deny her own risk.

*This is part of the prevention lesson.*

Researchers have known for years the conditions that predispose a person to stroke—smoking, diabetes, high cholesterol and an irregular heartbeat known as atrial fibrillation. But the major one is high blood pressure.

"Of all the modifiable risk factors, high blood pressure leads the list," Dr. Sacco said. "With heart disease, you think more of cholesterol; with stroke you think of high blood pressure."

The reason, Dr. Sacco said, is that with high blood pressure, the tiny blood vessels in the brain clamp down so much and so hard to protect the brain that they can become rigid. Then they get blocked. The result is a stroke.

*More of the science lesson.*

Often, people decide they do not need their blood pressure medication or simply forget to take it because they feel well. But, Dr. Sacco said, patients are not solely to blame. Doctors may not have time to work with patients, monitoring blood pressure, telling them about changes in their diet and exercise that might help, or trying different drugs and combining them if necessary.

And it is not so simple for people to keep track of their blood pressure. Machines in drugstores and supermarkets are not always accurate. Doctors may require appointments to check blood pressure.

Even when people do try to control their pressure, doctors may not prescribe enough drugs or high enough doses.

"They're on a couple of drugs, and the doctor doesn't want to push it," said Dr. Jeffrey A. Cutler, a consultant to the National Heart, Lung and Blood Institute and a retired director of its clinical applications and prevention program.

The result is that no more than half the people with high blood pressure have it under control, Dr. Cutler said. He estimated that half of all strokes could be prevented if people kept their blood pressure within the recommended range.

*Numbers give the prevention lesson context.*

Another lost opportunity to prevent strokes is the undertreatment of atrial fibrillation, in which the two upper chambers of the heart quiver. Blood can pool in the heart and clot, and those clots can be swept into the brain, lodge in a small blood vessel and cause a stroke.

*And still more of the science lesson.*

Strokes from atrial fibrillation can largely be prevented with anticlotting drugs like warfarin. Yet many who have the condition do not know it and many who know they have it were never given or do not take an anticlotting drug.

Some strokes can also be prevented by procedures to open obstructed arteries in the neck that supply blood to the brain.

*Kolata picks up the narrative again with her main character.*

As for Dr. Fite, she completely recovered. And she has changed her ways.

*Don't forget cost; very important in any medical story.*

She was sobered by the cost of her treatment and brief hospital stay—$96,000, most of which was paid by her insurance company. But she was even more sobered by how close she came to catastrophe.

*And don't forget prevention.*

Now, Dr. Fite takes three blood pressure pills, a drug to prevent blood clots and a cholesterol-lowering drug. She plans to take those drugs every day for the rest of her life.

"I was so stupid," she said. "Boy, when you go through this, you never want to go through it again."

*Strong quote to end the story.*

"I have been given that precious second chance," she said. "I was so blessed."

## Selection 10.2

*In the next series example, Denise Grady writes about the primitive state of maternal care in Africa and, in particular, Tanzania. The second part of the series deals with the deadly toll of abortion by amateurs, while the last part focuses on some of the 50 million orphans in Africa, many of whom lost their mothers as a result of childbirth. Grady selectively uses details to clue readers into the poor maternal care offered to pregnant African women. When painting a word picture, the writer needs to be very specific and choose only those details that tell a bigger story. For example, Grady writes that the hospital is "6 miles from the nearest paved road and 25 miles from the last electric pole." That gives us a feeling for the remoteness of the medical facility. The crowning detail that Grady provides is the maternal death rate in Tanzania—900 times higher than that in Ireland. Nine hundred times. That's an eye-popping statistic. Through detailed reporting, dramatic anecdotes and an excellent graphic, Grady puts maternal death rates in Tanzania and Africa in perspective.*

### DEATH IN BIRTH
### Where Life's Start Is a Deadly Risk

By DENISE GRADY

BEREGA, Tanzania—The young woman had already been in labor for two days by the time she reached the hospital here. Now two lives were at risk, and there was no choice but to operate and take the baby right away.

---

*Published: May 24, 2009.*

It was just before dawn, and the operating room, powered by a rumbling generator, was the only spot of light in this village of mud huts and maize fields. A mask with a frayed cord was fastened over the woman's face. Moments later the cloying smell of ether filled the room, and then Emmanuel Makanza picked up his instruments and made the first cut for a Caesarean section.

Mr. Makanza is not a doctor, a fact that illustrates both the desperation and the creativity of Tanzanians fighting to reduce the number of deaths and injuries among pregnant women and infants.

Pregnancy and childbirth kill more than 536,000 women a year, more than half of them in Africa, according to the World Health Organization.

Most of the deaths are preventable, with basic obstetrical care. Tanzania, with roughly 13,000 deaths annually, has neither the best nor the worst record in Africa. Although it is politically stable, it is also one of the world's poorest countries, suffering from almost every problem that contributes to high maternal death rates—shortages of doctors, nurses, drugs, equipment, roads and transportation.

There is no single solution for a problem with so many facets, and hospital officials in Berega are trying many things at once. The 120-bed hospital here—a typical rural hospital in a largely rural nation—is a case study in the efforts being made around Africa to reduce deaths in childbirth.

One stopgap measure has been to train assistant medical officers like Mr. Makanza, whose basic schooling is similar to that of physicians' assistants in the United States, to perform Caesareans and certain other operations. Tanzania is also struggling to train more assistants and midwives, build more clinics and nursing schools, provide housing to attract doctors and nurses to rural areas and provide places for pregnant women to stay near hospitals so that they can make it to the labor ward on time.

But there is a shortage of Emmanuel Makanzas, too. As he began to operate, he said he should have had another pair of skilled hands to assist him. But, he said, "we are few."

He made a quick, vertical cut, working down from just below the navel, through one layer at a time: skin, fat, muscle, the peritoneal membrane. Within three or four minutes he had reached the uterus, sliced it open and wrestled out a limp, silent baby boy exhausted by the prolonged labor and knocked out by ether. It took a nurse 5 to 10 minutes of vigorous resuscitation to get him breathing normally and crying.

There are many nights like this at the hospital here, 6 miles from the nearest paved road and 25 miles from the last electric pole. It is not uncommon for a woman in labor to arrive after a daylong, bone-rattling ride on the back of a bicycle or motorcycle, sometimes with the arm or leg of her unborn child already emerging from her body.

Some arrive too late. In October, a mother who had been in labor for two days died of infection. In November and December, two bled to

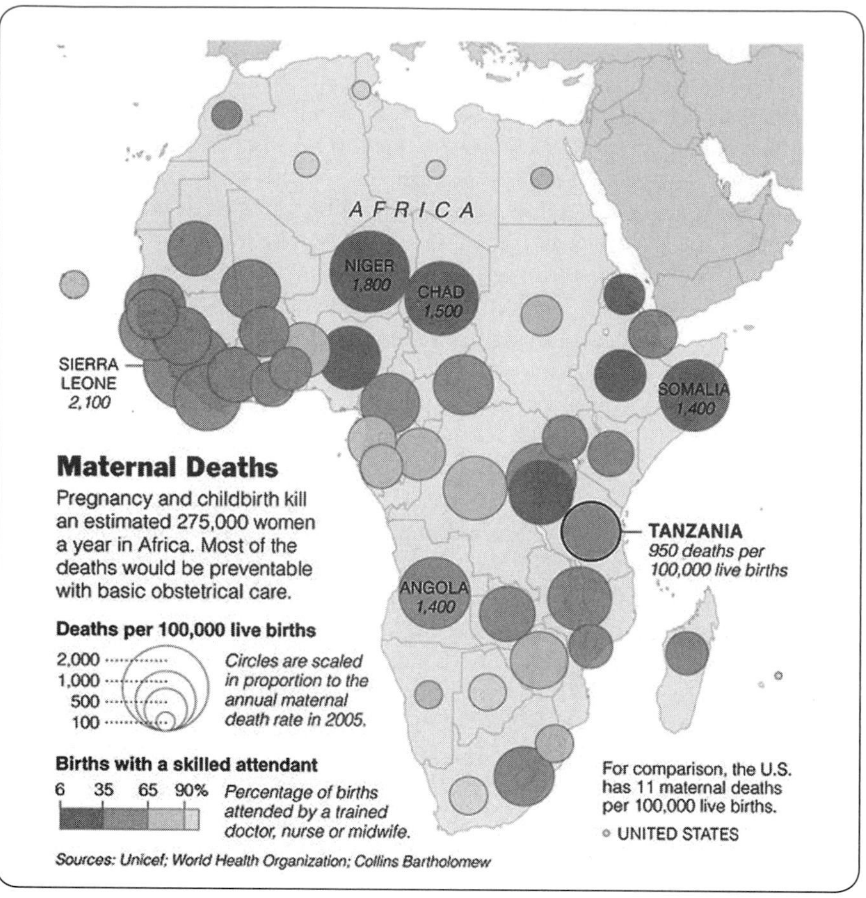
AFRICA
NIGER 1,800
CHAD 1,500
SIERRA LEONE 2,100
SOMALIA 1,400
ANGOLA 1,400
TANZANIA
950 deaths per 100,000 live births
Maternal Deaths
Pregnancy and childbirth kill an estimated 275,000 women a year in Africa. Most of the deaths would be preventable with basic obstetrical care.
Deaths per 100,000 live births
2,000
1,000
500
100
Circles are scaled in proportion to the annual maternal death rate in 2005.
Births with a skilled attendant
6 35 65 90%
Percentage of births attended by a trained doctor, nurse or midwife.
For comparison, the U.S. has 11 maternal deaths per 100,000 live births.
UNITED STATES
Sources: Unicef; World Health Organization; Collins Bartholomew

The New York Times

death. Doctors say they think that more deaths probably occur outside the hospital among the many women who try to give birth at home.

A few minutes' walk from the hospital is an orphanage that sums up the realities here: it is home to 20 children, all under 3, nearly all of whose mothers died giving birth to them.

"You can never get used to maternal deaths," said Dr. Siriel Nanzia Massawe, an obstetrician and the director of postgraduate studies at Muhimbili University of Health and Allied Sciences in Dar es Salaam, the country's largest city. "One minute she's talking with her husband, then she is bleeding and then she is gone. She's gone, very young. You cannot sleep for one week. That face will always come back to you. Too many die, too young. But the people in power, they have not seen it. We need to make them aware."

Over the course of several days at Berega, the difficulties became clear. At times, Mr. Makanza performed one Caesarean after another, sometimes in the middle of the night. One mother was only 15.

Another had already had two Caesareans, adding to the risk of this operation or any future pregnancies, but she declined Mr. Makanza's recommendation to be sterilized.

Others had hoped to speed their labor by taking herbal medicine but were suffering dangerously strong contractions. Hospital staff members struggled to keep up with the operations, handwashing bloodstained gauze and surgical drapes in basins and mopping blood from the floor between cases.

Two women had severe problems from high blood pressure. One came to the hospital after giving birth at home and having a seizure. Another delivered a full-term infant who had died in her womb at least a week before; her only other pregnancy had ended the same way.

A mother in the maternity ward had arrived in labor with twins, one already dead. A Caesarean had saved the second.

## The Global Perspective

Women in Africa have some of the world's highest death rates in pregnancy and during childbirth. For each woman who dies, 20 others suffer from serious complications, according to the W.H.O. "Maternal deaths have remained stubbornly intractable" for two decades, Unicef reported last year. In 2000, the United Nations set a goal to reduce the deaths by 75 percent by 2015. It is a goal that few poor countries are expected to reach.

"Why don't we have a global fund for maternal health, like the one for TB, malaria and AIDS?" Dr. Massawe asked.

Tanzania has reduced its death rate for young children, but not maternal mortality. The Ministry of Health says its maternal death rate is 578 per 100,000 births, but the World Health Organization puts the figure at 950 per 100,000. By contrast, the health organization estimates the rate in Ireland, the world's lowest, to be 1 per 100,000.

The women who die are usually young and healthy, and their deaths needless. The five leading causes are bleeding, infection, high blood pressure, prolonged labor and botched abortions. Maternal deaths from such causes were largely eliminated nearly a century ago in developed countries. In poor countries a mother's death leaves her newborn at great risk of dying as well.

Experts say that what kills many women are "the three delays"—the woman's delay in deciding to go to the hospital, the time she loses traveling there and the hospital's delay in starting treatment once she arrives. Only about 15 percent of births have dangerous complications, but they are almost impossible to predict.

## A Medical Emergency

A case in the Tanzanian city of Moshi late last year reveals how suddenly a seemingly normal labor can turn into an emergency in which every second counts. Hawa Khalidi, 36, who had five normal births, gave birth to her sixth child a few hours before dawn on Nov. 19 at a health center staffed only by nurses in one of the poorer sections of the city.

Then she began to hemorrhage, and by daybreak she was dead.

An autopsy found that Mrs. Khalidi bled to death because the nurse who delivered her baby failed to perform one basic task, essential to prevent deadly bleeding: removing the placenta after she gave birth.

Normally, pulling on the umbilical cord will extract the placenta. But the autopsy revealed that the cord broke off. The nurse apparently did not know how to reach into the womb to remove the placenta. She sent Mrs. Khalidi to a hospital, but by then Mrs. Khalidi had lost so much blood that doctors could not save her.

In an interview, Mrs. Khalidi's husband said nurses at the clinic had scolded her because she was too poor to bring her own "delivery kit" containing gloves, clamps and other supplies. Some maternity wards are so crowded that women sleep two or three to a bed, or lie on the floor, along with their newborns. Although the government has promised to build more clinics and to put one within three miles of every village, it cannot even fully staff the clinics it already has. Health workers—overworked, underpaid and sometimes poorly trained—often become demoralized and resigned to the high death rates.

Women lack education and information about birth control, and some become pregnant too young to give birth safely. Husbands and in-laws may decide where a woman gives birth and insist that she stay at home to save money. Malnutrition, stunted growth, malaria and other infections, anemia and closely spaced pregnancies all add to the risks.

In rural areas, many women use traditional birth attendants instead of going to the hospital. The attendants usually have no formal training in medicine or midwifery. Many doctors blame them for high rates of maternal death and complications, saying they let labor go on for too long, cannot treat complications and fail to recognize emergencies that demand hospital care. But many women are loyal to them. For one thing, the price is right. Around Berega, they charge about $2 per birth. A normal birth at the hospital costs about $6, an emergency Caesarean $15.

Dr. Jeffrey Wilkinson, an obstetrician from Duke University who is working at the Kilimanjaro Christian Medical Center in Moshi, pointed out that other African countries, like Niger, had even higher maternal death rates. Despite the many obstacles in Tanzania, "there is hope here," he said.

## A Hospital's Shortages

Even though it serves an area with about 200,000 people, the hospital in Berega has no obstetrician or pediatrician. It has only one fully trained doctor, Dr. Paschal Mdoe, 31, who became the medical director in August, fresh out of medical school.

Like most hospitals in Tanzania, the one in Berega tries to compensate for the doctor shortage by relying on assistant medical officers like Mr. Makanza to perform many Caesareans and a few other relatively simple operations like hernia repairs. Although such assistants eventually become quite adept in such operations, most other countries do not recognize their credentials and so do not try to lure them away, a big plus for Tanzania, which loses doctors and nurses to Botswana and other countries that pay more.

Periodically, visiting surgeons repair fistulas, a severe childbirth injury that causes incontinence in the mother. Other outside experts like Dr. Wilkinson have also taught staff members how to resuscitate newborns and treat obstetrical emergencies like hemorrhages and severe high blood pressure.

To persuade more women to give birth at the hospital instead of at home, the hospital is sending health workers with that message to marketplaces, churches, village elders and religious leaders.

In addition, the hospital is creating a "maternity waiting home" so that pregnant women who live far from the hospital can travel to Berega before labor starts and have a place to stay until it is time to give birth. Officials are also negotiating with the government to cover all fees for pregnant women and children, and to acquire an ambulance. (The hospital, a mission institution supported partly by the Anglican Church and the government, does not receive enough money to cover its costs, so it charges fees to make up the difference.)

But there is a long way to go. Only 20 percent of women in the area give birth at the hospital, and many do so only when they need Caesareans. Many women say they simply cannot afford the hospital. More than 50 percent stay home to give birth, and the rest go to local clinics that cannot handle emergencies or perform Caesareans.

"We lost four or five babies this week," the Rev. Isaac Y. Mgego, an Anglican priest and the hospital's director, said in an interview in January. "Our doctors have to play with two bad things, to save the mother or save the child."

It is not easy to lure doctors and nurses to Berega, where most people live in mud huts with no electricity, flush toilets or running water. Malaria is common.

To attract staff members, the hospital provides concrete houses with access to a pump. The church "tops up" government salaries for doctors and nurses, and Dr. Mdoe successfully lobbied church officials to give his staff a raise. A nursing school is being built, with the hope that it will draw local students who will want to remain in Berega.

The hospital has four nursing officers, 10 midwives and 2 other workers known as clinical officers, a total of 16.

"We used to have 34," Mr. Mgego said. "People leave. We are struggling to retain them. They don't want to live in villages. Some go without saying goodbye. Those who are committed, they are working tirelessly."

It costs about $200,000 a year to run Berega Hospital, Mr. Mgego said. He said he hoped the hospital would find ways to prevent the serious problems that required mercy missions and visiting surgeons from groups like Amref, the African Medical and Research Foundation, also known as the flying doctors.

"Coming here to cure people is good, but what can we do to prevent this?" Mr. Mgego asked. "So that one day we can say, flying doctors, you can come, but we have only one patient, or nobody, around here."

## A Conversation with . . . Gina Kolata

MEDICAL REPORTER

© The New York Times

*Gina Kolata is a senior writer at The New York Times, where she reports on science and medicine. Before joining The Times in 1987, she was a senior writer for Science magazine. During her tenure at The Times, Kolata has also written articles for magazines including Smithsonian, American Health, Discover, Ladies Home Journal, Cosmopolitan, Redbook, Seventeen, Ms., Glamour, GQ, and Psychology Today. Kolata graduated from the University of Maryland and studied molecular biology on the graduate level at the Massachusetts Institute of Technology for a year and a half. She later returned to the University of Maryland and obtained a master's degree in applied mathematics. The following is an edited transcript of a telephone interview.*

**What's the biggest difference between writing a medical story and writing a story on a nonmedical topic?**

With medical stories you have to know the history of the issue. It helps to understand what makes a study credible and what makes it not credible. It helps to know which experts have a good reputation in the field and which people are fringy. A lot of these things you acquire over the years.

**What's the biggest challenge facing you as a medical reporter in reporting breaking medical news?**

The biggest problem is that you don't have a lot of space. You're not writing a textbook. There are so many things that are commonly misunderstood that it's hard to write a story that gets these things across. Like why would observational study not be as credible as a randomized controlled clinical trial? Or, even worse, for cancer there's this whole question of overdiagnosis. It's very hard to explain this concisely and convincingly. The biggest challenge is to get what's really pretty sophisticated logical reasoning into a story and make it readable and short enough for the newspaper.

**When you're writing a story, whom are you writing for?**
I write for myself. I am easily bored. I have a short attention span. I never think about an ideal reader. I just think about myself.

**Do you ever think about the educational level of the reader?**
No, I don't. I think about me. If I'm not interested, then who else would be? Sometimes my editor, Barbara Strauch, will say things like "People don't know what metastasis is." I say, "You know. You're right." So, yeah, there are things I'm explaining where I think, "Well, I know this." But I have to say it so if I didn't know it, I would understand it right away.

**What are some criteria you use for newsworthiness?**
If it's newsworthy it's usually something that's just been discovered or exciting or goes against conventional wisdom, and all of a sudden people say, "Oh wow. We've been wrong all along. This is the way we should be thinking about this." It has to be something that really engages. It has to have something that captures my imagination, or it has to be a breaking news story.

**What are the hardest stories to cover and why?**
The hardest stories are the ones that deal with things like overdiagnosis. Things where it goes so against conventional wisdom. Everybody believes that if you catch cancer early, that's the best thing for you. To try to talk to people about length bias and lead-time bias—though we'd never use those words—that's really hard because people just don't get it. It goes so against what they've been told all along.

**What's your favorite story and tell me why?**
I don't have a favorite because I fall in love with—it sounds so silly for a reporter to fall in love with her own stories—I fall in love with a lot of stories. Usually it's the one that I'm working on now or the one I just wrote. I loved that stroke story. I loved that stroke story because I will never forget that woman in the lede. I still think about her. So those stories [in the Six Killers series] were really a challenge to write because we were trying to take the six leading killers and tell people something that they didn't already know. Like heart attack, you think, "Oh boy, what a bore. They're going to tell me to get my cholesterol down." So it was a hard story. To figure out where I'm going to go with the whole field of heart disease was really a challenge. The same thing with strokes. But once I got it going and I had the perfect people to put in it, I loved those stories.

**How did you find Dr. Diana Fite, the protagonist in the stroke story?**
Actually it was pretty hard. I went to the National Institutes of Health, and they said they had people all the time that would be the kind of person I wanted, the kind of narrative I wanted. I went there and spent a couple of days and wouldn't you know nobody came into the stroke unit who was really appropriate for what I wanted. So I said, "Okay, I'll e-mail a bunch of people who see a lot of stroke patients and tell them what I'm looking for and see if they have anybody that would fit it." And a guy in Texas said, "Oh, you wouldn't believe, we have the most incredible person that came into our stroke unit." That's how I found her. She was amazing. It was an incredible story. At that point I knew what I wanted. You have to know what you're looking for.

**What do you think is the most common error that beginning medical reporters make?**
People don't appreciate why one study is more credible than another. Why would you believe this one instead of that one? So they give a lot of credibility to things that really should not be getting it at all. Often that means that they will exaggerate the important studies which are not very important, or they will take criticisms—which are ridiculous criticisms of something that really is important but that people don't want to hear—and they'll blow the criticisms up as though they were of equal importance with the study. You have to have a lot of confidence in your own knowledge and judgment. That's something that comes with experience. It's hard not to be swayed when someone at a leading medical school is saying something for reasons that have nothing to do with science, and what they're saying is an exaggeration of what the facts really are. You have to have a lot of confidence. You have to be willing to check things out to death with other people and know who to believe and who not to.

**What's your level of medical or scientific training?**
First, I was a microbiology major. Then I was going to get a Ph.D. in molecular biology, but I left after a year and a half because I didn't like the lab. Then I went back to school, and I was going to get a Ph.D. in math. I was in graduate school again, and I decided I wasn't cut out to be a mathematician. I was going to quit, but my adviser said I should write a thesis or people would think I was an idiot dropping out of graduate school. So I got a master's in math, but only because my adviser said people will think you're dumb if you drop out of graduate school and never get a degree. That's really why I got a master's.

**If you were advising college students who wanted to be medical reporters, what would be the two or three most important courses they should take?**
They should know statistics. Not at the level of a statistician but the level so they can understand what's going on when people talk about the design of studies. It would be very nice to understand at least enough so that you could appreciate a good study from a bad one. It would be really nice if they knew something about medical history. It's amazing how much knowing a little bit about medical history helps inform what you see today. It also helps you

write a better story. And I guess it would help if they took at least one writing course.

I taught a course at Princeton on medical writing. Nobody had ever told them that it wasn't enough just to throw all your thoughts on the paper in some sort of random order. In the beginning every single paper I read, I would put at the bottom, "I finished your story, and I didn't know what your point was." One thing that I think that they all came away with was an ability to say what is my point. I told them that in a newspaper story you should tell the reader right away: why am I reading this and why am I reading this now.

Some people really have a gift for this kind of writing, and some people don't. For seeing the story. It's not just writing it. It's seeing what the point is. Seeing what you want to tell. Seeing why is this interesting right away and glomming onto that. With writing, so many people think, "Oh, I can write, anybody can write." That's always what happens. "I don't know what to do with my life. I guess I'll become a journalist like you, Gina." It actually takes a lot of work, a lot of work. What we do is pretty hard, and it takes a lot of experience. I don't think people quite appreciate what goes into these stories, which, if we're lucky, seem so easy to read. Not anybody could write like that.

**When you have an embargoed journal article, what's your approach in reporting and then writing it?**

We get these things in advance from the journal. It's usually five or six days in advance of when we're allowed to publish them. We always honor these embargoes because you have to. Otherwise you're cut off from the source of the articles. Then I e-mail them to people who I think are experts, or I ask the author who are other experts as well. You have to show it to people. Maybe I missed some fatal flaw in the way that they have done their statistics. I have to show them all the details because these are experts who know what they're looking at, and I'm not. I can look at the bottom line, but I'm not a reviewer. I'm not a scientist. So I absolutely share those articles with other people and so do other reporters, to my knowledge.

**Talk about the need for putting a human face on your stories.**

It always helps, but it's a problem because you don't want to make that story overwhelm everything else. You see this all the time with medical reporting. For example, I saw this all the time with the breast implant stories. People would put in a story [about] somebody who had silicone breast implants and now has every health problem in creation. Then maybe they would have this person have the implants taken out and, guess what, the health problems are gone. You have a story like that, and you could have the scientists talking as much as they want about how, guess what, the science doesn't support a connection. But the reader sees this person who had the implants put in and was so sick and now feels better, and they don't believe a word the science says. That's why I call it the tyranny of the anecdote. They can be so, so, so powerful, so I think you have to use them carefully. I think they can make a story come alive, but you've got to make sure that they don't become the story because an anecdote is not a story. I think of it like an illustration. It's like a photograph.

**When you're writing about a complicated topic that's difficult for you to understand, do you ever go back to the scientist and ask that person, "Have I got it right?"**
I do that all the time. I'll go back to them as many times as it takes. I figure it's better to go back to them and embarrass myself by looking like an idiot than to get it wrong in the paper and embarrass myself in front of millions of readers. If there's any question about whether I have the nuance right, whether I have the point right, I'll always go to them.

**How far do you go in sharing material? Do you paraphrase it or do you ever send [your source] a paragraph or two of your actual story?**
I send a paragraph or two, and I'll say, "Is this right?" All the time. I put this as the subject head: Fact Check. I say, "Is this right?" Any question in my mind about whether it's right, I send it to them right away. No hesitation. Because I don't know. If I try to paraphrase it, often they'll say, "Oh, this one word is a little bit wrong. It gives the wrong impression." And I'd rather have them see that one word.

**You wrote a very controversial story back in 1998, Hope in the Lab (see Selection 8.1 Introduction, page 156), the one about tumors in mice [treated] with angiostatin. If you had it to do over, how would you change that story, given 11 years of experience and 20/20 hindsight?**
What I would have done was when [Nobel laureate James D.] Watson told me that Judah Folkman was going to cure cancer, I would have e-mailed him afterwards and said, "You told me that Judah Folkman was going to cure cancer. I want to use that, so I want to make sure that's absolutely the way you feel." Now I have it in writing if he says yes. If he says no, I'm not going to quote somebody saying that if they're going to then turn around afterwards and say, "I never said it." It's a statement so strong that [it] overwhelms the whole story. Without that statement in there, it's a story about mice. With that statement in there, it's a story that says this is the answer to cancer, and it turned out not to be the answer to cancer.

**How about the first couple of paragraphs [of the angiostatin story]? If you didn't read it carefully, you might miss the mice and think it had to do with humans. It says, "Within a year, if all goes well, the first cancer patient will be injected with two new drugs that can eradicate any type of cancer, with no obvious side effects and no drug resistance—in mice."**
I think I would have started out, "In mice these drugs can eradicate any type of cancer in the future." I think people thought that I was saying this is a cure for humans for sure, and I think I would have emphasized the mice.

**Is that the one story that you wish you could do over if you had the opportunity?**
I definitely would do that one over. Yeah, for sure. I probably wouldn't even write it these days because I'd be more skeptical.

**Is there a lesson for students to learn when they're interviewing a Nobel Prize winner or some other esteemed scientist?**
I would say be very careful. Be very careful of something that's going against everything that you've always heard. That doesn't mean it's not true. It just means be really careful with it—and be really careful when you're writing about cancer that people understand what's a mouse and what's a person.

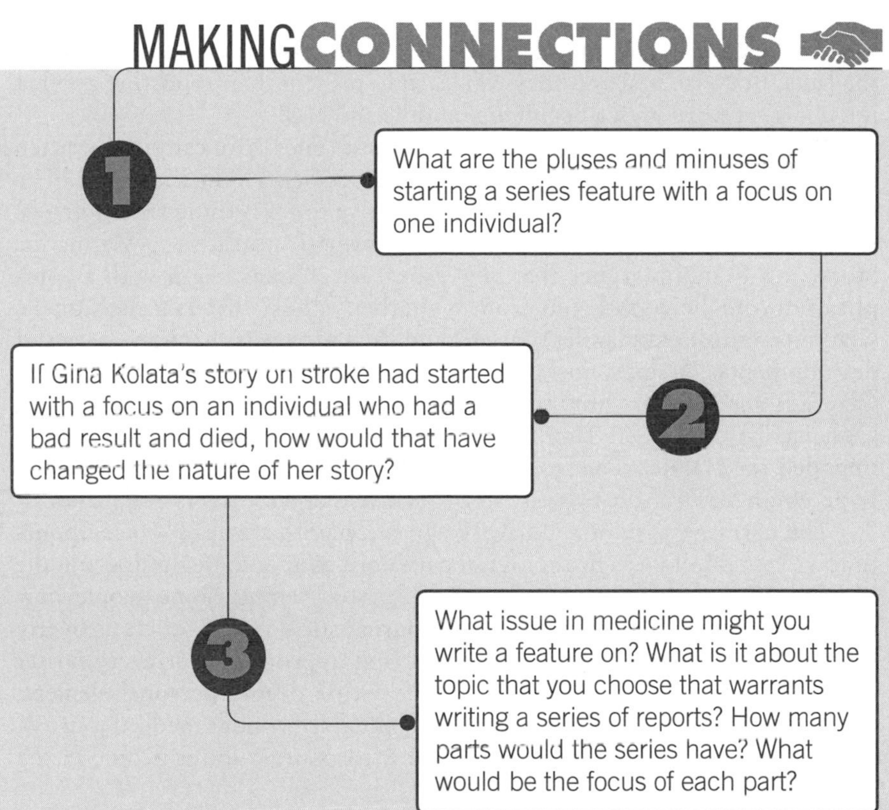

MAKINGCONNECTIONS
1
What are the pluses and minuses of starting a series feature with a focus on one individual?
2
If Gina Kolata's story on stroke had started with a focus on an individual who had a bad result and died, how would that have changed the nature of her story?
3
What issue in medicine might you write a feature on? What is it about the topic that you choose that warrants writing a series of reports? How many parts would the series have? What would be the focus of each part?

# CHAPTER 11

# narratives

THERE'S BEEN A LOT OF BUZZ ABOUT narrative journalism in recent years, but narrative nonfiction (also called literary journalism or creative nonfiction) has been a popular story form for a long time. Narrative nonfiction uses the tools and techniques of fiction writing—character development, scene setting, description and dialogue—to tell true stories. Journalists can't make up dialogue; they can't concoct scenes; and they can't stray from the facts. But with practice, they can learn to present their reporting as what it truly is—a story with a beginning, middle and end.

People have been telling tales since earliest times. You can trace written fictional narrative at least back to the Greek epic poems "The Iliad" and "The Odyssey." You'll find the elements of narrative in everything from nursery rhymes to Shakespeare. In his book about dramatic nonfiction, Writing for Story, Jon Franklin argues that Shakespearean dramas begin with a complication (our hero finds out from his father's ghost that Hamlet's uncle, Claudius, murdered Hamlet's father) and then proceeds through a series of developments.[1] Hamlet mistakes the father of his girlfriend, Ophelia, for Claudius and murders him; then, insane with grief over her father's death, Ophelia drowns herself; later, Hamlet's mother drinks the poisoned chalice intended for Hamlet. The story ends with a resolution of the sort that you hope you never to have to write in a journalistic piece: Everybody dies.

The narrative is in our DNA. We grow up with stories ("Once upon a time . . .") that follow a chronological path until their end. Beginning, middle and end. It's a simple form ideally suited for storytelling. Some people view narrative journalism as the salvation of journalistic writing, others as overly long puffery. Using narrative techniques isn't appropriate for every writer or every story. But for the kind of story with a deeply personal element, narrative can grab readers and capture real life. No wonder medical journalists have taken this formula and adapted it for stories about people facing medical crises.

Sally Ryan for The New York Times

*Deborah Lindner, 33, did intensive research as she considered having a preventive mastectomy after a DNA test.*

## Selection 11.1

*In the first story in this chapter, Amy Harmon introduces us to a 33-year-old woman with a defective gene that raises her risk of developing breast cancer. The discovery of the mutant gene—in the absence of any symptoms—is the complication that drives the story forward. The development in this narrative is the series of steps that she takes to deal with the threat of breast cancer. The resolution? Well, I won't spoil the story for you. As the narrative unfolds, note how the reporter weaves a series of science lessons into the story. This piece works on two levels—as a compelling narrative and as a review of the risks, benefits and psychological turmoil associated with a preventive mastectomy.*

## The DNA Age
## Cancer Free at 33, but Weighing a Mastectomy

By AMY HARMON

CHICAGO—Her latest mammogram was clean. But Deborah Lindner, 33, was tired of constantly looking for the lump.

Ever since a DNA test had revealed her unusually high chance of developing breast cancer, Ms. Lindner had agonized over whether to have a mastectomy, a procedure that would reduce her risk by 90 percent.

She had stared at herself in the mirror, imagining the loss of her familiar shape. She had wondered, unable to ask, how the man she had

*Published: September 16, 2007.*

just started dating would feel about breasts that were surgically reconstructed, incapable of feeling his touch or nursing his children.

But she was sure that her own mother, who had had chemotherapy and a mastectomy after a bout with the cancer that had ravaged generations of her family, would agree it was necessary.

"It could be growing inside of me right now," she told her mother on the phone in February, pacing in her living room here. "We could find it any time."

Waiting for an endorsement, she added, "I could schedule the surgery before the summer."

But no approval came.

"Oh, sweetheart," her mother said. "Let's not rush into this."

Joan Lindner, 63, is a cancer survivor. Her daughter, by contrast, is one of a growing number of young women who call themselves previvors because they have learned early that they are genetically prone to breast cancer, and have the chance to act before it strikes.

As they seek to avoid the potentially lethal consequences of a mutant gene, many of them turn to relatives who share its burden. But at a moment when a genetic test has made family ties even more tangible, they are often at their most strained.

Parents who have fought cancer typically have no experience with the choices that confront their children, and guilt over being the biological source of the problem can color their advice. Siblings and cousins who carry the risk gene evangelize their own approach to managing it, while those who dodged its inheritance seem unqualified to judge.

Even as she searched for her own answer in the year after her DNA test, Deborah Lindner, medical resident, found herself navigating her family's strong and divergent opinions on the imperfect options that lay before her.

Her father, who once feared he would lose his wife to cancer, encouraged the surgery. Her sister reminded her that cancer might be cured in a few years if she could wait.

Her aunt said she hated to see her niece embrace a course of action akin to "leechings of the Dark Ages." A cousin declined even to take the DNA test.

But it was her mother's blessing that Deborah most eagerly sought.

Mrs. Lindner, who had passed her defective gene to her daughter, wanted to will her more time. When she had her own breasts removed she had been married for 27 years and had raised two daughters. Now Mrs. Lindner couldn't shake the fear that her daughter might trade too much in her quest for a cancer-free future. What if taking such a radical step made it harder for Deborah to find someone special and become a mother herself?

"I have this amazing gift of knowing my risk," her daughter told her over the phone that winter night, gazing out over the frozen city from her apartment on the 38th floor. "How can I not do anything about that?"

The Lindners share a defective copy of a gene known as BRCA1 (for breast cancer gene 1) that raises their risk of developing breast cancer sometime in their lives to between 60 and 90 percent. Only 30,000 of more than 250,000 American women estimated to carry a mutation in BRCA1 or a related gene, BRCA2, have so far been tested. But their numbers have doubled in the last two years, and with a sharp increase in genetic testing, are expected to double again in the coming one.

About a third opt for preventive mastectomies that remove the tissue where the breast cancer develops. A majority have their ovaries removed, halving their breast cancer odds while decreasing the risk of highly lethal ovarian cancer, to which they are also prone. Some take drugs that ward off breast cancer. Others hope that frequent checkups will catch the cancer early, or that they will beat the odds.

Their decisions, which require weighing an inborn risk against other life priorities, are highly individual. But with DNA forecasts of many other conditions on their way, BRCA carriers offer the first clues for how to reckon with a serious disease that may never arise—and with the family turmoil that nearly always does.

## A 50–50 Chance

Deborah Lindner's sister, Lori French, got her results first.

Long ago, before she knew about the DNA test, Ms. French, 37, had resolved to have her breasts and ovaries removed by age 40 to avoid the family cancer. Nor did she want reconstructive surgery, having seen her mother struggle with the pain and cosmetic disappointment of hers.

"Plan on it," she had told her husband before they got married a decade earlier. "I'm going to get old and have big hips and no breasts."

The envelope with the test results that Ms. French opened with shaking hands in the summer of 2005 offered a reprieve. She and her husband sobbed, hugging each other in the knowledge that she was free of the genetic defect. While she still had the 12 percent chance any woman has of developing breast cancer, she could not have passed on the steep BRCA risk to either her daughter or son.

"It's done!" Ms. French told her family. "In our line, it's ended."

For years, the sisters had united in a common dread. Now it was Deborah's alone.

"I'm so sorry you have to be the one," Ms. French said when her sister called a week later with the news that she had tested positive for the mutation.

"I'm so glad it's not you," Deborah replied.

It could have been either, neither or both of them—each sister, she knew, had had a 50 percent chance of inheriting the defective gene from their mother, dictated solely by a roll of the genetic dice. But if it was going to be one of them, Deborah thought she was in a better position to handle it. Her sister taught at a missionary school in the Philippines, where she lived with her family, while Deborah was single and in the second year of her medical residency program at Northwestern University, with ready access to quality health care.

Yet in the weeks that followed, Deborah fought off pangs of jealousy and the fantasy that fate could somehow be rearranged.

"She already has a husband, she already has kids," Deborah thought on morning runs along Lake Michigan.

She enrolled in a stepped-up surveillance program that required alternating mammograms and sonograms with M.R.I.'s every six months. But on the mornings of her appointments, and at unpredictable moments in between, she was overwhelmed with fear. Often, she would examine her breasts every other day.

"It's taking over my mind," she told Erin King, a close friend and fellow resident in the obstetrics and gynecology program.

Ms. King, 33, who had had breast implants for cosmetic reasons, and another resident friend were proponents of pre-emptive surgery.

"Get them off and get new ones," they told her. "They'll be awesome and perky and cute."

But they sympathized with her distress at the appearance of traditional reconstruction, with skin grafts molded into a fake nipple that can never quite match the texture of a real one and the areola simulated by a tattoo.

"They just don't look normal," Deborah sighed as they debated the question over the barbecue grill at Ms. King's apartment one night.

Accustomed to seeking her mother's counsel, Deborah kept her distance in those months, not wanting to worry her. Instead, she pestered breast specialists. How many cancers do you actually catch? How many in an early stage? The answers were vague. Still, they discouraged her from surgery. Most women who had a preventive mastectomy, a breast surgeon told her, already had a family.

## A Frightening Pattern

In the fall of 2006, Deborah turned her residency research requirement into a personal quest for better information, analyzing the records of BRCA mutation carriers who had been counseled at Northwestern.

One file told of a woman who had developed cancer and chosen a lumpectomy, a procedure that leaves the breast mostly intact. The cancer came back—while she was pregnant. When she had an early Caesarean section so she could get chemotherapy without harming the baby, doctors discovered an ovarian tumor that had already spread to her abdomen.

The pattern was not uncommon. BRCA-related breast cancer usually strikes early, before age 50, and is more likely to recur in the other breast. Ovarian cancer, which strikes about 50 percent of BRCA1 carriers, compared with 2 percent of the general population, is rarely detected early and is fatal three-quarters of the time.

"It's like I'm reading this book and I know what's coming," Deborah told her fellow residents. "I see the note, 'Patient opts for surveillance,' and I'm like, 'No, don't do it, don't do it!' "

Several times during her oncology rotation that term, she slipped out of an ovarian cancer patient's room to cry in the stairwell. To eliminate her risk of ovarian cancer, doctors had recommended that she have her own ovaries removed by age 40, or as soon as she had children. Removing her ovaries would halve her breast cancer risk as well, but the hormones that are generally used to treat the harsh menopausal symptoms brought on by the procedure, Deborah learned, would then raise the risk again—unless she had her breasts removed first.

## Unspoken Questions

Over Thanksgiving at her parents' winter home in Florida, Deborah ran through her risk analysis. Her father, Philip Lindner, listened and nodded. Mammograms and ultrasounds, she noted, may miss more than half of cancers in younger women with denser breasts. Magnetic resonance imaging tests are more reliable but produce more false positives, which can lead to unnecessary biopsies and worry. And it is not yet clear that early detection improves survival rates in women with BRCA mutations.

"You can't argue with statistics," said Mr. Lindner, a financial executive. "You don't want to get cancer and then say, 'I wish I would have done thus and so.'"

Deborah's mother agreed it was important to know the risks. But not knowing them could be a luxury, too. Had she had the same options as her daughter, would she have found a man and had a family? It might have altered her whole life.

"I know the joy that my girls have brought to me," she confided to a friend. "If Deb misses it, she won't know what she missed. But having experienced it, I would never have wanted to miss it."

Tentatively, she broached the subject of breast-feeding with her daughter. "That was something very special to me," Mrs. Lindner said.

"Wouldn't it be more special," Deborah shot back with uncharacteristic edge, "if I was around to have children in the first place?"

But if her mother worried that surgery would make her less attractive to men, Deborah shared those concerns.

"Do fake boobs freak you out?" she often imagined asking Jeff Zehr, the man she had begun dating a few months before.

Mr. Zehr, a fellow marathon runner who attended her church, had told her she was special to him, and she felt similarly. But she didn't want to scare him away or, worse, put pressure on the relationship to proceed faster than it otherwise would.

As Deborah felt increasingly torn between life events that couldn't be rushed, and surgeries that shouldn't wait, there was one more piece of information she thought would sway her mother.

"Will you do something for me?" she asked. "Look through the family tree and find out how old everyone was when they got their cancer."

The answers were chilling. One of her first cousins, Mrs. Lindner learned, had breast cancer at age 33. Now the cancer had returned, and she was losing the fight.

Another first cousin got her breast cancer diagnosis at 34; she died. Her daughter, at 33, had recently learned she had the disease.

Mrs. Lindner called her daughter. "Have the surgery as soon as possible," she said.

But a few days later, Mrs. Lindner called back. Her mother's ovarian cancer, she remembered, had not surfaced until she was in her 70s—and she had survived. Joan Lindner had been 48 when the doctors detected her breast cancer, and she had survived too.

"We were really on the far side of the bell curve," she said.

## Memories of Chemotherapy

Deborah remembered her mother's cancer diagnosis, which came just before her graduation from high school. Her school choir had been selected to sing at Carnegie Hall, and her parents had planned to come as chaperones. Instead, she went alone while her father accompanied Mrs. Lindner to chemotherapy appointments. During that summer, her mother's bedroom door, always open, stayed closed.

Now Deborah reminded her what she had always said about her chemotherapy. Her eyelashes, once long and curly, had been rendered short and stubby. Food tasted different. It had, in so many subtle ways, aged her.

"I don't want that for myself," Deborah said. "I don't want to treat cancer. I just never want to get it."

She began to seek support elsewhere. A genetic counselor gave her a brochure for Bright Pink, a group of young women who have tested positive for the BRCA genes. Lindsay Avner, its 24-year-old founder, lived in Chicago, and their meeting over coffee in the hospital lounge one evening in March lasted four hours. Ms. Avner had had a prophylactic mastectomy last year.

"You've got to see my breasts," she told Deborah, escorting her into the bathroom.

Ms. Avner's surgeon at Memorial Sloan-Kettering Cancer Center in Manhattan had used a technique that preserved the breast skin and nipples, leaving a scar only under the breast.

Deborah, still in her scrubs, said, "Wow."

Mr. Zehr drove her to an appointment with Geoffrey Fenner, the chief of plastic surgery at Evanston Memorial Hospital one evening in mid-April. If she could find a surgeon to perform the mastectomy, Dr. Fenner said he would perform the reconstruction.

The nipple-sparing technique, the doctor explained, is not popular in the United States; a decade-old study suggested that leaving the nipple increased the risk of cancer. But more recent research indicated that the risk was perhaps only 1 percent greater than with traditional reconstruction.

"I can live with that," Deborah said.

Mr. Zehr, a corporate insurance underwriter, waited outside. On the car ride home, Deborah lobbed her question into the darkness.

"Does the thought of plastic surgery bother you?" she asked.

A moment passed.

"It would if I thought the person I was with was doing it because they didn't like the way they looked," he said. "But that isn't this situation."

He looked at her. "So, no, it doesn't bother me."

Deborah announced her intention to have surgery in a long e-mail message to family members at the end of April.

"I want to share with you what I feel is the right answer for me," she wrote.

Like anyone who carried the defective gene, she might never get cancer, she acknowledged. Or she might only get it when she was old. "But I'm not a gambler," she wrote.

Her aunt, Gloria Spurlock, a music teacher in Louisville, Ky., immediately called Mrs. Lindner, her sister, at her home in Des Moines.

"How could you let her dismember her body?" she demanded. "You have to talk her out of it."

Stung, Mrs. Lindner tried to defend her daughter. But Mrs. Spurlock was voicing some of her own worst fears.

"Gloria," she replied. "This is Deb's decision."

It was the first of several heated phone calls between the sisters. Mrs. Spurlock had considered getting tested after Mrs. Lindner found out she had a BRCA mutation. The sisters knew the gene must have come from their mother, who had had ovarian cancer a decade earlier, and whose own mother had died of the same disease. But Mrs. Spurlock concentrated instead on a healthy diet, rest and positive thinking.

The medical profession, she had long believed, was far too eager to administer drugs and remove body parts that could be healed.

Mrs. Spurlock's daughter, Lisa Spurlock, 24, also expressed dismay.

"I'm sorry you have to be so scared of this disease," Ms. Spurlock wrote to her cousin.

The reactions gave Deborah pause. Then they made her angry.

"Why are they saying things like this to me?" she demanded of her mother.

From the Philippines, her sister suggested that Deborah was exposed to the worst-case scenarios as a doctor. Can't breast cancer often be cured?

"You're right, it can often be cured," Deborah wrote back. "The problem is that the cure involves cancer, surgery, chemotherapy, sometimes radiation and the possibility of metastasis and death."

When a second surgeon in Chicago gave the idea of the preventive mastectomy a lukewarm reception because of her age, Deborah flew to New York for a consultation with the doctor who had performed Ms. Avner's surgery. She invited her mother to come with her.

On the plane, Deborah showed her mother a PowerPoint presentation she had created, making the case for preventive surgery. Mrs. Lindner listened. But mostly she watched the relief in her daughter's face as she talked about escaping her genetic prognosis.

It was there again the next day in Dr. Patrick I. Borgen's office on Park Avenue, when the doctor supplied the first unconditional medical affirmation of Deborah's view.

"Maybe your grandchildren will have better options," said Dr. Borgen, director of the Brooklyn Breast Cancer Project at the Maimonides Cancer Center. "But right now a draconian operation is the best thing we can do for you."

Back home in Iowa, Mrs. Lindner asked her husband: "What would we have done? What if we had known when we were dating?"

"We would have done the same thing," he said. "We would have wanted you to live."

At Dr. Borgen's recommendation, Deborah scheduled the double mastectomy with Dr. D. J. Winchester at Evanston Northwestern hospital for the last weekend in June, three days after her medical board exam. Her insurance agreed to pay after requesting a letter of support from her surgeons. There would be just enough time to recover before she began practicing in the fall.

## A Glance in the Mirror

But with the date fixed, Deborah, for the first time in months, began to doubt her decision.

Glancing in the mirror on her way out for a run, she looked herself over.

"I was like, all right, there's me, those are my breasts," she told a friend. "That is what I see."

It did not help that Mr. Zehr did not seem to quite understand what the surgery entailed. "I won't be able to breast-feed," she reminded him.

"I thought you were having reconstruction," he said, puzzled.

"Yes," she said, "but they'll be silicone."

With three days to go, Deborah met with a nurse to go over the details of the procedure she had discussed with the surgeon. She wanted to be sure about where the incisions would be, and the size of the implants.

"We had talked about the scars on the side," she told the nurse, "and not touching the nipple."

"Oh, you may have incisions everywhere," the nurse said. "There may be one up the front and underneath and up the nipple."

Deborah burst into tears.

"Am I doing the right thing?" she asked her mother from her cellphone after she left the office.

Mrs. Lindner, packing for the drive to Chicago to be with her daughter during her hospital stay, knew she was not just asking about the scars. And she had the answer.

"Yes," Mrs. Lindner said. "You are doing what is right for you."

On the morning of the surgery, Mr. Zehr was there, holding Deborah's hand. "You look cute in your gown," he told her.

In the lounge, Mrs. Lindner waited. The surgery and reconstruction took seven and a half hours, twice as long as the doctors had expected. The incisions were small, Dr. Winchester explained when he came out, and hidden under the breast, so it had taken a long time to scrape out all the breast tissue.

Then Mrs. Lindner rode up in the elevator with her daughter, still unconscious from the anesthesia. As they arrived at their floor, Deborah opened her eyes.

"Mom," she said, and managed a small smile.

## Selection 11.2

*In the next story reporter Pam Belluck gives readers a window into childhood mental illness. It's an especially tough assignment since families are understandably reluctant to share their problems with reporters. Before profiling a child, a reporter must obtain the child's and the parents' consent. A reporter also has to make her best ethical judgment about whether the benefit of informing readers about childhood mental illness outweighs the possible harm to the child and family being profiled. Even if a reporter gains access, explaining the science behind childhood mental illness is difficult. Psychiatrists don't have a complete understanding of the origins of childhood disorders. Parents have an even harder time coming to grips with their children's psychological demons.*

*In the first of an occasional series on troubled children, Belluck conveys what it's like for a child and her family to live with mental illness. Belluck chooses a narrative format in telling the story of 10-year-old Haley's long history of emotional problems. As with most narratives, this story begins with a complication, when Haley started seeing things that were not there. The complication—Haley's mental illness—then leads to a series of developments that draw other family members into the child's emotional maelstrom. The resolution of this story isn't clear . . . an ending that may be emblematic of the nature of childhood mental illness.*

## TROUBLED CHILDREN
# Living With Love, Chaos and Haley

By PAM BELLUCK

PLYMOUTH, Mass.—When Haley Abaspour started seeing things that were not there—bugs and mice crawling on her parents' bed, imaginary friends sitting next to her on the couch, dead people at a church that housed her preschool—her parents were unsure what to think. After all, she was a little girl.

"I thought for a long time, 'She's just gifted,'" said her father, Bejan Abaspour. " 'This is good. Don't worry about it.'"

But as Haley got older, things got worse. She developed tics—dolphin squeaks, throat-clearing, clenching her face and body as if moving her bowels. She heard voices, banging, cymbals in her head. She became anxiety-ridden over run-of-the-mill things: ambulance sirens, train rides. Her mood switched suddenly from excitedly chatty to inconsolably distraught.

"It's like watching 'The Sound of Music' and 'The Exorcist' all at the same time," Mr. Abaspour said.

For her family, life with Haley, now 10, has been a turbulent stream of symptoms, diagnoses, medications, unrealized expectations. Diagnosed as a combination of bipolar disorder with psychotic features, obsessive-compulsive disorder, generalized anxiety disorder and Tourette's syndrome, her illness dominates every moment, every relationship, every decision.

Haley's fears, moods and obsessions seep into her family's most pedestrian routines—dinnertime, bedtime, getting ready for school. Excruciating worries permeate her parents' sleep; unanswerable questions end in frustrated hopes.

"The first time we took Haley to the hospital, I guess I expected that they would put it all back together," said her mother, Christine Abaspour. "But it's never all back together."

At least six million American children have difficulties that are diagnosed as serious mental disorders, according to government surveys—a number that has tripled since the early 1990's. Most are treated with psychiatric medications and therapy. The children sometimes attend special schools.

But while these measures can help, they often do not help enough, and the families of such children are left on their own to sort through a cacophony of conflicting advice.

The illness, and sometimes the treatment, can strain marriages, jobs, finances. Parents must monitor medications, navigate therapy sessions, arrange special school services. Some families must switch

---

*Published: October 22, 2006.*

neighborhoods or schools to escape unhealthy situations or to find support and services. Some keep friends and relatives away.

Parents can feel guilt, anger, helplessness. Siblings can feel neglected, resentful or pressure to be problem-free themselves.

"It kind of ricochets to other family members," said Dr. Robert L. Hendren, president-elect of the American Academy of Child and Adolescent Psychiatry. "I see so many parents who just hurt badly for their children and then, in a sense, start hurting for themselves."

Ms. Abaspour, 39, struggles to master the details of Haley's illness, to answer her obsessive questions, to keep her occupied. Mr. Abaspour, 50, who long believed that "Haley was going to grow out of it," has been gripped by anxious thoughts and intrusive images that rattle him to tears on the hourlong commute to his job as an anesthesia engineer at a Boston hospital. He imagines people being crushed by trucks, someone hurting Haley, his own death.

Haley's sister, Megan, 13, has been so focused on Haley and determined not to add to her family's burden that in June, after a quarrel with her parents, she tied a T-shirt around her neck in a suicidal gesture.

"I feel like she gets all the problems and I feel like I have to take some of that off of her," Megan said. "It's really difficult a lot to try to stay away from babying her and helping her. I try to stay still but it just hurts, it hurts inside."

Haley, with her shy smile and obsidian eyes, is increasingly aware of her own problems, although she cannot always express exactly what is going on inside. "My mind says I need some help" is the way she explained it recently.

Her illness has caused great financial strain; although the Abaspours have health insurance, they have been forced to draw on their savings and lean heavily on their credit cards for living expenses. Still, they have bought a trailer in a New Hampshire campground because there Haley finds occasional solace, and relatives nearby understand the family's ordeal.

The family wrestles with deciding whom to tell about Haley's illness, and what to say. Her worst symptoms are most visible at home and less apparent at the public school and the state-financed therapeutic after-school program she attends. Her parents say she works hard to hold herself together during the day and then later, feeling more comfortable with her family, falls apart.

This disparity in behavior is not uncommon, said Dr. Joseph A. Jackson IV, Haley's psychiatrist, and "parents often get the brunt."

Because of the contrast in Haley's public and private behavior, her parents are wary of telling people that she is mentally ill, as they might not notice.

"I don't want anybody to pity her," Mr. Abaspour said. But they also get frustrated when teachers or relatives play down the seriousness of Haley's illness, or conclude that she is being manipulative or that another child-rearing approach would help.

In the middle of last year, for example, a teacher did not understand Haley's need to leave the classroom to quiet the voices or relieve anxiety. Haley grew so frustrated that she "would sit there in her chair and cry," her father said. The parents pressed school officials to switch her to another class.

"We're sick and tired of trying to prove it to people," Ms. Abaspour said.

Her husband added, "Everybody thinks they have the solution. When Joe Schmo comes over for a drink, he says, 'Try this, this will work.' No, it won't."

## Visions and Voices

From birth, it was clear that "I was dealing with something different," Ms. Abaspour said. Displaying a photo album with picture after picture of Megan all smiles and Haley "crying, crying, crying," she added, "We just thought we had a very difficult child."

Yet exactly what was wrong puzzled them for years, and even now, Ms. Abaspour said, "Every day it's something new, I swear."

While increasing awareness of childhood mental illness has helped many children and families, it can also create a misimpression that everything can be treated, said Dr. Glen R. Elliott, chief psychiatrist at the Children's Health Council, a community mental health service in Palo Alto, Calif., and the author of "Medicating Young Minds: How to Know if Psychiatric Drugs Will Help or Hurt Your Child." That can make families with complex cases feel "either genuine confusion or pretend certainty," Dr. Elliott said.

The Abaspours decided to speak with a reporter about Haley's illness and its impact on their family because they hoped it would help other families and make society more hospitable for children like their daughter. Talking about it was sometimes emotional, especially for Mr. Abaspour, whose eyes often clouded with tears. But they also said they found it useful to articulate their feelings.

When Haley was 3 or 4, a pediatrician blamed tonsillitis-induced sleep apnea, predicting that after her tonsils were removed, " 'you'll see a totally different child,' " Ms. Abaspour recalled.

"We thought, 'This is what is wrong with our child. This is our answer,' " she said. Preschool teachers suggested a learning disability. Later, Haley repeated first grade. The Abaspours consulted therapists about the visions of friends in the liner of the family's pool and riding with Haley on her bike, and the voices criticizing her or telling her to touch a certain table. When a neurologist ruled out medical causes like Lyme disease, Ms. Abaspour recalled, her husband said, "I think we should just give her a placebo—it's all in her head."

They got a cat, "though we weren't cat people," Ms. Abaspour said. Then they got another because the first was "not the type of cat that Haley could throw over her shoulder and squeeze."

New symptoms kept emerging. For a while, when she was about 7, the voices "were telling her she was a boy," Ms. Abaspour said. "She had to constantly prove to them that she wasn't."

Haley became obsessed with penises, which she called "bums." She claimed to see them though she was looking at fully clothed men and boys, her mother said. "Then she felt guilty. She would come up to me and whisper, 'I saw his bum, I saw his bum.' The bus driver or the little boy, anyone. It was constant."

To halt the whispering, Ms. Abaspour suggested that they share a private signal: Haley could flash a thumbs-up after a sighting. Haley also seemed preoccupied with death, and on a highway would say that voices told her, "If that license plate didn't say such and such, she was going to die," her mother said.

Once, Mr. Abaspour recalled, Haley "kept yelling that she wants to start over."

## The Treatment Puzzle

When she was almost 8, Haley visited Dr. Jackson at his office at the Cambridge Health Alliance. He was struck by the results of a screening: Haley met full criteria for virtually every mental disorder listed.

"Her symptoms," he said, "suggested anxiety, morbid thoughts, obsessions possibly of a sexual nature, frequent fluctuations in mood, periods of euphoria, giddiness, irritability, rapid speech, auditory and visual hallucinations, thought disorganization, vocal tics, distractibility, poor socialization in school, sensory integration issues, attention impulse disorder, manic behavior, sleep disturbance."

Dr. Jackson wondered if the voices and the friends, which Haley told him were "nowhere but everywhere," were schizophrenic-like hallucinations or milder thought distortions.

He also saw Haley's mood swing from anxiety about a "disturbing dream in which her mother was killed" to euphoria, as she gleefully drew a large, brightly colored butterfly and a self-portrait with a too-big smile and a skirt that ballooned as if she were floating. The pictures, he said, "scream" manic sensibility, suggesting bipolar disorder.

Dr. Jackson prescribed an antipsychotic, Risperdal, one of a dozen drugs Haley would try. Some helped initially, but the voices returned or side effects developed.

Huge pills or bad-tasting liquid made Haley gag or throw fits.

"It was horrible, horrible, horrible," her mother said, "and she'd pull us into it because we had to make her take it."

Lithium caused weight gain: clothes that fit her one day no longer did the next.

When Haley was 8 1/2, Mr. Abaspour said, "Let's drop all of these medications and see what happens." He said, "I wanted to see her true self."

The results chastened them. "You see her fine one day," Mr. Abaspour said. "The second day comes and she's fine and you say, 'You see, honey, there's nothing wrong with her.' Then it's the third day and she goes crazy and you feel like an idiot."

Haley resumed taking Risperdal. Then, abruptly, her condition worsened.

"She couldn't function, she couldn't go to school," said Ms. Abaspour, who took Haley to a hospital; she had to handle the crisis with her husband away in London.

In the emergency room, Haley was manic and hyperarticulate, Ms. Abaspour recalled. "I was a basket case."

When Mr. Abaspour returned and saw Haley "like a zombie" in a hospital full of out-of-control children, his first reaction was, "She can't be in here."

But the eight-day hospital stay made him grasp the severity of her illness.

"You look at an X-ray and you say it's a fracture," he said. "But this thing. . . . Before then, there wasn't solid evidence."

A year later, school halls "would get scary because the voices would get louder," so Haley constantly visited the school's nurse and psychologist, her mother said. "She was going out of her mind."

Haley was hospitalized again, and another antipsychotic drug, Abilify, muffled the voices.

"I remember thinking, 'Am I supposed to be happy about this?,'" Ms. Abaspour said. She was grateful that something helped but distressed at the suggestion that Haley was psychotic. The Abilify has not soothed Haley's anxiety or stopped her outbursts. And despite increases in the dosage, back are the voices (four boys and a girl), the tics (eye squinting and hand clenching) and the "bums."

Dr. Jackson, her psychiatrist, said Haley's biggest asset was her "very caring family" that was "seeking ways to shore themselves up" to better help her.

Ms. Abaspour said: "We ask ourselves sometimes, 'Why? Why did it happen to us?' Other times we see a child bald, going through chemotherapy. That's the thing about this—it's on the inside, you can't see it."

## Megan's Heartache

I pretend no one is around me when my sister is there.

I feel a constant hurt inside.

I touch a rainbow of joyfulness in my mind when my sister and I are FINALLY having a fun laugh together.

I worry that when one day I die, I won't be there to help my sister.

I cry to the stars, pleading them to take me away from this madness at mind.

Megan's sixth-grade writing assignment was to write a poem called "I Am."

Virtually every line was about Haley.

Megan wrote of love, frustration, obligation, pain, embarrassment. Eighteen months later, those feelings erupted.

Told to do dishes before calling a friend, Megan felt that the chore should be Haley's and stormed to her room. When her father said it was Megan's responsibility, "I really got mad and slammed the door," she recalled. "He came and ripped my phone right out of the wall."

That was unusual for Mr. Abaspour, usually gentle or quietly humorous.

"I tried not to say something that would hurt her," he said. "And definitely not to touch her. So I took it out on the phone."

Megan said her reaction was, "Why should I live?"

"I took a T-shirt and I put it around my neck," she said. "Then I said, 'No I shouldn't do this. I want to live but I don't know another way out.' "

Siblings of mentally ill children often have such feelings, experts said.

Ten days of treatment helped Megan understand that "I felt pretty much like I was another mom for Haley," she said.

The Abaspours, who always gave Megan positive attention, were stunned. But Ms. Abaspour said she might have unconsciously been relieved that Megan could get Haley to laugh, or in other ways "take a little attention off me."

For Megan, a doctor prescribed Prozac, but she became edgy and the suicidal thoughts continued.

"When I'm doing dishes and I see a knife there, my mind's like, 'Pick up the knife and kill yourself,' " Megan said. "I kind of just think, 'Would things be easier without me?' "

Now she has stopped taking medication and is seeing a psychiatrist. Her parents are encouraging her to focus more on herself. She realizes, she said, "I'm important."

Still, trying not to help Haley is hard. "I don't really feel the pain that she feels," Megan said, "but I feel that I should to make it even between us."

Haley's mother calls it "the ongoing search"—Haley's obsessive quest for novelty and for objects to hold or to stroke over her touch-sensitive skin.

"I need something to calm me down so I can learn how to end my frustration," Haley said. "I just get, like, sometimes, mad. I need to, like, hold it or hug it or just play with it."

She and her family search through stores, scavenge through her crawlspace storage area and her bedroom full of Beanie Babies, toy cars, dolls. Megan said she sometimes offered her own belongings for Haley, thinking, "if I get excited about it she'll decide it's the right thing."

But, Ms. Abaspour said, "she's never satisfied." Because her parents sometimes brush the hair on her arm with a surgical brush from Mr. Abaspour's hospital, the family's therapist recently suggested getting a soft lambskin.

Haley fixated on buying one, always asking as if it were a new thought: "Oh my God, you know what just came to mind? If I get that animal fur . . ."

Megan found her a faux shearling vest to stroke instead, but Haley exploded.

"I wanted Megan to find something like that animal fur," she wailed, convulsing and weeping.

Anguished as he watched her, Mr. Abaspour said: "This is the point of no return. She'll scream and cry and kick. If the neighbors could hear, they would think we were abusing the kid."

Haley refuses to be consoled or touched, all the while saying, "Please help me, please make it stop, please make it go away," her mother said. The Abaspours look on helplessly or send her to another room.

Haley's eruptions, often 20 minutes long, occur almost daily, especially in the evenings. They often begin with Haley revved up.

Before the lambskin incident, for example, she marched around, chatting giddily about camp: "Today, today, today, we, um, instead of two periods of the game thingies, they call it sessions, periods, each session or whatever, we went to the picnic tables and we all went to the picnic tables and it was really fun."

Haley's parents struggled to track her unspooling sentences and scrambled thoughts.

"Did you follow the bouncing ball?" Ms. Abaspour asked her husband, who replied, "I don't even see the ball, honey."

Haley sighs, frowns and fidgets, eyes drooping before she falls apart. Sometimes she hyperventilates or crawls under a table. It always ends with crying, but sometimes she will start to laugh through her tears, becoming "all chipper again, like manic," Mr. Abaspour said.

Adds Ms. Abaspour: Later, "she says, 'I'm sorry, I'm sorry,' apologizing for who she is." Her father said: "It's not like a hurt that you can kiss better. It comes from within, and she doesn't know why, and you can't do anything about it."

## A Mother's Stoicism

Christine Abaspour, the youngest of four girls raised by a divorced mother, knew what she wanted early in life. At 19, she left

Massachusetts, joined a sister in Florida and became a waitress. At 25, she met her husband-to-be, who was 11 years older. She was engaged in two weeks, married in nine months and a mother a year later.

"We both wanted to have children right away, like you wouldn't believe," she recalled.

Ms. Abaspour said that she had no regrets, and that Haley "was given to us for some reason, and I keep waiting for the day when I realize why."

Still, the experience has tested her stamina, and she avoids capitulating to Haley's whims and outbursts by imposing structure, consistency, even distance.

"I'm her mother," Ms. Abaspour said. "I try to make it a better world for her, a more comfortable world. I stay very strong for her and very encouraging for her. If she comes out of a meltdown, I'll say, 'I knew that you could.' I don't make her feel totally hopeless. It doesn't give me any satisfaction, though, because I still feel helpless. Unfortunately it just bites you in the face all day long."

Ms. Abaspour's stoic approach, which her husband appreciates but cannot always emulate, is "a good coping skill for parents," Dr. Elliott, of the Children's Health Council, said. "It's what happens to a family system when you've got a source of chaos in the middle of it."

After getting Haley ready for school, Ms. Abaspour feels she has already lived an entire day. In the afternoon, "Haley walks in the door and I just want to hold her and give her a big kiss like most kids," Ms. Abaspour said. "Instead I get a frown and tears and 'Ooh, I had such a stressful day.' "

She said that every evening, a distraught Haley will "say to me her same 12 questions: 'What's going to happen when I need to go to school and I can't leave the classroom?' or 'What do I have to look forward to today?' "

By bedtime, Ms. Abaspour said, "your heart's just breaking."

To slake Haley's thirst for "something to do," Ms. Abaspour keeps her involved in activities outside of school. Otherwise, the family ends up stopping for ice cream or concocting other outings, because unstructured time allows Haley to focus on the voices and anxiety. "Staying home is not an option," Ms. Abaspour said. "Honestly I could not keep her busy. Sometimes being around here on a Saturday or Sunday, it's almost toxic. She has multiple episodes—it's like living hell."

Haley's fears of noises, crowded streets and surprises force the Abaspours to forgo amusement parks, apple picking or other traditional family activities. When relatives visit "and you think it's going to be relaxing and we'll watch movies and eat popcorn—that doesn't happen in this family," Ms. Abaspour said.

Instead, there are mood cycles, as when Haley marched around announcing, "I'm going to make a really great art project," then fell apart, wailing, "I don't know what to do."

Ms. Abaspour stays unflustered. When Haley bawled, "I don't have any markers," her mother replied, "Oh, don't tell me you don't have."

But she found Haley a T-shirt to cut up and draw on, saying, "If I can get her to do that kind of chop, chop, chop, mark, mark, mark, it kind of brings her back."

Ms. Abaspour said she had watched "everyone else in the family rush over to her, and I won't become a part of that. I make her be responsible for her own feelings because I can't be responsible for those. You still have to be a regular parent. Honestly, she has to learn to soothe herself."

But Ms. Abaspour doggedly monitors Haley's progress. This summer, she visited Haley at day camp and was dismayed that the child frequently declined to participate, asking for the nurse.

Sitting out the swim period one day, Haley, wearing a "Keep It Cool" T-shirt, listed her feelings on a worksheet: "stressed, axxouis, sick, shacky."

At lunch, she mostly licked salt off pretzels. Asked to choose a word-card matching her emotions, she picked "overwhelmed."

Ms. Abaspour worries that as Haley becomes a teenager, her poor social skills might get her "mixed up with the wrong kids" or lead her to use illegal drugs. So she arranges play dates, but if friends are unavailable "it's the end of the world," she said. If they are available, she said, Haley anxiously asks, "What do I say, Mommy?"

Ms. Abaspour was recently laid off from a medical assistant's job. Her former co-workers understood her need to interrupt work to deal with Haley's needs, she said, and "didn't look at me and say, 'Her child's crazy.' " Now she fears she will not find an employer who is as tolerant, though the family needs the income. Haley's illness, the Abaspours were dismayed to discover, does not qualify for disability assistance.

In August, Ms. Abaspour arranged an elaborate 50th-birthday surprise party for her husband. They were "not always on the same page" about Haley at first, she said, but their strong marriage helps her handle the strain.

So do bright spots, she said, like the day Haley "really kissed me."

Still, she can get overwhelmed.

Sometimes she bolts awake at night, but she declines medication.

"I can't climb in a shell and stay there forever," she said, "although it seems like some days where I'd want to be."

## A Father's Anxiety

As a young man, Bejan Abaspour worried, especially about family.

Twenty years ago, for example, when his sister's son was born, "I pictured my nephew getting Super Glue in his eyes and I was calling my sister saying, 'Make sure you keep Super Glue away from him.'"

But the worries were not that intense—until Haley's illness. After that, the intrusive thoughts and images got worse, horrific scenes in which he imagines himself as bystander or thwarted rescuer. "I'll be driving next to a semi tractor-trailer truck and all of a sudden I will picture someone getting crushed by the wheel," he said. "It's usually an older lady or a kid. You get them out from under the truck, but it doesn't stop. I'm in the emergency room, trying to help. I'm at the funeral. Then very easily, the tears come."

Mr. Abaspour said he sometimes pictured Haley "getting lost somewhere, or someone's going to hurt her. I'm involved and trying to get the guy who did it to stop. Sometimes I kill him. Sometimes it doesn't get that far."

Other times, he said, he imagines his death, seeing his family "at the funeral home and I'm laying there. I try to see what's going on at home, how Meggie's reacting to my death, how Haley's reacting, what Christine is going through."

He rehashes things Haley has said, like wanting to "start over" or her question: "When I get really old, can I come back home? Will you be there?"

He wonders if his worrying laid genetic groundwork for Haley's illness, "if I'm the cause of what Haley's going through."

Until recently, Mr. Abaspour, who also has trouble sleeping, told no one about his agonizing thoughts, not even his wife.

"I didn't want to burden her," he said. "I can handle it. So what if I'm driving to work and I cry? So what if I only sleep for four hours?"

But last spring, the family's therapist noticed "I had certain problems," he recalled. She encouraged him to tell his wife whenever he had disturbing thoughts. Mr. Abaspour said he hoped that confronting his own anxiety would help "get to the bottom of what Haley's going through."

He added, "It doesn't matter for me, but for Haley."

Families once kept illnesses like Haley's quiet, afraid of being shunned or disparaged.

Public acceptance has grown, but some misperceptions and prejudice remain, and families feel conflicted: they want people to understand so the child can get appropriate help, but they also fear that Haley will be mocked or ostracized.

"If they keep it a secret then they're bad parents," Dr. Elliott said. "If they start spewing diagnoses, they're subject to criticism because they're not taking responsibility, just laying it on the illness. Or they're social pariahs because there are some people who think that mental illness is contagious."

Like other families, the Abaspours sometimes hesitate to publicly label their daughter mentally ill. But they also want people to know, and they get frustrated if people do not fully accept or understand it, or see her symptoms "as a manipulative thing, or they feel like they can fix it themselves, maybe by distracting her," Ms. Abaspour said.

Her own family now understands and is very supportive, but it took some convincing, she said.

"My mother would say, 'She'll be fine, she'll be fine, there's nothing wrong with her,' " Ms. Abaspour said. "My sister says, 'Well, she didn't act like that when she was over here.' "

Mr. Abaspour has not told most of his family, who live in England, because they might worry excessively or not understand.

He told his sister, but "she was like I was when I first encountered the situation—disbelief or denial," he said. His sister, he said, has not told her husband or her 20-year-old son, which created an odd atmosphere when they visited the Abaspours in August. "When Haley did have one of her little episodes, they were all like, 'oh, oh,' and they wondered why we weren't running over to her," Ms. Abaspour said. "I would like to talk to them more about it. If she had diabetes, they'd know she had diabetes."

When, after reading a book for children with bipolar disorder, Haley said, "I can't wait to go to school and tell everybody I'm bipolar," the Abaspours were torn.

They discouraged her from announcing the diagnosis. But Haley did tell her classmates, " 'I have a lot of noise going on in my head and sometimes I feel anxious and sometimes I have to take a walk.' "

Some day, the Abaspours hope, Haley will have more effective drugs and better coping skills, and society will be more tolerant, so she can lead an independent life. But they have no illusions.

"This is not going away," Ms. Abaspour said. Not for Haley or her family. "The overflow of what Haley has is what has made all of us what we are today."

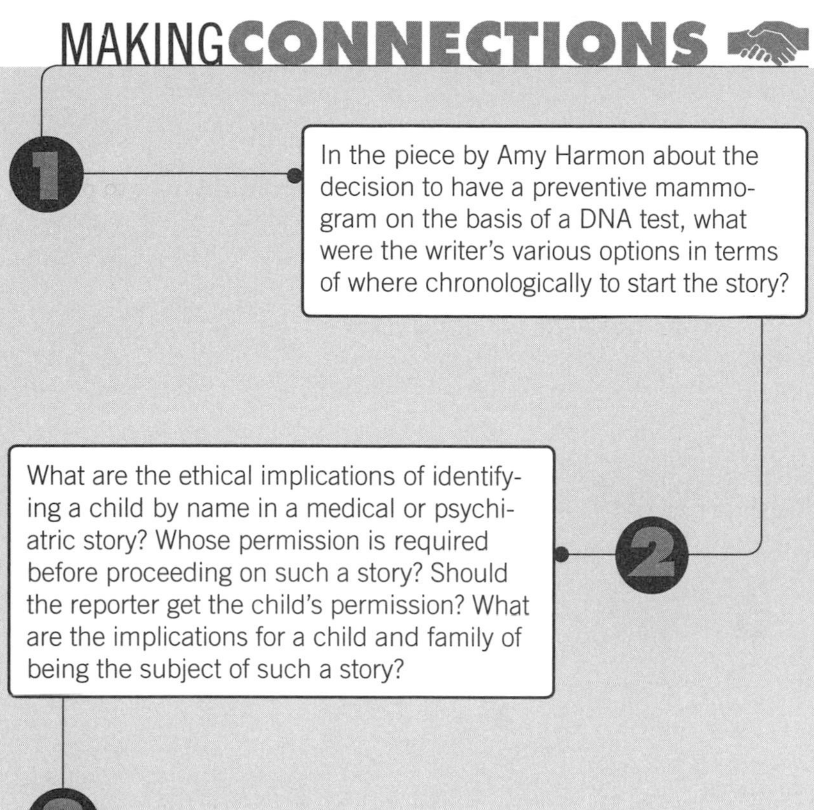

# MAKING CONNECTIONS

1. In the piece by Amy Harmon about the decision to have a preventive mammogram on the basis of a DNA test, what were the writer's various options in terms of where chronologically to start the story?

2. What are the ethical implications of identifying a child by name in a medical or psychiatric story? Whose permission is required before proceeding on such a story? Should the reporter get the child's permission? What are the implications for a child and family of being the subject of such a story?

3. What kinds of stories are best told in narrative form?

# Part III

# commentary

IN COMMENTARY, AS IN NEWS AND FEATURES, journalists depend on solid reporting and informed sources to lend substance to their writing. The range of what qualifies as commentary on the health beat extends from a fiercely worded opinion piece on the op-ed (opposite the editorial) page, to a painfully personal blog entry by a reporter undergoing cancer treatment, to "branded" columns in which a particular writer explores one or another beat every week.

The way journalists use the word "column" can be confusing, as it refers both to the kind of op-ed writing that advocates or judges and to another kind in which a reporter applies his or her unique perspective to a particular segment of the news. In The New York Times the latter kind of column—which appears in The Times news pages—should not contain personal opinion, notes Barbara Strauch, Times health and medical science editor. To see the variety of health and medical news columns in the health section, start at nytimes.com, click on HEALTH, and then scroll down until you see VIEWS.

In contrast with news-page columns, writers on the op-ed page can and do share their opinions, although relatively few op-ed pieces address health or medical topics other than policy issues like health care reform. The next chapter includes one of the rare pieces by a Times columnist that has a sharp medical (not policy) focus.

In another form of commentary, the essay, the writer pursues a thesis and through artful argument tries to convince the reader of the merit of his or her position. The most famous American medical essayist, Lewis Thomas, regularly wrote for The New England Journal of Medicine. Contemporary sometime essayists (like Dennis Overbye and Daniel Goleman, featured in this book) carry on that tradition in the pages of The Times.

In the online world, blogs fill some of the niche for commentary. Reporter Tara Parker-Pope anchors The New York Times health blog, known as Well (also the name of a column that she writes). Other writers also contribute regularly to the Well blog. In the chapter on blogs, we feature three posts from Well bloggers. To read the interactions between writers and readers, you'll need to go online.

The last type of commentary, called op-chart by The Times, may combine graphics, text and even cartooning. In the chapter Beyond Plain Text, we offer an example of this genre and explore alternative ways to tell stories.

CHAPTER 12

# columns

COLUMNS ABOUT HEALTH APPEAR both on the op-ed page of The New York Times and in the news sections, often in the Tuesday edition of Science Times. In op-ed pieces, columnists present points of view and freely offer opinions. Readers expect no less. But when a column appears on the news pages, Times editors want their writers to provide perspective and background, but avoid personal opinion.

Health and medical columnists tread a fine line between reporting and editorializing, especially when they deal with controversial issues where proponents offer conflicting claims. The best column writers cite research, consult multiple sources and offer balanced accounts if the definitive scientific verdict isn't clear. The Times slugs its columns (some might call it a branding) with names relevant to the beat: Personal Health, Personal Fitness, Well, Mind, The Doctor's World, Doctor and Patient, and Cases, among others. Column writers range from daily reporters to occasional contributors.

In this chapter you'll read a piece by Times op-ed columnist Nicholas D. Kristof, who doesn't often report on health but here relies on a keen eye and sharp pen to focus on a medical injustice. Tara Parker-Pope, one of the most popular Times columnists, has no formal health or medical training (see a conversation with her at the end of Chapter 14), but rather years of experience reporting on consumer health issues. In her pieces she often dispels medical myths; she's not afraid to counter popular wisdom. Our third columnist, Jane E. Brody, joined The Times in 1965, and her Personal Health column appears weekly in the Science Times. The last featured columnist, Dr. Lawrence K. Altman, has worked as a Times reporter for 40 years. Like other health professionals who write columns, he draws on his medical background to provide perspective, giving consumers an inside view into health issues.

To write an effective piece, columnists need to have a point of view and evidence to support that view. Storytelling skills discussed in earlier chapters apply to columns. Anecdotes that tell a bigger story, descriptions that transport the reader to particular settings and emotion conveyed through action all help make columns memorable.

# Selection 12.1

*This column by Nicholas D. Kristof uses one woman's plight to pull readers into an operating room in Pakistan—and into a global health problem. Because the piece ran on the op-ed page and not on the news or feature pages of The Times, Kristof was free to become a character in the story and to use a loaded word like blasphemy. Notice how the quotes, used only sparingly, convey Shazia's world as strongly as a scream. And Shazia, the subject of the piece, never says a word—one more way to show women's powerlessness in too much of the world.*

## OP-ED COLUMNIST
## Crisis in the Operating Room

By NICHOLAS D. KRISTOF

KARACHI, Pakistan

Afterward, they comforted each other with the blasphemy: "It was God's will."

It was the first pregnancy for Shazia Allahdita, 19. I was in the operating room at a public hospital here in Karachi as surgeons performed a Caesarean section on her to try to save her life.

As she lay unconscious under the anesthesia, doctors plucked a baby boy from her uterus and then labored to revive the child. "He has a heartbeat, but he's not crying," Dr. Aijaz Ahmed explained tersely as he gave the boy oxygen. "He's not responding. I think he's getting weaker."

These dramas play out constantly in poor countries. One woman dies a minute from complications of pregnancy or childbirth somewhere in the world, and 20 times as many suffer childbirth injuries.

There's no mystery about how to save these lives. Some impoverished countries, such as Sri Lanka, have succeeded stunningly well at saving mothers simply because they have tried. But foreign aid donors like the United States have never shown much interest in maternal mortality, and impoverished women are typically the most voiceless, neglected people in their own countries—so they die at astonishing rates. Here in Pakistan, 1 woman in 74 will die at some point in her life from complications during pregnancy.

Shazia's suffering is typically unnecessary. It all would have worked out fine if she had gone to a hospital to deliver her baby. She wanted to. Her husband and relatives all agreed, when I interviewed them later, that she had had her heart set on delivering at the public

---

*Published: July 29, 2009.*

hospital here. It's also free, so long as supplies haven't run out (other times, family members have to rush out to buy supplies).

But Shazia's female in-laws thought that a hospital birth was a silly extravagance, and a young Pakistani woman is at the mercy of her mother-in-law and sisters-in-law. (In Pakistan, men are little involved in such decisions about childbirth.) It didn't help that the in-laws resented Shazia because she and her husband, Allahdita, had breached tradition by marrying out of love rather than by family arrangement.

When Shazia went into labor, the family summoned a traditional birth attendant to help with the delivery. Hours passed. Nothing happened. Shazia asked to go to the hospital, but it was far away and would require what for them would be an expensive taxi fare of 300 Pakistani rupees, equivalent to about $3.75.

"If she went to the hospital, then every time the family visited it would be a long way to go and very inconvenient," explained an aunt, Qamarunnisa. "It was so much easier to go to the local health post. It seemed easier."

So the family eventually took her to a local clinic, where Shazia struggled to deliver for another 24 hours of labor. The family discussed taking her to the hospital, but the obstacle was the 300 rupee taxi fare. "If it hadn't been for the money, she would have come here," said Qamarunnisa.

But nobody wanted to pay. Shazia's in-laws truly are poor, but it's hard to imagine that they would have balked if it had been a man in the family who was in danger—or if they had known that Shazia was carrying a baby boy.

"If they had known it was a son, they would have come up with 500 rupees," said Dr. Sarah Feroze, as her colleagues struggled to save Shazia and her baby.

Finally, some 30 hours after Shazia's water had broken, an aunt paid for the taxi to the hospital. The doctors immediately saw that Shazia's baby could not fit through her pelvis and rushed her into the operating theater for the C-section.

Shazia lived. The baby died.

I visited Shazia the next day. She was in a crowded, stifling ward. The power had gone out. Her bedding was soiled. She was crying.

Outside, her husband, Allahdita, was grieving but philosophical. "It is God's will," he said, shrugging. "There is nothing we can do."

That's incorrect. If men had uteruses, "paternity wards" would get resources, ambulances would transport pregnant men to hospitals free of charge, deliveries would be free, and the Group of 8 industrialized nations would make paternal mortality a top priority. One of the most lethal forms of sex discrimination is this systematic inattention to reproductive health care, from family planning to childbirth—so long as those who die are impoverished, voiceless women.

Thankfully, there is the dawn of a global movement against maternal mortality. Prime Minister Gordon Brown of Britain and the United Nations secretary general, Ban Ki-moon, are trying to work with the United States and other countries to hold a landmark global health session at the U.N. focusing, in part, on maternal health. If that comes to pass, on Sept. 23, it will be a milestone. My dream is that Barack and Michelle Obama will leap forward and adopt this cause—and transform the prospects for so many young women like Shazia.

## Selection 12.2

*In the next column, Tara Parker-Pope cites three journal studies and quotes from an expert to support her message that statins (anti-cholesterol drugs) don't prolong life. Striving for balance, she also acknowledges another report that questions her thesis. Although she has a point of view, Parker-Pope presents both sides. As she says in an interview in this book, she knows how hard it is, for both patients and journalists, to distinguish good health recommendations from hype. This column is well researched and provocative. It counters the mountain of drug advertisements that lead some patients to ask their doctors for a drug that, critics say, they don't need.*

### Well

### Great Drug, but Does It Prolong Life?

By TARA PARKER-POPE

Statins are among the most prescribed drugs in the world, and there is no doubt that they work as advertised—that they lower not only cholesterol but also the risk for heart attack.

But in the fallout from the headline-making trial of Vytorin, a combination drug that was found to be no more effective than a simple statin in reducing arterial plaque, many people are asking a more fundamental question about statins in general: Do they prolong your life?

And for many users, the surprising answer appears to be no.

Some patients do receive significant benefits from statins, like Lipitor (from Pfizer), Crestor (AstraZeneca) and Pravachol (Bristol-Myers Squibb). In studies of middle-aged men with cardiovascular disease, statin users were less likely to die than those who were given a placebo.

But many statin users don't have established heart disease; they simply have high cholesterol. For healthy men, for women with or

---

*Published: January 29, 2008.*

without heart disease and for people over 70, there is little evidence, if any, that taking a statin will make a meaningful difference in how long they live.

"High-risk groups have a lot to gain," said Dr. Mark H. Ebell, a professor at the University of Georgia who is deputy editor of the journal American Family Physician. "But patients at low risk benefit very little if at all. We end up overtreating a lot of patients." (Like the other doctors quoted in this column, Dr. Ebell has no ties to drug makers.)

How is this possible, if statins lower the risk of heart attack? Because preventing a heart attack is not the same thing as saving a life. In many statin studies that show lower heart attack risk, the same number of patients end up dying, whether they are taking statins or not.

"You may have helped the heart, but you haven't helped the patient," said Dr. Beatrice Golomb, an associate professor of medicine at the University of California, San Diego, and a co-author of a 2004 editorial in The Journal of the American College of Cardiology questioning the data on statins. "You still have to look at the impact on the patient over all."

A 2006 study in The Archives of Internal Medicine looked at seven trials of statin use in nearly 43,000 patients, mostly middle-aged men without heart disease. In that review, statins didn't lower mortality.

Nor did they in a study called Prosper, published in The Lancet in 2002, which studied statin use in people 70 and older. Nor did they in a 2004 review in The Journal of the American Medical Association, which looked at 13 studies of nearly 20,000 women, both healthy and with established heart disease.

A Pfizer spokeswoman notes that a decline in heart disease death rates reported recently by the American Heart Association suggests that medications like statins are having an impact. But to consistently show a mortality benefit from statins in a research setting would take years of study. "We've concentrated on whether Lipitor reduces risk of heart attacks and strokes," says Halit Bander, medical team leader for Lipitor. "We've proven that again and again."

This month, The Journal of the American College of Cardiology published a report combining data from several studies of people 65 and older who had a prior heart attack or established heart disease. This "meta-analysis" showed that 18.7 percent of the placebo users died during the studies, compared with 15.6 percent of the statin users.

This translates into a 22 percent lower mortality risk for high-risk patients over 65. A co-author of the study, Dr. Jonathan Afilalo, a cardiology fellow at McGill University in Montreal, says that for every 28 patients over 65 with heart disease who take statins, one life will be saved.

"If a patient has had a heart attack," Dr. Afilalo said, "they generally should be on a statin."

Of course, prolonging life is not the only measure that matters. If preventing a heart attack improved the quality of life, that would be an argument for taking statins even if it didn't reduce mortality. But critics say there's no evidence that statin users have a better quality of life than other people.

"If you can show me one study that people who have a disability from their heart are worse off than people who have a disability from other causes, I would find that a compelling argument," Dr. Golomb said. "There's not a shred of evidence that you've mitigated suffering in the groups where there is not a mortality benefit."

One big concern is that the side effects of statins haven't been well studied. Reported side effects include muscle pain, cognitive problems and impotence.

"Statins have side effects that are underrated," said Dr. Uffe Ravnskov, a retired Swedish physician and a vocal critic of statins. "It's much more frequent and serious than has been reported."

Dr. Ebell acknowledges that there are probably patients with heart disease who could benefit from a statin but who aren't taking it.

But he added, "There are probably more of the opposite—patients who are taking a statin when they probably don't need one."

## Selection 12.3

*Columnists write for many reasons: to inform, to persuade and sometimes just to satisfy their curiosity. "This is really interesting to me, this business of how people convey health and vitality," says Tara Parker-Pope in an interview for this book. "What is it about the push-up that does that for all of us?" To find out she researched the medical science behind push-ups and found that they're a good indicator of upper body fitness. To hook readers' attention, she begins by invoking three prominent people known for their high-visibility push-ups. Using a technique common in narrative features, Parker-Pope goes full circle, ending with one of the characters whom she introduced at the top of the piece. Another distinguishing feature of Parker-Pope's work is her conversational style, which she manages to maintain even while loading her columns with facts and details—for example, that people lose as much as 30 percent of their strength between age 20 and age 70. Notice, too, how many ways this column answers the essential audience question: Why should I bother reading this? Parker-Pope uses her Well column both to inform and to motivate. After reading this piece, what reader isn't going to drop down to see how many push-ups he or she can do?*

Stuart Bradford

## WELL
# An Enduring Measure of Fitness: The Simple Push-Up

By TARA PARKER-POPE

As a symbol of health and wellness, nothing surpasses the simple push-up.

Practically everyone remembers the actor Jack Palance performing age-defying push-ups during his Oscar acceptance speech. More recently, Randy Pausch, the Carnegie Mellon professor whose last lecture became an Internet sensation, did push-ups to prove his fitness despite having pancreatic cancer.

"It takes strength to do them, and it takes endurance to do a lot of them," said Jack LaLanne, 93, the fitness pioneer who astounded television viewers in the 1950s with his fingertip push-ups. "It's a good indication of what kind of physical condition you're in."

The push-up is the ultimate barometer of fitness. It tests the whole body, engaging muscle groups in the arms, chest, abdomen, hips and legs. It requires the body to be taut like a plank with toes and palms on the floor. The act of lifting and lowering one's entire weight is taxing even for the very fit.

"You are just using your own body and your body's weight," said Steven G. Estes, a physical education professor and dean of the

---

*Published: March 11, 2008.*

college of professional studies at Missouri Western State University. "If you're going to demonstrate any kind of physical strength and power, that's the easiest, simplest, fastest way to do it."

But many people simply can't do push-ups. Health and fitness experts, including the American College of Sports Medicine, have urged more focus on upper-body fitness. The aerobics movement has emphasized cardiovascular fitness but has also shifted attention from strength training exercises.

Moreover, as the nation gains weight, arms are buckling under the extra load of our own bodies. And as budgets shrink, public schools often do not offer physical education classes—and the calisthenics that were once a childhood staple.

In a 2001 study, researchers at East Carolina University administered push-up tests to about 70 students ages 10 to 13. Almost half the boys and three-quarters of the girls didn't pass.

Push-ups are important for older people, too. The ability to do them more than once and with proper form is an important indicator of the capacity to withstand the rigors of aging.

Researchers who study the biomechanics of aging, for instance, note that push-ups can provide the strength and muscle memory to reach out and break a fall. When people fall forward, they typically reach out to catch themselves, ending in a move that mimics the push-up. The hands hit the ground, the wrists and arms absorb much of the impact, and the elbows bend slightly to reduce the force.

In studies of falling, researchers have shown that the wrist alone is subjected to an impact force equal to about one body weight, says James Ashton-Miller, director of the biomechanics research laboratory at the University of Michigan.

"What so many people really need to do is develop enough strength so they can break a fall safely without hitting their head on the ground," Dr. Ashton-Miller said. "If you can't do a single push-up, it's going to be difficult to resist that kind of loading on your wrists in a fall."

And people who can't do a push-up may not be able to help themselves up if they do fall.

"To get up, you've got to have upper-body strength," said Peter M. McGinnis, professor of kinesiology at State University of New York College at Cortland who consults on pole-vaulting biomechanics for U.S.A. Track and Field, the national governing body for track.

Natural aging causes nerves to die off and muscles to weaken. People lose as much as 30 percent of their strength between 20 and 70. But regular exercise enlarges muscle fibers and can stave off the decline by increasing the strength of the muscle you have left.

Women are at a particular disadvantage because they start off with about 20 percent less muscle than men. Many women bend their knees to lower the amount of weight they must support. And while anybody can do a push-up, the exercise has typically been part of the male fitness culture. "It's sort of a gender-specific symbol of vitality," said R. Scott Kretchmar, a professor of exercise and sports science at Penn State. "I don't see women saying: 'I'm in good health. Watch me drop down and do some push-ups.'"

Based on national averages, a 40-year-old woman should be able to do 16 push-ups and a man the same age should be able to do 27. By the age of 60, those numbers drop to 17 for men and 6 for women. Those numbers are just slightly less than what is required of Army soldiers who are subjected to regular push-up tests.

If the floor-based push-up is too difficult, start by leaning against a countertop at a 45-degree angle and pressing up and down. Eventually move to stairs and then the floor.

Mr. LaLanne, who once set a world record by doing 1,000 push-ups in 23 minutes, still does push-ups as part of his daily workout. Now he balances his feet and each hand on three chairs.

"That way I can go way down, even lower than if I was on the floor," he said. "That's really tough."

## Selection 12.4

*Jane E. Brody has written her Personal Health column for more than 25 years, keeping it fresh by choosing newsy topics relevant to her readers' health. This column, written in 2007, is pertinent today as Americans continue to consume alcoholic and nonalcoholic beverages of all kinds—sugared, artificially sweetened and caffeinated. Brody's columns, like Parker-Pope's, make excellent use of facts, research and expert opinion, yet are written in an informal style. Here she talks directly to you, the reader, asking you to think about what you drink. At one point she groups herself with the experts, talking about what "we" found, but later she uses first person to show ways that her own views diverge from theirs. Although Brody is not writing an advice column, her message comes across clearly: Sugary liquid calories are making Americans fat.*

### Personal Health
### You Are Also What You Drink

By JANE E. BRODY

What worries you most? Decaying teeth, thinning bones, heart disease, stroke, diabetes, dementia, cancer, obesity? Whatever tops your list, you may be surprised to know that all of these health problems are linked to the beverages you drink—or don't drink.

Last year, with the support of the Unilever Health Institute in the Netherlands (Unilever owns Lipton Tea), a panel of experts

---

*Published: March 27, 2007.*

on nutrition and health published a "Beverage Guidance System" in hopes of getting people to stop drinking their calories when those calories contribute little or nothing to their health and may actually detract from it.

The panel, led by Barry M. Popkin, a nutrition professor at the University of North Carolina, was distressed by the burgeoning waistlines of Americans and the contribution that popular beverages make to weight problems. But the experts also reviewed 146 published reports to find the best evidence for the effects of various beverages on nearly all of the above health problems. I looked into a few others, and what follows is a summary of what we all found.

At the head of the list of preferred drinks is—you guessed it—water. No calories, no hazards, only benefits. But the panel expressed concern about bottled water fortified with nutrients, saying that consumers may think they don't need to eat certain nutritious foods, which contain substances like fiber and phytochemicals lacking in these waters. (You can just imagine what the panel would have to say about vitamin-fortified sodas, which Coca-Cola and Pepsi plan to introduce in the coming months.)

## Sweet Liquid Calories

About 21 percent of calories consumed by Americans over the age of 2 come from beverages, predominantly soft drinks and fruit drinks with added sugars, the panel said in its report. There has been a huge increase in sugar-sweetened drinks in recent decades, primarily at the expense of milk, which has clear nutritional benefits. The calories from these sugary drinks account for half the rise in caloric intake by Americans since the late 1970s.

Not only has the number of servings of these drinks risen, but serving size has ballooned, as well, with some retail outlets offering 32 ounces and free refills.

Add the current passion for smoothies and sweetened coffee drinks (there are 240 calories in a 16-ounce Starbucks Caffè Mocha without the whipped cream), and you can see why people are drinking themselves into XXXL sizes.

But calories from sweet drinks are not the only problem. The other matter cited by the panel, in its report in The American Journal of Clinical Nutrition, is that beverages have "weak satiety properties"—they do little or nothing to curb your appetite—and people do not compensate for the calories they drink by eating less.

Furthermore, some soft drinks contribute to other health problems. The American Academy of General Dentistry says that noncola carbonated beverages and canned (sweetened) iced tea harm tooth enamel, especially when consumed apart from meals. And a study of 2,500 adults in Framingham, Mass., linked cola consumption (regular and diet) to the thinning of hip bones in women.

If you must drink something sweet, the panel suggested a no-calorie beverage like diet soda prepared with an approved sweetener, though the experts recognized a lack of long-term safety data and the possibility that these drinks "condition" people to prefer sweetness.

Fruit juices are also a sweet alternative, although not nearly as good as whole fruits, which are better at satisfying hunger.

## Coffee, Tea and Caffeine

Here the news is better. Several good studies have linked regular coffee consumption to a reduced risk of developing Type 2 diabetes, colorectal cancer and, in men and in women who have not taken postmenopausal hormones, Parkinson's disease.

Most studies have not linked a high intake of either coffee or caffeine to heart disease, even though caffeinated coffee raises blood pressure somewhat and boiled unfiltered coffee (French-pressed and espresso) raises harmful LDL and total cholesterol levels.

Caffeine itself is not thought to be a problem for health or water balance in the body, up to 400 milligrams a day (the amount in about 30 ounces of brewed coffee). But pregnant women should limit their intake because more than 300 milligrams a day might increase the risk of miscarriage and low birth weight, the panel said.

Mice prone to an Alzheimer's-like disease were protected by drinking water spiked with caffeine equivalent to what people get from five cups of coffee a day. And a study of more than 600 men suggested that drinking three cups of coffee a day protects against age-related memory and thinking deficits.

For tea, the evidence on health benefits is mixed and sometimes conflicting. Tea lowers cancer risk in experimental animals, but the effects in people are unknown. It may benefit bone density and help prevent kidney stones and tooth decay. And four or five cups of black tea daily helps arteries expand and thus may improve blood flow to the heart.

## Alcohol

Alcohol is a classic case of "a little may be better than none but a lot is worse than a little." Moderate consumption—one drink a day for women and two for men—has been linked in many large, long-term studies to lower mortality rates, especially from heart attacks and strokes, and may also lower the risk of Type 2 diabetes and gallstones. The panel found no convincing evidence that one form of alcohol, including red wine, was better than another.

But alcohol even at moderate intakes raises the risk of birth defects and breast cancer, possibly because it interferes with folate, an essential B vitamin. And heavy alcohol consumption is associated with several lethal cancers, cirrhosis of the liver, hemorrhagic stroke, hypertension, dementia and some forms of heart disease.

### Dairy and Soy Drinks

Here my reading of the evidence differs slightly from that of the panel, which rated low-fat and skim milk third, below water and coffee and tea, as a preferred drink and said dairy drinks were not essential to a healthy diet. The panel acknowledged the benefits of milk for bone density, while noting that unless people continue to drink it, the benefit to bones of the calcium and vitamin D in milk is not maintained.

Other essential nutrients in milk include magnesium, potassium, zinc, iron, vitamin A, riboflavin, folate and protein—about eight grams in an eight-ounce glass. A 10-year study of overweight individuals found that milk drinkers were less likely to develop metabolic syndrome, a constellation of coronary risk factors that includes hypertension and low levels of protective HDLs. To me, this says you may never outgrow your need for milk.

The panel emphasized the need for children and teenagers to drink more milk and fewer calorically sweetened beverages.

"Fortified soy milk is a good alternative for individuals who prefer not to consume cow milk," the panel said.

## Selection 12.5

*Dr. Lawrence K. Altman's column of March 2006 could have been written, with minor changes, in 2009 when a new influenza pandemic occurred. Altman uses the 1976 swine flu outbreak in Fort Dix, N.J., as a case study of how public health officials can go wrong in warning about an infectious threat. In those days, he writes, officials focused much more on reassuring the public than on providing facts—an approach that he argues has now changed for the better. Using a historical case study gives readers perspective on current outbreaks. Because of his background as a former chief of the U.S. Public Health Service's Division of Epidemiology and Immunization in Washington, Altman draws on his own experience to frame the story. As a physician, he understands the medical science behind his stories. As a journalist, he knows how to source others. This blend of physician perspective with journalistic skills makes The Doctor's World a compelling column.*

### The Doctor's World
### With Every Epidemic, Tough Choices

By LAWRENCE K. ALTMAN, M.D.

To warn. Or not to warn.

That classic dilemma in public health has been brought into sharp focus by the A(H5N1) avian influenza virus that is spreading

*Published: March 28, 2006*

around the world and has led to the death of tens of millions of birds in Asia and Europe.

For health officials, few decisions can be as crucial as deciding if and when to sound early warnings when they believe that an epidemic is possible but do not know whether it will become a real catastrophe.

The dilemma often concerns the influenza virus because it continually mutates, leading to human pandemics that predictably occur unpredictably. Although scientists lack the knowledge to predict when and what strain will cause the next influenza pandemic, they say they are convinced that another one is inevitable and so preparation must start as soon as a threat is detected.

That kind of immediate action occurred in 1976 after four cases of swine influenza were detected at Fort Dix, a military base in New Jersey. Fearing that the cases represented an early warning of an impending pandemic of influenza, Public Health Service officials rushed President Gerald R. Ford, who was running for re-election, into recommending a swine influenza shot for every American.

Mr. Ford proposed a $135 million program to make enough vaccine to immunize 200 million people, about 95 percent of the United States population at the time. It was the government's first effort to immunize all Americans against one disease in one program, and Congress authorized it.

But the effort was suspended shortly after it began because a paralyzing ailment, Guillain-Barré syndrome, occurred among a small number of the 42 million vaccine recipients.

A few cases of the syndrome had been linked to influenza vaccine, but government officials failed to mention the risk in the consent form or to discuss it publicly.

The feared killer disease never came. But by the time the effort ended, 535 cases of Guillain-Barré had been diagnosed, including 23 deaths, outnumbering the mostly mild 230 cases of swine flu at Fort Dix. The virus did not spread. The immunization plan was a fiasco. Health officials were dismissed, some say unfairly.

The episode has become a textbook case in training a new generation of health officials about the dangers of sounding warnings too early without having a well-thought-out plan.

The opposite problem—failing to warn about preparations for an outbreak—occurred in 2001.

Shortly after Sept. 11, Tommy G. Thompson, then the secretary of health and human services, went on national television to assure Americans that the government was fully prepared to respond to any bioterrorism attack.

Within days, the deliberate release of anthrax spores through the postal system proved him wrong. The outbreak was small—22 cases, including 5 deaths. But it showed how poorly the government communicated in a timely way to doctors and the public. It left many government officials wanting never to be perceived as underreacting to a health threat.

The two episodes led many people to lose trust in government health warnings, or in the lack of them.

Warnings about A(H5N1) avian influenza began in 1997, when scientists in Hong Kong discovered that that strain of virus had jumped directly to cause disease in humans without first mixing in pigs, which had been the pattern until then. With the spread of the virus among birds, officials have warned that it could mutate, combine with a human influenza virus and create a new one to cause a human pandemic.

That has not happened, although 105 of the 186 people in the world who have developed A(H5N1) avian influenza have died.

Should health officials risk issuing stern warnings that may frighten people? Or should officials play it safe, going about their business and informing the public only when a pandemic becomes real?

If officials do issue early warnings, and nothing happens, they stand to lose credibility among people who say that scientists promoted the worst possibilities to grab more grants and waste taxpayer dollars.

If officials do not issue early or timely warnings, and a pandemic occurs, critics will say the public was not informed and protected in time.

The situation also leaves health officials vulnerable to charges of "I told you so," even though there is often no way to prove that the Monday morning quarterbacks actually made their criticisms known at the time key decisions had to be made.

Two types of dilemmas are often involved in deciding when and what warning to give, said Dr. Harvey V. Fineberg, who wrote a book with Richard E. Neustadt in 1978 analyzing the government's and industry's responses to the swine flu immunization program.

One is like a Category 5 hurricane with long odds on its occurring, but with devastating consequences if it does.

"In such cases, the naysayer is most often going to be right," said Dr. Fineberg, president of the Institute of Medicine of the National Academy of Sciences, said in an interview, referring to those who contend preparation is unnecessary.

The second dilemma involves a tension that can arise when scientists believe that political leaders and the public do not understand risk as well as scientists do. Problems can arise if an expert believes action is needed because the risk of an outbreak is, say, 10 percent, but perceives that government officials will consider 10 percent to be too low for action to be taken.

So the scientist may choose a way to present the facts and estimates to persuade government officials to do what the scientist believes is correct.

In deciding whether to warn and act, the tendency is often "reluctance to do something that may cause harm as opposed to allowing nature to create its own harm," Dr. Fineberg said.

Last year, the Bush administration released a comprehensive plan to counter an influenza pandemic. Even with it, the dilemma of when to warn will remain.

## MAKING CONNECTIONS

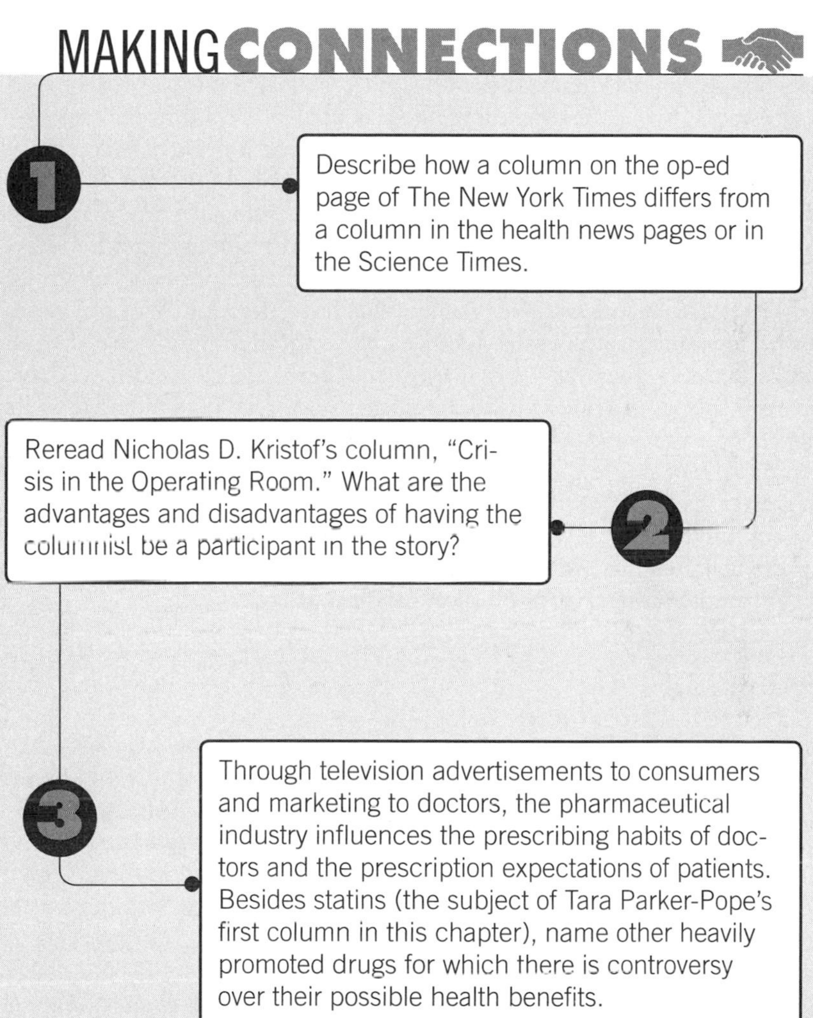

1. Describe how a column on the op-ed page of The New York Times differs from a column in the health news pages or in the Science Times.

2. Reread Nicholas D. Kristof's column, "Crisis in the Operating Room." What are the advantages and disadvantages of having the columnist be a participant in the story?

3. Through television advertisements to consumers and marketing to doctors, the pharmaceutical industry influences the prescribing habits of doctors and the prescription expectations of patients. Besides statins (the subject of Tara Parker-Pope's first column in this chapter), name other heavily promoted drugs for which there is controversy over their possible health benefits.

# essays

ANY CHAPTER ON MEDICAL ESSAYS HAS to begin with Lewis Thomas, one of the most prolific and certainly the most widely read medical essayist of the 20th century. Thomas died in 1993, but his essays—many of them originally written for The New England Journal of Medicine—live on in books like Lives of a Cell and The Medusa and the Snail.

Thomas, a Harvard-trained physician and president of the Memorial Sloan-Kettering Cancer Center, knew medicine and biology, and he knew how to write: "We have language and can build metaphors as skillfully and precisely as ribosomes make proteins. We have affection. We have genes for usefulness, and usefulness is about as close to a 'common goal' for all of nature as I can guess at. And finally, and perhaps best of all, we have music. Any species capable of producing, at this earliest, juvenile stage of its development—almost instantly after emerging on the earth by any evolutionary standard—the music of Johann Sebastian Bach, cannot be all bad."[1]

It wasn't just Thomas' writing or his knowledge of science that made him a great essayist. Ultimately, it was the power of his thinking and his ability to express insights that resonated with readers. Dennis Overbye and Daniel Goleman, among others, carry on that tradition today.

## Selection 13.1

*Dennis Overbye, The Times science reporter who covers what he calls "cosmic affairs,"[2] muses in the following essay about the connections between democracy and science. Overbye borrows from the essayist Thomas in likening scientific activity to an anthill. And, like Thomas, Overbye is an unabashed admirer of science. He disputes what he calls "the knock on science," that it is "arrogant and materialistic." Instead, he argues science is "the most successful human activity of all time." As with Thomas' writings, Overbye's essay is notable not so much for the language (which is elegant) as for the power of his ideas. That, essentially, is the definition of an essay: a writer giving his or her mind free rein to explore a topic in a literary way. Whatever its content and methods—memory, observation, research or some combination—the strength of an essay comes not from events developing in the world but from connections developing in the writer's mind. In that sense an essayist and a scientist have a lot in common.*

# Essay
# Elevating Science, Elevating Democracy

By DENNIS OVERBYE

All right, I was weeping too.

To be honest, the restoration of science was the least of it, but when Barack Obama proclaimed during his Inaugural Address that he would "restore science to its rightful place," you could feel a dark cloud lifting like a sigh from the shoulders of the scientific community in this country.

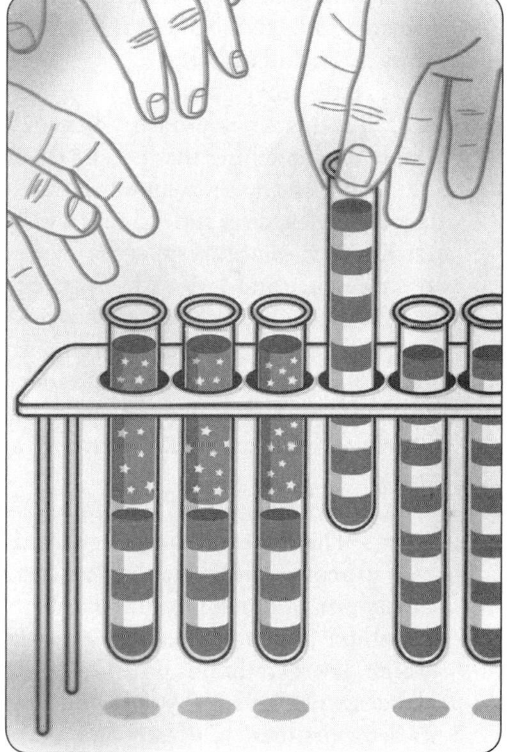

Harry Campbell

When the new president went on vowing to harness the sun, the wind and the soil, and to "wield technology's wonders," I felt the glow of a spring sunrise washing my cheeks, and I could almost imagine I heard the music of swords being hammered into plowshares.

Wow. My first reaction was to worry that scientists were now in the awkward position of being expected to save the world. As they say, be careful what you wish for.

My second reaction was to wonder what the "rightful place" of science in our society really is.

The answer, I would argue, is On a Pedestal—but not for the reasons you might think.

Forget about penicillin, digital computers and even the Big Bang, passing fads all of them.

The knock on science from its cultural and religious critics is that it is arrogant and materialistic. It tells us wondrous things about nature and how to manipulate it, but not what we should do with this

*Published: January 27, 2009.*

knowledge and power. The Big Bang doesn't tell us how to live, or whether God loves us, or whether there is any God at all. It provides scant counsel on same-sex marriage or eating meat. It is silent on the desirability of mutual assured destruction as a strategy for deterring nuclear war.

Einstein seemed to echo this thought when he said, "I have never obtained any ethical values from my scientific work." Science teaches facts, not values, the story goes.

Worse, not only does it not provide any values of its own, say its detractors, it also undermines the ones we already have, devaluing anything it can't measure, reducing sunsets to wavelengths and romance to jiggly hormones. It destroys myths and robs the universe of its magic and mystery.

So the story goes.

But this is balderdash. Science is not a monument of received Truth but something that people do to look for truth.

That endeavor, which has transformed the world in the last few centuries, does indeed teach values. Those values, among others, are honesty, doubt, respect for evidence, openness, accountability and tolerance and indeed hunger for opposing points of view. These are the unabashedly pragmatic working principles that guide the buzzing, testing, poking, probing, argumentative, gossiping, gadgety, joking, dreaming and tendentious cloud of activity—the writer and biologist Lewis Thomas once likened it to an anthill—that is slowly and thoroughly penetrating every nook and cranny of the world.

Nobody appeared in a cloud of smoke and taught scientists these virtues. This behavior simply evolved because it worked.

It requires no metaphysical commitment to a God or any conception of human origin or nature to join in this game, just the hypothesis that nature can be interrogated and that nature is the final arbiter. Jews, Catholics, Muslims, atheists, Buddhists and Hindus have all been working side by side building the Large Hadron Collider and its detectors these last few years.

And indeed there is no leader, no grand plan, for this hive. It is in many ways utopian anarchy, a virtual community that lives as much on the Internet and in airport coffee shops as in any one place or time. Or at least it is as utopian as any community largely dependent on government and corporate financing can be.

Arguably science is the most successful human activity of all time. Which is not to say that life within it is always utopian, as several of my colleagues have pointed out in articles about pharmaceutical industry payments to medical researchers.

But nobody was ever sent to prison for espousing the wrong value for the Hubble constant. There is always room for more data to argue over.

So if you're going to get gooey about something, that's not so bad.

It is no coincidence that these are the same qualities that make for democracy and that they arose as a collective behavior about the same time that parliamentary democracies were appearing. If there is anything democracy requires and thrives on, it is the willingness to embrace debate and respect one another and the freedom to shun received wisdom. Science and democracy have always been twins.

Today that dynamic is most clearly and perhaps crucially tested in China. As I pondered Mr. Obama's words, I thought of Xu Liangying, an elderly Chinese physicist and Einstein scholar I met a couple of years ago, who has spent most of his life under house arrest for upholding Einstein's maxim that there is no science without freedom of speech.

The converse might also be true. The habit of questioning that you learn in physics is invaluable in the rest of society. As Fang Lizhi, Dr. Xu's fellow dissident whose writings helped spark the 1989 Tiananmen Square demonstrations and who now teaches at the University of Arizona, said in 1985, "Physics is more than a basis for technology; it is a cornerstone of modern thought."

If we are not practicing good science, we probably aren't practicing good democracy. And vice versa.

Science and democracy have been the watchwords of Chinese political aspirations for more than a century. When the Communist Party took power it sought to appropriate at least the scientific side of the equation. Here, for example, is what Hu Yaobang, the party's general secretary, said in 1980. "Science is what it is simply because it can break down fetishes and superstitions and is bold in explorations and because it opposes following the beaten path and dares to destroy outmoded conventions and bad customs."

Brave words that have yet to be allowed to come true in China. Mr. Hu was purged, and in fact it was to mourn his death that students first began assembling in Tiananmen Square in 1989.

Dr. Fang got in trouble initially because he favored the Big Bang, but that was against Marxist orthodoxy that the universe was infinitely unfolding. Marxism, it might be remembered, was once promoted as a scientific theory, but some subjects were off-limits.

But once you can't talk about one subject, the origin of the universe, for example, sooner or later other subjects are going to be off-limits, like global warming, birth control and abortion, or evolution, the subject of yet another dustup in Texas last week.

There is no democracy in China, and some would argue that despite that nation's vast resources and potential, there will not be vigorous science there either until the Chinese leaders take seriously what Mao proclaimed back in 1955 and then cynically withdrew: Let a hundred flowers bloom, let a hundred schools of thought contend.

In the meantime I look forward to Mr. Obama's cultivation of our own wild and beautiful garden.

## Selection 13.2

*Sometimes an essay is simply a meditation transformed into words. Daniel Goleman, the former psychology reporter for The New York Times, writes in the next essay about the psychobiology of emotional healing. He begins the essay by introducing his "dear friend," who we learn has been fighting cancer for a decade. In the third paragraph, Goleman links his friend's seeming longevity with his rich network of friends and family. The essayist uses this link to expound on a growing body of scientific knowledge supporting his thesis that, even for the sickest individuals, loving friends can sustain or give meaning to life. To make his points, Goleman explains the concept of "mirror neurons" and describes the "biology of emotional rescue." He presents this science to set up the real payoff of the essay that you'll find in the final two sentences. As in the Overbye essay, it's insight that counts.*

### Essay

### Friends for Life: An Emerging Biology of Emotional Healing

By DANIEL GOLEMAN

A dear friend has been battling cancer for a decade or more. Through a grinding mix of chemotherapy, radiation and all the other necessary indignities of oncology, he has lived on, despite dire prognoses to the contrary.

My friend was the sort of college professor students remember fondly: not just inspiring in class but taking a genuine interest in them—in their studies, their progress through life, their fears and hopes. A wide circle of former students count themselves among his lifelong friends; he and his wife have always welcomed a steady stream of visitors to their home.

Though no one could ever prove it, I suspect that one of many ingredients in his longevity has been this flow of people who love him.

Research on the link between relationships and physical health has established that people with rich personal networks—who are married, have close family and friends, are active in social and religious groups—recover more quickly from disease and live longer. But now the emerging field of social neuroscience, the study of how people's brains entrain as they interact, adds a missing piece to that data.

The most significant finding was the discovery of "mirror neurons," a widely dispersed class of brain cells that operate like neural WiFi. Mirror neurons track the emotional flow, movement and even intentions

---

*Published: October 10, 2006.*

of the person we are with, and replicate this sensed state in our own brain by stirring in our brain the same areas active in the other person.

Mirror neurons offer a neural mechanism that explains emotional contagion, the tendency of one person to catch the feelings of another, particularly if strongly expressed. This brain-to-brain link may also account for feelings of rapport, which research finds depend in part on extremely rapid synchronization of people's posture, vocal pacing and movements as they interact. In short, these brain cells seem to allow the interpersonal orchestration of shifts in physiology.

Such coordination of emotions, cardiovascular reactions or brain states between two people has been studied in mothers with their infants, marital partners arguing and even among people in meetings. Reviewing decades of such data, Lisa M. Diamond and Lisa G. Aspinwall, psychologists at the University of Utah, offer the infelicitous term "a mutually regulating psychobiological unit" to describe the merging of two discrete physiologies into a connected circuit. To the degree that this occurs, Dr. Diamond and Dr. Aspinwall argue, emotional closeness allows the biology of one person to influence that of the other.

John T. Cacioppo, director of the Center for Cognitive and Social Neuroscience at the University of Chicago, makes a parallel proposal: the emotional status of our main relationships has a significant impact on our overall pattern of cardiovascular and neuroendocrine activity. This radically expands the scope of biology and neuroscience from focusing on a single body or brain to looking at the interplay between two at a time. In short, my hostility bumps up your blood pressure, your nurturing love lowers mine. Potentially, we are each other's biological enemies or allies.

Even remotely suggesting health benefits from these interconnections will, no doubt, raise hackles in medical circles. No one can claim solid data showing a medically significant effect from the intermingling of physiologies.

At the same time, there is now no doubt that this same connectivity can offer a biologically grounded emotional solace. Physical suffering aside, a healing presence can relieve emotional suffering. A case in point is a functional magnetic resonance imaging study of women awaiting an electric shock. When the women endured their apprehension alone, activity in neural regions that incite stress hormones and anxiety was heightened. As James A. Coan reported last year in an article in Psychophysiology, when a stranger held the subject's hand as she waited, she found little relief. When her husband held her hand, she not only felt calm, but her brain circuitry quieted, revealing the biology of emotional rescue.

But as all too many people with severe chronic diseases know, loved ones can disappear, leaving them to bear their difficulties in lonely isolation. Social rejection activates the very zones of the brain that generate, among other things, the sting of physical pain. Matthew

D. Lieberman and Naomi Eisenberg of U.C.L.A. (writing in a chapter in "Social Neuroscience: People Thinking About People," M.I.T. Press, 2005) have proposed that the brain's pain centers may have taken on a hypersensitivity to social banishment because exclusion was a death sentence in human prehistory. They note that in many languages the words that describe a "broken heart" from rejection borrow the lexicon of physical hurt.

So when the people who care about a patient fail to show up, it may be a double blow: the pain of rejection and the deprivation of the benefits of loving contact. Sheldon Cohen, a psychologist at Carnegie-Mellon University who studies the effects of personal connections on health, emphasizes that a hospital patient's family and friends help just by visiting, whether or not they quite know what to say.

My friend has reached that point where doctors see nothing else to try. On my last visit, he and his wife told me that he was starting hospice care.

One challenge, he told me, will be channeling the river of people who want to visit into the narrow range of hours in a week when he still has the energy to engage them.

As he said this, I felt myself tearing up, and responded: "You know, at least it's better to have this problem. So many people go through this all alone."

He was silent for a moment, thoughtful. Then he answered softly, "You're right."

## MAKING CONNECTIONS

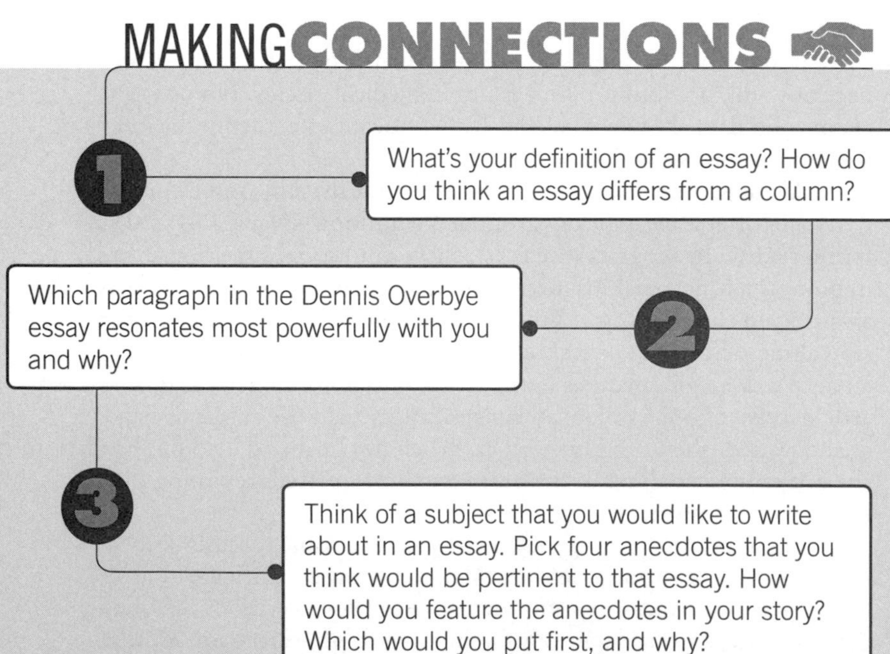

1. What's your definition of an essay? How do you think an essay differs from a column?

2. Which paragraph in the Dennis Overbye essay resonates most powerfully with you and why?

3. Think of a subject that you would like to write about in an essay. Pick four anecdotes that you think would be pertinent to that essay. How would you feature the anecdotes in your story? Which would you put first, and why?

CHAPTER 14

# blogs

AN ONLINE COUSIN TO THE COLUMN, the blog allows reporters to have a dialogue with readers and to point them to journal articles and other primary sources that enhance the credibility of the reporting and deepen the discussion. In the broader online world, blogs range from highly researched journalistic accounts to ramblings of true believers. In The Times, bloggers practice traditional journalism, but sometimes with a personal edge.

Tara Parker-Pope, the most prolific Times blogger on health topics, has a blog and a column, both named Well. Compared with her column, most of her blog posts are shorter but never lack sourcing or reporting. She also uses the blog to link to other health stories and columns in The Times, giving readers a chance to discuss those pieces (and to comment on another person's comments). And she invites guest bloggers. In 2008 and 2009, for example, Times writer and editor Dana Jennings wrote a series of highly personal Well posts about the "transformation, transition and trauma" of his experiences with prostate cancer. Readers responded by the hundreds with experiences of their own. Read even a sampling of those pages and pages of blog posts, and you'll tap into the reality and drama of people's everyday lives in a way that you'd be hard-pressed to do if you relied just on traditional print journalism.

One of Parker-Pope's particularly controversial posts—at least in terms of the number of reader responses—examined the research on whether vitamins provide real health benefits. Parker-Pope concluded that, with a few specific exceptions, the answer is no. To support her points, Parker-Pope provided extensive documentation with multiple links, often to source material. Despite the many research studies backing up her points, Parker-Pope's post attracted 625 comments, many of them negative. Rather than feeling overwhelmed by the response, Parker-Pope sees it as an example of the benefits of new technology.

In an interview for this book she explains her role as a blogger: "The blog gives me this opportunity to say, OK, you decide. I'm not going to tell you what to think, but I'm going to give you all the information. I'm going to link to these studies. I can do that online. I couldn't do that before in a paper, but I'm actually going to show you the study. I'm going to summarize it. I'm going to do all the work, and it was a heck of a lot of work, putting all that together and citing all that research."

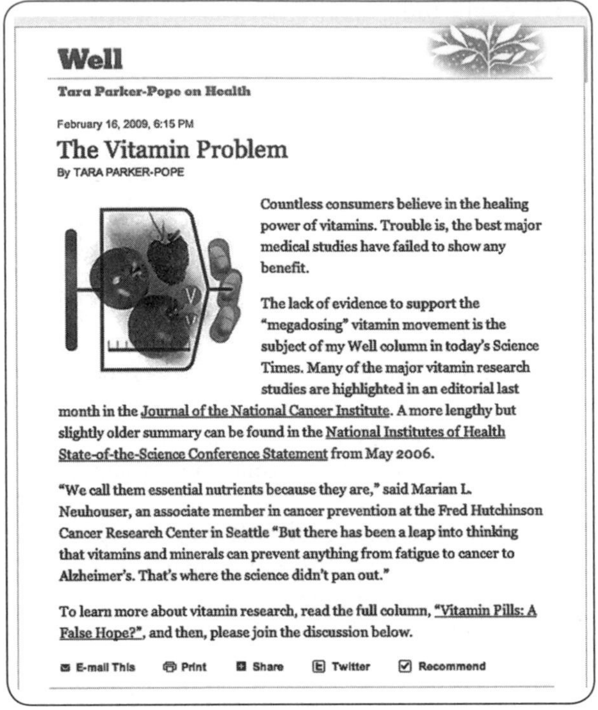

**Well**

**Tara Parker-Pope on Health**

February 16, 2009, 6:15 PM

**The Vitamin Problem**

By TARA PARKER-POPE

Countless consumers believe in the healing power of vitamins. Trouble is, the best major medical studies have failed to show any benefit.

The lack of evidence to support the "megadosing" vitamin movement is the subject of my Well column in today's Science Times. Many of the major vitamin research studies are highlighted in an editorial last month in the Journal of the National Cancer Institute. A more lengthy but slightly older summary can be found in the National Institutes of Health State-of-the-Science Conference Statement from May 2006.

"We call them essential nutrients because they are," said Marian L. Neuhouser, an associate member in cancer prevention at the Fred Hutchinson Cancer Research Center in Seattle "But there has been a leap into thinking that vitamins and minerals can prevent anything from fatigue to cancer to Alzheimer's. That's where the science didn't pan out."

To learn more about vitamin research, read the full column, "Vitamin Pills: A False Hope?", and then, please join the discussion below.

E-mail This Print Share Twitter Recommend

The New York Times

## Selection 14.1

*In this blog post, note the standard journalistic lede and the 13 studies that Tara Parker-Pope cites, with links to either earlier news reports or scientific journal articles. This is solid journalism. If a health blogger strives to be more than an online gossip, then she can take Parker-Pope's blog as a model. After the piece on vitamins, you'll see a selection of the comments that followed. Parker-Pope responded to some of them online.*

### WELL
### News Keeps Getting Worse for Vitamins

By TARA PARKER-POPE

The best efforts of the scientific community to prove the health benefits of vitamins keep falling short.

This week, researchers reported the disappointing results from a large clinical trial of almost 15,000 male doctors taking vitamins E and C for a decade. The study showed no meaningful effect on cancer rates.

*Published: November 20, 2008.*

Another recent study found no benefit of vitamins E and C for heart disease.

In October, a major trial studying whether vitamin E and selenium could lower a man's risk for prostate cancer ended amidst worries that the treatments may do more harm than good.

And recently, doctors at Memorial Sloan-Kettering Cancer Center in New York warned that vitamin C seems to protect not just healthy cells but cancer cells, too.

Everyone needs vitamins, which are critical for the body. But for most people, the micronutrients we get from foods usually are adequate to prevent vitamin deficiency, which is rare in the United States. That said, some extra vitamins have proven benefits, such as vitamin B12 supplements for the elderly and folic acid for women of childbearing age. And calcium and vitamin D in women over 65 appear to protect bone health.

But many people gobble down large doses of vitamins believing that they boost the body's ability to mop up damaging free radicals that lead to cancer and heart disease. In addition to the more recent research, several reports in recent years have challenged the notion that megadoses of vitamins are good for you.

A Johns Hopkins School of Medicine review of 19 vitamin E clinical trials of more than 135,000 people showed high doses of vitamin E (greater than 400 IUs) increased a person's risk for dying during the study period by 4 percent. Taking vitamin E with other vitamins and minerals resulted in a 6 percent higher risk of dying. Another study of daily vitamin E showed vitamin E takers had a 13 percent higher risk for heart failure.

The Journal of Clinical Oncology published a study of 540 patients with head and neck cancer who were being treated with radiation therapy. Vitamin E reduced side effects, but cancer recurrence rates among the vitamin users were higher, although the increase didn't reach statistical significance.

A 1994 Finland study of smokers taking 20 milligrams a day of beta carotene showed an 18 percent higher incidence of lung cancer among beta carotene users. In 1996, a study called Caret looked at beta carotene and vitamin A use among smokers and workers exposed to asbestos, but the study was stopped when the vitamin users showed a 28 percent higher risk for lung cancer and a 26 percent higher risk of dying from heart disease.

A 2002 Harvard study of more than 72,000 nurses showed that those who consumed high levels of vitamin A from foods, multivitamins and supplements had a 48 percent higher risk for hip fractures than nurses who had the lowest intake of vitamin A.

The Cochrane Database of Systematic Reviews looked at vitamin C studies for treating colds. Among more than two dozen studies, there was no overall benefit for preventing colds, although the vitamin was linked with a 50 percent reduction in colds among people who engaged in extreme activities, such as marathon runners, skiers and soldiers, who

**Comments from News Keeps Getting Worse for Vitamins:**

'All these studies are done by bitter scientists upset that they can't get funding from Big Vita. It's sloppy, biased science.'

'All I know is, I feel better when I take vitamins than when I don't and I definitely seem to fight off looming colds much more successfully.'

'It's said that extremes are always dangerous and moderation the key to a long and fruitful life, and I think this article proves it. Vitamins are like cosmetics—too much hoopla but not much substance.'

'My parents eat a terrible diet and are completely sedentary, yet they take vitamins. My wife's parents are vegetarians who get a lot of exercise but don't take vitamins. Who do you think is more healthy?'

'Thank you very much. I did read one of the abstracts. It really helps.'

**[Parker-Pope response:] Thanks; the great thing about blogging is you can actually provide the links!**

'Simply quoting little snippets about various so-called studies doesn't provide an argument for or against. Who funded the studies? How large and how long and how was the test conducted are the real questions people need answered. I always keep in mind that big pharm makes more money providing scripts for sick people than anything they could provide to keep them healthy.'

**[Parker-Pope's response:] I don't believe any of these studies are funded by industry. Most are by NIH, NCI or other non-industry sources.**

'I recently heard that women who take multi-vitamins tend to develop dense breast tissue and that dense breast tissue either leads to breast cancer or makes it harder to find. Does anybody know if this was a real scientific study or just an internet rumor?'

**[Parker-Pope's response:] Yes, multivitamins have been linked with breast density. Click here [linked to study].**

'Love the blog, Tara! The best Well for feeling well! There is always something to learn every time I pop in.'

*Web audiences take health journalism personally, as you'll see in these excerpts from the more than 600 responses to Tara Parker-Pope's blog post on vitamins. A few of the excerpts include Parker-Pope's response.*

were exposed to significant cold or physical stress. The data also suggested vitamin C use was linked with less severe and slightly shorter colds.

In October 2004, Copenhagen researchers reviewed seven randomized trials of beta carotene, selenium and vitamins A, C and E (alone or in combination) in colon, esophageal, gastric, pancreatic and liver cancer. The antioxidant users had a 6 percent higher death rate than placebo users.

Two studies presented to the American College of Cardiology in 2006 showed that vitamin B doesn't prevent heart attacks, leading The New England Journal of Medicine to say that the consistency of the results "leads to the unequivocal conclusion" that the vitamins don't help patients with established vascular disease.

The British Medical Journal looked at multivitamin use among elderly people for a year but found no difference in infection rates or visits to doctors.

Despite a lack of evidence that vitamins actually work, consumers appear largely unwilling to give them up. Many readers of the Well blog say the problem is not the vitamin but poorly designed studies that use the wrong type of vitamin, setting the vitamin up to fail. Industry groups such as the Council for Responsible Nutrition also say the research isn't well designed to detect benefits in healthy vitamin users.

## Selection 14.2

*While Parker-Pope's posts focus on providing information, the Well blog has also included a series called Cancer Journal by Times writer and editor Dana Jennings. Each painfully personal piece of writing brought responses in droves from others who have cancer and their loved ones.*

*In his first installment in November 2008, Jennings described his goal this way: "In these posts I hope to provide an antidote to the averted eyes and the retreat into medical jargon that sometimes characterize talk about prostate cancer. Prostate cancer isn't just about surgery, treatment and survival—it's also about relationships, sex, self-esteem, embarrassment, hope and fear. By writing about my own experiences, I hope I can start a personal, honest and down-to-earth conversation about the disease—in all its bewildering sadness and, yes, in all its strange humor—with fellow prostate cancer patients, their caregivers and anyone else who is interested."*

*That post drew responses from 614 people, most of them men saying some version of thank you, and many sharing stories that they'd never talked about before. Sometimes Jennings responded online. (To one man with a bad prognosis: "We're dealt this dark and difficult hand. But, I say, keep on bluffing until we're told we can't play anymore. All the Best, Dana.") Over the months, the Web audience followed Jennings' journey. At first they saw his fear and anger: "There's a book-jacket photo taken of me early last year, before I learned that I had cancer, and I can't stand to look at it. Can't bear to look at my floppy mop of Glen Campbell hair, the innocent grin. I want to smack that cheery and naive face and bellow: 'Boy, you don't know nothing.'" But months later, as in this next post, he began to feel better and to see some good in what he had endured.*

## WELL
## After Cancer, Gratitude for Simple Pleasures

By DANA JENNINGS

I've been thinking a lot about gratitude lately, trying to put my finger on what exactly I'm grateful for in the year since I had surgery to remove my cancerous prostate.

When you have cancer, when you're being cut open and radiated and who knows what else, it can take a great effort to be thankful for the gift of the one life that we have been blessed with. Believe me, I know.

And sometimes, in the amnesia of sickness, we forget to be grateful. But if we let our cancers consume our spirits in addition to our bodies, then we risk forgetting who we truly are, of contracting a kind of Alzheimer's of the soul.

Not that I'm feeling grateful each moment of each day. I'm well past the anger that I felt after my diagnosis, but I still get frustrated sometimes by the physical challenges I face in the wake of prostate cancer, wishing that by mid-afternoon my brain wouldn't become a test pattern as my body begs for a nap.

Gratitude is an antidote to the dark voice of illness that whispers to us, that insists that all we have become is our disease. Living in the shadow of cancer has granted me a kind of high-definition gratitude. I've found that when you're grateful, the world turns from funereal gray to incandescent Technicolor.

There are, of course, the obvious things to be thankful for. There's the love and care of my wife, sons and extended family; the concern and support of my friends, colleagues and community; the skill and insight of the doctors and all the other medical staff who have brought me to this very moment:

The nurses who spooned ice chips into my cotton mouth after surgery; the therapists who blasted Black Sabbath and Pink Floyd for me when I had radiation last winter; the blood technicians who made a steel needle feel like cold silk; the hospital aides who took a couple of minutes to talk to me about movies, comic books and mortality at three in the morning when I couldn't sleep.

The small moments of gratitude are the most poignant to me because they indicate that I'm still paying close attention to the life I'm living, that I haven't yet succumbed to numbing obliviousness.

These days I'm grateful for:

---

*Posted: August 4, 2009.*

The Friday morning breakfasts with my friend Gary, who had his prostate removed last February. As we both continue to recover, we've turned into prostate cancer cronies.

Those nights when I sleep through, and don't have to get up and do the zombie shuffle to the bathroom.

When just the right song vaults and shimmers from the oldies station: Tunes like "Walk Away Renee" by The Left Banke, or "G.T.O." by Ronny and the Daytonas, or "You Didn't Have to Be So Nice" by the Lovin' Spoonful.

The pollen-encrusted bumblebees patrolling the blue-purple cat mint that frames our front steps.

An iced green-tea lemonade, sweetened.

The healing sound of our dog, Bijou, drinking her water.

The latest issues of The Mighty Thor, The Incredible Hulk and The Invincible Iron Man, which still have the superhuman power to ferry me back to the summer of 1967 and being 9 years old and pulsing with wide-eyed innocence.

A tuna sub slabbed with roasted red peppers and sliced deli pickles.

The warm shaving cream that prickles my neck at Balonze Barber Shop after a buzz cut—I get the "triple-zero" these days—and then the brisk and bracing alcohol rub-slap on my scalp.

And gratitude, finally, for the readers of these posts. I am grateful that I get to share my prostate cancer tales with you and, in turn, get to hear your stories.

## Selection 14.3

*In the next example Parker-Pope looks at the relationship between teenagers who watch steamy television and their chances of becoming pregnant or causing a pregnancy. The hook for the post was a study published in the journal Pediatrics. In an interview for this book, Parker-Pope says she was no fan of the study: "I felt like this was a very predictable study: TV is bad for your kids, and it's going to make them do bad things. Nothing is ever that simple or clear." Instead, she focused on what the researchers were studying, what questions were asked and answered and, finally, what could be concluded from the data. In this case Parker-Pope used the blog as a springboard for readers to discuss the study and vent on the pluses or minuses of television shows geared to sexually inquisitive teenagers. One commenter, a physician, questioned the study authors' methodology, and another commenter wrote that the study results are "incongruent with our current understanding of emotion and empathy." One of the study's authors even wrote a comment.*

*In all, Parker-Pope's post attracted 51 comments—far fewer than the number of comments on the vitamin blog, but enough to add dimensions to the study that Parker-Pope didn't address. That, of course, is the beauty of the blog: Readers can flesh out parts of the story that the reporter either missed or didn't have space to examine.*

## WELL
# Behind the Statistics on TV and Teen Pregnancy

By TARA PARKER-POPE

A new study making headlines today suggests teenage girls and boys who watch a lot of steamy television are more likely to become pregnant or cause a pregnancy.

But a closer look at the data shows the relationship between television, sexual content and teen pregnancies is complex. The same study, published today in Pediatrics, also found that teens who watch a lot of television in general are less likely to become pregnant.

How can that be? The answer may be that kids who watch a lot of television obviously aren't out dating and socializing with friends. So as unhealthy as it may be to spend hours in front of a screen, the behavior appears to be oddly protective against teen pregnancy.

The link between television and teen pregnancy only shows up when a high proportion of the television shows watched by a teen are filled with sexual content. When most of the television a teen watches is sexual in nature, risk for teen pregnancy doubles compared to kids who watch little or no sexually-themed television.

The study only shows an association between steamy TV and teen pregnancy, which means some other factor may be influencing the data. It could be that shows like "Gossip Girl" and "Degrassi High," with their depictions of casual, consequence-free sex, prompt sexually active teens to have more partners or to be less careful about birth control. Or it may be that kids prone to risky or problem behavior also are more attracted to shows with high sexual content.

While the answer isn't clear, the study findings do suggest that parents should be aware of what kids are watching on television and be ready to offer an alternate viewpoint.

"If the type of sexual portrayals that teens see on TV are the only messages they're getting about sex, then they're likely to approach sexual relationships in a way that might not be the healthiest way," said Steven Martino, study co-author and a behavioral scientist at the RAND Corporation, the nonprofit health care research firm that conducted the study. "It's important to talk to them about that and see how they're reacting, and offer other perspectives to them about sex that they might not be getting on television."

---

*Posted: November 3, 2008.*

## A Conversation with . . . Tara Parker-Pope

HEALTH REPORTER, COLUMNIST AND BLOGGER

© The New York Times

*Tara Parker-Pope has been a consumer health columnist for The New York Times since August 2007. Along with her column, she writes the health blog, Well, on NYTimes.com. Before joining The Times, Parker-Pope wrote the weekly Health Journal column for The Wall Street Journal from 2000 to 2007. She joined The Wall Street Journal in 1993. From 1987 to 1993, she worked for the Austin American-Statesman and the Houston Chronicle, where she covered state and local politics, transportation and suburban news. Parker-Pope received a bachelor's degree in sociology from the University of Texas in 1992. The following is an edited transcript of a telephone interview.*

**What was your medical or science background before you started doing reporting?**

My background is as a journalist and as a beat reporter. I studied social sciences in college. I don't have an academic science background at all. Everything I know about reporting has basically been through my journalism experience. I was a government reporter. I covered transportation. I covered consumer products, marketing, advertising, and it was actually that coverage that got me into health coverage. I started covering consumer issues that often would be health issues. It was from that consumer products experience that I started writing the health column. I started writing for The Wall Street Journal because my editor said, "I want somebody writing this column who doesn't have a medical background, who is the same person who's reading the story, who has the same questions the average reader has. I want you to approach it as a real person, not as a medical person." So, that's how I got into health writing.

**Why did you start writing a blog?**

I had been working for The Wall Street Journal for 14 years and had been trying to have more of an online presence. I had a very interactive relationship with my readers in terms of e-mails. It was incredibly time-consuming. Yet it was only for that individual reader. I get a lot of questions from readers, not medical questions, but information questions. They're trying to understand how to get answers about different things, and I was a resource. But at the time I didn't have an online outlet with which to share information with readers.

At that time The New York Times wanted to start a health-oriented blog, a daily dose of health information. I started talking to them and had a very strong idea that I wanted to do a very consumer-oriented blog. I have this belief system that once you're in the medical system everything changes. The time to really be proactive about your health is before you are at the doctor's office. So, my whole mantra is that health doesn't happen at the doctor's office. It happens in the small decisions that we make every day. It was [with] that philosophy that I created the Well blog.

**How is your blog different from your column? They both go by the same name, so how do you differentiate the two?**

The branding is the same for a reason. I write stories that are actionable consumer health information. A Well story is a story that you can act on now. It's very much for the individual. I would not write about things happening on the frontiers of medicine. I wouldn't write about the discovery of the gene that may lead to a cure for Alzheimer's, but I would write about how somebody who is caring for a family member with Alzheimer's might better cope. Or, I might write about a new treatment that is helping delay some of the symptoms of Alzheimer's, but it needs to be something that is available to readers now. That's what distinguishes Well from other medical coverage.

So, the Well brand is about this idea [that] health doesn't happen in the doctor's office. It happens in the small decisions we make every day. We, as individuals, have the power to take charge of our health, to arm ourselves with information, and be partners in prevention and in our wellness and our health. A Well post could be something that I linked to on another Web site. It's not always original work, but it's something I'm interested in and I think readers would benefit from knowing. A Well column in the paper is always going to be my work, my reporting, and it's going to be a little bit longer and a more involved exploration of a particular topic.

**Do readers respond any differently to your blog than to your column?**

The blog is really conversational. It's where I get together a lot with readers, and we share information and we talk. What really distinguishes the online content is this incredible feedback you get from readers. It's very much about wellness and prevention. It's actionable. A reader can read it, and they can change their behavior immediately. The blog is two or three or four posts a day. It's often going to be linked to other stories. If another blogger writes something that I think our readers will find interesting, I create a blog post.

One thing that distinguishes the blog from other parts of the paper is flexibility. While the blog has to maintain the same standards as the rest of the paper, on the blog there aren't space rules or decisions about placement that need to go through several layers of editors to make a decision. I still work with an editor every day, but the format makes for a very nimble place to do journalism. Things don't always happen that quickly in newspapers. They happen very quickly online.

**How is your writing different in the blog from your column?**

Whether it's the blog or the newspaper, I want people to read a story that I've written. I don't want them to have to work very hard to absorb it. Somebody once studied my columns at The Wall Street Journal and found that I tended to use much shorter words than most reporters. I was really just thrilled about that.

When I write any story, I try to pick small slices of big issues, and I try to translate it for the reader in a very accessible way so that they don't have to spend a lot of time trying to figure out what it's about. They can get it immediately. My writing is the same, in that regard, in the paper and on the blog. On the blog I am sometimes more conversational. I almost never use "I." I rarely inject myself into a column. I think readers want information. They want issues. They don't really care about me although my opinion counts for them sometimes. I share more of my personal experiences in the blog because I have conversations with readers. I have a hard time separating the comments from the content because the reporting continues once the blog post is up. The readers will have a question, and I will go and research it. Or maybe go interview somebody, or pull something from my notes that I didn't include in the original story and post it in the questions. Then readers will share something else. And I'll say, "You know, that's really interesting, I haven't heard about that." Then another reader will say, "Yeah, I'm a physician, and this is what my experience is." So it's really very dynamic. It's time consuming, but a lot of fun.

**What's the best mix for you among first-person journalism, second-person journalism and third-person journalism in the blog?**
I really do not like first-person journalism. I think most of the time telling other people's stories is what we should do as journalists. We should be very careful about when we decide to put "I" in the story. Readers want to read about themselves. They want to hear about their lives. They want me to tell them about them.

**Do reporters question the assumptions of scientists and doctors often enough?**
I think there's another problem sometimes in medical reporting and health reporting, in that we automatically assume a layer of skepticism about anything that's funded by the pharmaceutical industry. Yet we don't apply that layer of skepticism to research that's funded by the government, by the NIH. There's always an agenda with every piece of research. So, if you're completely convinced C-reactive protein is a great predictor for heart attacks, then that person has an agenda. They might be right. But just because that research isn't funded by a drug company doesn't mean we shouldn't stop and think, "OK, what are the issues here? How do we present balance?" We can only present both sides. I know enough about health and medicine to know nothing is ever that cut and dried. What is the evidence? Let's look at it, let's look at the data, and what are we going to find? You don't know what you're going to find. I was surprised that there was not a lot more evidence that statins save lives. [See Chapter 12 column, "Great Drug, but Does It Prolong Life?"] Statins prevent heart attacks. That's different than saving a life. And that kind of nuance is very hard to appreciate unless you've been covering health for a very long time.

So every study is compromised by somebody's bias, by somebody's thought process. All of these decisions bias research. The challenge for us is to say, "Okay, this is an important finding. What are the limits of this finding? What questions have really been answered?" That's the mistake we make so often as reporters and as readers, interpreting information. You have to be very specific about what the finding is. As a reporter, the way you protect yourself, the way you don't make those mistakes, is double the amount of people you talk to. It's just better to add a couple more phone calls.

The most important thing any health writer could do is to compare relative risk to absolute risk. If what you're saying is going to frighten people, then you need to be absolutely certain that you explain to them what it means to them as an individual.

There's a study that linked alcoholic beverages to breast cancer, and it completely panicked women. It was a major study out of Oakland, California, out of Kaiser. It was 70,000 women, and it looked at their drinking habits for not quite 20 years. This analysis found a 30 percent increase in your risk of breast cancer if you had three drinks a day. Thirty percent increase really scares people, and that's a relative risk. It's a very scary sounding percentage, but it translates into a very small risk for the individual. The typical 50-year-old woman has a five-year breast cancer risk of 3 percent, so if her risk increases by 30 percent, her individual risk is only 4 percent. So, going from 3 to 4 percent sounds a lot less scary than 30 percent.

Of everything I've said, I think that issue of absolute risk is the most important thing that we can do.

**What's the most fun about your job?**

I would say the reader interaction. I really like that part of it. I've been a journalist now for more than 20 years. In [my] early days of journalism you would write a story, and you might get a phone call or you might get a letter a few days later. There was definitely this delay. It was a very static process. What we have learned in the online world is that readers are a wealth of knowledge. Readers know so much, and they're an incredible resource to journalists. Having the opportunity now to look at comments and input and ideas from readers, it's fantastic.

I wrote a post on resistant bacteria. Several readers on that post said, "What about doctors wearing their scrubs on the subway? This is gross. I get upset. They've got blood [on their clothing]." I had never thought about this issue before, but how interesting. What's happening with doctors and the clothes they wear? It turned into a really good story and a very lengthy discussion with readers, and it was completely generated by readers. It's an idea I wouldn't have had if we didn't have this way of communicating. I just love that interaction. Even when they are hard on me, and they often are, I have learned so much. I have changed as a journalist, because readers will consistently be bothered by something. I have to stop and say, "Okay, all of these people can't be wrong. Maybe this word that I'm using or this choice is not the right way to convey this." So, I've definitely changed and grown because readers have given me the feedback. So, I'm really grateful for that.

We just have to be vigilant in our reporting. We have to certainly be open to the information the readers have because they're very wise. We have to really think every time we write a story, "Are we scaring people? Is this a call to action? Am I giving them everything they need to know? Am I really giving them how this issue affects their individual life?" If you think about the fact that every health story you write, a reader is going to make a decision, they're going to call their doctor, they're going to stop their medicine, they're going to start medicine, they're going to do something, then you realize the stakes as a health reporter are very high. People are directly affected by what we do. It's incredibly rewarding because the stakes are high, but it's also an incredible responsibility.

## MAKING CONNECTIONS

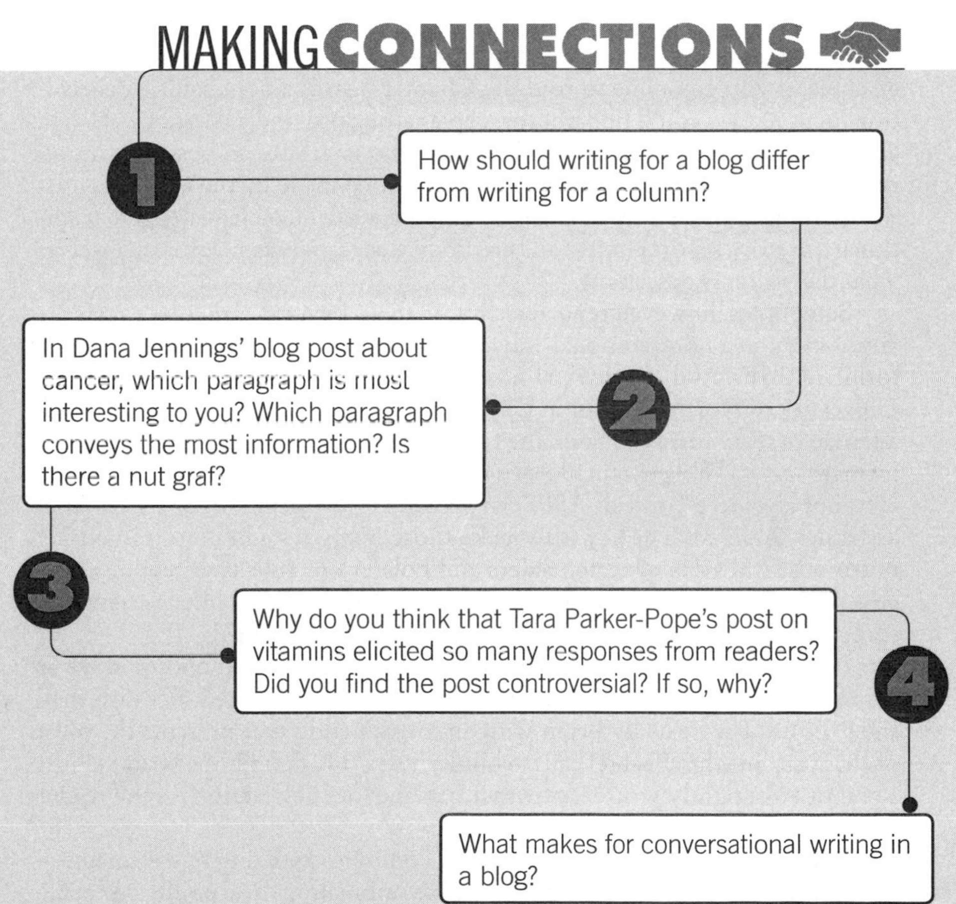

1
How should writing for a blog differ from writing for a column?
2
In Dana Jennings' blog post about cancer, which paragraph is most interesting to you? Which paragraph conveys the most information? Is there a nut graf?
3
Why do you think that Tara Parker-Pope's post on vitamins elicited so many responses from readers? Did you find the post controversial? If so, why?
4
What makes for conversational writing in a blog?

CHAPTER 15

# beyond plain text

ONLINE READERS CAN GET HEALTH AND medical information in a variety of ways, including video, audio and interactive multimedia. The traditional text story is still a staple of health and medical reporting, but journalists are also finding new ways to tell stories with words and pictures.

One common device is to supplement a text story with a graphic (for example, if you go online to read the Chapter 7 story about calorie deprivation in monkeys, you'll find photos, explanatory text and a diagram). Also in Chapter 7, in the story about a blind man who navigates an obstacle course, reporter Benedict Carey includes a link to a video made by the neuroscientist whose findings Carey reports. These graphic and video elements give traditional text stories more context and credibility, as readers can see for themselves what the writer is describing.

Sometimes, however, reporters choose to go beyond plain text to tell the entire story in a nontraditional way. Some people call these alternative story forms, or ASFs. Andy Bechtel, a former copy editor and now a professor at the University of North Carolina at Chapel Hill, writes that with some topics an alternative story form can hook the reader in ways that a story in a traditional format cannot: "Well-executed ASFs inform readers, providing not only quick facts but also deep context. ASFs can provide information in 'bite sizes' that are easier to digest. The key is to make those bite sizes add up to something nutritious. ASFs can educate readers and bolster our role as watchdogs over government and other powerful institutions. ASFs can also offer variety and surprise the reader, and they can bring visual pizzazz to a page."[1]

In The New York Times, most graphics, bar charts and photos serve as adjuncts to a text story. Alternative story forms are different because they stand alone. They usually begin with an introduction that presents the meat of the story in what Bechtel calls "chunky text." He defines the term as "just a graf or two, tightly written, often with a label or subhead to give the reader an idea what it will contain."

In various kinds of ASFs, chunky text combines with different elements—charts, graphics, timelines, a Q&A or any combination. The point is to make the information easy to digest. Ideally, all those chunks of words and graphics add up to a story of substance that readers can scan for the information that they want.

Alternative story forms don't work for all stories, but they can work well with information-heavy ones that don't have plots and characters. Take

PRESIDENTIAL PHYSIQUES OF THE MODERN AGE
2008 CANDIDATES
BARACK OBAMA 6'1½"/ 180 lbs.
JOHN McCAIN 5'7"/ 165 lbs.
PAST PAIRINGS WINNING CANDIDATES IN BLACK
2004
JOHN KERRY 6'4"/ 185 lbs.
43RD GEORGE W. BUSH 6'0"/ 190 lbs.
2000
AL GORE 6'1"/ 195 lbs.
43RD GEORGE W. BUSH 6'0"/ 190 lbs.
1996
42ND BILL CLINTON 6'2"/ 230 lbs.
BOB DOLE 6'0"/ 178 lbs.
1992
42ND BILL CLINTON 6'2"/ 230 lbs.
GEORGE H.W. BUSH 6'2"/ 195 lbs.
1988
MICHAEL DUKAKIS 5'8"/ 160 lbs.
41ST GEORGE H.W. BUSH 6'2"/ 195 lbs.
1984
WALTER MONDALE 5'11"/ 180 lbs.
40TH RONALD REAGAN 6'1"/ 185 lbs.
1980
JIMMY CARTER 5'9"/ 160 lbs.
40TH RONALD REAGAN 6'1"/ 185 lbs.
1976
39TH JIMMY CARTER 5'9"/ 160 lbs.
GERALD FORD 6'0"/ 195 lbs.
38TH ASSUMED PRESIDENCY ON RICHARD NIXON'S RESIGNATION
1972
GEORGE McGOVERN 6'0"/ 170 lbs.
37TH RICHARD NIXON 5'11½"/ 173 lbs.
1968
HUBERT HUMPHREY 5'11"/ 160 lbs.
37TH RICHARD NIXON 5'11½"/ 173 lbs.
1964
36TH LYNDON JOHNSON 6'3"/ 200 lbs.
BARRY GOLDWATER 6'0"/ 185 lbs.
1960
35TH JOHN F. KENNEDY 6'0"/ 175 lbs.
RICHARD NIXON 5'11½"/ 173 lbs.
1956
ADLAI STEVENSON 5'10"/ 185 lbs.
34TH DWIGHT EISENHOWER 5'10½"/ 173 lbs.
1952
ADLAI STEVENSON 5'10"/ 185 lbs.
34TH DWIGHT EISENHOWER 5'10½"/ 173 lbs.
1948
33RD HARRY S. TRUMAN 5'9"/ 167 lbs.
THOMAS E. DEWEY 5'8"/ 160 lbs.
1944
32ND FRANKLIN D. ROOSEVELT 6'2"/ 188 lbs.
THOMAS E. DEWEY 5'8"/ 160 lbs.
1940
32ND FRANKLIN D. ROOSEVELT 6'2"/ 188 lbs.
WENDELL WILLKIE 6'1"/ 220 lbs.
1936
32ND FRANKLIN D. ROOSEVELT 6'2"/ 188 lbs.
ALF LANDON 5'8"/ 155 lbs.
1932
32ND FRANKLIN D. ROOSEVELT 6'2"/ 188 lbs.
HERBERT HOOVER 5'11"/ 185 lbs.
1928
ALFRED E. SMITH 5'8½"/ 175 lbs.
31ST HERBERT HOOVER 5'11"/ 185 lbs.
1924
JOHN W. DAVIS 6'0"/ 190 lbs.
30TH CALVIN COOLIDGE 5'10"/ 169 lbs.
1920
JAMES M. COX 5'6"/ 170 lbs.
29TH WARREN G. HARDING 6'0"/ 240 lbs.
1916
28TH WOODROW WILSON 5'11"/ 170 lbs.
CHARLES E. HUGHES 5'11"/ 170 lbs.
1912
28TH WOODROW WILSON 5'11"/ 170 lbs.
THEODORE ROOSEVELT* 5'10"/ 200 lbs.
1908
WILLIAM J. BRYAN 5'10"/ 180 lbs.
27TH WILLIAM H. TAFT 6'0"/ 332 lbs.
1904
ALTON B. PARKER 6'0"/ 200 lbs.
26TH THEODORE ROOSEVELT 5'10"/ 200 lbs.
1900
WILLIAM J. BRYAN 5'10"/ 180 lbs.
25TH WILLIAM McKINLEY 5'7"/ 185 lbs.
1896
WILLIAM J. BRYAN 5'10"/ 180 lbs.
25TH WILLIAM McKINLEY 5'7"/ 185 lbs.
TOTAL VICTORIES BY HEIGHT & WEIGHT
TALLER 17
SHORTER 8
HEAVIER 18
LIGHTER 8
PRESIDENTIAL ANOMALIES
16TH TALLEST ABRAHAM LINCOLN 6'4" 180 lbs.
4TH SHORTEST JAMES MADISON 5'4" 100 lbs.
27TH HEAVIEST WILLIAM H. TAFT 6'0" 332 lbs.
DEMOCRATS ON LEFT; REPUBLICANS ON RIGHT. * THEODORE ROOSEVELT RAN AS A PROGRESSIVE IN THE 1912 ELECTION.

Open N.Y.

a political piece on presidential physiques that appeared on October 6, 2008, on the op-ed page of The New York Times. This alternative story from Open N.Y., a design studio, used both graphics and text to compare the heights and weights of presidential candidates. A text-only treatment of this story would have made for tedious reading. A short text introduction preceded the graphic.

The whole point of the ASF is to convey selected information in a more effective and entertaining way. Researchers, supported in part by The Poynter Institute for Media Studies, have also focused on how online readers scan computer screens. They call their research "eyetracking."

Eyetracking research doesn't lead to an easy formula for capturing readers' attention, but it does suggest that page designers and editors can create story formats that take advantage of readers' viewing patterns. Increasingly, you may see health or medical stories presented in an ASF rather than in the traditional inverted pyramid or narrative feature format. As Bechtel says, "If you're tired of writing or editing that story in a traditional form, you can be certain your reader is tired of reading it."

Research shows that test subjects retain more information when they read information presented in an ASF than when they read text and photos presented in a traditional way. In an eyetracking study carried out by EyeTrack07, 582 subjects read one of six stories about bird flu—three in print and three online.[2] "Readers of prototype 3—the most visually graphic version, without a traditional narrative—answered the most questions correctly," writes Sara Dickenson Quinn, EyeTrack07 director.[3] "Alternative story forms seem to work best with fact-laden stories, providing a way to handle numbers, time, location and juxtaposition references in a simple, comparative way."

In the bird flu study Quinn tracked readers' comprehension skills as they read a feature story, but ASFs can also work in commentaries. In a feature called Op-Chart on The Times op-ed page, contributors use multiframe cartoons, text, graphics and charts to make their points.

## Selection 15.1

*The following op-chart by Howard Markel and Sam Potts uses an alternative story form to review the history of American epidemics. There's no traditional story with experts spouting facts and figures, but the chart did run with three paragraphs of text. The text and chart together give the reader multiple ways to take in information. You can scan the chart and then read the text, read the text and then scan the chart, or hop back and forth. This storytelling technique cedes control to the reader by providing multiple points of entry to the story.*

# OP-CHART
# American Epidemics, a Brief History

By HOWARD MARKEL AND SAM POTTS

ALL epidemics are different in their own way, and the current swine flu outbreak—which by Friday had sickened 141 people in 19 states, and caused deaths and illness in Mexico and 13 other countries—is no exception. Yet, as you can see from the chart below, which provides details on a selected handful of epidemics in American history, all outbreaks share certain themes. While some of these events killed many thousands and others affected only a few, in each case public health officials felt a grave threat was imminent and did what they could using the science of the day.

History also shows us, unfortunately, that epidemics lead to reflexive scapegoating of those thought to have caused the problem. Just as European immigrants were blamed for importing cholera in the late 19th century, we are now seeing reports of American politicians saying that Mexican migrant workers should be turned away from hospitals and a rash of scurrilous posts on the Internet attributing the outbreak to their "dirty" ways of life. Another common feature is misinformation. There are now boycotts around the world of Mexican pork, despite well-established science that humans do not contract swine flu from eating pork. And then there was Vice President Joe Biden's premature suggestion that we all avoid airplanes and the subway.

Confusion and blame games aside, we can take heart that our public health professionals are working around the clock to prevent this crisis from getting out of control. One thing the history of epidemics teaches us is that given our remarkable arsenal of treatments, public health measures and rapid surveillance and communications ability, there's never been a better time to have a pandemic than today—except, that is, tomorrow.

*Howard Markel, a doctor and professor of medical history at the University of Michigan, is the author of "Quarantine" and "When Germs Travel." Sam Potts is a graphic designer.*

---

*Published: May 3, 2009.*

| Year | Disease | Location | Cause | Symptoms | Transmission | Public Health Strategy | Number of Sick or Dead | Scapegoats |
|---|---|---|---|---|---|---|---|---|
| 1892 | CHOLERA | WORLDWIDE/ NEW YORK CITY | VIBRIO CHOLERAE BACTERIA | Profuse vomiting and diarrhea leading to dehydration and death | Gastrointestinal; usually contracted from contaminated food or water | Isolation and quarantine of all cases | Nearly 1 million cases worldwide; in New York City there were 11 cases and 9 deaths; there were 44 deaths at the New York quarantine station and an additional 76 aboard ships en route to New York Harbor | Several thousand Russian Jewish immigrants were quarantined at Hoffman and Swinburne Islands, near Staten Island. Several hundred first-class cabin passengers were restricted to the Surf Hotel on Fire Island |
| 1900 | BUBONIC PLAGUE | SAN FRANCISCO | YERSINIA PESTIS BACTERIA | High fever, intense muscle and headaches, fatigue, bloody vomiting, followed by swollen and painful lymph nodes | Fleas carried by rats | Quarantine and forced vaccinations in Chinatown | By 1904 there had been 121 cases and 113 deaths; of the dead 107 were Chinese, 2 were Japanese and 4 were Caucasian | Chinese immigrants; many protested and some brought successful legal suits against mandatory vaccination laws |
| 1917 | TYPHUS FEVER | EL PASO, TEX. | RICKETTSIAE PROWAZEKII | Extremely high fever, joint and muscle pain, delirium, reddish-purple rash spreading from the chest; 20 percent to 40 percent of victims died in the years before antibiotics | Body lice carrying rickettsia bite humans; when they scratch themselves, tainted feces enter the bloodstream | Isolation of the ill and quarantine of those with contact with them. Intensive medical inspections at the Texas-Mexico border; kerosene disinfecting baths for all Mexicans crossing the border | 3 cases | Thousands of Mexican day workers crossing the border were subjected to daily kerosene baths; in one case an explosion occurred, killing 28 men and severely burning 25 to 30 more |
| 1918 | SPANISH INFLUENZA | WORLDWIDE | INFLUENZA VIRUS (A/HN1) | Fever, cough, fatigue, chills, possibly progressing to pneumonia; in severe cases, patients suffocate as their lungs fill up with fluid | Respiratory; highly contagious and easily spread | Widespread closures of schools and public places and prohibitions against public gathering; orders to keep mass transit and buildings well ventilated; isolation and quarantine in some communities | Estimated at 650,000 deaths in the U.S., and 50 million to 60 million worldwide | Pandemic was too widespread for any one group to be blamed |
| 1947 | SMALLPOX | NEW YORK CITY | VARIOLA MAJOR VIRUS | Fever, headache, severe fatigue, severe backache, malaise, followed by rash that turns to blisters; 30 percent or more infected died | Respiratory or physical contact with infected person; highly contagious | Vaccination of all who had contact with the ill, followed by general public vaccination | 3 cases | There was not enough vaccine produced for every American, causing panic among those turned away |
| 1952 | POLIO | NATIONWIDE | POLIOVIRUS | Fever, sore throat, headache, vomiting, fatigue, pain or stiffness of neck, back, arms or legs, muscle spasms; in serious cases, paralysis and death | Gastrointestinal; victims ingest the virus, which infects the lymphatic glands and nerves until it reaches the spinal column and possibly brain | Social distancing measures like canceling summer camps for children and closing public pools. (The Salk polio vaccine was not widely distributed until 1955.) | Approximately 60,000 cases and 3,000 deaths, primarily children | Children of upper socio-economic classes contracted polo out of proportion to poorer children who had unclean drinking water and thus developed antibodies through low-level exposure to the virus |
| 1976 | SWINE FLU | FORT DIX, N.J. | INFLUENZA VIRUS (A/H1N1) | Fever, cough, fatigue, chills, possibly progressing to pneumonia | Respiratory | Isolation and quarantine of ill soldiers and their contacts at Ford Dix; nearly 40 million vaccinations given to civilians. After the vaccination program there was an increase of Guillain-Barré syndrome, a neurological disorder causing paralysis. Scientists still debate whether there was a connection | 1 death and fewer than 200 confirmed cases | The government officials involved in the widespread vaccination program; the head of the Centers for Disease Control lost his job and President Gerald Ford was accused of using the crisis for political gain |
| 1982 | H.I.V./AIDS | SAN FRANCISCO/LOS ANGELES/ NEW YORK; THEN A GLOBAL PANDEMIC | HUMAN IMMUNODEFICIENCY VIRUS | TK | Sexual activity, blood transfusions, needle sharing among drug abusers, blood exchange between mother and baby during pregnancy, breastfeeding | Public health education, safer sexual practices, scrutiny of the blood-banking system, needle exchange programs | More than 25 million people have died worldwide; experts expect 45 million more deaths | Gay men, intravenous drug abusers, Haitians |
| 2003 | SARS | FIRST IN ASIA, THEN NORTH AND SOUTH AMERICA AND EUROPE | SARS CORONA VIRUS | High fever, headache, chills, malaise, coughing, possibly severe pneumonia | Respiratory and gastrointestinal | Chinese government concealed the outbreak for several months, helping the disease to spread; quarantine and isolation policies in Hong Kong, Canada and Singapore | 8,098 cases, 774 deaths worldwide; 8 cases in the United States (all had traveled to SARS-afflicted areas abroad) | Asians and those who had traveled to affected parts of Asia. University of California at Berkeley briefly ordered a ban on Asian students visiting the campus |

Howard Markel and Sam Potts

# MAKING CONNECTIONS

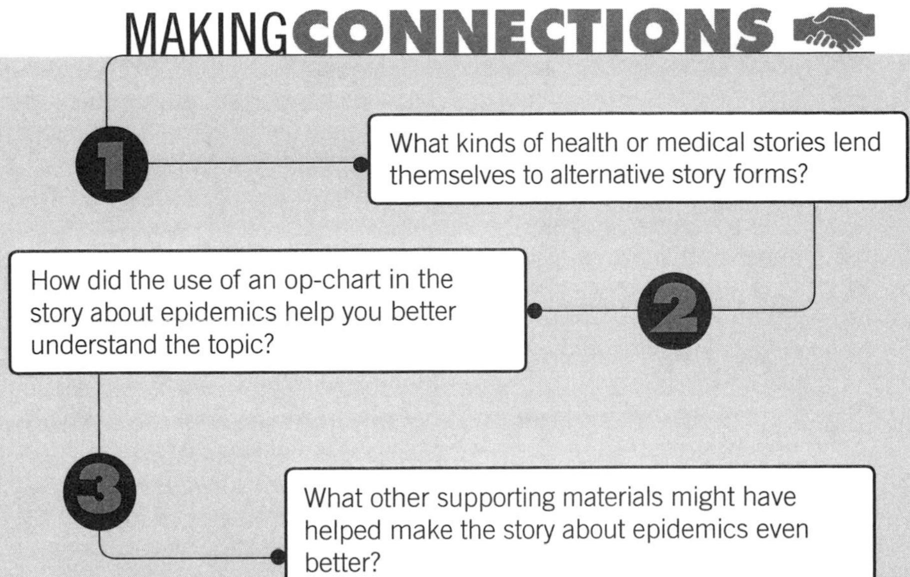

1
What kinds of health or medical stories lend themselves to alternative story forms?
2
How did the use of an op-chart in the story about epidemics help you better understand the topic?
3
What other supporting materials might have helped make the story about epidemics even better?

# references

## sources cited

Arango, Tim, "Fall in Newspaper Sales Accelerates to Pass 7%," The New York Times, April 27, 2009, www.nytimes.com/2009/04/28/business/media/28paper.html.

Bechtel, Andy, "Alternative Story Forms and Copy Editing," The Editor's Desk, Oct. 5, 2007, http://editdesk.blogspot.com/2007/10/alternative-story-forms-and-copy.html.

Collins, Glenn, "Berton Roueche, Medical Writer For The New Yorker, Dies at 83," The New York Times, April 29, 1994, www.nytimes.com/1994/04/29/obituaries/berton-roueche-medical-writer-for-the-new-yorker-dies-at-83.html.

"Eli Lilly Agrees to Settle Zyprexa Marketing Cases," The Wall Street Journal, January 15, 2009, http://online.wsj.com/article/SB123201838370585347.html.

"Eyetracking the News: A Study of Print & Online Reading," The Poynter Institute, 2008, http://eyetrack.poynter.org.

Franklin, Jon, "Writing for Story: Craft Secrets of Dramatic Nonfiction by a Two-Time Pulitzer Prize Winner," Plume Books, 1994.

"Freedom of Information Act (FOIA)," United States Department of Justice, www.usdoj.gov/oip/index.html.

Kolata, Gina, "Hope in the Lab: A Special Report; A Cautious Awe Greets Drugs That Eradicate Tumors in Mice," The New York Times, May 3, 1998, www.nytimes.com/1998/05/03/us/hope-lab-special-report-cautious-awe-greets-drugs-that-eradicate-tumors-mice.html.

National Center for Health Statistics, "Health, United States, 2007, with Chartbook on Trends in the Health of Americans," Hyattsville, MD: 2007.

Quinn, Sara Dickenson, "Visual Voice," The Poynter Institute, Sept. 11, 2007, www.poynter.org/column.asp?id=47&aid=129587.

Schmeck, Harold M., Jr., "Dr. Jonas Salk, Whose Vaccine Turned Tide on Polio, Dies at 80," The New York Times, June 24, 1995, www.nytimes.com/1995/06/24/obituaries/dr-jonas-salk-whose-vaccine-turned-tide-on-polio-dies-at-80.html.

Seward, Zachary M., "Top 15 Newspaper Sites of 2008," The Nieman Journalism Lab, www.niemanlab.org/2009/02/top-15-newspaper-sites-of-2008/#more-1881.

Shaw, David, "A Case Study in How a Story Can Set Off a Frenzy," Los Angeles Times, February 13, 2000, http://articles.latimes.com/2000/feb/13/news/mn-64006.

"Talk to the Newsroom: Dennis Overbye, Science Reporter," The New York Times, July 7, 2008, www.nytimes.com/2008/07/07/business/media/07askthetimes.html.

Thomas, Lewis, "The Medusa and the Snail: More Notes of a Biology Watcher," Penguin Books, 1995.

Watson, James D., "High Hopes on Cancer," The New York Times, May 7, 1998, www.nytimes.com/1998/05/07/opinion/l-high-hopes-on-cancer-838411.html.

# notes

## introduction

1. Tim Arango, "Fall in Newspaper Sales Accelerates to Pass 7%," The New York Times, April 27, 2009, www.nytimes.com/2009/04/28/business/media/28paper.html.
2. Zachary M. Seward, "Top 15 Newspaper Sites of 2008," The Nieman Journalism Lab, www.niemanlab.org/2009/02/top-15-newspaper-sites-of-2008/#more-1881.
3. "Health, United States, 2007, with Chartbook on Trends in the Health of Americans" (2007), fig. 20, www.ncbi.nlm.nih.gov/books/bv.fcgi?rid=healthus07.figgrp.152.

## chapter 4 • investigative stories

1. "Freedom of Information Act (FOIA)," United States Department of Justice, www.usdoj.gov/oip/index.html.
2. Glenn Collins, "Berton Roueche, Medical Writer For The New Yorker, Dies at 83," The New York Times, April 29, 1994, www.nytimes.com/1994/04/29/obituaries/berton-roueche-medical-writer-for-the-new-yorker-dies-at-83.html.
3. "Eli Lilly Agrees to Settle Zyprexa Marketing Cases," The Wall Street Journal, Jan. 15, 2009, http://online.wsj.com/article/SB123201838370585347.html.

## chapter 5 • obituaries

1. Harold M. Schmeck Jr., "Dr. Jonas Salk, Whose Vaccine Turned Tide on Polio, Dies at 80," The New York Times, June 24, 1995, www.nytimes.com/1995/06/24/obituaries/dr-jonas-salk-whose-vaccine-turned-tide-on-polio-dies-at-80.html.

## chapter 8 • perspective stories

1. Gina Kolata, "Hope in the Lab: A Special Report; A Cautious Awe Greets Drugs That Eradicate Tumors in Mice," The New York Times, May 3, 1998, www.nytimes.com/1998/05/03/us/hope-lab-special-report-cautious-awe-greets-drugs-that-eradicate-tumors-mice.html.
2. David Shaw, "A Case Study in How a Story Can Set Off a Frenzy," Los Angeles Times, Feb. 13, 2000, http://articles.latimes.com/2000/feb/13/news/mn-64006.
3. James D. Watson, "High Hopes on Cancer," letter to the editor, The New York Times, May 7, 1998, www.nytimes.com/1998/05/07/opinion/l-high-hopes-on-cancer-838411.html.

## chapter 11 • narratives

1. Jon Franklin, "Writing for Story: Craft Secrets of Dramatic Nonfiction by a Two-Time Pulitzer Prize Winner" (1994), p. 21.

## chapter 13 • essays

1. Lewis Thomas, "The Youngest and Brightest Thing Around," in "The Medusa and the Snail: More Notes of a Biology Watcher" (1995), pp. 16–17.
2. "Talk to the Newsroom: Dennis Overbye, Science Reporter," The New York Times, July 7, 2008, www.nytimes.com/2008/07/07/business/media/07askthetimes.html.

## chapter 15 • beyond plain text

1. Andy Bechtel, "Alternative Story Forms and Copy Editing," The Editor's Desk blog, Oct. 5, 2007, http://editdesk.blogspot.com/2007/10/alternative-story-forms-and-copy.html.
2. "Eyetracking the News: A Study of Print & Online Reading," 2008, http://eyetrack.poynter.org.
3. Sara Dickenson Quinn, "Visual Voice," Sept. 11, 2007, www.poynter.org/column.asp?id=47&aid=129587.